D0094963

The Climate of Treason

The Climate of Treason

Five who Spied for Russia

ANDREW BOYLE

HUTCHINSON
London Melbourne Sydney Auckland Johannesburg

Hutchinson & Co. (Publishers) Ltd

An imprint of the Hutchinson Publishing Group

3 Fitzroy Square, London W1P 6JD

Hutchinson Group (Australia) Pty Ltd
30–32 Cremorne Street, Richmond South, Victoria 3121
PO Box 151, Broadway, New South Wales 2007

Hutchinson Group (NZ) Ltd
32–34 View Road, PO Box 40–086, Glenfield, Auckland 10

Hutchinson Group (SA) (Pty) Ltd
PO Box 337, Bergvlei 2012, South Africa

First published 1979
Reprinted November 1979 (twice)

Set in Monotype Garamond by The Anchor Press Ltd

Printed in Great Britain by The Anchor Press Ltd
and bound by Wm Brendon & Son Ltd
both of Tiptree, Essex

British Library Cataloguing in Publication Data
Boyle, Andrew
The climate of treason.
1. Espionage, Russian – Great Britain –
History – 20th century
I. Title
327'.12'0947 UB271.R9

ISBN 0 09 139340 X

CONTENTS

ILLUSTRATIONS

(between pages 224 and 225)

PROLOGUE

'Any fool may write a valuable book,' observed the eighteenth-century poet Thomas Gray, 'if he will only tell us what he heard and saw with veracity.' Those were wise words; but no writer seeking to unravel the double lives of that small group of British middle-class undergraduates recruited in the 1930s to serve as Soviet secret agents can hope to follow Gray's advice to the letter. Such obstacles as Britain's highly restrictive Official Secrets Act and the natural deceitfulness of the spies themselves rule out the possibility. However, I plead 'not guilty' to the implicit charge of folly in tackling so difficult a theme. For other writers ventured into the field before me, clearing some of the ground and helping to uncover a trail which the said security authorities would have preferred to see left well alone. The earlier efforts of the *Sunday Times*'s journalists Bruce Page, David Leitch and Phillip Knightley, of the *Observer*'s Patrick Seale and Maureen McConville, of Professor Hugh Trevor-Roper, E. H. Cookridge, Geoffrey Hoare, Anthony Purdy and Douglas Sutherland, among others, proved both an incentive and a disincentive to me. Unless I had succeeded in breaking fresh ground and producing some startling new evidence, I would not have written this book. I had no wish simply to add just another volume to the bulging list of espionage titles.

The reader must be the final judge of the book's intrinsic worth, for it is not exclusively concerned with spies and spying. The historical background of the previous half century, with the steady decline in Britain's power, wealth and status, helped to create the unhealthy political and social climate in which Philby, Maclean, Burgess, and their close associates grew up. Yet the distemper of the thirties affected thousands of other students and intellectuals. How and why it should have fatally affected these three in particular seemed a suitable subject for an experienced biographer and contemporary historian. The full facts will never be known, of course, certainly not until the archives of the KGB and the British Secret Service are thrown open to public scrutiny. The United States's Freedom of Information Act offers the researcher a partial glimpse of the truth. The files of the CIA and the FBI, with a number of sensitive exceptions, did help me to penetrate several obscure corners. Without the personal guidance of former members of the American intelligence community, however, I would never have stumbled on 'Maurice' or 'Basil', the code-names given to the Fourth and Fifth Men in the conspiracy. There may be further accomplices still to be uncovered. If so, I leave the field as open as I found it for future sleuths to track them down.

Why did I decide to follow the arbitrary convention, largely created by the press in the mid 1950s, of playing the often misleading 'numbers game' with the five British subjects now definitely known to have spied for the Soviet Union? The answer is simple. Once Kim Philby had conclusively identified himself in 1963, after twelve years of suspenseful debate and doubt inside the secret service, as the Third Man involved in arranging with Guy Burgess the flight to Russian sanctuary of Donald Maclean, there could be no going back to a different and more logical order of numbering. I have called 'Maurice' and 'Basil' the Fourth and Fifth Men not because they were necessarily less industrious or successful in their clandestine roles than the trio whose names have been notorious for so long, nor because their recruitment necessarily came later, but only because they happened to be the two further accomplices whose trails I found.

For obvious reasons, I have refrained from identifying most of my American and British informants who possess inside knowledge of the case. For still more obvious reasons, I cannot identify 'Basil' and 'Maurice'. These unnamed Englishmen also spied for the Soviet Union. Both confessed: the first when cornered and unmasked by the CIA in Washington, the second to the security authorities in London about two years after Burgess and Maclean reappeared publicly in Moscow. Since both men duly received the equivalent of 'Royal Pardons' for their pains, it would have been tempting Providence to 'name names'. They were exonerated at the discretion of the two secret services concerned, partly for the sake of expediency and partly as a reward for the important light they were able to shed on the pattern of treachery inside the British Establishment.

Espionage is the second-oldest and arguably the least honourable of the professions. Moses employed spies before taking Canaan, Julius Caesar before landing in England, William of Normandy before crossing the sea in turn to wrest the Anglo-Saxon crown from Harold, the Tudor and Stuart monarchs in self-defence against Catholic recusants who would have preferred to see a Spanish co-religionist on the throne. In commending Philby's cool but misleading justification of his double career in the British and Soviet Secret Service, Graham Greene drew the following parallel:

> Like many Catholics who, in the reign of Elizabeth, worked for the victory of Spain, Philby has a chilling certainty in the correctness of his judgement, the logical fanaticism of a man who, having once found a faith, is not going to lose it because of the injustices or cruelties inflicted by erring human instruments....

The agony of the thirties was an agony of conflicting beliefs. The choice between fumbling democratic procedures for intractable local problems and the final revolutionary solution of the Communist International seemed a simple one for rebellious and discontented idealists to make. That is why Donald Maclean, the lapsed Scottish Calvinist, swallowed the bait so quickly. That is partly why the brilliant but irresponsible Guy Burgess cast himself in the improbable role of *éminence grise* to his fellow conspirators. Philby, a more hard-headed and calculating character, played a deeper waiting game. He enjoyed the taste of power. He was more of an adventurer than an idealist. He thrived on deception and became an unprincipled pastmaster at it. Graham Greene, I think, has erred in regarding Philby as an ardent believer – the stuff of martyrdom was not in him. What kept him going was less the fanatic's faith than the delight he took in perfect craftsmanship. He betrayed his lack of conviction (as he was bound to do) first in Washington after Burgess joined the British Embassy staff towards the end of 1950, and again in Beirut shortly before deciding that the game was up and escaping to Moscow.

I do not expect everyone to accept my interpretation of the mixed motives and oddly contrasting characteristics of the individual conspirators. I knew none of them personally, perhaps a distinct advantage in the cause of a rigorous objectivity. As the reader will discover, my understanding of the period and of their places in it has been sharpened by the testimony, oral and written, of nearly 500 witnesses whose paths crossed theirs from childhood and schooldays onwards. I would like to mention them all by name, but space forbids. Besides, a number of them have expressly asked me not to include them in the customary roll-call of acknowledgements. Their modesty is impressive if a little puzzling. I respect their wishes, nonetheless, just as I must preserve the anonymity of those former agents of the British and American intelligence community whose first-hand evidence was sometimes oddly contradictory. Some of them will doubtless quarrel with my comments and conclusions as passionately as they quarrelled with each other when Anglo-American relations came under heavy strain as a result of MI5's failure to prevent the escape of Maclean and then trap Philby. However, the Americans were merely paying for the mistakes of the recent past, their own and Britain's.

The Soviet Union had good reason to fear the British after the Revolution. 'We may abandon Russia,' Winston Churchill had warned at the end of 1918, 'but Russia will not abandon us. We shall retire and she will follow. The bear is padding on bloody paws across the snows to the Peace Conference. . . .' Churchill, then Secretary for War and Air in the post-war Coalition Government of Lloyd George, consistently favoured military intervention to save the Russian people and the world from Bolshevism. He was firmly overruled. His stance as the enemy of Red Russia left him 'politically isolated and personally discontented', in the words of his biographer, Martin Gilbert. Yet the majority of politicians in Britain also feared and mistrusted Communism as a disruptive force. So in his heart did King George V; and successive British governments were in no hurry to recognize or to trade with the 'Workers' State'. Only in the Labour Party was there any practical wish to acknowledge the facts of international life and reach some accommodation with the new rulers of Russia. At the same time, Labour leaders and the majority of their supporters firmly resisted repeated overtures on the part of the tiny British Communist Party to affiliate: extremists were best left out in the cold to fend for themselves, especially at a difficult period when Labour had already replaced the fragmented Liberals as the official Opposition at Westminster.

The ineffectiveness of Labour in office, first in 1924 and again in 1929, was less surprising than the moderation and manifest good intentions of its ministers. They had been admitted by right, but still on sufferance, to Britain's ruling class. After sending for Ramsay MacDonald on 22 January 1924, and inviting him to form a Socialist administration, the King noted in his diary: 'Today twenty-three years ago dear Grandmama died. I wonder what she would have thought of a Labour Government.' In theory at least, Britain had entered the era of the common man. But real power eluded an inexperienced Cabinet dependent for its day-to-day survival on the backing of the traditional ruling parties. Labour, of course, had no ready-made cures for industrial strife, for growing unemployment, for social injustices. Political heirs to complex problems beyond the competence of any party or combination of parties to solve, Macdonald and his colleagues bought experience dearly and simply marked time. The British Communists had to bide theirs. Their inability to exploit the General Strike of 1926, which fizzled out after nine days of tension but relatively little violence, suggested that the trade unions themselves were not yet dominated by a hard core of extremists.

Nevertheless, a pathetic fallacy underpinned the attitude towards Communism of all British governments between the two world wars. Partly because ministers, in common with other members of the Establishment, seldom if ever bothered to study the writings of Marx and Lenin, they continued to look askance at members of the Communist Party as the only enemies within. The possibility of a Soviet-directed initiative to subvert from their allegiance young intellectuals of the upper and middle classes seemed altogether too far-fetched a proposition to be taken seriously. On the other hand, plotting and minor espionage by Soviet representatives could never be ruled out. The police raid on the ARCOS headquarters of the Soviet Trade Mission in 1927 confirmed to the authorities that their judgement on this score had been well founded. Ignorance and complacency blinded them to the increased likelihood of covert attempts to win over, and recruit, selected agents among the privileged sons of the widening ruling class at Oxbridge and other places of higher learning. The actual process was gradual. The plan owed much to the inspiration of well-travelled Soviet leaders like Maxim Litvinov, the former Russian envoy to London, who appreciated the tightly enmeshed web of trusting relationships which were at once the strength and weakness of the class structure in troubled Britain. The last people to be suspected of disloyalty by the authorities would be young undergraduates already training to take their places on the lower rungs of the Establishment ladder.

The humiliating downfall of the Labour Government in the financial and economic crash of 1931 created the right conditions for this bold plot. Disaffection sprang from political disillusionment; Cambridge, the more earnest of the two ancient universities, led the way. Neither the police nor MI5 paid undue attention to the spread of Communist ideas among students. Only card-carrying Party members interested them; and comparatively few card-carrying Party members at university stayed the course, a fact which could safely be put down to the passing restiveness of the young in every generation. This, then, was the climate in which Philby, Burgess, Maclean, Nunn May, 'Maurice', 'Basil', and others blossomed out as left-wing dissidents and potential Soviet agents during their undergraduate days. It was the climate of treason. Only the final solution of Karl Marx could save Britain from her own worst enemy, the ruling class of which the defeated and divided Labour Party now formed part.

It still seems puzzling, in retrospect, why a minority of young middle-class intellectuals and idealists were so easily seduced. Marx's second coming was, by any stretch of imagination, a distinct improbability in a country as politically stable as Britain. Nevertheless, shame and a desperate pessimism had become deeply rooted in many middle-class minds: the young felt particularly betrayed by their political elders, most of whom were relics of the Victorian age. Many of those who might have lifted the nation out of the political and economic doldrums had been killed off in 'the war to end wars'. The generation gap had grown too wide for comfort, particularly in the upper and middle classes from which leaders were drawn. It is not irrelevant to reflect that, almost without exception, the political elders looked back nostalgically to the past as if to a golden age of prosperity and tranquillity – an age which they vainly hoped to restore after the 1918 Armistice. They did little, in fact, to build on their hopes. One of the few leaders to see the vanity of such futile day-dreaming was Lloyd George; but Lloyd George was rejected in 1922 as an unscrupulous political adventurer who had contrived both to destroy the Liberal Party and to lower the tone of public life. He never came back.

The political elders also blundered in supposing that Britain's troubles stemmed from the immense sacrifices made to defeat Germany and her allies on the battlefield. In truth, the nation's economic decline had set in almost half a century earlier, coinciding with the steady expansion of the British Empire in its final and most stridently patriotic phase. Imperial preoccupations had obscured the many shortcomings in the state of home-based trade and industry. Germany and the United States had begun to overtake Britain before the end of the 1870s in the volume and quality of their steel and chemical products. Soon cheap American wheat, harvested on the prairies of the Middle West by mechanical means, undercut the prices of home-grown crops. There were, of course, new markets in British territories overseas to offset the strain and disguise the threat of this competition. Trade continued to follow the flag until the outbreak of the First World War, and a spirit of coarse superiority marked the mighty Empire, covering a quarter of the earth's surface, on which 'the sun never set'.

In the history of every country there come turning points at which the arrogance, called *hubris* by the ancient Greeks, seems to invite its own cruel nemesis. This was such a turning point. Eventually, at an unbearable cost, the British contributed to the overthrow of Imperial Germany and Imperial Austria on the battlefields of 1914–18, while Imperial Russia destroyed herself and enabled a Marxist tyranny to build a new police state on the ruins. There were no real victors of the First World War. Lloyd George should never have forgotten, if he ever remembered, the warning given by the American multi-millionaire industrialist, Andrew Carnegie, to English steelmasters in the 1890s: 'Most British equipment is in use twenty years after it should have been scrapped. It is because you keep this used-up machinery that the United States is making you a back-number.' By the early 1920s not only the machinery but the very industries which had once been the basis of Britain's wealth were outmoded. The politicians, now confronted by increasingly powerful trade unions wedded to restrictive practices and by employers unwilling to modernize, could only hope, in the negative conviction that other countries were probably still worse off.

Only the British Empire remained, but its impregnable foundations had been imperceptibly breached by the needless and ill-managed Boer War. The struggle to subdue the Irish people had temporarily ceased in 1921 with the partitioning of the island between a free state in the Catholic south and the province of Ulster in the largely Protestant north-east, an unhappy compromise which merely sowed fresh seeds of bitterness and violence. Nor did it do anything to arrest the decline of the British Empire which, as George V foresaw, was no longer a power to be reckoned with. 'What of the Empire?' were said to have been the King's last words, in 1936.

By then, as it happened, the Litvinov master plan to recruit middle-class undergraduates as Soviet agents had been put into effect. The probationers, once committed, could not easily turn back. What I find more astonishing in retrospect is the rapidity with which the anti-Establishment ferment caught on and spread in the 1930s, even allowing for the rise of Hitler and the subsequent anti-Fascist campaign.

I belong to the generation born between the two world wars. I can remember well how at school in the late 1920s we were encouraged as boys of eight to believe that the British Empire, recently enlarged in size by the peace settlement, would endure for the rest of our life-time. We celebrated Empire Day each 24 May, the anniversary of Queen Victoria's birth, parading before the flag and singing Kipling's hymn of dedication:

> Land of our birth we pledge to thee
> Our love and toil in years to be.

Kipling was exactly the same age as George V, and also died in 1936. The poet-laureate of the Empire had, I presently discovered, been deluding himself, the King, most of the ruling Establishment, as well as myself, by extolling the grandeur of an entity as impermanent as the Cheshire Cat's grin. I naturally came to prefer the simple realism of G. K. Chesterton:

> The Men who rule in England
> In stately conclave met.
> Alas, alas for England,
> They have no graves as yet.

While researching for my last book, the biography of the Anglo-Irish patriot Erskine Childers, I stumbled upon two other relevant and interesting facts. Firstly, Childers was far-sighted enough to perceive, partly through his experiences as a gunner in the Boer War and partly as a result of his subsequent impatience with Britain's clumsy handling of the Irish problem, that the British Empire was already doomed. He reached this conclusion well before 1914. Others, by no means all of them Socialists, shared Childers's bleak premonition. The second was this: there are always time lags between certain turning points and the public's awareness that such turning points have been passed. These time lags were doubtless longer then than they are now; but it is strange how persistent and firm were the illusions which comforted so many people in Britain, young and old alike, in the troubled 1920s. The next decade would force everyone to shed these illusions.

It was commonly held, for instance, before the crash of 1929, that Henry Ford's achievements had utterly refuted Karl Marx's grim prophecies. The repercussions of the American depression were swiftly felt throughout the civilized world. The Soviet Union alone escaped the worst consequences, due to its economic backwardness and self-imposed isolation. In London, when the crisis hit Britain in the summer of 1931, George V persuaded the Labour Prime Minister Ramsay MacDonald, to lead an emergency National Government, an apparent betrayal which split and demoralized the Labour Party. Still the centre of an Empire from which food and raw materials could be imported cheaply, Britain managed during the 1930s to avoid violent disturbances in areas of high unemployment and poverty. Exports fell off; but the British, increasingly forced since the 1880s to sell manufactured goods abroad, staved off bankruptcy with the earnings from overseas investments, shipping, insurance and financial services. This remained at best a short-term remedy: the stagnant heavy industries of Britain, in which these capital assets might have been usefully invested, were left to rot.

The Communist Party began to attract new members. The Comintern and the NKVD exerted themselves to take the fullest advantage of this cosmic crisis of capitalism. As Harold Macmillan, then the Tory MP for a depressed constituency in the stricken industrial north-east of England, justly noted:

> It had become evident that the structure of capitalist society in its old form had broken down, not only in Britain but all over Europe and even in the United States. The whole system had to be reassessed. Perhaps it could not survive at all; it certainly could not survive without radical change. . . . Something like a revolutionary situation had developed, not only at home but overseas.

It was no accident that, almost without exception, the young men recruited one by one as probationer-spies had passed through public schools before going up to university. These institutions had long been the natural forcing houses for sons of the ruling class; and in the Victorian heyday of imperialism, many new establishments had sprung up to supply the need for administrators, teachers, doctors, lawyers, as well as pro-consuls, military leaders and bishops in overseas territories. Reforms introduced originally at Rugby by the zealous Dr Thomas Arnold had since been copied or adapted in the oldest schools as in the new, from Eton, Harrow and Winchester to Haileybury, Cheltenham and Radley. The classics and a diluted form of Christianity were drummed into pupils; a frequently savage discipline was imposed to inculcate character and obedience to authority. Arnold had set his face against instruction in scientific subjects: 'Rather than have physical science the principal thing in my son's mind,' he said, 'I would gladly have him think that the sun went round the earth.... Surely the one thing needful for an Englishman to study is Christian moral and political philosophy.' The bias against the thorough teaching of science persisted, doing nothing to alleviate the competitive problems of British industry. Only in the twentieth century did attitudes gradually change. Science, while still considered a subject unsuitable for real gentlemen, was at least taught. Like engineers, manufacturers and tradesmen, of course, all but outstanding scientists ranked in the social scale as just a cut above ordinary people.

By the time Burgess went to Eton, Maclean to Gresham's, and Philby to Westminster School in the mid twenties, matters had belatedly improved. Yet most public schoolboys continued to be grounded in the classics. Those who sought to specialize in science remained few. In rare establishments, such as Oundle and Bedford, far-sighted headmasters took science more seriously. At Bedford, for instance, J. D. Bernal, the Marxist biochemist who exercised a sometimes sinister influence over the minds of many Cambridge undergraduates in the 1930s, received his formation after an unsatisfactory start at Stonyhurst, a Catholic public school run by

English Jesuits and steeped in the classical tradition. It is an intriguing fact that the scientific 'illiteracy' of the average public school product proved no bar to a convenient marriage of minds between Marxist scientists and Marxist non-scientists once Communism gained a grip on Cambridge. For Marxist visionaries like Bernal were exceedingly rare both in their cultural breadth and in their charismatic charm. Moreover, Cambridge had far outstripped Oxford as a world centre of scientific research, drawing the best brains from the grammar schools and technical establishments to the Cavendish Laboratory and the Dunn Biochemical Institute. The two cultures, normally as divisive as the more obvious class distinctions between rich and poor, rulers and ruled, were thus partly bridged by a shared belief in the Communist recipe for national survival. An Alan Nunn May could make common cause with a Donald Maclean, however incompatible the two might appear. 'Nothing could have been worse for the development of my mind than Doctor Butler's school,' Darwin had lamented in his autobiography of the five years he spent at Shrewsbury in the early nineteenth century. By a latter-day process of natural selection, Soviet recruiting sergeants wasted no time in tapping the available talent at Cambridge in the early 1930s. Scientists would have their future uses as much as non-scientists.

In the written records of the public schools attended by Burgess, Maclean and Philby, I discovered a number of useful clues to their developing characters in boyhood and youth. These sources were supplemented by the recollections of masters and fellow pupils. I am indebted to Michael McCrum, the present headmaster, and to Patrick Strong, the archivist of Eton College, for information which sharpened my perception of Guy Burgess as a schoolboy; to Sir Robert Birley, who taught him history; to Lord Hartwell, Evan James and other contemporaries who were friends of his; to the Director of Studies at the Royal Naval College, Dartmouth, for first-hand evidence about the intervening period Burgess spent there as a trainee-cadet; and to assistants at the Public Records Office in London for enabling me to unearth the basic facts of his father's comparatively undistinguished career as a regular officer in the Fleet. The present headmaster of Gresham's, Logie Bruce Lockhart, went out of his way to qualify my preconceptions regarding the status and tone of that small but ancient foundation at the time Donald Maclean was sent there. I am grateful to him, to the late John Pudney, and particularly to the late James Klugman, among other contemporaries, for their vigorous recollections, oral and written, of Gresham's as they knew it. Similarly, I wish to thank Dr John Rae, the headmaster of Westminster, and Charles Keeley the archivist, for allowing me to explore the records leading me not only to Joseph Grigg and several other fellow pupils of Philby's but to that remarkable octogenarian, Laurence Tanner, who was one of Philby's teachers.

It is impossible to provide an exhaustive list of the many individuals responsible for enlightening me on the heady atmosphere which Burgess, Maclean and Philby found on reaching Cambridge. To the late Sir Herbert Butterfield, a former Vice-Chancellor and Master of Peterhouse, I owe a special debt of gratitude for the clarity of his personal memories, for his balanced historical judgement, and for introducing me to Fellows who knew one or other of my subjects during their undergraduate days. The present Professor of German at Cambridge, Dr Leonard Forster, to name but one, shared with Maclean the same supervisor in French in his first year at Trinity Hall and formed his own rather unflattering opinion of the future spy–diplomat's mannerisms and personality. Sir Michael and Lady Clapham knew Maclean in quite a different context, the latter as a transitory girl friend and the former as a successful rival, while Christopher Gillie and Lady Felicity Rumbold added to my knowledge of his home and family background. At this point I should stress that, in order to spare them embarrassment, I did not approach the relatives of any of my subjects. The objective views of outsiders, whether sympathetically disposed or not, seemed to me preferable and altogether more valid. My understanding of Philby's less ostentatious life as an undergraduate at Trinity was deepened by the memories and reflections of a number of critical contemporaries, again including James Klugman and Joseph Grigg; and the testimony of Charles

Madge, Sir Robert Birley again, Dr Goronwy Rees, and Mrs Miriam Lane (*née* Rothschild), among dozens of equally acute eye-witnesses, strengthened my appreciation of the Rake's Progress through the same college of Philby's noisy companion and future accomplice, Guy Burgess.

'Really cogent evidence is what you need,' remarked an eminent historian during the preliminary stages of my research. 'If you don't succeed, don't publish.' Similar counsel, more colloquially and pungently expressed, was offered by Malcolm Muggeridge, Goronwy Rees and Arthur Koestler, who were not entirely unfamiliar with the secretive ways of spies. Conscious that Soviet agents in British Establishment guise would be the last people to keep diaries or leave incriminating notes lying about, I set about the hardest part of my task without much hope. Admittedly, I enjoyed discovering and piecing together the scattered fragments of an immense jigsaw puzzle. I was not alone in my growing suspicions about the identity of the so-called 'Fourth Man'. I disliked this numbering business, convenient though it was, because it falsely suggested that the spies concerned were of equal importance and intimately bound together operationally. This, I realized, was most unlikely, though a degree of 'inter-consciousness' did exist, exceptionally, between them, a dangerous concession which the Russians seldom appear to have authorized elsewhere. Maybe the presence of Burgess as a kind of joker in the pack forced this insecure expedient on the Russians. Maybe they felt that the British had to be treated as 'a special case' in the confused circumstances of the 1930s. At any rate, without disclosing my sources, I can say that gradually this chance element of 'inter-consciousness' led me to the trail of the so-called 'Fifth Man' as well, just as it had led American agents to the same quarry some thirty years earlier after a tip-off by two members of the future Israeli intelligence service. The 'Fifth Man', code-named 'Basil', freely confessed. 'Maurice', the Fourth Man, did not give himself up at once. Had the British been told of 'Basil's' confession to the Americans in 1948, all the conspirators, 'Maurice' included, could have been rounded up in quick order. And the humiliating fiasco of the Burgess–Maclean escape to Moscow, where Philby eventually joined them, would never have happened. Unfortunately, the Americans decided otherwise. They had their reasons, of course, but the British Secret Service is still smarting from the heavy blow to its self-esteem. Their curiosity, not to say the pestering of me by latterday representatives of the service, became only too apparent during the final phase of my work. It was quite understandable, if tedious and fruitless.

The full measure of the help I have received can be found on every page that follows. I must single out for special mention Malcolm and Kitty Muggeridge, Lady Llewellyn-Davies, Lord Rothschild, John Lehmann, Sir Roger Chance, Dr Goronwy Rees, David Footman, the Rt Hon. Jo Grimond, MP, and Laura Grimond, Nicholas Elliott, Colonel Felix Cowgill, Tom Howarth, Lord (C. P.) Snow, E. H. Cookridge, Sir Isaiah Berlin, Dr Michael Posnan, Walter and Tanya Bell, Lord Sherfield (the former Roger Makins), Lord Boothby, Lord Inchyra, Frank Gillard, Sir William Haley, Harman Grisewood, Christopher Mayhew, the Rt Hon. J. Enoch Powell, MP, Sir John Balfour, Sir Ashley Clark, Sir Frederick Warner, David Astor, Miss Clare Hollingworth, George Carey-Foster, Sir Robert Mackenzie, Robin Denniston, Neal Ascherson, Lord Adrian, Lord Shinwell, James R. Murphy, J. O. Roach, C. W. Crawley, Sir John Colville, Ralph Dreschfield, Dr Aristide Grosse, Sir Rudolf Peierls, Dr Conor Cruise O'Brien and Professor Hugh Seton-Watson. In my efforts to reconstruct, step by step, the careers of my subjects and to place them in the setting of the period, I was also greatly assisted by dozens of others too sensitive to permit their names to appear. As for the BBC's sensitivity in protecting the good name of its former employees, this was surely carried to excess when I was refused permission, under existing rules, to consult Guy Burgess's personal file. By contrast, I wish to acknowledge the large debt I owe to the efficient and painstaking custodians of the National Archives in Washington.

I must thank both authors and publishers for permitting me to quote extracts from the following works: *Communism and British*

Intellectuals by Neal Wood (Gollancz); *English History 1914–1945* by A. J. P. Taylor (Oxford University Press); *A History of England* and *Neville Chamberlain*, both by Keith Feiling (Macmillan); *Our Own People: A Memoir of Ignace Reiss and His Friends* by E. K. Poretsky (Macmillan); *My Lives* by Francis Meynell (Bodley Head); *A Chapter of Accidents* by Goronwy Rees (Chatto & Windus); *I Believed* by Douglas Hyde (Heinemann); *Memoirs* by Harry S. Truman, vol. 2, *Years of Trial and Hope* (Doubleday); *Chronicles of Wasted Time*, vols. 1 and 2, by Malcolm Muggeridge (Collins); *The Philby Affair* by Hugh Trevor-Roper (Kimber); *Philby: The Spy Who Betrayed a Generation* by Bruce Page, David Leitch and Phillip Knightley (Sphere); *The Missing Macleans* by Geoffrey Hoare (Cassell); *Harold Nicolson, Diaries and Letters*, 3 vols., *1930–62*, edited by Nigel Nicolson (Collins); *The Diaries of Sir Robert Bruce Lockhart*, edited by Kenneth Young (Macmillan); *The Mist Procession* by Lord Vansittart (Hutchinson); *Edward VIII* by Frances Donaldson (Weidenfeld & Nicolson); *John Strachey* by Hugh Thomas (Eyre Methuen); *Cambridge between the Wars* by T. E. B. Howarth (Collins); *Baffy, The Diaries of Blanche Dugdale, 1936–1947*, edited by N. A. Rose (Valentine Mitchell); *The Invisible Writing* by Arthur Koestler (Hutchinson); *Ramsay MacDonald* by David Marquand (Jonathan Cape); *Kim Philby, the Spy I Loved* by Eleanor Philby (Pan); *World within World* by Stephen Spender (Faber); *Bodyguard of Lies* by Anthony Cave Brown (W. H. Allen); *The Distant Drum, Reflections on the Spanish Civil War* by Philip Toynbee (Sidgwick & Jackson); *A World Destroyed: The Atomic Bomb and the Grand Alliance* by Martin J. Sherwin (Vintage); and *My Silent War* by Kim Philby (André Deutsch).

A concluding word of gratitude is due to my agent, Graham Watson of Curtis Brown, to James O. Wade of The Dial Press/James Wade, New York, and Harold Harris of Hutchinson, London, respectively, to Christina and to Eleanor Ransome, without whom there would have been no legible typescript, and to a former senior executive of the British Secret Service whose spasmodic intellectual pleasure in reading certain crucial sections of the finished article may have been offset by ingrained professional reservations. Like his American counterparts, this person must remain anonymous. Both to him and to the formidable array of independent witnesses who willingly answered when asked, I am obliged for the facts and impressions they furnished. Responsibility for the conclusions I elicited from these is mine, and mine alone.

1. RULING-CLASS RADICALS

The Communist Party of Great Britain was founded in the summer of 1920, but its rules were not drawn up until April of the following year. Dwarfed from the beginning by its gigantic neighbour, the British Labour Party, which already boasted four million members, it has remained ever since the smallest in numbers of any Communist Party among the major industrial nations. Membership jumped to merely 11,000 during 1926, the year of the General Strike; by 1930 it had fallen to a new low level of 1376. The figures soared again during the troubled 1930s, but not remarkably. There were still less than 16,000 card-carrying members in 1938 at the time of the Munich crisis. After another sharp drop a year later, prompted no doubt by the unpopular Nazi–Soviet Pact, membership rose again to a peak of 55,000 in the middle of the Second World War when the life-and-death struggle of the Red Army against the German invader commanded the admiring respect of the British people as a whole.[1*]

No table of official statistics can be taken, however, as a true guide to Communist strength. For Party leaders had been quick to learn from their Russian mentors that sympathizers and covert, or hidden, members could help to outweigh the disadvantages of inferior numbers. By skilful propaganda and underground manoeuvring, the Party could sometimes prove that it had a nuisance value out of all proportion to its size. It is oddly ironical then that, unlike early Communists elsewhere, the British comrades managed to attract and hold few intellectuals. Those who did become Leninist–Marxist converts out of conviction were regarded with suspicion; most of them failed to stay the course. This

* Superior figures refer to the Notes on pages 453–72.

distrust of intellectuals was an understandable prejudice which both Labour and Communist Party members instinctively shared. The tangled roots of that prejudice lay buried deep in the collective unconscious of the British working class: pride and a stubborn self-respect reinforced it. Why should they demean themselves by letting a handful of would-be mental superiors patronize or lead them?

As opposed to the Communists, however, Labour supporters usually succeeded in disguising their distrust, drawing on the ideas, enthusiasm and moral support of upper- and middle-class radical sympathizers. The Fabian Society, with George Bernard Shaw, H. G. Wells, Sidney and Beatrice Webb particularly active after its foundation in 1884, had helped to provide British socialism with a philosophy of moderation and 'gradualism' which orthodox Marxists spurned as altogether too timid.

Not even Karl Marx in his London exile created any stir among British radical thinkers. Expelled as an agitator from continental Europe during 1848, the 'Year of Revolutions', the prophet and founding father of Communism found freedom and leisure (thanks to the selfless support he received from his friend and collaborator, Friedrich Engels) to elaborate his own inhuman philosophy under the domed roof of the British Museum's Reading Room. He had no hopes of the British as revolutionaries. Despite oppression and exploitation, the working class appeared too law-abiding, too long-suffering, too willing to wait for legislative reforms to improve conditions of life. As an amphitheatre for playing out the Marxist drama of the class struggle, in accordance with the concepts of dialectical materialism, Britain was perhaps the least suitable of places. Karl Marx resigned himself to that fact as he pressed on with his research and writing.

The first volume of *Das Kapital*, which required a tactical genius such as Lenin to translate into practical revolutionary terms, was published in 1867. The second and third volumes, edited by Engels, appeared after Marx's death in 1883. Few educated British of the period had the taste or endurance for these turgid tomes; of those who pretended or claimed to have done so, fewer still accepted the Marxist recipe for salvation. One notable contemporary who swallowed it, hook, line and sinker, was the eccentric

English financier and radical writer Henry Hyndman, who remained permanently influenced by Marx. The Social Democratic Federation which he founded in the 1880s was a small body, rigidly doctrinaire and, despite its name, somewhat exclusive. It exerted little popular appeal, though its active members displayed considerable courage in the industrial upheavals of that time when extremists were often met with physical force.[2]

Britain's first Labour Prime Minister, Ramsay MacDonald, fell briefly under the spell of Hyndman's simple Marxist cure-all as a romantic young Scot down from his native Lossiemouth to his first job as a clerk in Bristol. MacDonald left the Federation without regret, thoroughly disillusioned with its autocratic leadership and ruthless tactics. Like many other British Socialists, the young MacDonald disliked the crude materialistic basis of the Hyndman school of Marxism. Nor did he believe that Marx was right to assert that Socialism would necessarily be imposed by revolution. Indeed, MacDonald contended that Marx would have done better to study 'the full implications of Darwinian biology' rather than Hegel's dialectic, for Darwin had demonstrated that higher forms of life emerge slowly from lower forms, 'not from a clash between opposing forces'. If Marx had taken the trouble to study Darwin, he might have better predicted how British society did, in fact, evolve in the late nineteenth century. There had been no revolutionary cataclysm. 'The Marxian today still wonders why England fell from grace,' wrote MacDonald. 'England did not fall from grace. Neither Marx nor Engels saw deep enough to discover the possibilities of peaceful advance which lay hidden below the surface.'[3]

The British brand of Socialism eventually adopted by the Labour Party owed more to Methodism than to Marx. The practical idealism of early reformers like Robert Owen was not forgotten. And constructive change was still the watchword of the Fabian luminaries. Into the amorphous mass of radical opinion they inserted leaven, which gradually permeated the whole. Their theories were founded on solid facts, so that Socialism could be applied in terms of society as it was. MacDonald felt as much at home among the Fabians as he did working with his fellow Scot,

Keir Hardie, to promote the aims of the Independent Labour Party, which also favoured moderate, undogmatic Socialist aims. Hardie had the vision to recognize that any future parliamentary group claiming to represent the working class must have unqualified trade union support. To leave the sponsorship of working-class MPs to the Liberals, as happened during the last quarter of the nineteenth century, would neither promote the cause of Socialism nor serve the interests of the working class. Hardie's insistence that the handful of worker-MPs should withdraw their allegiance to 'capitalist parties' like the Liberals at last won the day. The new Labour Party, representing all strands of moderate Socialist opinion from Fabians to trade unionists, emerged. Hyndman and his extremist followers chose to stay out in the cold.

Appropriately enough, the decision was reached in 1900. It laid down that future Labour candidates should not be drawn entirely and exclusively from the working class, since the Labour movement must always be open to anyone who earned his living by hand or by brain. This characteristically British departure, tolerant and practical, would not have earned the approval of Karl Marx; but such a bourgeois compromise would not have greatly surprised him, any more than it surprised that intolerant doctrinaire Henry Hyndman. The political climate of Britain did not yet seem conducive to bloody revolution, or bloody-minded revolutionaries. No Lenins lurked in the loosely knit British Labour Party in its early, struggling days. Its first big test came in the General Election of 1906, when the Liberals were swept to power. Of the twenty-nine victorious Labour MPs,

> only a minority acknowledged any debt to Socialist theory. When they were asked to name the books which had influenced them most, the Bible, Ruskin, Carlyle and Dickens figured most prominently in their replies; only two mentioned Marx. . . . Most of them were trade unionists who had come to Westminster to win tangible benefits for their members and their class, not socialist evangelists who saw it as a stepping stone to a new Jerusalem.[4]

No love was lost between the Labour Party and the out-and-out Marxist supporters of Hyndman. Peaceful evolution, not violent revolution, remained the cornerstone of the faith. Nor did the Bolsheviks' triumph in Russia and the subsequent formation in Britain of the Communist Party lessen the antagonism of Labour to Marxist extremism. On the other hand, the aggressive concept of 'workers' control', derived from French syndicalism, was propagated by A. G. Orage in his journal *New Age*; and from 1910 the Guild Socialists, as a small, independent organization, attracted numerous young idealists. In fact, the Fabian Research Department, set up by the Webbs in 1912, was dominated by them. Among the office-holders were the future economist G. D. H. Cole, and the future 'guru' of the Communist Party, R. Palme Dutt; and among ordinary members were the journalists Ivor Brown, William Mellor, Raymond Postgate, W. H. Ewer, George Lansbury and Francis Meynell.

Meynell, a product of Downside, one of England's leading Catholic public schools, and of Trinity College, Dublin, was a son of the poet Alice Meynell. He has shed revealing human light on the political mood of his own generation of young intellectuals during and just after the First World War. Slowly veering from the Catholic idealism in which he had been reared towards what he described as 'conscientious agnosticism', this able but restless youth joined George Lansbury's Socialist paper, the *Daily Herald*, alongside such colleagues as William Mellor, G. D. H. Cole, W. H. Ewer, Gerald Gould and Harold Laski, in 1913. Except for one war-time interval, when he expedited his release from prison as a conscientious objector by a twelve-day hunger strike, Meynell continued to work on that paper, whose secret benefactor was an unusual American millionairess. This lady, Mary Dodge by name, kept out of the public gaze by invariably letting her friend and fellow radical, the gracious Lady de la Warr, act discreetly for her. Discretion of the kind was necessary: both ladies had been active in the prewar suffragette demonstrations aimed at securing votes for women from the otherwise preoccupied Liberal Government of Mr Asquith. Meynell's friend and colleague, Raymond Postgate, held similarly emotional views. Postgate's father was Professor of Latin at Cambridge University, and Raymond had himself graduated from St John's College, Oxford. A double link bound him to

Lansbury: his devotion to the same ideals of social justice, and his recent marriage to Daisy, the daughter of this socialist stalwart and employer. Lansbury's *Daily Herald* staff earned a good deal of unpopularity for the paper's critical and allegedly unpatriotic attitude to the war, yet few of its writers were doctrinaire Socialists. As Postgate admitted: 'To get into its columns a writer had only to be called a rebel: he had to be an enemy of the existing capitalist system, and what he was in favour of mattered less.'[5]

Meynell's qualifications as a rebel could not be denied. His precise recipe for saving Britain from herself had not yet been thought out; but he remembered vividly for the rest of his life how the overthrow of the Czar 'thrilled the whole Labour Movement and many outside it'. The Russian revolutionaries appeared to be the best available models to follow: 'For me and the rest of "Lansbury's Lambs" Lenin's was a most hopeful programme – the beginning of a new Socialist International. We did not foresee its slow degradation by Stalin after Lenin's death in 1924.'[6] Needless to say, Meynell had read none of Marx's ponderous works. In this he was anything but alone. A smattering of William Morris and of the ex-Cambridge, ex-parson Edward Carpenter, one of Morris's later disciples, faintly coloured the young man's vague aspirations for building a better world.

An unofficial representative of the new Soviet régime arrived in London to spy out the land not long after the 1918 Armistice. Maxim Litvinov was already on friendly terms with the Meynells. As a refugee from Czarist Russia, Litvinov had married an English girl called Ivy Low; and Ivy happened to be a close companion of Francis Meynell's sister, Violet. In the summer of 1920, a few weeks before the founding of Britain's Communist Party, Litvinov left Britain on a sudden visit to Copenhagen. His ostensible aim was to negotiate an exchange of British and Russian soldiers taken prisoner in Winston Churchill's newly 'undeclared war' against Bolshevism; his unavowed aim was to seek an end to that war itself. Francis Meynell, aware that the *Daily Herald* was badly short of newsprint, partly because of a boycott initiated by some wholesale suppliers, crossed the sea to obtain Litvinov's conspiratorial assistance. At the hotel where they met, the Russian leader studiously left the door of his room wide open for the benefit of any eavesdroppers in the vicinity, and greeted Meynell:

I said, 'Here, dear Maxim, is a present from Ivy,' and gave him a carefully parcelled tie in which was sewn a note from [Theodore] Rothstein who was substituting for Litvinoff in London. Maxim thanked me with an understanding glance and went into his bedroom. In a few minutes he returned, wearing the new tie. When we were seated and chatting, the door open all the time, he said, 'You English are great pipe-smokers. Here is some Russian tobacco to try,' and he tossed me a tobacco pouch. I knew that he knew that I never smoked a pipe, so I guessed that the pouch contained an answer to Rothstein. It did – a practical one; for when I got back to my hotel I opened the pouch and found two strings of pearls.[7]

Meynell had to be careful not to be caught smuggling the pearls into England, so he sank them deep in a fancy jar of Danish butter and delivered the contents safely to Rothstein. It was the first of several such trips he undertook as a carrier of jewels, each more hazardous than the last as Scotland Yard's Special Branch grew increasingly suspicious. Once, after vainly searching his baggage, 'the sleuths were helpful in repacking, but I found it difficult to thank them and at the same time prevent three large diamonds in my mouth from rattling'. In the end, unable to supply the necessary newsprint, Litvinov was persuaded by Meynell to consult Moscow about a suggested unconditional gift to the *Daily Herald*. Meynell duly received £75,000 worth of jewels. These he tried to dispose of openly on the London market, a somewhat foolhardy move which in itself was bound to attract attention. However, the authorities were already on the alert, and waiting, not for the first or last time; messages between Moscow and the Russian Trade Mission in London had meanwhile been intercepted and decoded. There were injudicious references in them to funds for the *Daily Herald*; and since Meynell had unwisely failed to consult Lansbury or anyone else in advance, he chose now to resign rather than be sacked by his co-directors, one of them Ernest

Bevin, a young and rising trade union leader. Proceeds from the sale of the jewels were handed back intact to the Russians.

This did not end Meynell's unconventional if relatively brief career as a left-wing sympathizer and activist. Towards the end of 1920 he was buttonholed by the recently appointed chairman of the new Communist Party, Arthur McManus, and persuaded to redesign the title and to edit the *Communist*, the organization's weekly organ. Thus Meynell became a card-carrying comrade, though his motives were mixed. McManus, a tolerant Clydeside shop steward, did not mind nearly so much as other members of the Party's provisional executive that this recruit 'had never heard of dialectical materialism. . . . I had awkward summonses before them.' Nevertheless, Meynell's editorship produced quick results. Sales of the newspaper quadrupled from 8500 to over 40,000 in the first two months of 1921. Its layout was as presentable as its editor, already a superb typographer, could make it; its contents were no better than might have been expected from a confused idealist. Its comments on current events were 'allusively quizzical', according to Meynell:

> For instance, whenever we quoted from *The Times*, we referred to 'the bloody old *Times*, as Cobbett called it'. I cannot think that the out-of-work miner knew or cared who Cobbett was. The simple fact is that we wrote and cartooned for ourselves.[8]

The editor was obliged to resign in the early summer of 1921. Most of the Party's senior officials were relieved to see him go, but it is only fair to add that they did not push him. What happened, in fact, was that Meynell, after lampooning the leaders of the railwaymen and transport workers for their failure to back an ultimatum of the miners, which might have resulted in a General Strike and improved wages all round, had been unexpectedly served with a writ for libel. The offending cartoon, a realistic impression of The Last Supper, cruelly depicted the railwaymen's spokesman, J. H. Thomas, in the guise of Judas Iscariot. Of the abortive triple strike – called off at the eleventh hour, so Meynell alleged, as a result of J. H. Thomas's weak-kneed treachery – King George V had noted anxiously:

There is no doubt that we are passing through as grave a crisis as this country has ever had. All the troops have been called out: Kensington Gardens is full of them. The public are on the side of the Government.

The writ for libel had already been accepted by the offending editor on the last Saturday of April 1920 when the Monarch, relieved but still a little bemused, wrote in his diary:

I went to a football match at which there were 73,000 people: at the end they sang the National Anthem and cheered tremendously. There were no bolsheviks there! At least I never saw any. The country is all right: just a few extremists are doing all the harm.[9]

Months passed before the Meynell case came to court. The judge directed the jury that 'vindictive damages' would be in order. Meynell promptly went bankrupt, unable to find the necessary £2000 – a large amount at that time. He was eventually discharged from bankruptcy when Lady de la Warr once more came discreetly to the rescue. From mid 1921 onwards, Francis Meynell devoted himself increasingly to typography and his famous Pelican and Nonesuch presses, gradually shedding his extremist opinions though not his left-wing friends.

The flirtation with Communism of Francis Meynell, whom the ultra-Tory newspaper the *Morning Post* had once described as 'a conscientious cad' and who was later honoured with a knighthood, seemed fairly typical of the period. Not many of the small group of radical intellectuals with whom Meynell was originally associated joined the Party or, if they did, stayed in it. Karl Marx had expressed his faith in the intellectual as the 'head' while the workers provided the 'heart' of the revolutionary movement. Unfortunately, owing to the traditional class antipathy between British intellectuals and workers, Marx's prescription did not work too well. William Mellor, a powerful orator of Evangelical fervour with a marked regional accent, would openly deride the idea that the only good Communist was necessarily one 'whose arse stuck out of his pants'; and Mellor, a former divinity student at Oxford, had warned as early as 1920 that he did not think it wise for the Communist Party at its birth to begin 'bureaucratizing its administration'. The bureaucracy took control, nevertheless; and before the end of the 1930s most of the original intellectuals had quit, Mellor among them.

The precise reasons for this varied, of course, with the individual member. Sylvia Pankhurst, a daughter of the militant advocate of women's rights, Emmeline Pankhurst, was a founder-member of the British Communist Party and the only intellectual among the eight delegates who went to Moscow in 1920 for the Second Congress of the Comintern. On the original provisional Executive of the Party, three intellectuals were elected out of a committee of fourteen. Apart from Mellor, the middle-class members were Colonel Cecil L'Estrange Malone, a distinguished war-time aviator who had served in the Royal Navy with the Anglo-Irish patriot Erskine Childers, author of the famous thriller *The Riddle of the Sands*. There was also a lady called Dora Montefiore. Malone, then a Liberal MP, was sentenced to six months in gaol for 'incitement to revolution' when, on the third anniversary of the Russian Revolution, he asked a large audience in the Royal Albert Hall, London: 'What are a few Churchills or Curzons on lamp-posts compared to the massacre of thousands of human beings?'

That gesture of martyrdom did not mollify Malone's colleagues on the British Politburo. They distrusted his motives, disliked his argumentativeness and were not sorry to see him leave gaol and go to the Labour Party. Dora Montefiore in due course died; and J. Walton Newbold, another rare intellectual voted on to the Executive, soon followed Malone's example. Later, he was appointed by MacDonald's second Labour Government of 1929 to the Macmillan committee on finance and industry, whose published findings precipitated that government's collapse.

Nearly two-thirds of prominent British Communists or Party sympathizers during the twenties had studied at Oxford or Cambridge. Their numbers fluctuated but probably never exceeded 300. They included R. Palme Dutt and his brother Clemens, sons of a Swedish mother and an Indian father who had a medical practice at Cambridge. Rajani Palme Dutt, like Tom Wintringham and Andrew Rothstein, was a graduate of Balliol; John Strachey, Ralph Fox and Montagu Slater were graduates of Magdalen, and

Raymond Postgate of St John's. Trinity College, Cambridge, had helped to sharpen the minds of M. Philips Price, W. N. Ewer, Emile Burns and Maurice Dobb, the last-named settling down to a long and eventful career as a Marxist intriguer and academic economist of subtlety and virtuosity. He came from a Gloucestershire family of landowners related to the Huxleys and Trevelyans. Philips Price, like Ewer, was a journalist who later became a Labour MP. So in due course did John Strachey, a future Labour Cabinet minister and the scion of an ancient West Country family of landed gentry. Philips Price had been educated at Harrow, Strachey at Eton. Ellen Wilkinson, a graduate of Manchester University with outspoken left-wing views, was to win notoriety as a fiery Labour MP whom Attlee promoted as Minister of Education in his 1945 administration. Andrew Rothstein, whose father Theodore happened to be a Russian Bolshevik posted to Britain, found less difficulty than most in accepting Party discipline and dogma. Along with the Palme Dutt brothers and, perhaps more surprisingly, Emile Burns, Rothstein earned a place in the hierarchy of the small but rigidly organized British Communist Party.

Burns was the son and grandson of senior colonial administrators in Britain's best Victorian pro-consular tradition. His grandfather, Sir Patrick, had been Auditor-General of the Leeward Islands; Emile Burns's brother took the same path, which would lead eventually to a knighthood and to the post of permanent British representative to the United Nations' Trusteeship Council. Two other women worthy of mention were a London School of Economics graduate, Freda Utley, whose father had been a friend and former associate of George Bernard Shaw's on the Liberal newspaper the *Star*, and Dona Torr, the daughter of a canon of Chester Cathedral.

As an outlet for youthful idealism, rebelliousness and confused anti-Establishment fervour, the new Communist Party managed to attract non-conformists of radical instincts, quite unprepared in most cases to be ordered how to think and what to say by an uncompromising leadership drawn mainly from the working class. They revelled in free and wide-ranging debate, and therefore found it intolerably hard to swallow policies and tactics which omniscient officials tried to ram down their throats. Moreover, the general post-war mood of indiscipline did not help Party organizers who insisted on stiffly disciplined acceptance of the Party line. For though the Communist Party had to feel its own way forward, it based itself slavishly on the Soviet model, too readily adopting the principle: 'When father turns, we all turn.'

What ultimately played into the hands of the Communists was the inability of the traditional Conservative and Liberal parties to restore the nation to prosperity and power. When Churchill as Minister for War had sought boldly to reassert outmoded British values in 1919 by promoting armed intervention against the emergent Soviet Union, moderate trade unionists like Bevin had rallied with Labour Party stalwarts, Communists, and intellectuals to force Lloyd George, then Prime Minister, to disown an unacceptable plan. Francis Meynell, incidentally, had been instrumental in persuading Sir Osbert Sitwell to write a poem damning Churchill's bellicosity, which replaced the *Daily Herald*'s leading article on 22 July 1919:

> The Daily Herald
> is unkind.
> It has been horrid
> about my nice new war.
> I shall burn the Daily Herald.
> I think, myself,
> That my new war
> Is one of the nicest we've had;
> It is not a war really,
> It is only a training for the next one,
> And saves the expense of Army Manoeuvres.
> Besides, we have not declared war;
> We are merely restoring order –
> As the Germans did in Belgium,
> And as I hope to do later
> In Ireland . . .[10]

Eccentrics as brilliant as Sitwell simply could not be dragooned or silenced. They belonged to that rare breed of highly articulate individualists which, regardless of class distinctions, had always tended to flourish in Britain. The politically inclined, especially the middle aged and the moderates, preferred the less claustrophobic atmosphere of the post-war Labour Party and regarded Communism as a plaything for young extremists. It came as no great surprise when C. P. (later Sir Charles) Trevelyan, a Northumberland landowner and a great-nephew of Macaulay, forsook the Liberals and became a Labour MP in 1922. He was joined on the back-benches by Arthur Ponsonby, another ex-Liberal whose father had been Queen Victoria's private secretary and who had himself served in childhood as one of Her Majesty's pages of honour. The not unfamiliar gibe that such turncoats deserved to be shot as 'traitors to their class' became more pronounced in 1924, during Ramsay MacDonald's brief first term as Labour Prime Minister, when Trevelyan and Ponsonby accepted ministerial posts. The composition of the parliamentary Labour Party in the early twenties reflected the marked shift in the radical outlook. Trade unionists no longer dominated; they formed just over half the total of Labour MPs, the remainder being drawn from the middle, even the upper class.

The Communists thus had an uphill struggle, not least because Labour kept them at arms' length, excluding them rigorously from affiliating in any way. Walton Newbold, a Quaker intellectual, was returned as Labour MP for the Scottish industrial town of Motherwell in 1922, but lost the seat the following year and left the Communist Party shortly afterwards. A second Communist, Shapurji Saklatvala, who was a Parsee and a member of the immensely wealthy Tata family of Bombay, also won the Labour working-class seat of Battersea North as an official Labour candidate in 1922, losing it the next year, then regaining it under his true colours in 1924. This was the peak of parliamentary achievement for the Party then and later. It stood no chance against the gigantic, expanding Labour movement, whose leaders would have no truck with official extremists. It lost ground, too, in failing to gain and hold many more intellectuals. By curbing the spontaneity of malcontents whose bourgeois thought might otherwise corrupt doctrinal purity, the Communist leaders sacrificed strength to safety. Hence the Party in Britain remained until the end of the decade the weakest of all the extremist left-wing movements in the advanced countries of Europe.

Engels had once complained as vigorously as Marx about the unsuitability of the British as potential revolutionaries. Even the proletariat, he said, was bourgeois. The public took little practical interest in politics. The majority voted in general elections only, and, to the chagrin of the press lords, barely one householder in two bothered to buy a daily newspaper. Political apathy went hand in hand with an indefinable spirit of discontent, probably a reaction to the awesome destruction and loss of life in the recent war. Where merely one trade unionist in every ten troubled to attend his branch meetings, the well-organized Communist militants could, and often did, move in and exert an influence wholly disproportionate to their actual strength.

Beatrice Webb, who with her husband Sidney had charted the historical growth of British trade unionism, probably spoke for many upper- and middle-class radicals of the period in writing-off the handful of Communist intellectuals as 'mild-mannered desperadoes'. Among the mass of workers throughout the Labour movement, the Soviet experiment roused some sympathy and admiration. Here at last was 'the Workers' State'; no paradise, but a brave experiment. They deplored the reign of terror and dictatorship which accompanied it, but blamed Churchill and other Allied power-maniacs for forcing the Russians to ruthlessness in the interests of survival. The King might harbour recurring fears that the foundations of British society were in danger of crumbling. The loyalty of his ministers, of his armed services, of his police, and of the bulk of his people, did not waver during the 1920s. Indeed, now that the Irish Question had been temporarily shelved, the Special Branch at Scotland Yard could concentrate on the Communists, tapping telephones, opening letters, even raiding the Russian Trade Mission for evidence of subversion. In 1925 two Communist intellectuals, Tom Wintringham and G. Page Arnot, were among the twelve Party members arrested, tried and convicted for attempting to incite troops to mutiny.

Yet the deeper disillusionment of the next generation of intellectuals had already begun. And it owed far more to the political disenchantment of individual teachers in the public schools and universities with the arid complacency and hopelessness of Labour's efforts to save the nation by aping the values of the traditional ruling class than it owed to the example and propaganda of the struggling Communist Party.

2. THE YOUNG MISFITS

The end of hostilities on 11 November 1918, had been greeted in Britain with almost universal joy and relief. Belief in material progress, a vague substitute for the diluted Christianity in which relatively few people now believed, encouraged the false hope that the nation would soon reap the fruits of victory. Nothing could prevent the British from resuming their accustomed role as the proud and prosperous leader of the world: German militarism had been finally crushed after four and a quarter years of terrible ordeal. The full cost had yet to be calculated; in treasure it had left Britain far more impoverished than she knew, but the price in blood was too daunting to contemplate. Three-quarters of a million young men had perished on the battlefields; a further million and a half had been disabled or severely damaged in health from wounds or the effects of gas. If one added the death toll among soldiers from lands of the Empire, the total of British war victims was in excess of a million dead. Beneath the frenzied jubilation at the triumph of Allied arms, there were undertones of grief and a sense of irreparable loss that lingered on.

Perhaps that sense was strongest among Britain's sadly decimated ruling class. Death is never a respecter of rank or status; but in the trench warfare of Flanders, death had discriminated cruelly against the young subalterns fresh from the public schools. Proportionately three times more young British officers were wiped out than non-commissioned men in the Army, Navy and Air Force. The thought crossed some minds – minds of a reflective bent – that the nation could not afford such a huge human sacrifice. Those missing tens of thousands of tomorrow's leaders stood for all that was finest in the national character. This absence would make it harder for their elders and juniors to live easily together. It has been suggested since that contemporaries tended to exaggerate the problem, all the more so since the survivors included three future British Prime Ministers, Anthony Eden, Harold Macmillan and Clement Attlee. Outstanding exceptions such as these to the grim norm of mass killing can scarcely be cited as good evidence. The British losses in irreplaceable talent and spirit far outweighed the damage to trade, property or wealth.[1]

The resulting generation gap did not pass unnoticed at Oxford and Cambridge. In the public schools, too, from which most of the young officers had gone gaily to meet their violent ends, the rolls of honour listing the names of the fallen were a mute reminder of the magnitude of the sacrifice. The ritual of remembrance sometimes served as a spur, sometimes as a reproach. For the rising generation was being invited to take up additional burdens of responsibility, prematurely shed by these shining exemplars, when they had difficulty enough shouldering their own. Some dutifully tried to comply. Others, in the naturally rebellious mood of boys who resent being imposed upon, risked ill will by refusing. All suffered in the process from guilt because, try or refuse to try as they might, no schoolboy felt remotely capable of living up to the standards set by the missing immortals.

The tendency to cherish old illusions persisted everywhere, but most notably in Britain. As if to suggest that King George V's beloved grandmother had not yet vacated her throne, Empire Day continued to be celebrated on 24 May, Queen Victoria's birthday. Children at State schools were encouraged to salute the flag and hymn Rudyard Kipling's verses about the sublime imperial destiny of the race. Whether the words had any relevance to known facts did not concern the children, who were simply grateful for the half-holiday from their desks. Besides, the British Empire was held to be a solid and impressive entity, a splatter of red across the earth's surface, at least in the school atlases.

If the mass of the public, young as well as old, seemed as obsessed as the traditional ruling class with a frustrated longing to restore every possession and relic of past greatness, they wanted also to enjoy life to the full after all the sorrowing and suffering.

So the pursuit of pleasure became an end in itself, especially for emancipated sons of the upper and middle classes who could still afford to indulge themselves. This escapist mood accounted for the changed behaviour of many public schoolboys on reaching university, and the observations of the future novelist Evelyn Waugh on the subject were relevant and quite typical. At Lancing, an Anglo-Catholic foundation on the Sussex Downs near the town of Worthing, Waugh had noticed that 'my introduction to public school coincided with my first experience of hunger'. He had disliked the starvation diet occasioned by the enemy's effective submarine blockade in 1917. He had equally disliked the petty bullying and the undeviating routine and uneven discipline. His older brother, Alec, had been expelled from Sherborne, the public school for which Evelyn's name had been entered, departing under something of a cloud, and subsequently leaving for France with his machine-gun unit only to be taken prisoner by the Germans. Evelyn Waugh's anxiety for his brother's safety, an anxiety that cut to the heart of millions of families throughout Britain, did not reconcile the younger brother to his lot:

> I have heard it said that when in the last century, criminals were removed from the squalor and corruption of the old gaols and confined in the modern houses of correction prescribed for them by the humane, many went out of their minds. An analogous process transformed English public schools at the same period. The system worked well under men and boys of good-will, imagination and enthusiasm in a time of plenty and bright prospects. These were temporarily lacking at Lancing. The boys in authority were too young, the masters too old. Everything was of necessity a makeshift – the clothes we wore, the food we ate, the books we worked with, the masters who should have taught us. We were cold, shabby and hungry in the ethos, not of free Sparta, but of some beleaguered, enervated and forgotten garrison.[2]

On going up to Hertford College, Oxford, Waugh was only too happy to compensate for recent woes by leading a gay and work-free life with like-minded undergraduates. Conscious of all that separated them from the battlefield survivors then finishing their interrupted studies, they sedulously went their own way and improvised their own convivial rites through exclusive little centres like the Hypocrites' Club. They were rebels against convention and remembered austerity; such assured leaders of fashion as Harold Acton set new aesthetic standards in dress, manners and literary tone, so that members of the cult entertained an exaggerated sense of their own importance. The 'hearties', young men equally devoted to organized games and more concerned with exercising their bodies than their minds, provided an opposite and contrasting pole; but there were numerous groups of more or less ordinary people between. The right to shock their elders was probably the highest common factor they possessed. To play the dandy with style, an undergraduate needed a liberal allowance as well as panache. Waugh's father was a London publisher and an occasional author of moderate means, and his younger son not only felt comparatively poor but fell repeatedly into debt. Some older men, returning soldiers like Anthony Eden and Harold Macmillan, more restrained and self-possessed, already had their eyes on the political arena. They had been seasoned by the miracle of survival to waste no time in preparing to campaign for a peace that would endure.

Of course, would-be politicians of a less settled sort flourished at Oxford too. John Strachey, two years older than Waugh, had ampler funds to follow his fancy. When his married sister, Amabel, called on Strachey at noon one day in his rooms at Magdelen, she was a little surprised to find him at late breakfast eating 'chocolate cake and crème-de-menthe'. His father St Loe Strachey was editor of *The Spectator*. Lytton Strachey, the historian and critic, was a kinsman. The young man thought it modish to affect advanced radical opinions. On joining the Labour Party in 1923, he was asked by Bertrand Russell: 'Why are you a Socialist? Did you hate your father, your childhood or your public school?' To which Strachey, an old Etonian, promptly replied: 'A bit of all three.' Facetiousness of the kind served as a characteristic English veneer to disguise any underlying seriousness. More than a decade later, when Strachey wrote an article explaining why he had embraced the Marxist creed, he still could not resist the impulse to joke about it: 'I have a stock answer to dear old ladies who ask me, "And why, Mr Strachey, did you become a Communist?" "From chagrin, madame!" I reply. "From chagrin at not getting into the Eton cricket XI." '[3]

Strachey stood politically head and shoulders above most undergraduates who had been too young for the ordeal of trench warfare. His later collaboration with Sir Oswald Mosley, another returning warrior who had broken with the Conservative Party over the treatment of Ireland to emerge as a dazzling meteorite of the Socialist movement, continued throughout the 1920s. Strachey, the disciple, parted from Mosley, the ingenious mentor, when the latter's overbearing impatience with Ramsay MacDonald's over-cautious approach to the problem of chronic unemployment caused Mosley to resign from the second Labour Government and launch an increasingly sinister and reactionary organization of his own. That ruined partnership between two politically able scions of the traditional squirearchy was accidentally important in hardening the divisions between extremists of the Left and Right among young intellectuals during the early thirties. For Strachey quickly established himself as the most effective single propagandist of Communism, while Mosley just as quickly demonstrated a perverse taste for authoritarianism as leader of the British Union of Fascists.

By a quaint coincidence, it was Strachey's friendship with the cricket-loving, but now politically inert, Francis Meynell which induced the younger man to take a farmhouse in the Essex countryside where his best writing was done. Haunted by the fear that his former associate, Mosley, might have him assassinated, Strachey bought a revolver to protect himself, and slept with it under his pillow. It was an unnecessarily theatrical gesture, as far-fetched in its ways as Strachey's denigration of a particular group of modern novelists, Aldous Huxley, H. G. Wells and the young Evelyn Waugh among them, for trying to bite the withered capitalist hand that fed them. Waugh, he declared, had only three alternatives open to him after writing *Decline and Fall*: 'to commit suicide, become a Communist, or immerse himself within the Catholic Church. He chose the last (and easiest) alternative.' It was an interesting sidelight on the exclusiveness of small sets in the closed society of Oxford that Waugh's cousin, Claud

Cockburn, a contemporary whose paths seldom crossed his own, had become a maverick kind of Communist sympathizer and a buccaneering friend of Graham Greene, while still an undergraduate at Christ Church. The Oxford University authorities did not care for Marxist agitators; but they were more lenient than had been the case during the war, when R. Palme Dutt, not yet the professional ideologue of the Communist Party, was expelled for propagating subversive views.

Cambridge University went through a similar phase of mild unrest immediately after 1918. Undergraduates fresh from public school felt uneasy and self-conscious among the slightly older and hardened ex-officers, with their contempt for established authority and their rough dismissiveness of young fools rash enough to parade unorthodox opinions. Maurice Dobb, who arrived from Charterhouse on a scholarship to Pembroke College, made no secret of his Marxist convictions and quickly suffered the consequences. A group of 'hearties' seized him and threw him 'fully dressed into the River Cam' in a futile effort to teach him sense.[4] This happened to Dobb more than once; but his persecutors became bored and eventually left him alone. In general, the 'hearties' had no more tolerance for believers in the Soviet Workers' Paradise than for simpletons who swallowed the Lloyd George line about transforming Britain into a Home for Heroes. Apart from half-a-dozen prominent scientists, J. D. Bernal and Joseph Needham among them, whose advanced left-wing ideas would certainly have provoked the 'hearties' if the latter had discovered them, Communist sympathizers at Cambridge were few and mainly secretive. Active Labour men seemed just as thin on the ground.

One detached if slightly jaundiced observer of the post-war Cambridge scene was a lonely young man called Malcolm Muggeridge. The son of a lower-middle-class Fabian Socialist, he instinctively grasped the advantages and disadvantages of his position. Not having attended a public school or even a recognized grammar school, he felt at odds with most of his contemporaries. He had been admitted to Selwyn College to read the only subjects open to him at his secondary school in the outer suburbs of South

London, namely, the quite unsuitable disciplines of chemistry, physics and zoology:

This was my first acquaintance in their own native habitat, with the English middle and upper classes, whose characteristics were, I think, more noticeable at Selwyn than at more fashionable and famous establishments like King's and Trinity. . . . The Dean, in the course of an address to freshmen in the college chapel, remarked in an aside, that none of us were ever likely to be in want, or lack for the essential requirements for a bourgeois way of life. . . . I had absorbed sufficient of my father's sense of economic insecurity, as well as of my Booler relatives' attitude to unemployment as a kind of natural catastrophe over their heads, to find this remark completely novel. . . . As I came to realize after the Dean's address, it was more or less true that a boy who had been to a public school and taken a degree at Cambridge could assume that his livelihood was assured; especially as we still had an Empire on which the sun never set, as distinct from a Commonwealth on which it never rises, offering him all sorts of openings, from governorships and colonial bishoprics to affluence and a good chance of a knighthood on the banks of the Hooghly. Hence the self-assurance, and in the more ill-mannered among them arrogance, which struck me among my fellow-undergraduates. The converse face of this self-assurance or arrogance was the highly developed system of sycophancy which prevailed; fags required to be sycophantic to their masters, players to the captain of games, boys to prefects, prefects to housemasters, housemasters to headmasters and so on. I found the undiscriminating application of this sycophantic attitude of mind to anyone of note or in authority quite surprising until I got used to it. . . .

It was hardly a matter for astonishment that Malcolm Muggeridge quickly came to dislike Cambridge as a fraudulent, second-rate institution; a 'place of infinite tedium, of idle days, and foolish vanities, and spurious enthusiasms'. Bereft of public schoolboy pretensions, he remained an outsider with sharp ears and a mocking tongue:

Public schoolboys, whatever their particular school – from the most famous like Eton, to the most obscure – had a language of their own which I scarcely understood, games they played which I could neither play nor interest myself in, ways and attitudes which they took for granted but which were foreign to me – for instance, their acceptance of sodomy as more or less normal behaviour.... The University, when I was there, was very largely a projection of public school life and *mores*, and a similar atmosphere of homosexuality tended to prevail. There was also a hangover from Wildean decadence, with aesthetes who dressed in velvet, painted their rooms in strange colours, hung Aubrey Beardsley prints on their walls, and read *Les Fleurs du Mal*. The nearest I came to being personally involved with these was when a High Church ordinand after dinner read to me from Swinburne's *Songs Before Sunrise* in a darkened room faintly smelling of incense. I emerged unscathed....[5]

The Socialist upbringing of Muggeridge was by no means the only or the chief element in his studious aversion to politics, commerce, the Church, even authorship, as likely or desirable professions. Already an agnostic who yearned to believe in something, he had a touch of Cobbett's passionate loathing of the world as it was, but lacked the vision and maturity as yet to diagnose and expose its corrupting ways. On completing his studies at Cambridge, he drifted like so many others of his generation, first into teaching then into journalism. His low-grade pass degree prompted him to roam far afield in search of paid work. He taught English in Christian College, South India, for instance, where he began to realize why the splendours of the British Empire were fading fast, later moving to Egypt where nationalist outbursts and incipient signs of nervousness among British officials and businessmen confirmed his worst suspicions. It was in Cairo that his luck turned. There he met Arthur Ransome, the author, a man he revered as once the *Manchester Guardian*'s correspondent in Moscow who knew Lenin, Trotsky, Litvinov and the other Soviet leaders, and who had even witnessed the Russian Revolution, an event Muggeridge deemed of greater moment for mankind than Christ's Crucifixion itself. Through Ransome's good offices, the young man next obtained a staff post on the *Manchester Guardian*. By now he had married Kitty Dobbs, a niece of the distinguished Fabians Beatrice and Sidney Webb; and the bonds of matrimony secured his doubtful entry into the self-important aristocracy of British socialism, now half accepted as part of the aspirant ruling class.

The Webbs at this period had no faith whatever in the Soviet experiment. Having patented the theory of political and economic gradualism as the only civilized cure for the evils of capitalism, they tended to deplore all revolutionaries and to denounce their handiwork. The self-importance of the Webbs subconsciously reflected a monumental complacency which Muggeridge ascribed to inverted snobbery. When Beatrice Webb remarked that Stafford Cripps and other in-laws of hers were already earning some £20,000 per annum, thereby criticizing this ne'er-do-well for condemning Kitty Muggeridge to live on a pittance, the gibe stuck in his memory like a burr. 'There is no snobbishness,' commented Muggeridge, 'like that of professional equalitarians.' He had not the slightest intention of aping these upper-crust radicals. He was sure in his heart that their quiet revolution would peter out in Britain. Events seemed to confirm his unkindly verdict. The economic collapse of 1931 – which led to Ramsay MacDonald's defection, split the Labour Party, and cost his own father his parliamentary seat – roused Muggeridge to a fresh pitch of furious desperation. On impulse he volunteered to go to Moscow and work freelance for the *Manchester Guardian*. His offer was accepted promptly and almost gratefully by his employers.

So Malcolm Muggeridge set off for Russia, not as a would-be journalistic disciple following the masterful Arthur Ransome, not as one of those 'mild-mannered desperadoes' or Parlour Pinks whom Beatrice Webb so often ridiculed for playing at Communism, but rather in the ingenuous spirit of a Marxist enthusiast only too happy to burn his boats and never return to Britain:

Kitty and I were confident that going to Russia would prove to be a definitive step, a final adventure.... We sold off pretty well everything we had, making, as it were, a bonfire of all our bourgeois trappings: my dinner jacket, for instance, and Kitty's only long dress, as well as some little trinkets and oddments, and most of our books. . . . We even wound up our bank account, taking what money we had – some £200 as I recall – in traveller's cheques. . . . I took particular pleasure in jettisoning our marriage lines, and my ridiculous BA hood and certificate; these being also, in my eyes, badges of bourgeois servitude to be discarded for ever. . . .[6]

The Muggeridges paid a farewell weekend visit to the Webbs before departing in March 1932. The Soviet Ambassador, Gregori Sokolnikov, and his ebullient wife were present and pressed the emigrants to call on them in Moscow. Stafford Cripps, another of Muggeridge's kinsmen by marriage, was also in attendance to wish him godspeed. If the drastic remedy of trying to become permanent settlers in the Workers' Paradise had been officially prescribed for all intellectual dissidents at that time, Britain would have spared herself much avoidable agony and self-doubt in subsequent years. But Ramsay MacDonald, Stanley Baldwin, Neville Chamberlain and their cautious Liberal colleagues in the National Government of 1931 had more pressing matters. Besides, whatever their nominal Party allegiances, the politicians had no misgivings about the integrity and utter trustworthiness of young men of good families who had attended the right schools and universities to acquire the same sort of vague and conventional virtuousness in training for public life as most of them had once received.

One of the staidest and least inspiring members of Ramsay MacDonald's hastily constructed National Government was the President of the Board of Education, Sir Donald Maclean. Like the rest of his colleagues, he had been reared in the climactic final quarter of the Victorian age, reflecting to a rare degree its private virtuousness, its public sense of probity and the inevitable limitations which accompanied these fine qualities. Sir Donald was a respected Liberal MP, one of the last of that short-lived pedigree of orthodox Liberal sectarians. Throughout the decade of bitterly split loyalties which had followed the displacement of Asquith by Lloyd George in an intricate coup at the end of 1916, Maclean had remained conspicuously faithful to the former. Lloyd George he deplored as an unscrupulous interloper and pretender, though, like the exemplary Christian he always tried to be, Maclean probably prayed for him. As a result of the split in the once-predominant Liberal Party, MacDonald and his supporters had twice managed to form minority Labour governments in the twenties dependent either on Tory or on factional Liberal support. Maclean's role as a hidden manipulator of such frail and fraying Liberal strings as could be safely pulled had invariably been that of an honourable but short-sighted subordinate. He detested the limelight; and, except in his capacity as deputy Speaker of the House of Commons, he preferred to work in the shadows and do what little good he could by stealth.

'A popular, respected but not particularly distinguished MP' is the summing-up which appears in the *Dictionary of National Biography*. The writer qualified that assessment by dwelling on the 'handsome presence, cool judgement and imperturbable good humour and patience' of Sir Donald when he sat in for the Speaker. Such attributes, together with a gluttonous appetite for detailed legal drudgery and an air of God-fearing righteousness wholly becoming to a life-long Presbyterian of ancient Scottish descent, misled superficial critics into dismissing him as a decent, simple, wholly unambitious fellow. Shortly after Lloyd George had first entered 10 Downing Street, plain Mr Donald Maclean received a knighthood for diligence behind the scenes as the chairman of the committee weighing such matters as enemy debts, or of the tribunal considering the appeals against military service of such resolute conscientious objectors as the volatile Francis Meynell. Perhaps Maclean's most notable contribution to social reform, anonymous as usual, was a report of 1919 which prepared the ground for Britain's new Ministry of Health. Yet he had proved himself only a few months earlier to be quite capable of rallying demoralized friends to the sticking point of decision.

The post-war election of 1918 had all but annihilated Asquith's still substantial following of independent Liberal candidates. Only twenty were returned to Parliament out of 266 who stood. Maclean retained his seat in the Scottish border district of Peebles; Asquith and every single one of his former ministers had lost theirs. At a dramatic meeting of the dejected handful of survivors of this electoral rout, an unnamed coward proposed that the Party of Gladstone should forthwith strike its colours and disband. The proposal was being formally discussed when the normally self-effacing Sir Donald Maclean broke in with unaccustomed heat,

'If we go out of that door without forming a party, Liberalism will go under for a generation.'[7]

From 1919 until his own defeat at the polls in 1922, Maclean served as chairman of the anti-Lloyd George Liberal remnant at Westminster, striving with blinkered dedication to salvage the Party's sinking fortunes. He was not a natural vote-catcher; the Scottish electors of Kilmarnock and the Welsh of East Cardiff found his charisma and prospectus wanting. They shut him out of the House of Commons until 1929. Then Maclean fought North Cornwall in the election which unexpectedly brought MacDonald's second Labour administration to office, and this time the reluctant outsider came top of the poll. By then he was over sixty years old; and his family of five children, four sons and a daughter, were all at school. The man whose high principles had forced him in 1919 to undertake the artificial resuscitation of an organization hopelessly divided against itself suddenly began to enjoy ten years afterwards a new and unforeseen lease of politicial life all the more rewarding for being so unexpected. The official Liberals had vanished as an effective Opposition or as an alternative ruling Party. Their 'Shadow Cabinet' in the crisis of 1931 was insubstantial indeed; but Maclean, again an esteemed member, entered fully into the earnest deliberations with Sir Herbert Samuel and other old Party friends while the anguished Ramsay MacDonald was trying to form his emergency Government. The prize which had eluded Maclean since 1906, when he had entered Parliament in the massive Liberal landslide of that year, was at last within reach. Articulate friends and supporters both inside and outside Liberal Establishment circles rejoiced with Sir Donald at his ministerial appointment, which was honoured with a seat in the Cabinet after the General Election of October 1931. MacDonald had made him President of the Board of Education.

Only one member of the family writhed inwardly at this belated preferment and found it difficult to explain why it upset him so badly. Donald Maclean, Sir Donald's second son, was then eighteen years old. A self-contained, studious, clever and apparently conventional youth in every way, he had passed out of his public school that summer with flying colours. The usual glowing reports on his continuing excellence at work and prowess at sport followed him home. Taller than his father, and with the same handsome cut of head and features, Donald had recently added to the family laurels by winning a scholarship to Trinity Hall, Cambridge, where he went as a freshman at the end of the summer holidays. Nobody seemed to notice anything amiss in Donald's testy attitude to the crowning of his father's hitherto grey and mainly unspectacular career in politics. Donald was too well trained in the art of politely dissimulating his feelings to venture even mild criticism of Ramsay MacDonald's incredible conduct in staying on as Prime Minister and betraying the Party he had led and helped to found. Secretly, he felt that the ex-Labour leader had behaved basely, cynically and almost criminally. Despite Sir Donald's warm approbation of MacDonald's unselfishness in putting country above Party, thereby ruining his own reputation in the embittered eyes of his former supporters, the young Maclean did not question or contradict his father. Donald had never been on close terms with a parent whose habit of gently laying down the law, and solemnly ensuring compliance with it, tended to discourage the free-and-easy discussion of contentious subjects. So Donald held his tongue and bottled up resentment with a disarming smile of assent. His mother could usually be counted on to listen sympathetically; but a knotty political point like this, touching her unqualified pride in her husband's political wisdom, was best left unspoken altogether.

In material terms Sir Donald and Lady Maclean had done well by their children, though not without a struggle. They had married in 1907, the year after his first election to Parliament as Liberal MP for Bath. Both of them came of lower-middle-class families, Gwendolen from Surrey, her husband from a small town in Carmarthenshire, in spite of his unbroken Scottish ancestry and name. John Maclean, his father, had insisted on describing himself as a cordwainer by trade, and the son honoured his memory by religiously using that obsolete term for a skilled shoemaker. The Macleans had hailed originally from the tiny island of Tiree in the Inner Hebrides, John moving south to escape the hand-to-mouth penury of fishing and crofting. He learned his craft in the

Bolton area of Lancashire, and later plied it with profit among wealthy textile manufacturers and the gentry of the district. He made a good marriage to another Scottish Highlander, Agnes Macmellin, a lady of gentle birth who spoke Gaelic as fluently as English. This remarkable woman lived in Sir Donald's household to the ripe old age of ninety-one, after her own husband's death. The frugal ways and rigorous routine of a Calvinist upbringing were thus visited on Donald the younger during and after the First World War, as they had once been visited on his uncomplaining father. A good grammar school grounding had enabled the future Sir Donald to pass his law examinations without trouble and gradually establish himself as a successful solicitor in Cardiff, until political ambition drew him to London.

The Maclean residence in Southwick Street, London, was a gloomy, solid, three-storeyed house. It stood conveniently near the Marylebone Presbyterian Church in Upper George Street, where the whole family, soberly attired and on their best behaviour, worshipped every Sabbath. It was a large church, with a mainly working-class congregation. A few middle- and upper-class families living in the neighbourhood would also attend the services, attracted by the eloquence and warm personality of Dr Robert Calder Gillie, the minister. As one of the church elders, Sir Donald became a close personal friend of Dr Gillie, and their respective children often played together. Christopher Gillie, today a lecturer in English at Cambridge, retains a clear impression of the Liberal politician, 'dressed in a morning coat with a grey silk hat', walking past on Sunday mornings:

> I was in some awe of him but not at all intimidated. I remember him as bland and friendly. As children we saw more of Lady Maclean, I suppose because she visited us more often. My own father was a very striking figure in the pulpit. He was as tall as Sir Donald, six feet three inches in height and squarer than the rest of us. Lord Eccles has described him as 'a very handsome man with a grand Scottish voice'. Actually he did not sound Scottish at all.[8]

What little leisure Sir Donald had left from running a busy legal practice, and nursing his uncertain political interests, went on lay preaching or in promoting his favourite charity, the National Society for the Prevention of Cruelty to Children, which he had helped to found. His own children, with the possible exception of the one girl in the family, loved and respected him at a distance. Presiding over family prayers, encouraging them all to read the Bible for its relevance to the difficulties which continuously confronted Christians in a diabolically wicked world, Sir Donald was too seldom off parade to relax easily with them. He was by no means a wealthy man. His parsimonious outlook, his great energy, his indifference to good food, coupled with an abhorrence of strong drink, did not help to widen the fairly restricted social circles which his children frequented. Young Donald was eleven years old when his grandmother died in 1924 and suddenly the familiar voice, crooning and scolding away in barely intelligible Gaelic, was stilled for ever.

Because young Donald had brains, his father decided to send him away to a public school. Dr Gillie spoke well of Gresham's, a small sixteenth-century foundation in north Norfolk with a liberal reputation and a consistently good academic record which other larger and better known institutions might justly have envied. John Reith, a fellow Scot who appeared to be stamping his stern personality on the new British Broadcasting Company, happened to be an acquaintance of both the Gillies and the Macleans; and Reith had nothing but praise for Gresham's, his old school. Besides, one of Dr Gillie's elder sons, Blaise, was already there and doing reasonably well. So the Macleans decided to send Donald there too. In Reith's day, there had been an innovative headmaster called Howson who introduced an honours system, under which boys were trusted to obey the rules and to own up when they broke them. There was also what has aptly been described by the present headmaster as 'a fanatical pursuit of purity'. This led to a considerable degree of artificial immunization against bad outside influences. No games were played against teams from other schools, 'in case the boys were contaminated'. Dr Eccles, a man of powerful character but small imagination who succeeded Howson as headmaster, carried on these inherited ideas with imitative conviction and reduced success:

There was still much trust, some freedom of study periods and less games worship than elsewhere, and perhaps above all, Howson admired those who were artists, musicians, craftsmen and scientists more than those who simply discussed the ideas of the dead.[9]

Donald Maclean moved into this closed atmosphere with a sense almost of liberation. Once his homesickness wore off, he adjusted himself dutifully to conditions which gradually became bearable and sometimes agreeable, despite the dismal lack of privacy, the little coarsenesses, and the tendency of certain individualists to abuse the honours system. Eccles, as headmaster, was a shadowy, menacing presence who stayed in the background, much as Sir Donald Maclean did at home. The boy shone in class. With a taste for reading, a retentive memory and a capacity for earnest concentration, young Maclean acquitted himself well without being ridiculed as a bookworm or a 'swot'. On the playing fields his long legs and commanding height earned him a place in his house hockey and rugby teams once he had mastered the rules and rudimentary skills of both games. The competitive spirit was easily stirred in him. He had a quick temper but knew how to control it. He struck some of his contemporaries as a shy boy who came out of hiding only when it suited him, and then had no inhibitions whatever about 'proving how charming, easygoing or even foolhardy he could be'. No crisis or unexpected dilemmas came to disturb the equanimity of young Donald's instinctive responses to the minor tribulations and challenges of this spartan, half-regimented existence. Self-preservation lay in seeking to maintain an inconspicuous posture, not always a simple course for a boy so conspicuously tall, self-conscious and easily riled that he would turn on those who tried to goad him or play stupid practical jokes.

On balance, he derived more pleasure than pain from the constant struggle to clear tiresome human hurdles with apparent effortlessness. His father did not regain a parliamentary seat until 1929. By then the son had adapted himself like a chameleon to the school régime. On occasions of earlier parental visits, Donald would emerge from his shell and take a keen proprietorial pride in showing off his father and mother. Sir Donald and Lady

Maclean would depart, invariably well pleased that they had chosen wisely in sending their brightest son to Gresham's. At first Donald might have agreed with them. In view of his father's inclination to preach and moralize, however, the wary adolescent kept his growing misgivings strictly to himself. Wild horses would not have dragged from him the fact that he was already deeply confused and uncertain about the two entities on which his father's whole existence was centred; the Liberal Party, or what was now left of it; and God, the alleged be-all and end-all of human destiny and endeavour.

The comparative freedom of the school routine did not extend to religious services. These were compulsory, and all the more tedious on that account. Slowly Donald Maclean began to grow weary of mouthing pointless entreaties to a God who never replied. His father would have counselled him to 'try praying harder', but then his father's practice had been to ram religion down the throats of all his children as soon as each learnt to talk. Donald no longer had much use for Christian teaching and behaviour which bore so little relation to human aspirations. Naturally, he did not confide this to any master, going through the ritual in the school chapel, and in the family pew at the Marylebone Presbyterian Church during holidays, with straight-faced mechanical conformity. Only towards the end of his time at Gresham's did he admit to James Klugman, a voluble and extremely able boy 'who always came top of nearly everything except games but was never made a prefect or given the least responsibility because of a total allergy to good order and discipline', that he had lost the little faith he might once have imbibed in childhood. Maclean kept his friendship with Klugman a secret from Sir Donald, from his mother, and from the rest of the family. Nor did he dare ask this short, dark, rather flabby youth, who lived with his rich parents and sister in a large, expensively furnished house in Hampstead, to visit him at Southwick Street. They would arrange to meet furtively instead at public houses or in cinemas. Donald was not in the least ashamed of this witty Jewish friend, merely afraid that his father might disapprove of him. Klugman admitted:

When I was at Gresham's, I felt so much out of things as the clever oddity who got most of the prizes, but not even the humblest office, that I cast around for a title to bestow on myself. I hit on an ingenious one in my last year, and I surmised at once that the authorities wouldn't like it. They certainly didn't. For I called myself 'The Communist', advertising myself as the only specimen for miles around. I hadn't any clear idea, to begin with, what a good Communist really stood for; but having a very inquisitive mind, I soon remedied that. The books I read opened my eyes a little. Being also one of nature's rebels, I became a distant sympathizer.[10]

Like a good conformist, Donald pretended not to be interested. He kept his mask skilfully in place. There was room for conformists as well as eccentrics at Gresham's, an institution which preened itself on the ease with which it managed to accommodate promising specimens of both breeds. Among the names of recent old boys spoken of respectfully as incorrigible characters who had left traces behind them, that of Wystan Auden, the future poet, often cropped up conversationally in the hearing of Maclean and Klugman. Auden had treated school rules and regulations with 'a patronizing indifference', yet he bore a charmed life and usually avoided any needless antagonizing of masters and senior boys set over him. Frank McEachran, an outstanding teacher who could draw out talent in the young by inspiration, had quietly encouraged Auden and another adoring disciple called John Pudney. McEachran's staff colleagues sometimes looked askance at what they mistook for a colleague's waywardness, shaking their heads sadly at the outrageous views he expressed freely on the most sacred subjects. Klugman became one of his debtors in turn; and so, indirectly and mainly through Klugman, did the ambivalent Maclean. Not even McEachran, however, could control or guide the madder impulses of the young. Early one summer's day, Auden roused Pudney and led him to a lake in the grounds. There he committed to the stagnant waters all his 'pretentious poems', but that same evening the poet had second thoughts and asked Pudney to help him retrieve the manuscript:

Fortunately it was afloat. It had scarcely penetrated the green scum of the surface. . . . There were sloshing sounds. An abominable stench drifted towards me, I called out to ask if he was all right. He snapped back that of course he was. Thus the works that eventually came under the eye of T. S. Eliot at Fabers and thereafter so quickly made their mark upon the thirties, were prudently salvaged from aqueous oblivion.[11]

Under what remained of Howson's earlier and enlightened dispensation two future composers, Benjamin Britten and Lennox Berkeley, had offered the first faint hints of musical creativity. Stephen Spender might have flourished at Gresham's, too, had not a sudden death in the family and his own vulnerable temperament sped his departure from the junior school. His brothers, being more robust, braved the ordeal and flourished there. It is interesting to note the number of Donald Maclean's contemporaries, exact or near, who afterwards profited from the régime. According to Pudney, Howson's less than comparable successor as headmaster:

divided his interests between God and physics. There was great emphasis on science, none whatever on classics or English. The lack of formal encouragement of the arts was healthy enough in that it went hand in hand with an atmosphere of 'live and let live'. Nobody was lauded for artistic activities, nor was anyone decried. Most important of all, nobody had the arts thrust down their throat.[12]

As headmaster, Eccles proved too obstinate a personality to be guided by an imaginative predecessor. In the words of a qualified judge, Gresham's present headmaster: 'The maintainer is never as effective as the innovator.'[13]

Nevertheless, the achievements in later life of Maclean's contemporaries indicated that the original system still worked. Apart from future scientists like Sir Alan Hodgkin, a president of the Royal Society; Sir David Wansbrough-Jones, a scientific advisor to the Ministry of Supply; the Keith-Lucas brothers, one of whom invented the vertical take-off aircraft; and Sir Christopher Cockerell, the inventor of the hovercraft, there were many others who became eminent doctors, university teachers, and lawyers. Each would retain some sense of indebtedness to Gresham's, as in their different ways would James Klugman, the future historian and savant of the British Communist Party, and Donald Maclean, a career diplomat who seemed likely to reach the top. Gresham's present headmaster commented:

> They were a collection more noted for their enterprise and intelligence than their orthodoxy. Donald Maclean is not, of course, one of the old boys of whom we are inordinately proud but, in fact, he was remembered with some admiration and affection by those who were contemporaries of his and who knew him well.[14]

Donald Maclean felt enormously relieved when the long vacation of 1931 ended. The political upheaval of the doleful summer months, starting with the break-up of the Labour Government, then the astonishing *volte-face* of Ramsay MacDonald, the suspension of the gold standard, and the emergence of Sir Donald as one of the few Liberals in the new emergency Cabinet, had filled the young man with confusion and doubt. His father's immediate delight at the good news from Gresham's that Donald had won a coveted Modern Language Scholarship to Trinity Hall, Cambridge, had not lasted. There had been differences of opinion between them about politics, and Sir Donald had taken stern exception to the dogmatic assertiveness with which his son assailed the so-called reactionaries and opportunists responsible for the downfall of Labour. After that sudden lapse, the young man held his tongue and watched events with a sullen passivity. His mother's attempts to draw him out were quite unavailing; his father's preoccupations in Whitehall and elsewhere, coupled with a new aura of undisguised cheerfulness at his unexpected political preferment, made young Donald Maclean impatient to escape. Cambridge would at least allow him to air his thoughts without being accused of dumb insolence or inexcusable ignorance.

He revelled in the unrestricted freedom of life as an undergraduate, but was careful at the start not to run up debts or otherwise aggravate his father's puzzled doubts about him. Klugman had rooms in Trinity, the biggest college in the University, fortunately situated just two minutes' walk from Trinity Hall, so that Klugman's new friends became Maclean's and the pair spent a good deal of time also with companions and old boys from Gresham's. This point remained fresh in the memory of a quiet, observant freshman who had been at a different school. Leonard Forster would likewise have preferred to pass the time of day with friends who had been at Marlborough with him; but as most of his fellow Marlburians had gone to Oxford instead, he had to make the best of it. Try as he would, Forster did not particularly warm to the slightly precious products of Gresham's:

A certain flabbiness and limpness was characteristic of all of them, especially Klugman. Perhaps it was the done thing at Gresham's not to be too intense and muscular. By 'flabby' I don't mean merely physically as though these fellows were running to puppy fat, I mean mentally so as well. I knew Donald Maclean quite well during our first year. We went to the same supervisor and often compared notes about our work. I found him a very flabby character, naïve about many things yet also unwilling to budge even when proved wrong or ridiculous. I didn't like his immaturity. He read a good deal, seldom laughed because he was very earnest, and had no marked sense of humour.

Forster, who is today the Professor of German at Cambridge, regarded Maclean as the 'most easily malleable' of the Greshamites, the two cleverest and most articulate of whom were R. L. Dreschfield, who later became a successful lawyer and Queen's Counsel, and the inevitable Klugman. 'Both of them roamed the place, proclaiming their brash left-wing views; and both appeared determined to influence others.' Leonard Forster was not deeply interested in politics. He therefore easily resisted their advances. Donald Maclean, while anxious to keep his rapidly changing ideas hidden from a father who was now a minister of the Crown, acquired Communist sympathies well before the end of his first year. Forster commented:

That should surprise nobody. It was then the fashion to voice such views if you happened to be politically inclined. Everyone seemed to be anti-government and anti-Tory. Labour had failed dismally. Only the Soviet Union seemed to have all the answers, and an active branch of the Communist Party had recently been founded inside the University.[15]

The founding of the first Communist cell had followed a visit to

Cambridge University during the summer of 1931 by Clemens Palme Dutt, the brother of the Party's leading ideologue and a specialist in proselytizing work among students, who had recently served as an agent of the Comintern in Paris and India. The fact that a nucleus of perhaps a dozen Communists and Marxist sympathizers already existed among the Fellows made Cambridge a natural choice. By now Maurice Dobb had established himself as a gifted economics lecturer at Trinity, combining donnish scrupulousness and charm with the zeal of a writer wholly dedicated to propagating Marxist theory and Soviet practice. Dobb, that young post-war undergraduate whom posses of anti-Bolshevik 'hearties' dumped in the river, had for some time been encouraging like-minded dons and undergraduates to visit the house in Chesterton Lane which he shared with Roy Pascal, a keen extremist Fellow of Pembroke College. Dobb, along with his bright young disciple Joan Robinson, Pascal and J. D. Bernal, the physicist and crystallographer, were the principal Marxist supporters of the move to found a Communist cell in Cambridge. Although Clemens Palme Dutt nominally proposed it, there can be no doubt that the initiative came from the West European Bureau of the Comintern, acting on instructions issued by Maxim Litvinov, Karl Radek and other leading policy-makers in Moscow. Their reasoning had unquestionable merit. The political vacillating of the Labour Party through the twenties had served to isolate and expose the deficiencies of a struggling Communist Party largely bereft of intellectual respectability and 'clout'. Thus with a fine sense of timing, virtually on the eve of the second Labour Government's helpless collapse, Moscow uttered the word, and Palme Dutt promptly obeyed.

Two undergraduates in particular had since helped to fertilize a small cell which, but for their energy, might have remained a sterile and clandestine study group. One of them was David Haden-Guest, the son of a Labour politician and future peer, who had arrived in 1930 to read philosophy and logic under the famous Cambridge savant Ludwig Wittgenstein. (The other was John Cornford.) Haden-Guest had interrupted his course at Trinity to spend a year at the University of Göttingen where, instead of gaining fresh insights into his chosen subject, he became gravely distracted during the winter of 1930–1 by evidence of the rising Nazi threat to the survival of German democracy. Taking part in a Communist demonstration on Easter Sunday 1931, he was arrested by the police, held for two weeks in solitary confinement, and eventually released as a result of going on hunger strike. The young man had left for Germany a pacifist and a Socialist. He returned blazing with conviction that only through revolutionary Marxism could the free world be saved from the ruinous, humiliating plight which was fast overtaking the Germans.

As for Britain, the failure of the Labour Party was scandalously clear. Only a strong Communist Party could lift the country out of the slump and put down capitalism and its political minions. Haden-Guest was one of the handful of undergraduates present that summer's day when Clemens Palme Dutt called on Dobb and his associates; and the young man's fiery enthusiasm had swung the meeting in favour of immediate action. It was decided there and then not only to create a Communist cell in the heart of Trinity College, but to concentrate on winning recruits in the town as well as in the University. The readiness of David Haden-Guest to assume responsibility for the organization had another useful effect. It lifted an unwanted load from the shoulders of Dobb, Bernal and Pascal who, as Fellows of their respective colleges, considered it wiser to remain discreetly in the background. The University authorities adopted a vaguely tolerant view of undergraduate excesses in the political field; but dons who were known to be active Communist officials would have been courting needless trouble. Apart from Haden-Guest, two working-class undergraduates attended the foundation meeting: Jim Lees, an ex-coal miner on a trade union economics scholarship; and Jack 'Bugsy' Wolfe, a Jew from the East End of London who was reading biochemistry under J. B. S. Haldane. Haldane himself, disgusted as he was with the dismal record of Labour, had yet to take the logical step leftwards and join the Communist Party.

The sheer size of Trinity College, with its undergraduate population of nearly a thousand, its scores of Fellows, and its numerous groups and clubs catering for a host of diverse activities, helped the cell to co-exist and quietly grow. It was possible for contemporaries to spend all their time in reasonably close proximity without meeting or getting to know one another. The young Enoch Powell was already there, slightly overlapping with Harold Philby, Guy Burgess and James Klugman but never once consciously setting eyes on any of these unknown contemporaries. Of course Powell's case, on his own frank admission, must be regarded as exceptional:

> I had one interest, and one alone, working. My single aim was to win all the glittering prizes. I succeeded by rising before dawn and retiring each night like clockwork, precisely at nine thirty. I probably wasted my time. I made no friends that I can remember, even as a Fellow.

There was one undergraduate over the wall at Trinity Hall, however, whom Powell had some reason to know and to remember:

> Oh yes, you mean Alan Nunn May? We had been at King Edward's School, Birmingham, together. There's actually a school photograph that shows us as prefects, standing side by side with our arms folded in the conventional manner. I hardly knew him at school. I lost track of him altogether at Cambridge.[16]

In much the same way, Robert Childers, the younger son of Erskine Childers, discovered only half a century later that he had been a close neighbour of Philby's at Trinity. They had one good friend in common, but this man 'did not think of introducing us and the opportunity did not arise of its own natural accord'.[17] Trinity College was like that. And so the incipient Communist movement created little stir, except among the faithful. Donald Maclean had less excuse than Enoch Powell for ignoring or forgetting the existence of Nunn May, a retiring, dreamy-looking character who, in Leonard Forster's phrase, 'managed to convey the distant impression of always being spiritually in his laboratory'.[18] Nunn May suffered from shyness and appeared to prefer his own company. Whether he had any political ideas, Maclean did not bother to enquire during his first three terms of acclimatization. Occasionally he caught glimpses of unknown undergraduates standing on windy street corners trying to sell copies of the *Daily Worker*, distributing leaflets, even haranguing indifferent bystanders from soap-boxes in public places; but Haden-Guest's uphill work among the townspeople seemed to interest few beyond the uniformed members of the Cambridge police.

The process of infiltration seemed to be advancing more effectively and rapidly inside the University itself. Klugman, eternally inquisitive and intellectually restless, gloated over the prospects. In him Haden-Guest found a willing and capable recruiting sergeant, who 'did his bit for the cause' by argument and persuasion. Yet Maclean himself still held back. Inhibited by the thought of his father's horrified indignation on learning that any son of his could stoop so abysmally low, he begged Klugman not to press him. He needed more time to brood over the problem before fully committing himself. He was sorely tempted at odd moments to kick over the traces boldly. For the young man believed that the treacherous MacDonald's so-called National Government was a pitiful sham and that his own father deserved all the ridicule and contempt that was going for remaining a member of it. Not for the first or last time, his heart and mind were at violent odds.

Donald Maclean's release from an agonizing dilemma brought to a head by a troubled conscience, a sensitive nature and the perverse effect on both of Gresham's honour system, came with mournful suddenness that summer. The young man was at home, idling and trying to relax during the early weeks of the long vacation. Parliament had not yet risen, and his father's accounts of difficulties within the Cabinet left the son unimpressed and even bored. As a 'pure' Liberal, battling for principle almost alone against hard-faced Tories and a few renegade Socialists, Sir Donald clearly had his work cut out. For months past, the majority had been pressing for abandonment of Free Trade as a means of protecting Britain's near-stagnant economy; the squabble had been temporarily shelved by Ramsay MacDonald's compromise formula, offering ministers the luxury of 'agreeing to differ'. Donald had listened in silence to his father's incessant soliloquies, choking back impatience and scathing comment. The Prime Minister, it appeared, would give anything for a quiet life, while

Neville Chamberlain, the new Chancellor of the Exchequer, had every intention of denying him that boon with plans for raising tariffs on foreign imports and promoting the dynastic Chamberlain family dream of a vast, new Empire Free Trade area. A Commonwealth conference would shortly be held in Ottawa to that end, and on its outcome Sir Donald would decide finally whether to stay in the Government or resign. He looked old and grey with worry and overwork; but he was evidently prepared to sacrifice everything for a principle which his son despised as tawdry and meaningless.

Providence rushed to Sir Donald Maclean's rescue. On the night of 15 June 1932, the dithering ended abruptly when he collapsed in his room and died soon afterwards of a massive heart attack. The shock brought the son momentarily to his senses: his stricken mother had to be consoled; there were innumerable family and business details to be attended to; and, with his elder brother Ian, Donald found relief in these mournful chores. His grief was natural enough, but the underlying tug of guilt was greater. Death had removed without warning a parent whose virtuousness he respected but whose views he secretly derided. It had simultaneously removed the one remaining obstacle to his openly making common cause with clever, altruistic Communist comrades at Cambridge.

Lady Maclean might disapprove, yet she would not oppose a son whom she still tended to spoil. Listening, however, to the moving oration preached by the Reverend Dr Gillie on the day of his father's burial, Donald could have been forgiven for concluding that he had all along been underestimating the sheer strength of the dead man's convictions. Dr Gillie was speaking from personal knowledge when he described a major crisis of belief which had beset the politician in earlier life, and which Sir Donald had faced and surmounted in utter loneliness. A phase of scepticism had once tempted him to renounce his harsh religious faith, but he could not do so without thorough soul-searching. So he locked himself in his study and spent a whole night at his desk, wrestling with the doubts that oppressed his mind. At one point he got up and paced the room, after drawing an imaginary line down the centre: 'On this side,' he told himself, 'I walk with Christ. One step across that line, and I shall turn away for ever from him.' The pacing continued, on the right side of the line, until daylight. He did not falter or stumble again, once that anguished night lay behind him, but clung tenaciously to the truth as he saw it.[19]

The preacher's words might have been fashioned with young Donald in mind, and their moral was not lost on him. If his will lacked the steely quality of his late father's, at least his keen brain had already analysed and rejected as bogus the timid prescriptions for recovery of the traditional parties. Only Marxism seemed to hold out hope of saving Britain from the political follies of the ruling class, whether Tory, Socialist or Liberal. As for the guilt gnawing at his spirit, that could be allayed at last by a detailed study of Marxist teaching. It was a vow he kept when he returned to Cambridge. His father, he knew, would have reproved him sternly for such a twisted choice of faith. Indeed, it is said that Donald Maclean, like an inverted Hamlet bent more on vindicating himself than avenging the alleged spectre's memory, claimed to have been visited by the ghost of his father one evening in the gardens of Trinity Hall. He mentioned this odd hallucination quite casually to several of his friends, but everyone assumed that Donald had his tongue firmly in his cheek. A person so dedicated to the self-imposed task of absorbing the Gospel according to Marx, it was felt, simply must be joking. According to Christopher Gillie, who arrived as a freshman at the College in October 1932, Donald Maclean's transition from a Calvinist upbringing and background to the equally rigid categories of atheistic Marxism had a simple logic about it: 'I saw a good deal of him after his father's death and he was cheerfully open now about his unreserved allegiance to the Communist cause.'[20]

The old inhibitions shed, Maclean's hunger for knowledge and thirst for the friendship of fellow crusaders could at last be freely appeased. The untiring, eager Klugman saw to that and to much else. The tactical position of Trinity Hall, lying snugly between its larger and more richly endowed sister colleges, Trinity and King's, enabled him to visit and receive like-minded visitors; and the big, pleasant rooms under the library which Maclean, as a scholar, still occupied, served as an alternative centre for meetings with leading members of the movement. Through Klugman he became more closely acquainted with several men from Trinity whose combined maturity and versatility made him despair at times of emulating them. There was Maurice Cornforth, like David Haden-Guest a philosophy student but one who already had a London degree and was working fitfully for a doctorate. Cornforth's conversion to Marxism had been sudden and unspectacular. The sight of Haden-Guest 'bubbling over with excitement' at the intellectual cogency of Lenin's *Materialism and Empirio-Criticism* roused his curiosity, so 'I went home and read the book, and thereupon decided to join the Communist Party.'[21]

This convert allowed himself little spare time for reading set books. It did not surprise Maclean to discover that Cornforth's fiancée happened to be Klugman's vivacious sister, Kitty, an ardent Party member herself. 'Verily, James Klugman, you are the universal provider,' he joked. The couple soon married, and their flat above a pawnbroker's shop in King's Street became an important centre for chosen members of the inner group.

Another Trinity man of a wholly different stamp needed no special prodding from Klugman to call, as he put it, on 'the bereaved son of the late Sir Donald Maclean', and present his commiserations. Guy Francis de Moncy Burgess was already a name to conjure with, and Maclean had done so often enough in the harrowing period before he felt at liberty to announce his beliefs. For fantastic anecdotes about Burgess's outrageous behaviour would circulate freely round the University, and nobody ever knew whether to swallow them or not. What drew these two oddly contrasted young men close together was, at any rate to begin with, the recognition that the one had something extra to place on the altar of Marxist–Leninism which the other did not possess. Maclean had acquired unfounded local renown for having 'stood out for principle' against the stuffy obduracy of his late father and family. Like all garbled absurdities, this one lent Maclean a spurious glamour which his exceptional height, good looks and faintly condescending manner seemed to enhance. He had not read much Communist literature, he admitted; he proposed to remedy that deficiency and was getting down to it. Burgess shamelessly teased the confession out of him, then advised Maclean not to worry. Acquiring knowledge was, of course, easy; but gaining recruits ripe for conversion to the movement must take equal priority.

Not only Donald Maclean but undergraduate Cambridge as a whole could not fail to remark, favourably or otherwise, on the paradoxical phenomenon of Guy Burgess at the age of twenty-one. His joie de vivre had immense appeal to the unwary. His charm could be switched on and off at will like electricity. He had epigrammatic wit and an air of omniscience which belied his years; yet his goatlike agility of mind went with an unguarded tongue. He would utter malicious and wounding comments at the drop of a hat against anyone blocking the maze of intersecting paths he followed. 'Not a person lightly to make an enemy of' fairly summed up the verdict of his contemporaries.

Burgess, as Maclean came to recognize, had a slightly older and quieter shadow. Anthony Blunt, one of the agnostic sons of an Anglican vicar, had displayed rare academic prowess at Marlborough. The promise seemed already on the verge of fulfilment at Cambridge. Blunt was so richly talented that he could have become a good philosopher or a great mathematician. He chose instead to specialize as an art historian. Now a Fellow at Trinity, he had instantly and irresistibly won the attentions of the flamboyant Burgess, from whom he was apparently almost inseparable. They were attached not merely by bonds of common interest but by membership of the exclusive club of cultural élitists known as The Apostles. Founded a century earlier by Alfred and Charles Tennyson, in association with Arthur Hallam, John Sterling, John Kemble and other precious souls, The Society (it reserved for itself the signal honour of initial capital letters) indulged at its dinners and discourses in the age-old quest for Beauty and Truth at their finest. In Tennyson's day the new Apostles had at one stage embroiled themselves foolishly in radical politics, not at Westminster but on Spanish soil. By and large, their opinions of alien revolutions reflected an amused and distinctly supercilious attitude. ''Twas a very pretty revolution in Saxony,' Hallam wrote in 1830, 'and a respectable one at Brunswick.' They affected the graces of experts, though they were more adept at splitting literary and metaphysical hairs, and should have stuck to that.

In the conspiracy of the exiled Liberal, General Torrijos, to overthrow the recently restored Bourbon, King Ferdinand, the nineteenth-century Apostles intervened irresolutely as harebrained adventurers, one of their associates, 'the only Englishman to die', as Graham Greene noted, ending up in a pool of his own blood when a firing squad summarily despatched him at Malaga. Neither Hallam nor the Tennysons had been present: they were happily held up by academic priorities at Cambridge. Nor, in later life, did Queen Victoria's poet-laureate wish to dwell on an escapade connecting The Apostles and himself with those best-forgotten Spanish rebels. The episode was glossed over in a few lines by Tennyson's official biographer, though Hallam may have accidentally hit on the truth in declaring: 'After revolutionizing kingdoms, one is still less inclined to trouble one's head about scholarships, degrees and such gear.'[22]

The Apostolic radicals of the 1930s, particularly Anthony Blunt, who secured the election of Burgess in 1932, felt as liberated as Hallam in that earlier, staider Cambridge. The objective of its Communist members was to disrupt the Society by provocation from within, just as the next aim of the rank and file was to split moderates from Marxists inside the University Labour Club until the extremist minority secured control. Since Burgess enjoyed living up to his boast of 'knowing everybody who was anybody, everywhere and anywhere', Maclean was then introduced to yet another Trinity undergraduate for whom the normally cynical and dismissive Burgess had nothing but adulation. At first sight there seemed to be little in the looks, manner, talk or scholarly credentials of Harold Philby to warrant it. Stocky, dark and of medium height, Philby proved conventionally pleasant but altogether too self-contained. He had a stutter; he studied others' faces as he fumbled with matches and pipe in a corner, listening and saying hardly a word. Maclean was all the more mystified because this young economics student, then in his third year, carefully pronounced himself a mere Socialist and seemed perfectly content with his ordinary bona fide membership of the detested Labour Club. What, he wondered, did Burgess really see in him?

As Maclean knew only too well, the process of becoming a Communist convert was bound eventually to create family discord. He therefore commiserated with Klugman who, towards the end of an enviably smooth academic course which finally earned him a Double First in Modern Languages, fell out with his parents over Communism. Such difficulties, however sad, had to be weathered. It appeared that Klugman's father, a fairly well-to-do businessman, was a lifelong Liberal: 'He voted for the Liberals,' said his son, 'in every election until 1931 because he believed in Free Trade and then, for the first and last time, he perversely voted Labour. It did him no good.' Klugman's mother, the main source of the family's wealth, was apolitical. Somewhat wistfully she felt obliged to support her husband when James, in the heat of a family argument, declared defiantly that he had been an active Communist Party member for some time. Klugman's personal ambition had been to make a career as a Cambridge Fellow. The notoriety of his political beliefs may have helped to rule that out; yet, in retrospect, he would not have had it otherwise:

> My commitment to the cause was for life, and it was an exhilarating moment to be alive and young. We simply *knew*, all of us, that the revolution was at hand. If anyone had suggested that it wouldn't happen in Britain, for say thirty years, I'd have laughed myself sick.[23]

Maclean echoed that blithely apocalyptic assessment. For Maclean shared Klugman's vision of Marxism rampant and soon triumphant in Britain. Yet, in his contrary way, he still contrived to enjoy the best of all attainable worlds at Cambridge as well as at home. With his natural aptitude for games, especially cricket, Maclean 'bridged the gulf between "hearties" and "aesthetes" almost without trying, and was popular with both', according to Christopher Gillie. 'The sporting types who rowed or kicked balls about, drank, swore and boasted about their amorous conquests, could overlook the left-wing bias of a person whom they accepted as one of themselves.'[24] Maclean's supervisors sometimes wished that he would concentrate a little more assiduously; yet the Dean of Trinity Hall, Dr Henry Dean, and other College Fellows who knew this versatile young man, saw no reason to disapprove of him: 'It was appreciated, of course, that he affected left-wing views as did many others,' said J. O. Roach, his supervisor in German. 'Nobody minded because it was felt that he, like most of his friends, would grow out of them.'[25]

If there was a whiff of rebellion in the air at Cambridge, some undergraduates were stung into mouthing the extremist sentiments of their Communist friends as a protest against the seemingly aloof and haughty indifference of the University authorities in general. The reaction of Christopher Gillie was not untypical. Far from being a naturally turbulent or politically conscious young man, Gillie resented 'the impression of weary omniscience given by so many of the Fellows who averted eyes and ears from our goings-on as though they had seen and heard everything before. This certainly provoked me. No doubt it provoked a lot of others, too.'[26]

Nevertheless, a good deal of self-questioning and uncertainty went on among the young dons, whatever their individual outlook. At Peterhouse, for example, Herbert Butterfield (later Master of his college and the University's Vice-Chancellor) realized as early as 1930 that the Communist germ had 'taken' and would not easily be contained. Now Peterhouse always was the smallest college in Cambridge; and Butterfield, an erudite historian but also a practical Yorkshireman of firm Methodist convictions, did not fall into the trap of trying to 'brainwash' students already infected by Marxist ideas:

I noticed that one particular grammar school at Lytham in Lancashire almost invariably sent us scholarship boys who arrived already full of Communist teaching. It proved difficult for some of them later on when they applied for jobs outside, especially in the public services. I remember the case of one of my students, a biblical fundamentalist of great seriousness. He was easily converted to Marxism by regular attendance at meetings of the Student Christian Movement which, at that particular time, went in for perhaps undue religious liberalism and caused this victim to look for an alternative version of fundamentalism. Again, I can recall the bubbling, Communistic enthusiasm of another undergraduate who seemed to regard the Soviet Union as more perfect than paradise. Charles Fletcher Cooke rose enthusiastically to the bait when the College agreed to let him visit Russia on a Travelling Scholarship. Charles was a tremendously keen letter-writer, and I wish I'd kept his letters from Moscow and elsewhere. Every single one of them expressed disillusion with the Soviet system – from the first to the last – and the young man returned an anti-Communist. He's still a Conservative MP, I believe.[27]

Not all dons acted with such intelligent restraint. Communist Fellows, of course, had other fish to fry; and the frying was usually done well, in decent privacy. To the discriminating Butterfield the two most attractive, in their quite dissimilar styles, were the biochemist Joseph Needham, who described himself as a 'Christian Marxist', and the many-sided Anglo-Irish scientist John Desmond Bernal. Needham, the son of a London doctor, believed quite simply that the Gospel teaching demanded Communist solutions to social problems; while Bernal chose to demonstrate 'a cavalier disregard for ascertainable historical facts' in praising the acceptable human face of Soviet planning:

> Bernal was a big man of captivating charm who certainly influenced hundreds of undergraduates [said Sir Herbert Butterfield]. He was that rare creature, a person of truly seminal ideas on a host of subjects, yet one who would never have exercised the cumulative persistence with detail required to win a Nobel Prize. I liked Bernal enormously.[28]

The year 1933 may well be regarded by posterity as a watershed in the political history of Britain. Among politically conscious undergraduates, in particular at Cambridge, it was a year when the cult of Communism established itself openly as something more pervasive and sinister than a passing fashion. By skilful propaganda and individual proselytizing, the movement consolidated its hold and eventually succeeded in forcing the once-dominant Labour Club to capitulate and close its doors. It also grieved the hearts of the novelist E. M. Forster, and John Maynard Keynes, the Bursar of King's, to find that the sacred enclave of The Apostles had been suddenly penetrated from within. In the words of Sir Roy Harrod, his biographer, Keynes

could not but observe the tendency towards Communism among the young at Cambridge, and most markedly among the choice spirits, those whom thirty years before he would have wished to consider for membership in 'The Society'. He attributed it to a recrudescence of the strain of Puritanism in our blood, the zest to adopt a painful solution because of its painfulness.[29]

Apart from Blunt and Burgess, there were other Apostles of the far Left. Julian Bell, the militant son of Keynes's Bloomsbury intimates, Clive and Vanessa Bell, was one; Hugh Sykes Davies, an amusing and clever young man who became a Fellow of St John's, was another; and Richard (now Lord) Llewellyn-Davies was a third. Though 'The Society', at Keynes's prompting, officially suspended its proceedings, the nucleus which had imported so much Marxist content into those proceedings continued to meet apostolically but unofficially. Their high-minded objective was to renovate the face of the earth, beginning with Britain, by Marxist–Leninist revolutionary means.

Cambridge, with its proud tradition of independent thinking and Cromwellian earnestness, had been well chosen first by Litvinov, then by the Comintern; but by 1933 Cambridge no longer stood alone. At Klugman's home in Hampstead, joint discussions had taken place during the Easter vacation of 1932 between delegates from Oxford as well as Cambridge, from the London School of Economics, and from University College, London. In the absence of Klugman's parents, this informal student gathering agreed on tactics to coordinate their activities. Representatives came from Communist Party headquarters; and the Party's National Organizer, Douglas Frank Springhall, 'something of an extremist and a tough hearty', intervened occasionally to clarify points or to sound an official note of encouragement. Guy Burgess needed no incentive to conduct his own extravagant reconnaissances at Oxford. A number of his Etonian friends were there; and his effervescent and sometimes dazzling conversational gifts made him a welcome guest at the table of Maurice Bowra, then a Fellow of Wadham College, and of other Oxford dons. To what extent Burgess, with his compulsive appetite for high living and good company, obeyed his own whims in thus mixing pleasure with Party business cannot now be accurately measured; but Dr Goronwy Rees, then a young Fellow of All Souls, first encountered him at an Oxford dinner party given by Bowra in the early summer of 1932 and was 'instantly captivated by his charm and intellectual vividness'. The fact that Burgess sought Rees out later, earning a mild rebuff for 'making a tentative pass' at him, did not prevent the pair from becoming close friends on the platonic level. Rees, a scholarship boy from a pious, lower-middle-class home in Wales, refrained from condemning Burgess for his shameless pursuit of any attractive young male, having already acclimatized himself to the prevalence of homosexual relationships in the rarefied, closed society of Oxford.[30]

The more 'dilettante' of the two ancient universities, sometimes dubbed by unkind critics as the 'home of lost causes', Oxford failed to overtake its rival's lead in the Communist campaign for undergraduate recruits. Yet the founding of the October Club at Oxford was not long delayed. On 9 February 1933, there was a debate in the Union on a motion so subversive in nature that the King, the Lords, the Commons, leaders of the armed forces and many lesser luminaries of the ruling class were momentarily stunned and scandalized. No public discussion at Cambridge could have produced a comparable effect. The motion, carried by a large majority, stated unequivocally that 'this House' would 'in no circumstances fight for King and Country'. The sensation spurred on the small, vociferous Communist faction at Oxford. Subsequently, however, it had a harder and less successful struggle than the well-entrenched Party branch at Cambridge University to disperse and demoralize loyal democratic Socialists. Even before the Spanish Civil War broke out, left-wing partisans began to cooperate, in keeping with the new Comintern policy line of the 'Popular Front'. By then, of course, Guy Burgess and his Marxist contemporaries in the cloistered atmosphere of Oxford and Cambridge had vanished into the outside world.

The value to the Communist movement of privileged but committed Marxist academics like Dobb and Bernal, Blunt and Pascal, can scarcely be overrated. In the liberal milieu of Cambridge they were accepted as respected members of a hieratic caste. Their political opinions, no matter how extreme, would not detract from their standing, always provided that the normal civilized rules and conventions were observed. Within these generous limits, they conspired to influence and keep a watchful eye on talented undergraduates likely to be of future use to the Party, whether as potential dons, who would remain to guide the next generation of students, or as yeast to leaven the bourgeois lump of the public services, journalism, the law, medicine or any other respectable profession. Clemens Palme Dutt and Douglas Springhall were the main links between Cambridge and Communist Party headquarters, with Andrew Rothstein a useful man in reserve; but Maurice Dobb, who was probably the first academic in Britain to carry a card (dated 1920), seldom hesitated to consult the top men when the urge took him. His Marxist faith was self-evident, unashamed yet subtle. He did not mind wearing his heart on his sleeve. A debate in the Cambridge Union with an orthodox, friendly adversary like his historian colleague George Kitson-Clark might exhibit him at his incisive best; but in lectures and supervisions he strove so sedulously to avoid 'playing the propagandist' that Fellows of other colleges could not be sure how thorough-going a Marxist Dobb really was. Yet the same Maurice Dobb, on crossing the Soviet frontier en route to Moscow by train in 1921, had flung his arms into the air and exclaimed to his comrade, Harry Pollitt, a jovial ex-boilermaker from Lancashire: 'How thrilling to be moving across this sacred soil at last.'[31] The effectiveness of Anthony Blunt was greater than Dobb's. It was he, according to informed contemporaries, who first opened Guy Burgess's eyes to the relevance of Marxism as a purifying, corrective force in every branch of decadent bourgeois endeavour – the creative arts, the sciences, history and philosophy as well as politics; and, as has been shown, the conversion of Burgess unleashed a wilful and sometimes malignant demon on the University.

No two religious conversions, of course, are ever exactly alike, and there persisted among the 'first wave' of Communist converts in the undergraduate body a faint uneasiness as to the total disinterestedness of Guy Burgess's convictions when at last he claimed to see the light. These reservations were understandable. For during his first year and part of his second, Burgess chose to indulge almost exclusively in socializing and pleasure-seeking, treating with scornful disdain every attempt to rope him into a movement which he abhorred as being quite un-English in its studied fanaticism. As a Trinity contemporary said,

> Only on finding that membership of the Party would not necessarily debar him from the high living that meant everything to him did Guy start to think again. Unlike Saul on the road to Damascus, our friend entered the true fold by turning all his previous objectives plumb on their heads.

Another critic, the poet and sociologist Charles Madge, who became a pioneer of the Mass Observation surveys in Britain later in the thirties, plainly had larger and more important targets than Guy Burgess in mind when he wrote these unoriginal lines in 1933:

> Lenin, would you were living at this hour:
> England has need of you, of the cold voice
> That spoke beyond Time's passion, and expelled
> All the half treasons of the mind in doubt.

For by 1933 Madge had left Magdalene and Cambridge in some haste,

> as a result of having gone off with Kathleen Raine [a fellow Communist writer], then married to Hugh Sykes-Davies. I had one year at Cambridge as an active Communist, 1931–32. Blunt and Burgess at Trinity were friends of a friend of mine, Guy Hunter, also at Trinity. I met Burgess a few times but did not know him well. At that time he was no Communist – in fact, when I became one he cut me dead in King's Parade. My brother John, two years younger than myself, came up to Trinity in 1932 and he was quite thick with Anthony Blunt and went with him

and possibly Burgess on a trip to the USSR in 1933 or 1934. My brother, Blunt and Burgess all became Communists, as did many others at Oxford and Cambridge. I met Burgess a few times after that and cordially disliked him.[32]

As a former naval cadet with the added distinction of having twice been accepted as a pupil at Eton, Burgess was more worldly-wise than most of his elders and contemporaries yet realized. Sir Robert Birley, as he has since become, had latterly taught Burgess history at Eton, noting how this precocious pupil distinguished himself by his exuberance out of class and his unforced brilliance in it. Birley, then an assistant master, thought very highly of Burgess's originality:

He had a gift for plunging to the root of any question and his essays were on occasion full of insights. His career in the upper school passed wholly without blemish. No evidence whatever of any weaknesses or defects of character came to light.[33]

As an Oppidan, a non-colleger, Burgess had stayed in a boarding house not far from the main school. If he ever felt the onset of homosexual temptations, it is not unlikely that opportunities to gratify them arose; at all events, he was never found out or caught. He was regarded as 'quite a card' by most of his companions. Burgess, among other talents, had a gift for drawing weird, swift, exotic caricatures, mostly of masters, and rounding them off with suitably wicked captions. His friends were fewer than his acquaintances, older and younger. These generally disliked him for being 'too clever by half', though Michael Berry (today Lord Hartwell, proprietor of the *Daily Telegraph* and *Sunday Telegraph*) retained a protective if distant regard for Burgess until the latter's defection to the Soviet Union. Another Etonian friend was Sammy (now Lord) Hood, who went up to Trinity College at the same time and afterwards became a diplomat. Hood's father had reached the rank of Rear-Admiral in the Royal Navy, and this probably helped to form a tenuous bond between the two boys. Guy's father also had served in the Fleet, and the boy would idly boast that, but for the misfortune of ill-health leading to premature retirement and death, Commander Malcolm Kingsford de Moncy

Burgess would almost certainly have risen to Flag rank as well. Naturally, the truth was simpler and somewhat starker.

Like many middle-class families of similar station, the Burgesses had a long and proud tradition of service to Crown and Empire. Guy knew, for instance, that his father had been born in Aden, and that his grandfather, a colonel in the Royal Artillery, automatically put down the name of his first-born son for Dartmouth, in accordance with clan ritual. Alas, Malcolm's naval career had never really prospered. His superiors found in him a youth 'of temperate habits', if somewhat deficient 'in zeal', and often 'inclined to be lazy'. It seemed at first that Malcolm may have been merely unlucky in his superiors. However, when at length he put to sea, an unfortunate collision occurred between HMS *Panther* and HMS *Thresher*. The court of enquiry solemnly judged 'sub-lieutenant Burgess to blame, but in view of inexperience [he was] only admonished by the C.-in-C. to be more careful in future'. His frustrations were unending. Limited powers of seamanship resulted in his being 'held unfit for service in destroyers'. His captain brusquely recommended him 'for trial in any other class of vessel'.[34] Undeterred, Lieutenant Malcolm Burgess persevered, earned slow promotion, fell in love with Evelyn Mary Gillman, an attractive daughter of wealthy parents, married her at Portsmouth on a December morning in 1907, and fathered two sons. The first was born at home, within sight of the naval dockyard at Devonport, on 16 April 1911. He was christened Guy Francis de Moncy Burgess, the French surname included as a tribute to distant Huguenot forbears; and because this child appeared brighter and more precocious than the young brother, Nigel, the father entered Guy's name for Dartmouth, as if determined to get his own back on the Admiralty.

Guy saw little of his father in childhood, catching only fleeting glimpses of an awesome, neatly uniformed figure who came home on leave occasionally during the 1914–18 war. The naval commander was on active service most of the time, combing the oceans on anti-submarine patrols. He came through unscathed; but tedium and strain had undermined his health. He also pined for his wife and family, especially after his posting in 1919 to the staff of the Rear-Admiral, Egypt. At his own request, Commander Malcolm Burgess was placed on the retired list in 1922. By then Guy was eleven years old and hardly knew his father. It was not a happy household at West Lodge, the Burgess country house at West Meon, Hampshire. The retired naval commander suffered from a mild heart condition; but this handicap did not prevent him from playing the tyrant with his two sons, whose mother had always tended to spoil them. He could console himself that Guy at any rate would be taught the meaning of real discipline at Dartmouth as soon as the boy was old enough to go.

The regulations governing entry to the Royal Naval College were precise and strict. According to the relevant Navy List Appendix of April 1924, 'Candidates for entry in January must be more than thirteen years and four months but not more than thirteen years and eight months of age on the preceding 1st December.' Since Guy would have to wait for admittance as a trainee-cadet, his father somewhat reluctantly fell in with his mother's eager wish that he should first spend a year in preparation at Eton. So to Eton they packed him off in January 1924, an unwilling new public schoolboy who knew in advance that his public schooldays were numbered. His name appears in the alphabetical lists of pupils in each number of the Eton College *Chronicle* for that year, including the Michaelmas 'Half', then disappears until Michaelmas 1927. The intervening period of thirty-three arduous months were spent at Dartmouth, where 'he clearly showed sure scholarly promise'[35] and carried off many prizes. His father would undoubtedly have been gratified had he lived to see his elder son's apparently effortless progress. But Commander Malcolm Burgess's sudden and horrifying death during the night of 15 September 1924 left a permanent scar on the mind of the boy just before his return to Eton at the end of the summer holidays.

The last terse entry in the father's official record of service merely states the date, place and medical cause of death. It occurred on the night in question 'at West Meon Lodge, West Meon'. It was technically ascribed to 'atheroma of the aorta and valvular disease of the aortic valve'. The circumstances, however, were so frighteningly dramatic, if Guy Burgess's description of the event can be credited, that they deserve to be briefly recounted. He was disturbed during that fateful night by an anguished cry for help from his parents' bedroom. Recognizing his mother's voice, he rushed in and found her pinioned down helplessly beneath the inert body of his father, who had apparently expired without warning in the act of making love. It demanded all the boy's strength to pull away the still-warm corpse and release her: somehow he managed. For many years afterwards he could never bring himself to speak about an incident, the recollection of which filled him with conflicting emotions of disgust and grief. Whether his adult aversion to sexual relations with women can be thus wholly or largely explained must remain a moot point. Guy Burgess was always so good at inventing excuses rather than giving reasons for his behaviour that even the friend to whom he confided the gruesome anecdote hardly knows to this day whether to believe it or not.[36]

As a beginner at Dartmouth, the boy settled down quickly. Reports on his progress were uniformly positive. He had the physique and the brains to shine equally in the classroom and on the playing fields; his aptitude for drill, sports and study marked him out among fellow cadets of his year as an all-rounder. His instructors, almost without exception, soon came to regard him as 'excellent officer material'. Perhaps, under the rigours of the régime, he found it simpler to conform and excel, thus compensating for the deficiencies of his late father's apprenticeship to the sea. The interests of Cadet Guy de M. Burgess, as he was listed, were wide and varied. He revelled in the writings of Mahan. He learnt to revere the history and traditions of the Royal Navy. He won prizes in 1926 for his own penetrating essays on naval operations, also scooping the pool in science, geography and other subjects. During what proved to be his final term, the summer of 1927, Burgess displayed versatility beyond the call of duty by taking further prizes for general history, for an analysis of Napoleon's military career, even for scripture and 'Notes on Picture Making'. He appeared deeply downcast at first when he underwent an eyesight test and failed it. There had been some complaints from instructors of this highly promising cadet's slowness in carrying out routine training exercises: they called in at ophthalmic specialist who assured them that defective vision rather than sloth was the cause. That summer Burgess had to withdraw from the Royal Naval College, armed with an honourable discharge and glowing references to the headmaster of Eton, who readily agreed to take back his old pupil forthwith.

Known henceforth as 'Burgess major' to distinguish him from his younger brother Nigel, who had entered the school in 1926, Guy was placed in the upper division of the fifth form, third remove.[37] From the start his housemaster, Francis Wellesley Dobbs, could not bring himself to like this precocious and opinionated young naval reject whom it was not easy to fit in academically and who vainly strove to earn Dobbs's good esteem. It was Robert Birley who first sensed the antipathy between Dobbs and Burgess. For that reason alone he was prepared to give the boy

> full marks for his dog-like devotion to a housemaster who knew a great deal about mathematics but precious little about human nature. . . . When Guy Burgess defected, some of his old friends were embarrassed. Naturally, too, some were more taken aback than others. I remember well Dobbs's stare of complete incomprehension at the news. 'I refuse to believe it,' he said. And he maintained that refusal to the last.[38]

Burgess turned out to be a reasonably keen footballer, a strong swimmer and a fitfully brilliant student who worked best when his interest and pride were challenged. He fully emerged from the chrysalis in his last year. Ranking sixth among the Oppidans, he hoped for election to the exclusive Eton Society, or 'Pop', which would have allowed him to wear braid on his jacket, to have a room of his own, and to lord it over small boys from other houses who would run errands and 'fag' for him. Michael Berry realized how much this privilege meant to Burgess, so 'I set about organizing a small ring of four other members who accepted my estimate of him and were prepared to vote him in.' It was soon borne in on Berry just how unpopular Guy had become. The majority simply 'preferred not to have him'.[39]

It is just conceivable that the intense and characteristically indiscreet affection of Burgess for another Eton friend, David

Hedley, offended the 'swells' who set the tone of the place. No hint of scandal could be traced to the pair while they were still at school, though their relationship attained some notoriety later. Hedley, under his bosom friend's influence, became a homosexual and remained a passionate Communist until his early death. Eton, rightly or wrongly, has always prided itself on being politically broadminded, partly perhaps because of the predominance of High Tories and scions of the old and new nobility among its pupils. Communism may have been discussed, but neither teachers nor boys saw any reason to take this alien, un-British creed seriously, a point which Burgess perversely grasped as somehow telling in Communism's favour. Robert Birley alone among the masters put himself out to keep this gifted youth well in his sights. After all, Guy Burgess did not leave this famous school without friends or honours to sustain him: he fully deserved to win the Rosebery and Gladstone history prizes in 1929, as well as his Scholarship in History to Trinity College, Cambridge. So, during the summer term of 1931, Birley dropped a line to Burgess, inviting himself to tea on a mutually agreeable date:

Of course Guy wasn't in when I arrived so I entered his room in New Court and waited. There were many books on his shelves, and I'm always drawn to other people's taste in reading. As I expected, his taste was fairly wide and interesting. I noticed a number of Marxist tracts and text-books, but that's not what really shocked and depressed me. I realized that something must have gone terribly wrong when I came across an extraordinary array of explicit and extremely unpleasant pornographic literature. He bustled in finally, full of cheerful apologies for being late as usual, and we talked happily enough over the tea-cups.

Naturally, Birley did not raise the one delicate question uppermost in his mind. When he had finished listening to Burgess, prattling on about his new friends and his interests without offering the slightest suggestion that anything might have gone wrong, Robert Birley said goodbye and returned to Eton, musing over the unpredictable waywardness of human nature. Guy had evidently fallen into some very queer company indeed, and Birley could not help wondering how and why. He did not confide his fears to anyone. The young man would seek him out eventually if the need arose, of that Birley was convinced. Had he been able to foresee in 1931 the strange circumstances in which Burgess would finally seek him out just before decamping to Moscow exactly twenty years later, this understanding and highly civilized teacher might not have held back so long. Whether he could ever have deflected Burgess from the wild course on which the young man was already thinking of embarking may well be doubted.[40]

3. THE TALENT SPOTTERS

Seriously as the Cambridge Communists took themselves, their activities were only loosely controlled. The results lacked the co-ordination which disciplined functionaries at Party headquarters in London deemed appropriate, but then functionaries had never trusted intellectual recruits. In theory, the Communist leadership laid down the duties expected of its members, regardless of class and social background. R. Palme Dutte, the high priest in such matters, had warned repeatedly that the Party's 'bourgeois elements' must constantly be on guard against individual prejudices and habits of mind which betrayed their upper- or middle-class origins. A modicum of humility was required of men who had to learn before they could begin to teach. The movement might need them, but certainly 'not as heaven-sent teachers of superior wisdom'.[1] If Marxism was then becoming all the rage, especially among university undergraduates, that in itself, according to Dutt, could be construed as yet another sobering example of bourgeois decadence. The last man in Cambridge likely to need such dreary pontifications was the mercurial, self-willed Guy Burgess, who always preferred to trust his own contrary instincts.

Some of his intimates at Cambridge had heard Guy holding forth on a favourite theme, his version of the causes of Britain's recent economic collapse. Few academic historians of the day would have endorsed his view that, for the past half-century, the British Empire had been in a state of steady and irreversible decline. The Germans and the Americans, he argued, had overtaken British production of steel and other industrial sinews of war and peace as long ago as the 1880s; since then nothing had gone right for the once-mighty British Empire. Its glorious image excited

Burgess. The fading of the image he resented with the passion of a man railing at fate by the bedside of a dying friend. Through all the years of imperial flag-waving and Kiplingesque patriotism that had since passed, and regardless of the costly race to maintain British naval supremacy against the battle fleet of the Kaiser, the British Empire had been dragged willy nilly by political lunatics into a disastrous and even costlier world conflict. The politicians of all parties had failed the people, so the people must rise against them. Burgess's consuming love for the vanishing Empire was matched by a corresponding affection for the shrinking Royal Navy. Thus his cup of bitterness was full to overflowing.

Whatever the motives of Burgess, his active scheming gave little pleasure to the functionaries at Communist Party headquarters. The Cambridge experiment was not, however, theirs to command, except indirectly and in the broadest outline. The Comintern and the Soviet NKVD had ordained that this Pandora's box should be opened, so with dutiful compliance the Party leaders at King Street watched developments passively and dubiously from a distance. They must have been as puzzled as the supercilious Donald Maclean, for instance, at the willingness of Burgess to dance attention on a pleasant, self-effacing member of the University Labour Club called Harold Philby. What Burgess did off duty might be no concern of the Party's, though his contradictory and often unpredictable behaviour would certainly have been denounced in any ordinary branch of the organization. Men of his type brought a disciplined movement into disrepute. It was all very well for him to charge about like a self-important Inspector General, bringing in improbable recruits on his own account and bypassing the normal channels, but this same Burgess also belonged to the vulgarly ostentatious Pitt Club, a decadent right-wing group, as well as to the élitist and secretive Apostles. Nobody had the right to question or reprimand him because of the tacit understanding that Communist undergraduates were to be treated with kid gloves. Moreover, their mentors among college Fellows usually seemed to deal at most with two or three principals of the ruling political executive, bypassing the statutory machinery as the unspeakable Guy Burgess did.

Halfway through his studies at Trinity, Harold Philby had decided to switch from history to economics; and it was in the rooms of Dennis Robertson, the University's Reader in this relatively new subject, that Kim first set eyes on Burgess. They met many times after that. For Burgess had not realized, until they were introduced, that there stood the only son of a famous father, and that Dennis Robertson happened to be an old friend of the redoubtable Arabist and explorer with his streaks of arch-rebel and adventurer. To any outside Communist it seemed highly improbable that anything of lasting value would come of the new-found companionship between these two wholly dissimilar young men, still less that the seeds of future treason could conceivably be sown through it. That, however, is where it was all too easy to underestimate the influence of Guy Burgess, whose very outrageousness proved an ideal disguise both in the early years of the Cambridge Communist ferment and later. Not that Burgess had yet been selected or briefed for any specific role; at this stage he was still making most of the running himself. But the favourable view taken of him by the nucleus of Fellows who could discreetly advance his career in the revolutionary cause was the one guarantee which mattered. If Burgess, with his restless intuition, wanted to win over the partly apolitical young Philby, then Burgess could count on their support.

Like his father Harry St John Philby before him, Kim was a Colleger and King's Scholar of Westminster School, which sent three of its cleverest products each year to Trinity. The other two successful candidates in 1929 were Hugh Burt, who chose to work for a medical degree, and Joseph Grigg, the son of an American journalist based in London, who went up with Kim, his close friend, to read classics. Grigg, an observant young man who intended to follow in his father's footsteps and became an accomplished foreign correspondent, remained on good terms with Philby at Cambridge. He knew that his friend was 'quite interested in politics' but held no extremist views. They frequently set off together on long walks or cycle rides into the countryside; and 'sometimes lively arguments arose between us over Kim's vaguely Socialist ideas'. Grigg, of course, did not 'live on top of Philby', as had happened in their schooldays. He noticed, especially during their rural outings, that Kim didn't care for drink; nor did he have much spending money:

> Like me, he worked hard, as most of us had to do. Don't forget that was a period of deepening economic depression, so that the prospects of earning a decent living were worrying for many Cambridge undergraduates. Kim kept himself to himself and led a fairly abstemious existence. Neither he nor I could afford to keep up with the wealthy young men who hunted and generally indulged themselves. We didn't fit into the category of the academically gifted, natural dons of the future. We belonged to the majority who had to slog away at our set books.

Grigg, in common with Tim Milne, another Westminster friend who had gone up to Oxford, had often visited Philby's home at weekends during schooldays. The family lived in Acol Road, Maida Vale. The house was rambling, plainly furnished and unpretentious. Kim's mother was 'a kind and understanding woman with a gentle smile and striking red hair'. Her husband was hardly ever there; and his son 'clearly idolized this absentee father who was then adviser to Ibn Saud, the King of Saudi Arabia, and would appear only when on leave'. Only once did Harry St John Philby manage to attend a school function with his wife in the customary gatherings of parents, and it was noticeable how the son's eyes shone with pride. In Grigg's opinion,

> Kim seemed to stand in considerable awe of his father, who had served in the Indian Civil Service before falling out with his superiors, resigning and then carving out a fresh and independent life of his own in a desert Kingdom of Arabia.[2]

It was perspicacious of Burgess to surmise, in a characteristic flash of insight, that the son of such a vigorous, self-willed and enterprising parent might be well worth cultivating as a likely recruit to the Communist cause. Plainly, in a slowly disintegrating British Empire, there would be fewer openings for future proconsuls of Harry St John Philby's calibre. If Kim wanted to emulate his father, he would find little room for adventure or manoeuvre in the hidebound British diplomatic service, with its stiff protocol and rigid career structure. That might just suit someone as outwardly conventional as Donald Maclean. Apparently, Donald's widowed mother was already pressing him to sit the entrance examination. It was probable, as Donald alleged, that she was following the advice of her Liberal friends and well-wishers; but Donald himself did not care much for the suggestion. His intention, so he insisted, was to visit the Soviet Union and undertake voluntary work as a teacher or a tractor driver. The Maclean family and their advisers appeared to assume that he was joking, or that if he happened to be serious, this absurdly romantic dream would evaporate once Donald, like everyone else, had to face the stern business of earning his own keep. In contrast to Lady Maclean, Harry St John Philby had nothing but contempt for the British Civil Service, whether home, foreign or colonial. It gratified Burgess that Kim not only shared his father's feelings on that score but seemed immediately and deeply impressed by Guy's favourite analysis of the reasons for Britain's decline as a nation and an imperial power. Agreement on these points bound the two men closely together. Besides, Philby could not help admiring the extraordinary verve and vitality of a person quite unlike anyone he had met before.

Nevertheless, Philby did not forsake the Labour Club just to please Burgess. His stammer inhibited him in any case from canvassing, debating or making speeches. At Westminster School, as Grigg remembered, Kim had never taken advantage of the privilege enabling King's Scholars to visit the House of Commons and listen to proceedings there. During the General Strike of 1926, when masters had donned the uniforms of special policemen and senior boys had volunteered – after obtaining parental permission – as junior clerks at the Foreign Office on the far side of Parliament Square, or as kitchen porters and bus or tram conductors, neither Philby nor Grigg had interested themselves in these activities, far less in the causes of the critical dispute; but they caught something of the national mood of intense relief afterwards. The headmaster, Mr Cosley-White, had summoned a special assembly and opened his address with the resounding words: 'The General Strike is over. This is a great day for Westminster and the Empire.'

Games had been compulsory, and Philby had evinced little taste or aptitude for football or cricket. Only once did he rate a mention in print. The *Elizabethan*, the school magazine, drew particular attention to the fate of the junior eleven in 'a good and fast game' against Ashburnham one wet afternoon in that same year, 1926. Influenza had weakened the Westminster side, and the visiting team proved heavier and more skilful. Nevertheless, 'Junior House Caps were deservedly won by H. A. R. Philby' among others.[3] A short, sturdy boy then, he had developed since physically and mentally without trying to acquire any liking for organized sport. The records at Trinity show that again he merited only a single mention for playing football during the four years he spent at Cambridge.

Application rather than brilliance was Philby's distinctive trait, both as a schoolboy and as an undergraduate. He tended to follow, not to lead, except in the mature ease with which he could express his thoughts on paper. The oldest surviving master of Westminster School, Mr Laurence Tanner, clearly recalled how Philby, inspired perhaps by Grigg, the aspirant-journalist, had edited a

rather scurrillous but well-written underground newspaper called the *Trifler*, on which a lot of time and trouble were obviously expended. A copy fell into my hands one day, and I felt obliged to tell the senior history class exactly what I thought of it since it contained a profile of myself, which was not flattering. 'You disappoint me, Philby,' I said, 'and I demand a public apology, not because I'm offended by your crude caricature of my mannerisms, my appearance and the shortcomings of my character. I'm simply appalled because you've not succeeded in being original or savage enough. Why didn't you consult me about my deficiencies? I could have helped. You really must try harder.'

Tanner's view of Philby was unreservedly kind and favourable:

I've only happy memories of him. I liked boys who used their wits and didn't shirk the grind of hard work. The régime of the school was liberal, and I believe young Philby benefited from that. He probably suffered by missing the guidance of a father whom in some ways he resembled. The boy had no problems of adjustment. I found him intelligent, amusing, charming. He was a rebel at heart, I knew, but he had little of his father's eccentricity. Perhaps he strove too slavishly to imitate him later when the maggot got into his brain at Cambridge.[4]

In one sense, this exceptional teacher did his pupil a slight injustice. Tanner was fond of telling boys in his class, including the actor John Gielgud and the novelist Angus Wilson, in their time: 'You must learn to think in centuries.' Westminster School, in its ancient setting beside the Abbey, hard by the Houses of Parliament and Whitehall, was one of the few public schools in the land which had preserved its high standards of humane education through the seven or eight centuries of its existence. Ben Jonson, Cowley and Dryden had studied there, as had Cowper and Southey, Sir Christopher Wren, John Locke and Edward Gibbon, Warren Hastings, Lord Raglan and Lord John Russell. If Eton and Harrow prided themselves on producing many prime ministers and politicians, Westminster School could lay claim to some of England's finest poets, thinkers, writers, architects, prelates and administrators, drawn from boys who had been born into middle-class homes. For what the notoriety might be worth, it also helped to drum into Harold Adrian Russell Philby qualities befitting a future clandestine Soviet agent.

If Philby had a fixation on the father whom he saw only at rare intervals, and Maclean rejoiced at his liberation from the religious oppressiveness of the late Sir Donald, then Burgess ranked as a special case wholly dissimilar from anyone else. A fellow Oppidan had once asked him at Eton: 'What exactly does your father do?' It was an innocent enough question, sparked off by doubt as to Guy Burgess's financial circumstances, which 'were apt to fluctuate between prosperity and penury', at least in the opinion of the questioner, Evan James.

'My own father died when I was thirteen years old', Burgess had replied. 'My stepfather, I'm afraid, is a professional gambler.'

Evan James hardly knew whether to believe him or not. That was one of the difficulties with Burgess the boy, Burgess the youth, and Burgess the man. He concealed his real self so well behind each of several garish and improbable masks that it became impossible to pin down the actual character. In fact, his widowed mother, Mrs Evelyn Mary Burgess, had since met and married a retired Army officer, Colonel John Retallack Basset. This happened not long after Guy's return to Eton from Dartmouth. The colonel enjoyed a mild flutter on the horses and was not ungenerous in advancing to his stepson extra pocket money from the occasional winnings. Mrs Basset was responsible for giving in so readily to every single one of Guy's importunate whims that he had become uncontrollable long before going up to Cambridge.

The boy who had enquired what Guy's father did for a living, Evan James, admitted long afterwards his inability to penetrate the mystery that was Burgess:

> Brought up in my respectable, middle-class way I was astonished never having heard of such a thing as a professional gambler. Since then, with the benefit of hindsight, I often wonder whether this was fact or fancy, or a bit of both. It may be that Guy hardly knew himself. . . .[5]

In contrast to Philby, who adhered strictly to his abstemious régime, never exceeding his small allowance and never borrowing money, Burgess lived well beyond his means at Cambridge. He cultivated wealthy young men like his amiable Trinity neighbour Victor Rothschild (now the banker, scientist and administrator, Lord Rothschild), who could afford to entertain fairly lavishly and no doubt felt that Burgess paid for his numerous luncheons, parties and dinners with the sparkling and frequently ribald tone of his conversation. On one occasion Jim Lees unwisely accepted an invitation to the Rothschild table where Burgess, seated next to this self-conscious, working-class guest, urged him to take a cigar. 'They're worth three and sixpence each,' he said in a deliberately audible whisper. Rothschild, who had been at Harrow, professed sympathy with Socialism but took no noticeably active part in proceedings of the non-Communist rump of the Labour Club to which Philby and Lees both belonged. Driving fast cars and leading a full social life amused him more, as reports in such current Cambridge periodicals as *Variety Weekly* amply testify:

Victor Rothschild provided a genuine thrill when his lovely Mercedes came into view. The manner in which he pulled up to avoid Denis Conan-Doyle's Austro-Daimler, which was lying broadside across his path, was masterly. He was travelling at over 100 miles per hour when he crossed the finishing line. . . . He seemed little perturbed by his accident, and was entertaining guests at an amusing cocktail party in Jesus Lane, later in the evening. . . .[6]

Through Rothschild's benevolence, Burgess visited the large and beautiful family home, and there met Victor's mother as well as his sister Miriam, an observant young lady with a sharp tongue and scientific aspirations who grew up to attain a worldwide reputation as an expert on fleas. Miriam was quick to see through the inconsistencies of her brother's talkative Cambridge companion.

I considered him intelligent, but rather babyish, with the slightly protruding teeth of the thumb-sucker. He was voluble to the point of spluttering, obviously neurotic, good looking with curly hair and fresh complexion, and his chief attraction was vitality and rather boyish enthusiasm. Before he graduated he talked the usual left-wing stuff, overemphasized the fact that he joined the hunger-marchers on their walk to London, and was obviously sincere about his sympathy for the underdog. But so was everyone else.

One of his outstanding weaknesses was his total lack of debating ability. In those days I used to argue with him, taking a conventional Socialist line, while he wanted a bloody revolution and was a self-styled Marxist. On one occasion I reduced him to floods of tears and thereafter felt he was scarcely fair game and I hadn't the heart to bait him in general discussions.[7]

Nevertheless, Burgess had already achieved what he sought: a foothold in the Rothschild entourage was his main objective. No matter how tiresome Miriam might prove to be at times, he had been accepted and welcomed as one of Victor's friends. For Burgess had as yet no clearer idea than Philby what to do in life when his undergraduate days came to an end. Anthony Blunt reassured him that a fellowship might reasonably be expected, if Guy did not wholly neglect his studies. There were too many distractions, however, and Burgess invariably succumbed to them. Neither he nor Philby had much inclination to branch out later, as Klugman, Haden-Guest and Cornforth proposed, and work as professional Communist standard-bearers. Philby in any case had disqualified himself by refusing to leave the Labour Club, politely declining suggestions that he would do far better to join the Communist Party. It must be re-emphasized that Philby at this stage was not yet a fully instructed or convinced Communist, only a vague sympathizer. There could be no question therefore of his 'going underground' or 'playing a covert game', as some commentators have supposed, though later on it would be easier for him than for any known Communist to do so.

All his life Philby had been an onlooker. Except on that one wet day at Westminster School when he had earned a Junior House Cap for unavoidable effort, he held back and let others with nimbler brains or bigger muscles do the striving in class or on the playing fields. A circumspect and watchful young man now, more self-conscious than ever about his father's remote yet bold example of independence, Philby kept his options open. He would have been untrue to his nature had he rushed into the Communist party as fecklessly as the gay Guy Burgess. It is doubly ironical therefore that Harry St John Philby's notoriety as a rebellious individualist, unintentionally promoted by Dennis Robertson, helped to heighten the regard in which the son gradually came to be held by Maurice Dobb, by Dobb's enigmatic Italian collaborator Pietro Sraffa, and by the unobtrusive Anthony Blunt. It is certain in any case that Harry St John Philby had no knowledge of the outwardly casual moves which led to Kim's being eventually introduced in London to a charming Russian, speaking fluent English, whose earnestness persuaded the young man that there were better ways in which a good Socialist like himself could effectively help the cause of progress and world peace than as a card-carrying Communist. The date of this meeting is unknown. Philby has carefully avoided offering any clues as to time and place, though he does admit that

> it was the Labour disaster of 1931 which first set me seriously to thinking about possible alternatives to the Labour Party. I began to take a more active part in the proceedings of the Cambridge University Socialist Society, and was its Treasurer in 1932/33. This brought me into contact

with streams of Left-Wing opinion critical of the Labour Party, notably with the Communists. Extensive reading and growing appreciation of the classics of European Socialism alternated with vigorous and sometimes heated discussions within the Society. It was a slow and brain-racking process; my transition from a Socialist viewpoint to a Communist one took two years. It was not until my last term at Cambridge, in the summer of 1933, that I threw off my last doubts. I left the University with a degree and with the conviction that my life must be devoted to Communism.[8]

Stated so laconically, Philby's conversion sounded like a natural progression upwards from religious doubt to religious certainty. What he studiously refrained from mentioning, for obvious reasons, were the circumstances and the people behind it. His name had already been brought to the favourable notice of Samuel Borisovich Cahan, the Resident Director of the Soviet Secret Intelligence Service in Britain.[9] Cahan, acting on instructions from his Comintern superiors, was on the lookout for talented young middle-class dissidents who, in time, would move into the upper echelons of Britain's power structure and control it from inside. This ambitious Trojan Horse strategy called for the recruitment and indoctrination of compliant intellectuals whom, until lately, the British Communist Party had been rather too inclined to cold-shoulder and neglect. It was not as though Harry Pollit, Rajani Palme Dutt and their colleagues had anything much to crow over as militant propagandists and missionaries to the British working masses. The results in that field since 1920 had been sadly disappointing. Gradual yet more devastating results could be expected in time by offering young intellectuals the chance to work in secret for the revolutionary cause, under Comintern rather than British Communist Party control. After his defection to the West in 1937, General Walter Krivitsky, the self-styled head of Soviet military intelligence in Europe, described how the pattern of Comintern policy in western Europe changed with circumstances:

For many years, while revolutionary prospects there seemed promising, the Comintern poured the greater part of its money into Germany and Central Europe. But when it became more decisively an appendage of the Soviet Government, and revolutionary objectives were side-tracked in favour of Stalinizing public opinion and capturing key positions in the democratic governments, Moscow's budgets for France, Great Britain and the United States were enormously increased.[10]

The one success registered at the King Street headquarters during the early 1920s had been the founding of a small but vigorous movement in the Indian subcontinent, and this development may well have accidentally accounted for the interest shown in Harold Philby. The Soviet Union in its early years was obsessed with the fear that Britain, France and other Western powers were scheming to overthrow the 'Workers' State'. The Kremlin rulers therefore relied on any diversions which local Communist Parties could create for heading off the capitalist enemy. Against the failure of the British Communists to turn the 1926 General Strike to advantage could be set their achievement in acting as a skilled midwife at the birth of the Party in India. Apart from the Palme Dutts, Ralph Sprat, a young intellectual from Cambridge, and Ralph Fox, a former Quaker relief worker in Russia who there 'saw the light', had been the main instruments of success, to the lasting annoyance and frustration of the British Raj and the India Office in London. Though Harry St John Philby had long ceased to be a thorn in the side of the Indian Civil Service, his notoriety as a forthright critic of British policy lingered on. What could be more natural than that the 'gurus' at Cambridge and their linkmen between King Street and the 'safe house' in London of the Russian Resident General should have seen in the son of such a father an ideal candidate for covert activities inside the unsuspecting British Establishment? The fact that he was a Socialist would be the best possible camouflage. No Fourth Man as such can be said to have 'engaged' Philby before he went down from Cambridge. The process of selecting and recruiting potential candidates owed little to the direct intervention of any of the Communist dons, though one of them (code-named 'Maurice') had earlier been 'nudged forward' and earmarked in much the same fashion, thus easing the subsequent recruitment of Burgess and Maclean in turn.

A profound secrecy enveloped the mysterious activities of

Cahan and his two trusted lieutenants, Leonid Tolokonsky and Georgi Askalov. Secrecy had become vital because of recent difficulties. L. B. Kamenev, L. B. Krassin and their aides during the early and precarious years of the Russian Trade Mission had displayed a zeal bordering on foolhardiness in obtaining classified information. The British security authorities had watched them, awaiting the chance to pounce. In due course a police search of the Russian Trade Mission's City headquarters caused a public sensation while Philby was still a schoolboy. According to the distinguished historian A. J. P. Taylor, the British Government 'blamed Soviet propaganda for much of India's unrest. Already, in May 1927, 200 police had raided the office of ARCOS, the Soviet trading organization, in the hope of discovering some evidence against the Communists. No evidence was found.'[11] To cover up what Taylor has called 'their blunder', the British Goverment retaliated by breaking off diplomatic relations with the Soviet Union. However, Taylor's assertion that the security authorities had acted in this instance on 'a false tip, presumably planted by a double-agent' does not really stand up to close examination. The police, it is true, failed to find one top-secret document on air strategy which had gone missing from the Air Ministry files; but they uncovered in the three tons of paper removed from the ARCOS building more than enough evidence of Soviet penetration to justify the raid, if not the rupturing of relations between London and Moscow.

After the sudden death of Krassin, the first Soviet chargé d'affaires, in November 1926, the Comintern and the NKVD agents in Britain had grown somewhat over-confident. Then they overreached themselves. The necessary machinery for controlling their activities hardly existed. Nor did the appointment of Arkady Pavlovitch Rosenholtz in Krassin's place improve matters. For Rosenholtz was a Red Army veteran and a specialist in political propaganda; and three of his 'trade experts' – including the commercial counsellor Igor Khopliakin – were agents of the Soviet Secret Service. One of the other five, N. K. Jilinsky, served as the link between a number of Communist 'front' organizations in Britain and the British Empire, quite apart from cooperating with

Ernst Wollweber, a leading Comintern agent based in Hamburg, the control centre of the international seamen's union. The third key person at the Trade Mission, L. B. Khinchuk, had been refused diplomatic status by a suspicious Foreign Office already aware that the directorate at ARCOS was topheavy with so-called 'experts'. Rosenholtz had good reason to worry at the ill-concealed energies of these colleagues of his, masquerading as commercial envoys, since he had no authority to reprimand or restrain them. Shortly before the ARCOS raid he advised his Foreign Minister, Litvinov, that it would be

a very useful precaution to suspend for a time the forwarding by post of documents of friends and neighbours from London to Moscow and vice versa. Telegraph your decision immediately. In your reply it is desirable to mention that the instructions emanate from the institution concerned.

This was an oblique reference to the Soviet Secret Service, which operated quite independently of the Soviet Foreign Ministry, much to Rosenholtz's frustration.

During the raid itself, men from Scotland Yard's Special Branch broke into the strongroom. There they found two men and a woman busily burning papers. One of the men, Anton Miller, tried to resist arrest. After being overpowered and searched, the police found in his underclothes a list of named contacts and secret 'post boxes' used by the Soviet Secret Service in North and South America, Australia, New Zealand and South Africa. The Prime Minister, Mr Stanley Baldwin, made no attempt either to exaggerate or to underplay the role of the Russian trade officials. As he informed the House of Commons: 'Both military espionage and subersive activities throughout the British Empire and North and South America were directed and carried out from the ARCOS and Soviet Delegation offices.'[12] Several governments, alarmed by what had been going on right under Baldwin's nose in London, resorted to similarly stern action against local Soviet trade representatives. A rudimentary spy ring was broken up in Canada barely twenty years before the much more effective and sinister atomic espionage net came to light. French counter-intelligence uncovered a laboratory for producing forged banknotes in various currencies. The example shown by Britain, Canada and France was presently followed by Belgium, the Netherlands, Yugoslavia, Hungary, Bulgaria and Czechoslovakia, which expelled Soviet emissaries and recalled their own. It was a very sharp lesson from which the badly rebuffed Soviet Secret Service ultimately benefited by changing its procedures and tactics. Gone were the days when amateurs like Francis Meynell could smuggle in precious stones given to him personally by Litvinov. Professional secret agents were needed, and the duty of Resident Director Samuel Cahan was to find, recruit and train them. Harold 'Kim' Philby merely happened to be among the first to catch his eye, thanks to the powerful undertow of the Marxist wave at Cambridge and the discreet liaison between the collective Fourth Man, those talent-spotting Cambridge dons, and Resident Director Cahan, via King Street. Only one professional Communist appears to have been used regularly as the go-between: a young man called Douglas Frank Springhall.

Surveying these events shortly before his death in 1977, James Klugman privately admitted to me that 'the Comintern's hard line on Bolshevization in the late twenties put off quite a few intellectuals, and there were numerous defections from the Party'.[13] On the lips of an intellectual who had served on the key political committee of the British Communist Party and spent most of his life directing its educational programme, such candour had a refreshing tang. During the Second World War Klugman served as a major on the staff of Brigadier Sir Fitzroy Maclean's military mission to the Yugoslav partisans, and before long his emotional as well as intellectual commitment to Tito gave rise to the kind of personal dilemma which every genuine Marxist intellectual must eventually experience. When Tito broke with Stalin and Yugoslavia was expelled from the Cominform (the Comintern under a new name), Klugman had to face a supreme test of faith and personal integrity. He chose to follow the latest shift in the Party line and to denounce Tito in a book entitled *From Trotsky to Tito*. Promotion to the hierarchy followed; then the Party line shifted again with Tito's return to the international Marxist brotherhood. Klugman's book was withdrawn from circulation on Party orders. As an isolated member of an enclosed bureaucratic élite, responding like an obedient puppet to any hierarchical pulling of the strings, Klugman had no choice in the matter; but he was human enough not to admire himself for this public abdication of private conviction. When we met, he was starting work on the latest volume of his history of British Communism, covering the crucial period from the late twenties to the middle thirties: 'I'm not looking forward to the task,' he said.

The policy of conformity and centralization had been laid down by Stalin to stamp his authority, first on his own inner caucus, then, through the Comintern, on Communist parties throughout the world. This tight, unrelenting control stifled initiative but ensured discipline. It also reduced the prospect of any further embarrassing incidents like the police swoop on the ARCOS headquarters in the City of London. If one side-effect was the disillusionment of open Communist intellectuals, their resignations caused no regrets to the hierarchy at King Street where intellectuals had always been distrusted. As for the departing rebels

> they were shocked to learn how much control over the policy of the Communist Party of Great Britain was being exerted by the Comintern. Had the Russians recognized the right of national Communism to assert itself, rather than forcing its own autocratic version upon people economically and politically more advanced than themselves, the course of history might have been radically different.[14]

That concluding comment by Neal Wood seems to stretch the possibilities too far. The biggest single weakness of the Party in Britain was its uncertain hold on the working class. The instinctive conservative outlook of many industrial and manual workers led them to steer clear of any 'foreign' movement advocating extremist remedies. What with alienating the intellectuals, failing to win mass support from the workers, and falling foul of the authorities, the record of the British Communist Party was neither good nor promising before the collapse of the Labour Government in August 1931. Then MacDonald's 'betrayal of his class' turned the tide. The intense but disciplined faith of individual Party members was at last justified; and the readiness of the public to swallow brilliantly tendentious Comintern propaganda, contrasting the unhampered social and economic progress of the Soviet motherland, under Stalin's benevolent direction, with the capitalist slump elsewhere, brought in a fresh stream of young idealists and romantics from the universities. These quickly outnumbered the disillusioned who had left the Party in the twenties.

The Comintern's skill in winning over young intellectuals did not guarantee that King Street would succeed in holding them indefinitely as Party members, especially when conflicts arose between individual consciences and awkward shifts in official policy. That remained a perennial problem for the bureaucratic comrades. Besides, the brief of Resident Director Samuel Cahan, the Soviet spy master in London, was clear-cut: to lure into his net as many volunteers as possible for clandestine work within the British Establishment, after a suitable period of probation. One secret agent thus entrenched would be worth one hundred open Communists. In the training, instructing and control of these candidates, the British Communist Party staff had no part. Their preliminary advice might be sought in rare cases. They also deputed a dependable official, usually Douglas Springhall, to serve as 'cut-out man', or intermediary, between the candidates and their 'talent-spotting' sponsors at Cambridge and elsewhere. So the sizing-up process, begun perhaps over a sherry in the rooms of a Communist undergraduate or a don during term, and continued intermittently until a consensus had been reached on the suitability of the candidate, would end with his being introduced by Springhall to Samuel Cahan or one of his aides.

It is certain that none of these meetings took place at the Soviet Embassy or any other building which might have been under police surveillance. The Russian spy master had a 'safe house' for a time at 3 Rosary Gardens in South Kensington; and it may well have been there that Philby went on an unknown date in the early months of 1933 to keep the appointment which changed the course of his life.[15]

One ex-Chief of the British Intelligence Service, who spent much time and thought in later years on the trial-and-error procedures adopted by the Russians in selecting probationary agents, insisted that no single university fellow was ever entrusted with 'the authority to recruit'. The Russians, in his view, were 'far too tough and cynical for that'. The suggestion that there must have been a 'Fourth Man' recruiting candidates at Cambridge in the early thirties he dismissed out of hand as 'ludicrous and quite impracticable'. Even if dons were occasionally recruited themselves in the sense of agreeing to help the cause by passing on useful information or assisting fellow agents in a small group, they would have been judged as 'too incompetent, unreliable and lacking in experience to discharge such a dangerous responsibility'.[16] It was firm Comintern policy to keep the selecting and running of candidates exclusively in Russian hands.

One Trinity College graduate of an earlier vintage whom the the Soviet vainly tried to recruit was the writer and publisher John Lehmann. A keen sympathizer with Communism, Lehmann lived abroad for several years after leaving Cambridge, acting as the 'secret correspondent' in Vienna for a Comintern 'front' organization called the Anti-War International, whose headquarters were in Paris. Its directors included Henri Barbusse and Romain Rolland, and the British office was run by John Strachey, the ex-Labour politician and author, who had since veered away from Sir Oswald Mosley to join the Communist Party. Lehmann witnessed the violent disturbances in Vienna in early 1934 which led to the crushing of the Social Democrats. There were several compatriots of his in the city at that time, Naomi Mitchison, Stephen Spender, Hugh Gaitskell and Harold Philby (to whom we shall be returning) among a score of others. When Lehmann was casually introduced to a swarthy young man who said that he wished to meet him privately, the Englishman obliged out of courtesy. Gradually the stranger's persistence in seeking him out twice more, finally disclosing who he was and what he wanted, and, 'refusing to take "no" for an answer', wore down Lehmann's calm:

My 'recruiting sergeant' was very pressing, appealing to my idealism, my sympathy for the workers' cause etc. but extremely vague about what he exactly wanted me to do. I smelt a rat in the end, that is I decided that he would finally reveal that he wanted me to become a Soviet agent. For that reason, while I was next in London, I went to seek counsel of John Strachey. Our discussions persuaded me that I was treading on too dangerous ground. The mysterious gentleman vanished from my life – perhaps because he had wind of John's enquiries among his own contacts. Of course I see now that I was peculiarly vulnerable, and perhaps lucky to swim past the lobster pot as easily as I did.[17]

Philby, whom Lehmann vaguely knew, doubtless became one of 'the mysterious gentleman's' contacts in Vienna; for Philby went to Austria under supervision, already a novice agent on probation. The previous June he had taken his finals in economics, emerging with a respectable second-class degree and a Trinity College prize of £14, which he spent on purchasing the collected works of Karl Marx. His father had come home again on annual leave; and when the proofs of *The Empty Quarter*, Harry St John Philby's new book on the Arabian desert which would make his name as an explorer, arrived from the publisher, his son willingly agreed to correct them and to prepare an index. As a reward for his accuracy and thoroughness, Kim's father gave him the princely sum of £50. Joe Grigg recalled:

He went out and bought a motor-bike. He seemed to be in no hurry to start looking around for a job, and the next thing I knew he announced that he was riding off to Austria for a few months. I already had a newspaper opening, but I envied him his carefree approach. When he reappeared several months later, he brought home a young Viennese wife, to the amazement of his mother and everyone else.[18]

Neither Grigg nor Philby's parents had any inkling that Kim had already embarked on the double life he had been persuaded and flattered into leading at the conspiratorial behest of a Russian. Before leaving London for the European mainland in the late summer of 1933, the young man had kept several secret assignations, probably with Leonid Tolokonsky, the knowledgeable and agreeable mentor, somewhat older than himself, whom Samuel

Cahan detailed to look after him. The first, difficult phase of dividing his mind into two halves, of learning to sort out and store things away in each sealed compartment, roused no suspicions at home or in the company of friends, though it meant weighing every word he uttered. Only once or twice had he slipped, fortunately without stumbling or having to brazen his way out. Dining one June evening at Trinity, at the table of Sir Dennis Robertson, his host had asked his two guests, Philby and Jim Lees, what they proposed to do with themselves after leaving Cambridge. Lees replied that he had hopes of landing a lectureship. Kim hesitated, then said blithely: 'I'm thinking of entering the Foreign Office.' Robertson was dumbfounded. 'The Foreign Office?' he echoed. 'I wouldn't advise it. Not with your left-wing politics. And I sincerely trust that you haven't offered me as a reference because I'd have to admit it.'[19] On such formalities, Robertson, Butterfield and the majority of Cambridge Fellows could not be easily budged; and for a moment Philby had felt awkward. The suggestion had not been his own but had come from his Russian mentor, and at first he had expressed a spirited defiance of which his father would have approved. Robertson's reluctance to help clinched the matter in Kim's favour, at least for the present. Cahan and Tolokonsky accepted the inevitable. They advised him to wait.

Then there had been long and heated arguments between articulate Communists and Socialists after Hitler gained power in Germany the previous January. Philby had spent the Easter vacation in Berlin with Tim Milne, that younger friend, now at Oxford, who had tended to look up to him since their time together at Westminster School. The two of them had travelled abroad before, visiting Hungary and other parts of Central Europe. Nobody could understand why the mighty German Communist Party had refused to combine with the Socialists in face of their common foe, still less why the German Communists had been so easily routed by the new and sinister Nazi leader of the Third Reich. Richard ('Otto') Clarke, who still regarded Philby as a calm, dependable Social Democrat, was as dumbfounded as the Labour Club's new secretary, Anthony Blake, by Kim's clear-cut, crisp refusal to blame Stalin for letting down his comrades in Germany. Stalin, a man interested wholly in power? Stalin, an anti-Communist who had betrayed the Left? 'Stuff and nonsense,' Kim stammered, 'what Stalin does IS Left.'[20]

It was a case of 'like father, like son' – but only on the surface. Harry St John Philby, himself the son of an Anglo-Indian tea-planter, was a man who put down shallow roots wherever the spirit moved him. His son had borne the nickname 'Kim' since his nursery days in Ambala, somehow absorbing the traits of Kipling's boy-hero but envying as he grew older the self-reliance and boldness of his own father. Who else would have openly flouted and rebelled against the Raj and the august Indian Civil Service? Who else would have dared to command, first the respect, then the protection of Ibn Saud, the desert monarch to whose primacy among the Arabian dynasts he had hitched his own star, ignoring the contradictory policy-makers of Whitehall and laying on the portable altar of Islam his ambitions and what little religious faith was in him? How Kim longed to emulate this godlike eccentric whose arrogant independence of mind he still envied. He was not cut out by nature to dictate his own destiny, and to do so unaided. He needed a universal faith to command his loyalty and, with it, an organization to sustain him materially. In Marxism he had discovered a truly modern materialistic creed, in the great Soviet experiment a painful panacea to cure systematically all the ills bedevilling the human race. The delusion was fantastic, yet it appealed to his practical, earth-bound mind. Unlike Guy Burgess, Philby had neither the fluency nor the gregariousness for active proselytizing. Unlike Maclean, he was not fitted for the solemn role of an aspirant diplomat, since this would inevitably mean having to live in the long crooked shadow cast by a notorious father. Something better and more desirable would turn up, if he benefited from his mentor's careful prompting. Of that Harold Kim Philby was fairly certain. Meanwhile, his outwardly easy-going and conventional appearance provided a natural cover that was almost perfect. In the words of Charles Madge: 'He seemed a pleasant fellow, very public school and not a fanatic. I still find his later career difficult to fit to his personality as I remember it.'[21]

Donald Maclean noticeably blossomed out during his final year, though in the phrase of his dispassionate younger friend Christopher Gillie, 'I felt there was something slightly dissolute about him, and I choose the word with care.' If Gillie suspected the worst, he was right. For Burgess had already introduced Maclean, the emancipated Calvinist-turned-Communist, to the sad pleasures of sodomy, the irrepressible Guy wryly boasting about it as if he had thereby earned the Victoria Cross for valour beyond the call of duty. Long afterwards he would deny the seduction, adding facetiously that the very thought of touching Maclean's 'large, flabby, white, whale-like body' nauseated him. Sexual demands apart, the two men were often seen consulting earnestly together in 1933 and 1934. In those days Gillie had moved to lodgings at 41 New Square and when Donald Maclean offered to take an adjoining room in the same house, Gillie felt genuinely honoured.

> Possibly because of family ties, Donald never ceased to show me an uncondescending kindness. After all, I was shy and comparatively innocent, he a walking epitome of the clever, successful undergraduate who knew exactly where he was going. I'm afraid it went to my head a bit because I looked up to him as a shining model. The walls of his 'digs' were adorned with large reproductions of nude bodies, and the landlady's mother didn't really care for them. She felt squeamish about the naked human form and would complain with meaningful gestures when Donald wasn't there – 'If only this bit were covered up decently, or that bit, I wouldn't mind so much!' He was often out. You see, he didn't have to overwork in preparing for examinations. One whole month set aside at the end saw him through his finals with first-class honours. The rest of his time seemed to be devoted exclusively to Communist Party activities. There were large red banners with slogans in one corner of his room and a lot of Marxist books and tracts.[22]

Burgess, not to be outdone by the impassioned Marxist fervour of a freshman called John Cornford, the son of the poet Frances, and a lineal descendant of Darwin, threw himself into organizing occasional demonstrations, such as the anti-war march to the War Memorial on Armistice Day 1933. The marchers endured taunts, jeers and a shower of rotten eggs and bruised tomatoes hurled by rowing men and 'hearties' from Jesus College and elsewhere, while policemen looked on stolidly. No truncheons were drawn, no bones broken. And Burgess, seated beside Julian Bell, his fellow Apostle, in the latter's veteran sports car, scattered the phalanx of counter-demonstrators like the navigator of a tank by guiding the vehicle's nose straight at them.[23] Christopher Gillie, though far from being a Communist, believed that 'the permissive but haughtily remote attitude of the University authorities led many undergraduates to pose as extremists out of cussedness'. Yet Burgess was ventilating more than frustration in the Great Hall of Trinity when he interrupted a soothing speech on the economy by the Chancellor of the Exchequer, Mr Neville Chamberlain, with shouts of 'Rubbish' and 'Tell that to the Marines.' Knowing that deeds spoke louder than words, the trouble-making Burgess obliged his College to reconsider its treatment of domestic staff by instigating a highly inconvenient strike of waiters for improved wages and conditions of service.

Maclean did not mind walking in processions but drew the line at competing with his friend in such time-wasting activities as fomenting strikes. He preferred to pour out his Marxist zeal on paper, an exercise which left the talkative, untidy-minded Burgess quite cold; and the unacknowledged influence on Maclean's thought of Strachey's writings peeped out between the lines of his occasional articles. The first of John Strachey's famous trilogy of clear, sophisticated and closely reasoned Marxist books, *The Coming Struggle for Power*, had been published in November 1931; the second, entitled *The Menace of Fascism*, appeared almost exactly a year later. With the unbridled faith of a convert, the author proclaimed that 'there is no force on earth which can long prevent the workers of the world from building a new and stable civilization for themselves on the basis of the common ownership of the means of production'. The stink of British capitalism in decay assailed everyone's nostrils; it was thus a matter of regret to Strachey that 'an appallingly large number of even the best intelligences' were still hanging back from 'the essential work of clearing the ground for the new order'. Fascism had recently put down fragile roots in Cambridge. Its supporters were few, far fewer than members of such fringe groups as the Christian Socialists and the Buchmanites; and Donald Maclean, taking a leaf from Strachey's book, regarded fascism as the logical last-ditch attempt of a doomed capitalist system to delay the inevitable revolution. The repressed instincts of Calvin seemed to dovetail perfectly in Maclean with the messianic certainties of Marx; and fellow undergraduates at Trinity Hall and beyond were struck by the seemingly unforced ease of his striving to be all things to all men.

In the end-pages of a current Weekend Book, Christopher Gillie filled in the blank squares of

a game in which other people's qualities are measured. My list of people were all relatives, except for a girl friend and Donald. For sense of humour I gave him eighteen out of twenty, so my impression was he had a good one. I gave him full marks under the headings Beauty, Charm, and Tact. The lowest mark is for willpower, twelve. He rated fourteen for Moral Sense and Common Sense, and fourteen for Discretion and Humility. These certainly look like over-ratings now, but then I admired him very much. . . .

Gillie also unearthed two direct references to Maclean in a diary of the period:

One reads – 'Donald, with his over-sweetened gracefulness, trying on the coloured handkerchief and looking like a beautiful peasant woman.' The other – 'When I had tea with Donald that day, he had only just got out of bed. He said, "Sleep is a grand thing. If I had my way, we should sleep all day."'[24]

For what it is worth, Maclean received the doubtful accolade of a searching, personal profile in the undergraduate journal *Granta* early in November 1933. The unnamed interviewer laid bare the self-mocking, mannered schizophrenia of his subject by letting him speak for himself:

'It is my job,' said the interviewer, 'to examine the undergrad's personality. Would it embarrass you if I took a glance at yours?'

'Not a bit,' replied Maclean. 'But which one? I have three dear little fellows. Here comes Cecil. Perhaps you would like to begin with him.'

Cecil: 'Oh my dear, you did startle me. I was just slipping into my velvet trousers when I heard you call. What *is* the fuss? Has anyone shaved off our hair, or destroyed the Picasso?'

DM: 'No, nothing like that, Cecil. I want to introduce you to the *Granta* representative.'

Cecil: 'Oh, how sweet! You must come to my next party. I am going to have *real* passion flowers, and everybody is going to dress up as a poem . . . *Do* come.'

Q: 'Delighted. But what are your favourite pursuits?'

Cecil: 'Oh, I usually spend the morning being a figure on a Greek vase – so Attic and delightful. Of course, I'm very keen on being critically aware: after all, as Mr Leavis says, it is the *only* thing.'

DM: 'Now, run along, Cecil, and get on with your tapestry work.'

Cecil [sulkily]: 'Very well, goodbye. I hear that dreadful creature Jack coming – I must fly.'

DM: 'Jack. This is the *Granta* representative.'

Jack: 'Hullo, chaps. I was just having a steak at The George. Awfully good fellows there – and damn' fine waitresses, too. [He winks] . . .'

Q: 'May I ask you how you spend your day?'

Jack: 'Oh, I just crack around, you know. Buy a few club-ties here, and smash up a flick there. Bloody marvellous.'

Q: 'Have you no ambitions, Jack?'

Jack: 'Rather. My heart's set on getting into the Hawks. They are such wizard blokes. Besides, the blazer is topping – it looks grand with a Crusader's tie and Sixty-Club trousers.'

DM: 'That's enough, Jack – you'd better go and oil your rugger boots.'

Jack: 'OK. Cheerio.'

DM: 'I hope I'm not boring you, but you haven't met Fred yet. He's very busy just now, trying to find out whether Middleton Murry is material or merely dialectic. Shall I get him?'

Q: 'Yes do, Mr Maclean. I'm anxious to see all your personalities.'

Fred: 'What do you want? I'm working. Who is this?'

DM: 'Be civil, Fred. This is the *Granta* representative. He wants to find out what you do and what you think.'

Fred [a large smirk of pleasure spreading across his face]: 'Oh, I see. Good morning. Have a cigarette.'

Q [suspecting a bribe]: 'No thanks.'

Fred: 'Well the point is this. Everybody ought to work. That's what I'm here for. I want to get on. Take Shakespeare or Henry Ford – they knew what was what. I belong to eleven societies and three lunch clubs. I once read a paper on Lessing's *Laokoon* (in German, of course). I hope to get a First. It's all due to *hard work*. Any questions? None – well that's all right. I am afraid I must go and see a man about a thesis. Goodbye.'

DM: 'Well that's that.'

Q: 'It was very interesting Mr Maclean – but, tell me, which is your favourite personality of the three?'

DM: 'I like them all equally. I see no standard against which to set them, no hierarchy in which to put them – they are all of the same value to me.'

Q: 'One more question. Why do you have these personalities at all?'
DM: 'Because society demands it. Cambridge expects one to be either Cecil, or Jack, or Fred. If one isn't, Cambridge is annoyed. It is a pleasant game – and I enjoy playing it.'[25]

Maclean had come far since his father's death. His widowed mother, encouraged by the protective concern and kindliness of her political friends, saw only the studious and superficially charming side of Donald's split personality. Having once succeeded in persuading him not to cause a scandal by going to Russia as a teacher or a tractor driver, she imagined that his left-wing vapourings must have been merely an immature phase which now lay safely behind him. Lady Maclean did her son an injustice, but then the ambitions she nursed on his behalf blinded her to the true reasons for the brooding moods of introspection which she sometimes noticed descending on him. At this time he had two or three girl friends who understood better than his incurious mother the political fanaticism of Donald; but the loyalty and affection they felt for him prevented any awkward scenes, especially as Donald could stand any amount of teasing about his convictions. What his pride could not abide was the indignity of having to explain and defend the obvious whenever a group of Lady Maclean's political friends were gathered together, the sole means of escape then being to adopt the pose of a silent, withdrawn listener whose blood boiled angrily within him.

He spent the Christmas of 1933 with a small house party of guests at Hawarden, the home of the Gladstone family. With his usual adroitness, he managed to avoid getting embroiled in political backchat, making excuses to retire to his room early and feast his mind on higher things. Among the volumes he had brought with him for bedside reading was a newly translated *Brief History of Russia* by M. N. Pokrovsky, with a congratulatory letter from Lenin to the author by way of preface. While the seasonal drinks circulated and the social chattering dragged on downstairs, Donald Maclean concentrated on the sacred text before him. Page 145 of Pokrovsky's work obviously held his attention, for he underlined the following passage.

Like the bourgeoisie, the intelligentsia lived on the surplus product that was extracted by force from the peasant and the workman. A communist revolution would mean that it would have to give up its advantages, renounce all its privileges and join the ranks of manual labour. And this prospect could be accepted only by a small number of the most sincere and devoted revolutionaries of the intelligentsia.

In the margin of page 145, like a reminder, half sardonic and half incredulous, that he had imbibed this Marxist–Leninist axiom on Christmas night in the home of the great father-figure of English liberalism, Maclean wrote: 'Hawarden, December 25th 1933', and added his initials.[26]

As in Philby's case the previous year, no record has come to light as to the precise timing of Maclean's first encounter with Samuel Cahan and his two aides, again with David Springhall as intermediary and contact man. This looked like an easier and more gratifying catch at first glance, given Maclean's sound theoretical grasp of Marxism and his matching willingness to serve the cause in any capacity, however humble. Yet, a major difficulty presented itself at once, for regardless of his keen intelligence, his pedigree, his social connections and his potentialities as a really malleable trainee-agent, Maclean laboured under the handicap of being a known Cambridge Communist and therefore a marked man. The unexpected irony of his position must have caused him anxiety and irritation; it also had the effect of making him all the more determined not to let this opportunity slip. Like a good soldier ready to fight and sacrifice himself for his ideals, Maclean could not have failed to impress these tough, cynical Russian mentors. His disposition was splendid. They urged on him the necessity of moderating the extremist views he expressed and of dropping out of the political limelight at the University. As for the idea of going to Russia for a while as a volunteer worker, that he must dismiss firmly from his mind.

Maclean's mother had been right, though for quite the wrong reasons. Cahan and his colleagues were unanimous that the young man would prove of greatest value to the cause in the British diplomatic corps. If he justified himself by studying hard, getting the best possible results in his final examinations, then applying for entrance to the Foreign Office in the normal way, the risks of his being turned down because of past sympathies with Communism would probably be lessened. Meanwhile, one meeting each month with Leonid Tolokonsky would suffice for liaison and basic training purposes.

During the long summer days and evenings of his last term at Cambridge, close friends noticed the mellowing of the young man's formerly unpredictable moods. He seemed to become more sociable, more interested in the mundane problems of others, less preoccupied with left-wing politics. Lady Maclean would appear more frequently for lunch or tea; one or other of his girl friends could be seen on the arm of the tall, handsome Donald as they walked together across the college lawns or went punting on the still waters of the Cam. One afternoon, while standing at the stern like a stooping sentinel, guiding his craft beneath one of the bridges, an attractive girl called Elizabeth Rea passed in a punt going the other way. Maclean shouted a friendly greeting, but his mother in her large hat sat up stiffly, staring straight ahead in disapproval. She had once hoped that Donald, who appeared to be fond of Elizabeth, would become engaged to this daughter of a prominent Liberal politician, the future Lord Rea of Eskdale; but her contrary son showed disappointingly little interest in settling down with anyone. And there, steering that punt upstream, stood another young man to whom Elizabeth Rea had since pledged herself, a slightly embarrassed-looking former graduate of King's, now working as an apprentice printer at Cambridge University Press, the future industrialist Sir Michael Clapham.[27] Maclean's friend Christopher Gillie recalled:

> Donald played a lot of cricket and tennis that summer. He got down to revision exactly a month before his finals, pacing himself to a nicety and romping home with the expected First. It's funny, but I have no recollections of his having any girl friends at all, certainly none that might be termed steady. Women were in short supply at Cambridge then. We made dreadful jokes about 'shaggy hag, the Newnhamite' etc. He did show me a postcard once inviting two Newnham or Girton undergraduates to a Party meeting. The card mentioned the date and the place, followed by the quotation: 'It is the cause! Let me not name it to you, you chaste stars, it is the cause!'[28]

The cause was scarcely ever mentioned now by Donald Maclean. Like Philby, yet without the latter's self-effacing competence, he strove to live his Communism inwardly while behaving with the easy grace of an apolitical man of the world. Trainee-agents on probation must be among the last people on earth to keep diaries, though doubtless they never miss assignations with their mentors and future controllers. When, where and how Maclean met his between June 1934 and January 1935 hardly matters now. What mattered most then, to mentor and trainee alike, was that the first hurdles had been cleared without trouble. Another, in the shape of the Foreign Office examination, lay immediately ahead. Once more, in consistently sharp form, Maclean surpassed himself. His name came high on the list, among the first half dozen successful candidates. Not until the very end of the oral examination did anything untoward happen; and afterwards he convinced his Soviet mentor, his mother, family and friends (in that order) that his open Communist sympathies at Cambridge need worry them no longer. Yet, as he freely told Lady Maclean, Cressida Bonham Carter, Elizabeth Rea and Felicity Bailey (the future Lady Rumbold), without even turning a hair:

> All went well, and I got on famously with the examiners at the *viva*. I thought they'd finished when one of them suddenly said: 'By the way, Mr Maclean. We understand that you, like other young men, held strong Communist views while you were at Cambridge. Do you still hold those views?' I'm afraid I did an instant double-take: Shall I deny the truth, or shall I brazen it out? I decided to brazen it out. 'Yes,' I said, 'I did have such views – and I haven't entirely shaken them off.' I think they must have liked my honesty because they nodded, looked at each other and smiled. Then the chairman said: 'Thank you, that will be all, Mr Maclean.'[29]

The hopes of Guy Burgess were meanwhile dashed by his failure to live up to his own, and to Anthony Blunt's, bright expectations. Having obtained a First in Part One, he squandered so large a measure of his energies on beguiling diversions, personal as well as political, that he took his Finals almost wholly unprepared. According to the shrewd Miriam Rothschild, he 'brought this on himself and deserved the setback. He was confidently expected to get a First and as far as I recall collapsed in tears during finals.'[30] He had to console himself with an Aegrotat. A hurried change of plans followed. Again nothing is known about the timing of Burgess's original meeting with Samuel Cahan, the Soviet Resident Director. Given his unquestionably energetic if injudicious part in the formative period of the Communist movement at Cambridge, Burgess may have been the first of the three to be looked over and earmarked for future clandestine work. It would equally have suited the Resident Director as well as Guy Burgess himself if Cambridge could have remained the professional centre of his activities. As he was shortly to demonstrate, a spectacular renunciation of his Communist past could be easily contrived; then, as a Fellow, he would have carried on clandestinely, in the role of a consultant 'recruiting sergeant', for Cahan's expanding underground network. The prospect, however, suddenly shrivelled into dust.

That summer, more in the spirit of a pilgrim than a tourist, Burgess paid a visit to Soviet Russia in the company of an Oxford friend, Derek Blaikie, who has since died. Blaikie, also a Communist and a homosexual, returned home with hilarious accounts of the trip, one memorable episode of which was his discovering Burgess, besotted with drink, sprawling on a bench in the Park of Rest and Culture. The miscreant had his sober interludes, too; and forearmed with the necessary letters of introduction, Burgess secured audiences with the Chief of the Comintern, Nikolai Bukharin, as well as with Ossip Piatnitsky, the man in charge of what Walter Krivitsky later described as 'the heart of the Comintern', its International Liaison Section, known in Russia as 'OHS'. It was Ossip Piatnitsky who had built up a worldwide web of resident directors like Samuel Cahan; yet it would be fatuous to suppose that Burgess in his wildest imaginings should have gone over Cahan's head and pleaded his own case with these two wily old Bolsheviks. Whether his success in seeing them impressed the Resident Director in London is still an open question. Like Philby and Maclean, Guy Burgess had to prove himself; and before he could begin to do so, the problem of finding suitable employment had to be tackled.

It was a strangely different Burgess who returned to Cambridge as a postgraduate in October 1934. His excesses as a seducer and a drinker did not diminish, but his formerly uncritical admiration of Soviet policies underwent an unaccountable change. He quarrelled with individual Apostles whose Communist beliefs he had helped to harden, declaring that Marxism had taken quite the wrong turning in the Soviet Union. Standing Marxist logic on its head, he asserted that the Fascist formulas of Hitler and Mussolini were dialectically sounder and less reactionary than the perverted State capitalism of Stalin. He waxed eloquent on the theme of Russian designs on British India, designs which, he said, seriously distorted the facts of 'historical necessity' and did more damage than Fascist expediency. With the unabashed solemnity of the born exhibitionist, Burgess finally announced that he had no choice but to break with the Party. He avoided his old friends, making great play of his Pitt Club and right-wing connections so that no noticeable break occurred in the pleasure-seeking side of his noisy existence. Perplexed and distressed as Anthony Blunt unquestionably was at Burgess's inexplicable *volte-face*, this young Trinity don patiently stood by a friend whom he did not wish to lose.

Temporary work as a lecturer and coach was found for him, not without the help of G. M. Trevelyan. The Regius Professor of Modern History at Cambridge thought well of Burgess's intellectual quality and chose to ignore, perhaps not even to notice, his rumoured defects of character. Indeed, Trevelyan genially advised him to sit for a prize fellowship at Pembroke as a suitable means of gaining a semi-permanent niche; and Burgess promised to think the matter over. Like James Klugman, he could have asked for nothing better of fate than the opportunity to shine as an academic; unlike the honest, straightforward Klugman, whose uncompromising allegiance to Communism had disqualified him, the devious Burgess was merely playing for time. He would have gladly settled for an assistant master's job at Eton as 'second best', but Dennis Robertson, whom he quoted as a referee, fouled his chances by politely declining to be drawn.[31] Burgess already had his instructions from Cahan, the Resident Director. When his former Communist associates had grown used to the fact that Burgess must be written off as a fickle renegade beyond all hope of redemption, it would be the moment to move out and start looking for work in earnest.

The element of deception involved in this elaborate ruse placed him under a strain, of course, but Burgess shrugged it off nonchalantly enough. Blunt was beside himself at the prospect of such an unnecessary separation. So Burgess promised to keep in touch. The journalistic job which he intended to take up sounded most improbable. The Anglo-German Fellowship, a loose association of Conservative and other well-wishers of Hitler, had been on the lookout for someone qualified to handle their publicity. The offer was too good to refuse, though Burgess remained mysteriously vague as to the nature of his duties. Goronwy Rees chanced to meet him shortly after he had embarked on his new line as a Fascist propagandist. It turned out that Guy had just moved into a flat at the top of a house in Chester Square, a short walk from where Rees lived in Ebury Street, Westminster. The Welshman had by now abandoned his cosy academic cocoon at Oxford in favour of journalism; and he had recently heard from mutual friends incredible reports of Burgess's renunciation of Marxism and of the acrimony and estrangements which had followed.

Guy was only too willing to give Rees a first-hand account; and presently the pair were locked in permutations and variations of the same arguments which had lately destroyed a number of beautiful friendships at Cambridge. Something very odd had evidently happened to Burgess since the previous summer when, as Goronwy Rees clearly recalled, Guy had invited him to accompany him to Moscow and Rees had been obliged for personal reasons to call off the trip at the last minute. Rees knew that this frivolous, debauched yet entertaining friend gave himself absurdly conspiratorial airs at times. Having once tried to prise out of him, quite unsuccessfully, why he had called on Nikolai Bukharin and what the Comintern Chief had said to him, Rees idly wondered whether that interview might not have put Burgess off his Communism, or indeed whether Guy might not have invented the whole story. The subsequent dramatic conversion to a typically extravagant version of Fascism-with-pink-edges defied rational explanation; and Goronwy Rees could only conclude that Guy must have some fell purpose of his own for performing ideological somersaults in public.

The two men met frequently during 1935 and the following year. Burgess was never short of cash; and despite his friend's delight in name-dropping, Rees grudgingly took his word for it that, among other part-time preoccupations, the ex-Communist Guy Burgess was being paid a handsome retainer by Lady Rothschild, the mother of Victor, as a specialist adviser on her investments.[32] Truth for Guy would always be a moving target, but the ability to dazzle friends and casual acquaintances with the lurid glare of his fantasies consistently prevented them from finding him out. It was perfectly true that Lady Rothschild did pay Burgess a generous monthly allowance, though her son Victor did not realize it. Miriam, her daughter, did, however; and her dismissal of Burgess's vaunted financial wizardry deserves to be recorded:

> He proved a good listener to my mother's discourses about the gold standard, on which she was quite an expert, and she might well have engaged in correspondence on such matters, but if she did so she never told me about it. I remember on one occasion at dinner Guy made some comment about *Mr Norris Changes Trains*, and my mother remarked afterwards that he was somewhat inconsequential, and I replied: 'Just a bit out of his depth, that's all.' I never got the impression he was remotely interested in the gold standard – or knew much about share movements, but I can say he appreciated good cooking. And had a weakness for claret! I can also say my mother rarely gave charitable gifts as lump sums, for the simple reason that they disappeared too rapidly and there were literally scores of people whom she assisted or supported by periodic and regular payments. These are the sorts of situation which, perhaps unfortunately, never interest the historian![33]

With a Rothschild stipend to supplement his modest salary, Burgess could indulge his expensive tastes within reason. His probationary period as a clandestine novice-agent, operating on behalf of the Soviet Union, a country he liked to compare fondly with Victorian England at the zenith of her ostentatious power and splendour, began enjoyably enough. His task was to pass over to Samuel Cahan regular summaries on the Anglo-German Fellowship's political activities and personalities, a task to which he brought his customary insight and flair for selective reporting.

If his Russian masters disapproved of someone so allergic to Marxist standards of self-discipline, they could at least console themselves with the knowledge that Guy Burgess, the apparent embodiment of bourgeois decadence, had no need whatever for camouflage or disguises. Just by being his natural self he would penetrate the tight, complacent social and intellectual coteries to which a remarkable talent for ingratiating himself with the most unlikely and unlikeable people usually guaranteed him access. Would his injudicious tongue and riotous conduct ever give him away? On balance, his masters and mentors evidently considered this a risk worth taking. For if nothing would have been easier than denouncing or disowning him in the event of his self-betrayal, it was just as probable that nobody would ever know when or whether to believe Guy Burgess or not. What better underground agent could there be than a human chameleon like this? Mosley once described his former friend and collaborator John Strachey as belonging to Freud from the neck down, to Marx from the neck up – 'and nowhere to John Strachey'; and Amabel, the latter's sister, added her own touch with the remark: 'He won't have a heart for years yet, I expect . . . he has grown up very irregularly.'[34] In the case of Guy Burgess, no critic, however ill disposed, could have pinned him down with precision. His essence was as bright and elusive as mercury.

4. THE DEVIL'S DISCIPLES

'Here [at Cliveden] we all assume the responsibilities of the Prime Minister, and imagine ourselves in his place or in that of the Foreign Secretary,' wrote Tom Jones of the Cabinet Secretariat in a revealing letter. 'For the talk is never of home but always of foreign problems, apart from the perennial game of remaking the Cabinet.'[1]

Lord and Lady Astor, the owners of Cliveden, a well-appointed country house by the River Thames not far from Maidenhead, would afterwards deny strenuously and publicly the existence of any organized group that deserved the name of the 'Cliveden Circle or Set'. A diversity of guests accepted invitations for the weekend, they contended; and not all of them went for the joy of talking politics. Even so, the Astors' house parties and the problems aired at them became an increasing source of divisive gossip and petty scandal during the 1930s. Like a dozen other political salons of the period, theirs had its hobby horses and *bêtes-noires*. Winston Churchill and Robert Vansittart, an uncompromising Foreign Office critic of Hitler, were not welcomed at Cliveden. Vansittart has written:

All sorts of pies were fingered at Cliveden. [There was] a scheme for making [Ramsay] MacDonald Ambassador at Washington when young Conservatives grew restive under him, a scheme for bringing back Lloyd George as either Foreign Secretary or Minister of Agriculture.... No question arose of including Winston.... Tom Jones' 'Cliveden Circle' deserves a niche in any history of our times. I respected its composition but not its ideas. Among these was a move to 'disarm the Germans by generosity', which found many sympathizers. Another was that Russia had ceased propaganda abroad.... 'There's no danger from Germany unless Vansittart provokes it,' said one of them to one of my secretaries, 'and we're going to have him out'.[2]

Self-deception about Nazi intentions proved to be as strong in various sections of the ruling class as was faith in Soviet Russia's messianic goals among its secret agents on probation like Maclean and Philby. Lloyd George stood out as an independent force among the pro-Germans. So, for that matter, did the heir to the throne himself. As will be shown, the sympathies of the Prince of Wales misled the Germans into expecting a favourable shift in British foreign policy as soon as he succeeded the ageing King George V. Many people in Britain laboured under a vague sense of guilt towards the Germans because of the unjust Versailles Treaty; ignorance of the barbarously cruel and intolerant nature of the Nazi régime remained surprisingly widespread, all the more so since evidence for its excesses was already available. The Prince's latest biographer, Frances Donaldson, has commented:

> It is understandable that the Prince of Wales, in common with so many young men of his generation, should have been looking for a cause, a philosophy which held out some hope for the future. In hindsight it is extremely unsympathetic that he should have found what he sought in Nazi Germany. Yet in justice it must be remembered that many another idealist found it in Soviet Russia, and that identification with either involved blindness, or at the very least confused thinking, in the face of murder, oppression and callousness on an unprecedented scale.[3]

When Kim Philby reached Vienna on his motor-bike in the late summer of 1933, he knew that he was entering a cockpit where a decisive and bloody battle might erupt from one day to the next between the Social Democrats, who controlled the city, and the anti-Socialist Coalition, under Chancellor Englebert Dolfuss, who had been ruling impoverished Austria by decree since the month of March. Philby had to live frugally, for he wanted to spin out his limited funds and learn as much as he could about the struggle for power by staying as long as possible. He found cheap lodgings in the home of a Polish Jew called Israel Kohlmann, a public employee, who lived there with his wife Gisella, and their only daughter Alice, a vivacious divorcée in her early twenties. 'Litzi', the diminutive by which everyone called her, was not a Social Democrat but that rare thing in the Vienna of the day, a militant Communist. The young Englishman was infatuated with this astute and untiring Party worker, whose grasp of local political complexities was as impressive as her range of underground contacts. Philby himself encountered during the nine or ten months he spent in Vienna not a few Socialist visitors from Britain, irresistibly drawn by press reports of tension and sporadic violence to a city that had appeared to be a working model of progressive Socialism at its best. After the overthrow of the great Austro-Hungarian Empire in 1918, the moderate Social Democrat leaders of Vienna had gradually transformed working and living conditions by energetic reforms, rehousing nearly 200,000 of the poorest citizens in massive blocks of well-designed suburban flats. There were free health clinics and baths; fine kindergartens and schools; organized facilities for sporting and other leisure activities. Public utilities such as gas, water and electricity were supplied at cost to residents of the Karl Marx Hof and other workers' estates. Austrian anti-Socialists, especially in the Christian Social Party which the Viennese scornfully dubbed the 'Clerico-Fascists', opposed these achievements of moderate Marxism in action and prepared to destroy them.

The Central European correspondent of the *Daily Telegraph* in Vienna from 1929 until 1939 was Eric Gedye, a capable and experienced Englishman from Somerset, who had been wounded in the Battle of the Somme, then served on the British Military Governor's staff in Germany before taking up journalism. The vivid despatches he sent to his newspaper were largely responsible for the influx of visitors from Britain during Philby's stay in Vienna. Gedye was a man of forty-three summers, exactly twice as old as Philby. When the latter eventually called to see him, Gedye sized him up swiftly and unerringly: 'He's no ordinary parlour pink,' he said to his Austrian assistant. 'I'll keep my eye on him.'[4] Philby responded to Gedye's offer to accept any worthwhile information for payment at the usual freelance rate, and before long the *Daily Telegraph* correspondent, who worked also for British intelligence, satisfied himself that Philby was 'a convinced Communist'.

The young Englishman lost no time in learning about the disagreeable complexities of Austrian politics. The Viennese Social Democrats had their own defence force, the *Schutzbund*, as a counter to the *Heimwehr*, the private army of the 'Clerico-Fascist' Party. It did not shock or surprise Philby to discover that the hard-line Communists chose to stay hidden on the sidelines, hopefully awaiting the inevitable clash. The orthodox Party line remained unchanged. Though these tactics had recently helped Hitler to seize absolute power in Germany, the bitter extremist refrain still was: 'Do not lift a finger to assist the pseudo-Marxists.' Yet Communist survivors still trickled across the German frontier, refugees alike from the Nazi terror and their blind subservience to Party dogma. The illogicality of it all did not cause Philby any heart-searching. He had no time for that. Besides, it was no longer his business to reason why.

As for Otto Bauer, the Social Democrat leader, Viennese Communists doubted whether he had the will or the nerve to defend his marvels of social engineering, and Philby doubted with them. The politics of non-provocation would not disarm Prince Starhemberg, the swashbuckling, loose-living Austrian aristocrat who commanded the *Heimwehr*, nor the implacable Chancellor Dolfuss, whose single aim was to maintain internal order and thus deny Hitler or Mussolini any excuse for moving into Austria. In so delicately balanced an alignment of forces, the intransigence of the Communists might have struck any informed, detached onlooker as suicidal; but Philby no longer depended on reflection or common sense to sustain him. He believed in Stalin as some men believed in God. The Austrian Social Democrats were equally contemptuous of the left-wing extremists: 'As long as we have a Bauer at the top,' they boasted, 'we do not need any Communists.'

In the autumn of 1933 the violently repressive measures enforced by Dolfuss tested Bauer and found him wanting, as the Communists had gleefully predicted. His unwillingness to meet force with force was no doubt prompted partly by the memory of what had happened to the Socialists in Germany, partly by fear that a premature battle with Starhemberg's *Heimwehr* would open the door wide to Hitler and/or Mussolini.

Much of Philby's attention was meanwhile absorbed with the illegal task of relieving the plight of the many Communist refugees from Germany. By the turn of the new year, however, the long-awaited trial of strength began. There were local outbreaks of Nazi violence, instigated by Hitler's supporters, in the border regions of the country. The *Heimwehr* was at once mobilized. Still Otto Bauer refrained from moving. Then a young Social Democrat in Upper Austria, Richard Bernasek, took the initiative, warning Bauer that he intended to fight rather than be crushed. The police intercepted the warning; and on 12 February 1934 they raided Bernasek's headquarters at Lintz. Bauer at last had to act; but his action came too late.

A strike by public transport workers in Vienna, the agreed signal for mobilizing the *Schutzbund*, was anticipated ruthlessly by Chancellor Dolfuss, who declared martial law and outlawed the Social Democrat Party. Armed police occupied civic buildings, then ringed the factories and great housing estates. Fighting broke out between the badly disorganized and leaderless members of the *Schutzbund* and the government forces. When sections of armed workers retreated to the blocks of flats, artillery was brought up to blast them out. Philby was as horrified by the expected bloodshed and destruction as were his notional compatriots, Eric Gedye and the poet Stephen Spender, the youthful Socialist Hugh Gaitskell and his future wife Dora. Beneath Philby's sense of revulsion lay a contrary element of satisfaction: at any rate, the underground Communist cadre to which he was attached had been proved right. After the shelling of the flats, there was some skirmishing; reprisals and counter-reprisals went on for days, while police and security forces searched Socialists' homes for weapons. Estimates of the dead and injured varied wildly in the confusion; but at least three hundred men, women and children were killed, and nearly a thousand hurt.

The methodical breaking up of the Social Democrat organization followed. The presses were confiscated, its clinics and leisure centres closed. Philby would have been less than human had he failed to help men on the run purely because they did not share his orthodox Marxist faith. Hugh Gaitskell, then a student of economics in Vienna, had been joined by his Welsh legal friend Elwyn Jones, a future Labour Lord Chancellor, and by the journalist and writer Naomi Mitchison. There were also some British Quaker relief workers and an enterprising American lady of means, Mrs Muriel Gardner. All of them worked hard distributing food and clothes to needy victims. Eric Gedye kept readers of the *Daily Telegraph* informed of these grim if predictable events, no doubt also passing on more detailed intelligence to MI6 in Whitehall.

Philby called on Gedye personally at the height of the drama. He wanted cast-off clothes for members of the *Schutzbund* who were hiding in the city's sewers, and the journalist parted with three old suits. The instinctive impulse to help momentarily outweighed political considerations. Yet Naomi Mitchison, looking back in her eighty-first year, could still recall the immediate doubts she had on first encountering Philby and Litzi in their own bare little flat. The meeting took place by appointment after this 'nice but oddly excited young Communist from Cambridge had rung me up with the suggestion that those in real distress were not Austrians but the hundreds of German Communists held in prison since the recent Reichstag Fire'. She wondered at first whether Philby might not have been duped. 'Everyone knew,' she said, 'that the Austrian Communist Party had been infiltrated by the agents of Dolfuss.' Then she made discreet enquiries only to learn that he was better informed than she had believed.[5]

> He lived at an address no taxi seemed to know. I found him at last, with a Viennese wife – a dark, untidy comrade – neither of them looking very domesticated. He struck me as too gentle to be a good politician. Probably the best politicians of all are really tough women.[6]

Philby, as it happened, had already yielded to another mildly bourgeois impulse of generosity by taking Litzi to the Vienna City Hall on 24 February and marrying her. On the marriage certificate he described himself as 'a student', compounding that small inaccuracy with the larger untruth that he was 'without religious faith'. He had fallen in love with Litzi. Yet it was a Marxist necessity rather than old-world gallantry that led him to take her, for better or worse. For Philby had a British passport; and she stood in danger of being questioned and put away. To leave her in the lurch might imperil all their comrades. So, personal sentiments apart, Kim took her as his wife to protect the movement, his only lasting love. The decision would no doubt cause complications on his return to London; but no young Communist living on his nerves, amid the chaos and sectarian hatreds of Vienna in the cruel late winter of 1934, could have been expected to spare much thought for the future. This was a different example of what T. S. Eliot meant by 'the awful daring of a moment's surrender'. Hugh Gaitskell and other conventional people might criticize Philby as much as they despaired of him for being an impulsive fool. He, the restless adventurer, did not care.

Attempts by the underground Communists in Vienna to rally the remnants of the broken and leaderless *Schutzbund* came too late to save either. The hunting down by the authorities of men on the run impaired Philby's value as an unofficial link between them. Besides, there were limits to the indulgence of the Austrian security police towards foreigners who took a hand in Austrian quarrels. Even the British, those much-favoured visitors, had to tread warily. So Philby said his farewells and prepared to leave for home with Litzi, his bride. He paid a last call on Eric Gedye, whose resolute spirit he admired. Their final exchanges convinced the *Daily Telegraph*'s Central Europe correspondent that Philby was more implicated in the activities of the Red underground than had first seemed credible. Gedye's visitor brought along an Austrian girl who offered to guide him to the secret hide-out of the revolutionary *Schutzbund* in a forest not far from the capital. Philby, with Litzi on the pillion of his motor-bike, was well on his way back to Britain when Gedye met parading members of the so-called 'Kirov Cadre' one Sunday morning in March 1934. 'Only later did I put two and two together and realize that these were Kim's friends,' Gedye afterwards admitted.[7]

At the Foreign Office in London, Vansittart foresaw the threat to divided Austria as primarily a Nazi threat. Equally he had little hope of interesting his obtuse political master, Sir John Simon, or the more influential 'regulars' at Cliveden, in the nuances. As he subsequently summed up the problem:

> A week of mad little civil war did small damage, though the Socialist fortresses were bombarded. Some mutineers fled to Czechoslovakia, some were caught and executed. Great bitterness remained and furthered Austrian debility. . . . Everywhere on the Left Dolfuss was pilloried as a tyrant, though tyranny was far from his nature. Worst of all, defeated Socialists joined the Nazis against Dolfuss – or the Communists against everyone. Encouraged by these internecine scuffles the local Nazis struck at Berlin's behest. . . . With the murder of Dolfuss came Nazi rebellions in Styria and Carinthia. . . . Lest the aggressors should go further Mussolini rushed divisions to the Brenner amid sighs of relief from all anti-Fascists. We [in Britain] should have done well to keep him there.[8]

What irked Vansittart was Britain's total absence of interest through lack of leadership. Nazi Germany had too many powerful friends in Britain for the isolated Vansittart's liking: they frequented Cliveden and other political salons. On this point at least he was accidentally in agreement with Philby, whose Soviet mentors, reasonably satisfied with his work under fire in Vienna, urged him next to infiltrate the main body of Anglo-German enthusiasts on the far right of the Conservative Party.

'I'm on *your* side of the barricades now,' Donald Maclean said one day with a smile of martyred affectation. It was the spring of 1936. The particular girl friend with him on that occasion noted and remembered the curious phrase, thanking her lucky stars that he seemed to have thrown off the Marxist distemper which had made him such a boring companion in his undergraduate days.[9] Donald was at last going straight. He greatly enjoyed his work as a lowly beginner at the Foreign Office; and, according to the family's numerous and highly placed Liberal friends, his Foreign Office superiors spoke encouragingly of his conscientiousness and adaptability. He was becoming quite the young-man-about-town, too, during off-duty hours, though the conversation of artists, writers and intellectual journalists appealed to him more than the gossip of wealthy and frivolous socialites. He cut a distinctive figure, striding through Chelsea in evening dress and black hat, with his silk-lined opera cloak swinging behind him. His bachelor flat in Oakley Street was too small for entertaining, but then he usually preferred to repay hospitality away from home in a few favourite restaurants and nightclubs. Only select men friends, of whom Guy Burgess was one, could count on occasional invitations to the flat. The writer Cyril Connolly noted:

> Donald Maclean was sandy-haired, tall, with great latent physical strength, but fat and rather flabby. Meeting him, one was conscious of both amiability and weakness. He did not seem a political animal but resembled the clever, helpless youth in a Huxley novel, an outsize Cherubino intent on amorous experience but too shy and clumsy to succeed. The shadow of an august atmosphere lay heavy on him and he sought escape on the more impetuous and emancipated fringes of Bloomsbury and Chelsea.

In Connolly's view, the devotion and attentiveness of 'an older woman' was precisely what the unformed Maclean lacked and needed, 'and it was Donald's misfortune that he was not quite able to inspire such an attachment'. It was evident to others, besides Cyril Connolly, that

> Guy Burgess, though he preferred the company of the able to the artistic, also moved on the edge of the same world. He was of a very different physique, tall-medium in height, with blue eyes, an inquisitive nose, sensual mouth, curly hair and alert fox-terrier expression.... [He] swam like an otter and drank, not like a feckless undergraduate, as Donald was apt to do, but like some Rabelaisian bottle-swiper whose thirst was unquenchable. . . . With all his toughness, however, Guy Burgess wanted intensely to be liked and was indeed likeable, a good conversationalist and an enthusiastic builder-up of his friends. Beneath the *terribilità* of his Marxist analyses one divined the affectionate moral cowardice of the public schoolboy. . . . Unlike Donald, he concealed his sexual diffidence by overconfidence.

What was common to both Burgess and Maclean at this time was their instability: both were able and ambitious young men of high intelligence and good connections who were somehow parodies of what they set out to be. Nobody could take them quite seriously: they were two characters in a late Russian novel, Laurel and Hardy engaged to play Talleyrand and the Younger Pitt. Burgess, incidentally, was a great reader of fiction: his favourite authors were Mrs Gaskell and Balzac, and later on, Mr E. M. Forster. . . . Donald was seldom heard to talk politics. Guy never seemed to stop. He was the type of bumptious Marxist who saw himself as Saint Just, who enjoyed making the flesh of his bourgeois listeners creep by his pictures of the justice which history would mete out to them. Grubby, intemperate and promiscuous, he loved to moralize over his friends and satirize their smug, class-conscious behaviour, so reckless of the reckoning in store. But when bedtime came, very late, and it was the moment to put the analyses away, the word 'preposterous' dying on his lips, he would imply a dispensation under which this was one house at least, this family, these guests, might be spared the worst consequences, thanks to the protection of their brilliant, hunger-marching friend whose position would be so commanding in the happy Workers' imminent Utopia. . . .[10]

The indiscretions of Burgess in the company of such intellectual friends as the journalist Cyril Connolly, who shared some of his tastes but none of his revolutionary fervour, would no doubt have guaranteed his instant dismissal if Captain Jack Macnamara, the Conservative MP for Chelmsford, had chanced to overhear them. Having been prompted not to apply for a Cambridge fellowship; having then been considered not wholly suitable for permanent employment in the Tory Research Department under its ex-MI5 Director, the friendly but careful Joseph Ball; and having finally and ineffectually pressed Victor Cazalet, MP, one of Baldwin's private secretaries, to get him a post in the Tory Central Office, Burgess had at last been willing enough to settle for fourth best: the post of personal assistant to Macnamara, a well-to-do bachelor and one of the leading members of the influential, Tory-dominated Anglo-German Fellowship. The pro-German cult, patronized by no less a personage than the Prince of Wales, was far more fashionable in 1935 than the anti-Nazi warnings of Winston Churchill and Vansittart. Sir Robert Bruce Lockhart's *Diaries* indicate how strongly Hitler's dynamic leadership commended itself to many leading members of the English ruling class at that time:

Friday, 14 September, 1934. Lunched at Sibyl's [Lady Colefax]. . . . Much talk about Mrs Ronnie Greville who has been at Nuremberg and who has come back full of admiration for Hitler. Her influence is very strong with [Sir John] Simon [then Foreign Secretary]. Her vanity is inordinate. In those countries where she is not given a special train, the local British ambassador or minister gets sacked.

Tuesday, 9th October, 1934. In afternoon took Prince Louis [the ex-Kaiser's grandson] to see the Prince of Wales. Prince saw him for nearly three-quarters of an hour, was very nice, told him that he was pro-German. Prince Louis talked to him about America and said that many people in America believed that the Prince did not want to be King and would step down in favour of his brother. 'That's all rot,' said our Prince.

Monday, 27 May, 1935. Dined tonight at Sibyl Colefax's. Although I had not been warned, I discovered that it was a large party for the Prince of Wales and Mrs Simpson. Room was divided into two tables. I sat at the Prince's table. . . . He drank a good deal, joked quite a bit, followed everything Mrs Simpson said with closest interest, and was very amused by Elsie Mendl's blue hair. After dinner we went into drawing room where Brendan Bracken [Tory MP and rising newspaper magnate, responsible for the rumour that he was Churchill's bastard son, more correctly regarded as his faithful shadow] and I drew into a corner. . . . Prince came over and said: 'Ah, there are the men I wish to hear,' and dragged us into his circle. Long discussion followed on foreign policy and France and Germany. Brendan very anti-German and war-like, I rather anti-French and our own foreign policy. Prince came out very strong for friendship with Germany: never heard him talk so definitely about any subject before.

Bruce Lockhart was a natural *boulevardier* and confirmed socialite, who had served both as secret agent and as British representative to the Bolshevik Government after the Revolution of 1917. By the mid thirties, when he was working as a journalist for Lord Beaverbrook, Bruce Lockhart had been on friendly terms with the Prince of Wales for almost a decade; and his observant diarist's eye missed little of significance. It did not really surprise him to find that the man soon to succeed King George V for eleven clouded and distracted months was so pro-

German; nor was he taken aback by the uncomfortable paradox that 'Russia does not hate Fascism so much as the jelly-bellied democracy of Britain.' For Fascism, whether of the Italian or the German variety, corresponded more closely to the ruthless form of personal tyranny imposed by Stalin. Like Vansittart of the Foreign Office, Bruce Lockhart saw something of Ivan Maisky, the Soviet Ambassador in London from 1932 to 1943, who coyly confessed to the diarist in January 1934 that 'already Stalin has established very nearly the same mental superiority over his colleagues as Lenin once enjoyed'.[11]

Virtually all London society cut Maisky dead and avoided like the plague any contact with Russians, a fact which obliged Burgess and Maclean as well as Philby to be vigilant whenever they went to see one or other of their mentors from the Resident Director's office. According to Vansittart, Maisky

> had begun as a Menshevik, and I thought that he might be killed if he were not a success. He was so closely surrounded by those bidden to inform on him that his gloomy Embassy gave me the creeps. Helping lame dogs over stiles is no duty when theirs is to bite, but my wife and I did our best to provide him and his with connections.... He achieved considerable diplomatic standing . . . and gave good service to his ghastly government which rewarded him by consignment to oblivion.... Working for Russia can be riskier than working against her.[12]

By an ironic coincidence, the Soviet agent who had given conditional approval, with the consent of Cahan, his master, to the recruitment of the young men from Cambridge, invited Bruce Lockhart to an unexpected meal in mid January 1934:

> Lunched with Tolokonsky at Simpson's. He is leaving London. His Foreign Office wants him to go to Washington. He wants to work in Russia. He says no one in Russia wants to live abroad (the times are too exciting and interesting), and those who do want to live abroad permanently are no use to the Bolsheviks and are therefore not the men to send. Tolokonsky, who was Commissar to the Vth Army in 1918 and took part in the Red Army's triumphal campaign from the Urals to Vladivostok, thinks war in the Far East is almost certain . . . chief danger is belief in this and other countries that Russia will be easily defeated. Russians today are much stronger in Far East. Japan has –

from her own point of view – waited too long. Sokolnikov, former Ambassador here, is now in charge of Far Eastern affairs. Tolokonsky also told me that the Bolsheviks have been paid the full £100,000 for the *Codex Siniaticus*. He tells me that the £10,000 which the public have to subscribe was put up by someone who figured in last honours list.[13]

Nominally the First Secretary at the Soviet Embassy, the vigilant Tolokonsky evidently missed little of importance that was happening in Britain or his own country. Bruce Lockhart merely recorded the titbits of the conversation and left it at that, accepting his Russian host at face value. It is clear from other diary entries referring obliquely to the British Secret Service, some members of which were well known personally to the diarist, that a spirit of unruffled smugness prevailed in both of its understaffed branches. Bruce Lockhart's principal source of inside information was Commander Reginald Fletcher (the future Labour politician Lord Winster). Like most of his colleagues in British intelligence, Fletcher had been recruited by 'C', otherwise the Chief, Admiral Hugh Sinclair, on the strength of a good military record. Sinclair, 'a terrific anti-Bolshevik', proved more energetic if no more subtle or inventive than his predecessor, Captain Sir Mansfield Cumming. As early as 1929, Fletcher had confided to Bruce Lockhart that 'the new C [Sinclair] is hard up for men for Russia'; yet not until the mid thirties was the first British university graduate recruited, and then by MI5, not MI6.

When six engineers from the British firm of Metro-Vickers, at work on Soviet heavy industrial projects, were put on public trial in 1933, charged with 'sabotage and espionage', Tom Jones of the Cabinet Secretariat in Whitehall 'voiced the majority opinion that we ought not to have assumed the prisoners' innocence', according to Vansittart of the Foreign Office:

Not one of them had been so employed, we should not have been so clumsy – and I told the truth to all enquirers. . . . This episode stirred some indignation, but we were impressed by the Five Year Plans and found more excuse for the OGPU than for the Gestapo. . . . My difficulty lay in stimulating our Government. I persuaded it to suspend trade negotiations and to inform the Soviet Government that we would take power to prohibit Soviet imports unless the trial was cancelled.

The two engineers who 'confessed' were sentenced to imprisonment, only to be released within three months because, in Vansittart's retrospective view, 'the Russians needed our exports more than we needed theirs'. Ramsay MacDonald and most of the Cabinet were afraid of 'going too far'. Indeed, the Prime Minister went out of his way to reproach Vansittart. 'The decision was wrong', he told him. 'You should not have pushed me into it.'[14] For MacDonald, who disliked trouble, at once came under fire from what his chief Foreign Office adviser, a patriot of the old school, witheringly dismissed as 'the brigade whose country is always wrong'. Like the armed forces of the Crown, though for longer than seemed compatible with safety, British intelligence had suffered from official neglect and unimaginative leadership. That state of affairs would continue until the end of the 'Devil's Decade' and the outbreak of the Second World War.

There were as many demons at large in the thirties as there were factions to tempt, infiltrate and lead astray. They flourished because the British ruling class had lost some of its self-confidence and, with it, its traditional sureness of touch. Britain had ceased to be the leader among nations; her Empire was beginning to disintegrate; her commerce and industry were stagnant; the rich were poorer; and the army of the unemployed in depressed areas far from the capital waited listlessly and without hope. People of all classes held most politicians of every party in contempt; the politicians responded uneasily by settling for uncourageous half-measures. Only the Communists rejoiced in their belief that the capitalist system, Britain's original gift to the universe, was irretrievably doomed. Malcolm Muggeridge, already cured of Marxism by his recent stint in Moscow as correspondent of the *Manchester Guardian*, could find no alternative promise of salvation in any political party or institution on his return. His case was typical, not exceptional:

> I have been unable to take completely seriously and therefore to believe in the validity or permanence of any form of authority. Crowns and mitres have seemed to be made of tinsel, ceremonial robes to have been hastily procured in a theatrical costumier's, what passes for great oratory to have been mugged up from the worst of Shakespeare.

Feeling this, I could not but assume that everything pertaining to this aspect of life must shortly come to an end. It was too absurd, too threadbare, too moth-eaten to endure. George Orwell was liable to break off a conversation to make statements like 'Eton's doomed', or 'Soon there won't be any more state openings of Parliament.' Such a disposition made one ostensibly irreverent, pessimistic, disloyal and – the commonest accusation – destructive in attitude of mind.[15]

On the political stage Stanley Baldwin, genially escapist in his methods as in his moralizing, groped his way forward a discreet step at a time. Ramsay MacDonald had faded dimly into the background. The National Government under Baldwin sought a quiet life, and the Prime Minister's worst delusion lay in his pretence that he could unerringly sense and interpret the national mood. He was largely correct in surmising that the British people disliked the thought of being dragged into another war, so this 'man of peace' delayed rearmament as long as possible and kept the bellicose Churchill fulminating vainly in the political wilderness against the underrated menace of Hitler. The Labour Party, still in disarray, nailed its tattered colours to the mast of an ill-starred ship, already sinking, called the League of Nations, proclaiming that 'collective security' would provide its own magical insurance policy against any aggressor.

Intellectuals, naturally, had more than enough blank ammunition to play with; and, with rare exceptions, intellectuals adopted an anti-Fascist and anti-Establishment posture. The proportion of Communists and Communist sympathizers among them was considerable. They believed, as Muggeridge had once believed, that the Soviet Union and its collectivist system offered mankind its one positive chance of happiness and security. They turned instinctively against their own elders in the ruling class of Britain, oblivious of the fact that they were stumbling in the darkness themselves. Stephen Spender, the poet, has recaptured the eerie spirit of the period in words well worth repeating:

Hitler forced politics on to non-political groups who suddenly became aware that they had interests in common. Not only the Jews, but also the intellectuals, because their position was directly attacked, and through sympathy with their colleagues who lived tormented under fascism, acquired an intensity of vision and a fury in their non-political politics which the professional politicians did not share. The intelligentsia also had more sinister reasons for understanding Hitler.... In Hitlerism the nightmares of Dostoevsky's *The Possessed*, of Nietzsche and of Wagner, were made real. The cultured European recognized in this political movement some of their own most hidden fantasies. Hatred of it was deeply involved with a sense of their own guilt.[16]

It was a measure of the Comintern's success that many intellectuals besides Spender were blinded by skilful propaganda to the equally hideous evils of Stalinist Communism. Ignorance played its part in the mirage as much as propaganda. For too few intellectuals in Britain understood that Russia, from her earliest Byzantine dreams of creating a theocracy on earth down to the latest Marxist–Leninist promises of world revolution and a classless paradise, had always been the home of messianic determinism. Her revolutionary thinkers like Bakunin were thus prepared, like their French precursor Robespierre, to wade through seas of blood to demonstrate their love for humanity in the abstract. How could the adventure-seeking but non-intellectual Philby, the solemn yet assuredly immature Maclean, or the brashly irresponsible Burgess have been expected to grasp so gruesome a paradox? They had been provisionally accepted to serve the Soviet Union in secrecy while being groomed for future service in some strategic corner of the British Establishment. No milieu, no atmosphere, no circumstances could have been more perfect for the grand deception, as the Russian Resident Director and his Comintern guides realized only too well.

The German Foreign Ministry documents clearly show how hard Hitler's Third Reich tried to capitalize on the known pro-German bias of the Prince of Wales during the last eighteen months of his father's reign. Inevitably, almost every foreign embassy in London became interested not only in the doings and sayings of the heir to the throne but in those also of Mrs Wallis Simpson, the twice-married American friend to whom he was most closely attached. The Russian emissaries, with their ambitious preoccupations, were slow off the mark. Eventually, however, two of their three young British agents on probation were instructed to gauge the strength of the movement in favour of Anglo-German understanding and friendship by joining it and posing as its ardent supporters. Burgess, as we have seen, did so in 1935 with a characteristic flourish, first breaking openly with his left-wing comrades at Cambridge, then ingratiating himself with Captain Jack Macnamara, the right-wing Tory MP for Chelmsford. Philby took longer to worm his way in. Before the end of 1935, nonetheless, both men were submitting regular reports to Soviet Resident Director Cahan. After the death of King George V in mid January 1936, these activities, largely social and undemanding, notably increased.

'One of the strangest aspects of Edward's reign,' Frances Donaldson has noted, 'is that he spent much of it under the surveillance of security officers. Mrs Simpson was the primary object of these attentions, but, since they were so often together, it was impossible to take this kind of interest in one of them without extending it to the other.'[17]

Lady Donaldson was referring, of course, to *British* security officers. Their aim was to discover whether Germany might not be using and manipulating Mrs Simpson, with whom the new King, in the phrase of one of his royal brothers, was romantically 'besotted'. Russian interest, if naturally more veiled and conspiratorial, proved to be no less genuine: Stalin, as Walter Krivitsky has testified, both admired and feared Hitler, seeking like a cynical suitor to woo a capricious fellow-dictator against whom the Russians were unready as yet to defend themselves. If Britain, through the known sympathies of her new monarch, were now to become an ally of the arch anti-Communist Hitler, the safety of the Soviet Union would be put at risk. Hence the urgency of the otherwise routine work to which Burgess and Philby were assigned.

Philby, on his return from Vienna, paid one last visit to Cambridge, leaving his wife Litzi at his parents' home in Acol Road, Maida Vale. Despite his stutter, he went up to address the University Socialist Society on the Austrian crisis, with a view to raising money for *Schutzbund* victims and their families. Guy Burgess, who was then in his fourth year at Trinity, readily accepted the task of collecting and forwarding the cash. The two men compared notes and kept in intermittent touch afterwards. Philby admitted that he intended gradually to drop all links with the Cambridge Left, in preparation for his new Anglo-German assignment. His aim was a practical one. He needed a job, preferably in journalism. In fact, this proved to be more difficult than he had expected. Unemployment was high among white-collar workers; and Philby had to suffer several disappointments and wait many weeks before he heard of a vacancy for a sub-editor and general assistant on an obscure monthly magazine called the *Review of Reviews*.

The staff of this once popular and now struggling Liberal periodical, which has long since disappeared, was small. Before Philby came, the recently appointed editor, a pleasant, hard-working intellectual called Wilfred Hope Hindle, had been helped by one girl-secretary who somehow contrived also to learn the rudiments of the craft for a pittance. Her name was Alison Outhwaite. She occupied the outer of the two small offices in Bedford Street where the *Review* was prepared for the press. From September 1934, when Hindle engaged him as his deputy for £4 a week, Philby applied himself dutifully to the dull, leisurely job of 'subbing' articles commissioned from outside contributors and writing the occasional uninspired piece himself at the editor's request. Hindle had previously worked for *The Times*, as had a more illustrious predecessor in the editor's chair, Wickham Steed. He had succeeded Sir Roger Chance, a remarkably energetic and kindly man, who happened to be an old Cambridge friend and admirer of Harry St John Philby's. When Hitler came to power, Chance gave himself sabbatical leave and went off to Germany

to see things for myself and to write about them. Some of my stuff appeared in the *Review*, of course, other articles were published by the *Fortnightly*. I didn't work with young Philby but remember him well. We met several times during my visits to London. He also invited me to his home where I met his Austrian wife. I must say I liked him. He struck me as a decent, intelligent young man with a sense of humour and no recognizable political views, quite unlike his father. I thought of him as vaguely Liberal. Of course he had that frightful stammer, so it would have been unkind to pin him down. Now, of course, I wish I had tried harder. He wasn't with the firm for more than a year at most.[18]

Sir Roger was not surprised that Philby moved on. Alison Outhwaite could not understand why a person of Philby's obvious gifts should have chosen to work there at all, and once or twice taxed him with her questions. Producing a monthly certainly did not over-exert his brain. Even when invited to lift the hem of his own political thoughts in print, Philby chose to parade conventional opinions which said nothing to which a sound Liberal could ever have taken exception. He was critical, for instance, of the weak and ambivalent stand of the Christian Churches against the aggressive neo-paganism of Hitler. Only once, after the sudden death in 1935 of T. E. Lawrence in a motor-bike accident, did he contribute anything marginally original. Whereas almost all other obituary notices poured out unstinted praise on the legendary career and exploits of the Uncrowned Prince of Arabia, Philby went out of his way to stress that Lawrence had misconceived the true source of future power in the Middle East:

> He was sent to Arabia to perform a concrete task, and performed it to perfection. But the surprising success of his operation and the brilliance of his personality lent a false glow to the material he had at hand. He was certainly deceived as to the permanence of his achievement.... The dominant figure in contemporary Arabia is not Lawrence, still less Feisal, but Ibn Saud....

The son's pride in a father who was Ibn Saud's personal adviser could not be concealed. The article virtually wrote itself.

Another venture which whiled away time was Philby's brief collaboration with Peter Smolka, a young Viennese acquaintance, in a small press agency registered as London Continental News Ltd, which supplied specialized items on events in Central Europe to the large Exchange Telegraph Company. This was an unprofitable sideline in more ways than one, since the British Foreign Office took note of its existence. The official archives for 1934 referred to it in passing, as the relevant Index proves, but the actual report on the enterprise was subsequently destroyed as being of no lasting interest. The main advantage of working as Hindle's assistant on the *Review of Reviews* was that it gave Philby ample opportunities for outside interests, including an intensive course in Arabic. Alison Outhwaite often saw him, head bowed, concentrating on grammatical exercises and laborious translations. What the secretary did not know was that a mysterious hand other than Philby's controlled these odd irons in the fire. As he put it himself some thirty years later, without offering more than the barest hint of the truth:

In the first year or two I penetrated very little, though I did beat Gordon Lonsdale to the London School of Oriental Studies by ten years. During that period I was a sort of intelligence probationer. I still look back with wonder at the infinite patience shown by my seniors in the service, a patience matched only by their intelligent understanding. Week after week, we would meet in one or other of the remoter open spaces in London; week after week, I would reach the rendezvous empty-handed and leave with a load of painstaking advice, admonition and encouragement. I was often despondent at my failure to achieve anything worthwhile, but the lessons went on and sank deep. . . . How, where and when I became a member of the Soviet intelligence service is a matter for myself and my comrades.[19]

Two or three former associates whom Philby met in the mid thirties were aware that he had moved politically to the Right. When at last, possibly with the help of Burgess, he was able to hand in his resignation to Hindle and join the expanding propaganda department of the Anglo-German Fellowship, this enervating interlude of marking time ended. Malcolm Muggeridge, who came to know Philby very well and worked under him in MI6 during the Second World War, contends that

a born adventurer like Kim, with very little political subtlety and an eye always to the main chance, was almost certainly attracted by this Anglo-German nonsense. It would have been quite in character. He admired Goebbels and once told me he could easily have worked with him. Don't forget at this stage, in 1936, the bandwaggon between London and Berlin hadn't stopped rolling, and Kim would have been quite ready to jump on it for that very reason.

In the judgement of Muggeridge, who met him for the first time in the 'pokey little place where Hindle presided', Philby

> protests too much in claiming that he already had settled convictions and was bluffing the Germans at the Russians' behest. I still think he was bluffing himself.[20]

In any case Philby, whatever the truth about his political convictions, swiftly made his mark as a promising young member of the Fellowship. The president, Lord Mount-Temple (the former Tory MP Wilfred Ashley), and the secretary, Mr E. W. D. Tennant, a prosperous City businessman, were reasonably impressed by his keenness. As a salaried official, he edited the propaganda sheet which purported to prove, by selective extracts from many sources, that the British press was misleading the British public about the policies of both British and German governments. The Foreign Office itself recognized that 'the Germans are spending more money and energy in this country than the Soviets'. Some of the cash was spent on entertaining aristocrats and other influential people at public banquets complete with swastikas and pro-Hitler speeches. Philby attended the dinner on 14 July 1936 when the Fellowship honoured the Duke and Duchess of Brunswick, the ex-Kaiser's daughter. Other names on the lengthy guest-list included those of Major-General J. F. C. Fuller, the military historian; Earl Jellicoe; Admiral Sir Barry Domvile; Baroness Bruno Schroder; and Lord Redesdale, the eccentric father of the Mitford sisters. Robert Bruce Lockhart, with whom Malcolm Muggeridge had worked until recently on the gossip column of Beaverbrook's *Evening Standard*, went as the guest of General Waters and noted later in his diary:

> Large crowd; many soldiers. Mount Temple in chair, Zetland as guest, Lord Lothian etc. Kaiser's daughter looked browned and athletic. Duke who had a very guttural voice speaks English indifferently. . . . The Brunswicks are pro-Nazi. The Kaiser is very angry with them. He thinks that they are trying to steal his chances and his monarchical thunder by currying favour with Hitler. If anything happened to Hitler tomorrow, they might have a chance.[21]

Part of Philby's routine consisted in flying at intervals to Berlin for discussions at the Propaganda Ministry, where he more than once consulted the former champagne salesman, Ribbentrop, who was Hitler's adviser on foreign affairs and later became German Ambassador in London. It was a decidedly odd way even then for a young English journalist to earn a living. Some of Kim's acquaintances in Fleet Street thought so and said so. They were unconvinced by his half-jocular stock excuse: 'I'm only doing it because it's well paid.' It was perhaps fortunate for his Soviet mentors that the Fellowship's plan to make him editor of a new trade paper financed by Germany was frustrated by supporters of Sir Barry Domvile, himself a fanatical pro-German who later founded his own extremist group, the Anglo-German Link.

After his father's death early in 1936, King Edward VIII by no means abandoned his quest for closer political ties between Britain and Germany; but his personal obsession with Mrs Simpson tended increasingly to distract him as the months passed. His Cabinet thought it expedient to humour him and play for time. Like a spoiled child, the new King kept on stressing the importance of an understanding with Mussolini, the invader of Abyssinia, as well as with Hitler. When German troops reoccupied the Rhineland in March 1936, anti-Fascist protests in Britain left the King unmoved. In the careful words of Frances Donaldson: 'No one could control the King, indeed no one seems to have been able to speak to him. . . .'[22] The growing tension between an impetuous monarch determined to have his way and a circumspect government determined to avoid trouble and prevent a scandal continued for the remainder of King Edward VIII's brief reign, so that the year 1936 deserves to be remembered as a wasted interlude when the slim outside chance of a British initiative to save the peace of the world finally slipped away. On the eve of the Spanish Civil War, in July 1936, the King went abroad, borrowing Lady Yule's luxurious yacht *Nahlin*, for a much-publicized cruise in the eastern Mediterranean. He was accompanied by Mrs Simpson and a party of chosen friends. So Britain drifted towards the distracting drama of a constitutional crisis in which the King would have to choose between his throne and marriage to the twice-divorced woman he loved and could, he claimed, no longer live without.

The Soviet Union had joined the League of Nations in 1934, and the League had imposed economic sanctions on Italy after Mussolini's attack on Abyssinia. The Labour Party was split on the question of sanctions, its left-wing idealists like Stafford Cripps denouncing the League itself as 'an international Burglars' Union'. On one issue all sections of the Party could agree: they opposed rearmament. But they failed to win the General Election of November 1935. The League also failed to stop the war in Abyssinia; and Britain, to the chagrin of King Edward VIII, next incurred the animosity of Mussolini for her pains. The Admiralty was as upset as the King. For the warships of the British Mediterranean Fleet were not equipped for offensive action.

'Admiral Sir Charles Forbes confided to me', wrote David Kelly, then a young diplomat stationed in Cairo, 'that his ships had enough ammunition to shoot for fifteen minutes and that, as he could take no war-time precautions to protect the Fleet crowded into Alexandria harbour, he sighed with relief each time dawn arrived'.[23]

Dissident intellectuals in Britain had meanwhile found an outlet for their confused ardour in the anti-Fascist campaigns inspired by Willy Muenzenberg, the Paris-based impresario conducting the Comintern's new Popular Front strategy. Arthur Koestler, a close associate and friend of Muenzenberg, has stated that 'Willy produced Committees as a conjurer produces rabbits out of his hat: his genius consisted in a unique combination of the conjuror's wiles with the crusader's dedication.'[24]

As Chief of the Comintern's West European Agitprop Department, Willy Muenzenberg had established its headquarters in France after escaping from Berlin on the night of the Reichstag Fire. His first venture, the World Committee for the Relief of the Victims of German Fascism, set the pattern for all future camouflaged 'front' organizations. It had branches in every Western country, with highly respectable non-Communist members, 'from

English duchesses to American columnists and French savants who had never heard the name of Muenzenberg and thought that the Comintern was a bogey invented by Dr Goebbels'. Such expert propaganda methods contrasted with the heavy-footed ingenuousness of official British measures like the Incitement to Disaffection Act of 1934, aimed at stamping out Communism in the armed services. When the Spanish Civil War broke out in July 1936, Muenzenberg's oblique and unseen influence on the public mind in Britain and other Western democracies was considerable.

No foreign question since the French Revolution caused greater excitement and controversy among British intellectuals than the conflict in Spain. Liberal and left-wing adherents swallowed the Muenzenberg bait, accepting that the Franco rebellion was part of a worldwide Fascist conspiracy against democracy itself. Spain became a battlefield of rival ideologies, for Franco had his minority of supporters among British Catholics, who detested Communism, and among right-wing Conservatives, who admired the efficiency of the dictators. Intellectuals had been talking and writing of 'the struggle against Fascism' since 1931. Now, in Spain, that struggle had become a reality: in the words of A. J. P. Taylor,

> They demanded 'arms for Spain'. Some of them visited Spain. Some of the younger ones fought for the republic. Some, of high intellectual lineage and achievement, were killed. 'Bloomsbury' rallied to Spain where it had once held aloof from political questions. This enthusiasm was by no means exclusively middle class. The working class, too, had its intellectuals of a vaguely Marxist cast. Of the 2000-odd British citizens who fought for the Spanish republic, the great majority were workers, particularly unemployed miners.[25]

Of the 500 British members of the International Brigade killed in action, many were Communists. Once the first wave of enthusiasm had spent itself, the British Communist Party pulled back its best members from the front and sent expendable 'volunteers' to brave the bullets in the front line. Baldwin and the British Cabinet laid down the safe policy of Non-Intervention, answering the accusation that they favoured Fascism with the counter-accusation that the Labour Party was simply warmongering.

Meanwhile the composer Ralph Vaughan Williams abandoned folk music for anti-Fascist symphonic composition; and the Left Book Club, which owed nothing directly to Muenzenberg's inspiration and was the brainchild of the non-Communist publisher Victor Gollancz and of the free-wheeling Communist intellectual John Strachey, distributed its mainly Marxist books each month to many thousands of subscribers throughout the land.

This was not an easy time for Guy Burgess or Kim Philby. In accordance with instructions, they carried on with their now-unpalatable task of watching and weighing up the political activities of their right-wing colleagues in the Anglo-German Fellowship movement.

Burgess often regaled his friends with tales of his riotous visits to Germany in the company of Captain Jack Macnamara. He boasted of having shepherded a group of English schoolboys to the Nuremberg Rally; of having attended the Olympic Games in Berlin; and of having completed a dissolute tour of the Third Reich with two friends, a War Office drinking companion, and a wealthy Anglican archdeacon, the Venerable J. H. Sharp. This cleric, who had adopted Macnamara as a child, seemed to have succumbed to his protégé's bad example as a 'gay adult'. One marginally useful result of Burgess's activities was the impressive number and range of personal contacts he made, and these his Soviet mentors obviously encouraged him to maintain. They expected him, as they expected Philby, to be patient until each managed to penetrate the official Establishment, preferably by joining the secret service. Their probationary tests would assist them towards that end, always provided they worked with a will.

Early in 1936, Guy Burgess obtained a month's trial in the sub-editors' room of *The Times*, but failed to impress his superiors and was finally turned down as unsuitable. Like Philby, he had grown restless and somewhat disenchanted with the Anglo-German chore, especially after Hitler's unopposed occupation of the Rhineland in March. The entry in Harold Nicolson's diary for 17 March reflected how sharp were the recriminations between France and Britain, ending with the casual remark: 'I dine with Mary Hutchinson, Maynard Keynes and Guy Burgess. Keynes is very defeatist.' Burgess himself had better reason than Nicolson or Keynes to know why Britain would not move or press France to move, since he was now starting to provide the British Secret Service with inside information as a freelance. He told them, for instance, that the French Cabinet had rejected by a majority of only one vote the proposal to send French troops into the Rhineland to expel Hitler's forces. In spite of his trifling with art and literature, his braggart's style, his air of loose, unconventional living, Burgess was still capable of pulling off the unexpected triumph and keeping it secret, thanks to the variety and range of his personal contacts. In this case his source was a highly placed homosexual, M. Edouard Pfeiffer, Communist *chef du cabinet* to M. Daladier, the French Prime Minister. According to his own account, Burgess received payment from the British Secret Service for this and other items of value from privileged sources. However, his friends had grown so accustomed to Guy's incurable impulse to exaggerate everything he did that they could not be quite sure if he was telling the truth or a vainglorious fable. What had once seemed a childish weakness had already become part of his hidden strength.

During the placid weekend that brought news of the outbreak of the Spanish Civil War, Philby and his wife entertained a friend. Jim Lees was genuinely amazed by the new-found right-wing sentiments of the quiet Socialist he had liked so well at Trinity College. He was particularly disturbed to hear him whisper that he would probably 'have to get rid of Litzi'. Nevertheless, like Baldwin in the more complex and dramatic case of Mrs Wallis Simpson, Philby chose not to rush matters and to let events take their own course. In this, we may be sure, he had the backing of his Soviet controller. It is not definitely known who this mysterious person was, though circumstantial evidence suggests that it might have been the Hungarian-born agent Theodore Maly, who was certainly sent to Britain in 1934 by the NKVD as Tolokonsky's special replacement. The tolerance, forbearance and persuasiveness which Philby ascribed to this controller were certainly qualities characteristic of Maly, a renegade Catholic priest who had turned to revolutionary Communism after being taken prisoner as an Austro-Hungarian chaplain by Czarist troops on the Carpathian front in 1915. In finding a new faith, Maly retained his capacity for stimulating zeal and dedication in others, though he seldom spoke of his past. Both Maly and Tolokonsky appear to have been recalled to Moscow and liquidated in the purges of 1938.[26]

Philby did not relish as keenly as Burgess, whom he saw from time to time, the routine of passing himself off openly as a pro-Nazi. He felt that he had got off to a false start; and his sense of inadequacy had increased during that first autumn of the fighting in Spain. He had spent two vacations there recently with his wife, who would naturally have preferred to visit her relatives in Vienna instead; and he could still vividly recall his boyish delight in accompanying his father to Granada as a reward for winning a King's Scholarship to Westminster School. When his controller hinted at one of their regular meetings that Philby might be of more use shortly in Spain than in London, the probationer responded enthusiastically. It was plain that very few Communists now remained at large behind Fascist lines. Many had been wiped out; and little information of any value was trickling through. If Philby went in, he would need foolproof credentials: a British passport was not sufficient. Only proper accreditation as a press correspondent attached to Franco's army would do the trick, and this might not be too easy to arrange quickly.

It is a matter of record that Walter Krivitsky, the self-styled coordinator of Soviet military intelligence in western Europe, was deeply concerned about the yawning gaps in his Spanish network at this time. The journalist Arthur Koestler, then working with Willy Muenzenberg in Paris, had been commissioned to go on a brief, hazardous trip to Franco's headquarters in Seville about a month after the war started to obtain first-hand evidence of German military involvement on the side of the Fascist rebels, and had been lucky to reach Gibraltar safely 'one hour before the warrant for my arrest was issued in Seville'. Koestler was representing a Hungarian newspaper and also carried credentials, provided for him at Muenzenberg's headquarters, from the London *News Chronicle*; but a former colleague at Ullstein's, the German newspaper group, had recognized him, and Koestler knew that this person knew him to be a Communist. Clearly, Philby would need a good cover; and his right-wing associations at last began to justify themselves.

While Baldwin and the British public were preoccupied with the sudden public sensation of the King's stubborn refusal to give up Mrs Simpson, and the constitutional crisis moved inexorably towards abdication, Philby was doing the rounds of Fleet Street, seeking an editor willing to use his services in Franco Spain. *The Times*, which already had a correspondent there, did not turn him down outright: if he would like to take his chance of submitting acceptable material on a strictly freelance basis, they would consider it carefully. What precise form of accreditation was given to him is no longer recorded, possibly a brief note 'to whom it may concern'. Obviously, Philby's journalistic *bona fides* required a firmer foundation than that for the trial period his controller urged on him as a first step. Whether it was the inventive Guy Burgess, working hand in glove with the wily Muenzenberg, who invented or 'discovered' the London General Press and a pliable director ready to sign the necessary card authorizing Philby to act as its correspondent, or whether the latter arranged it himself, is something that hardly matters now. He had cover enough at least to try his hand in the field. His Soviet mentors seemed anxious to pack him off, armed with detailed instructions on what to send them and how to send it. Every scrap of intelligence about enemy formations, dispositions and weapons would be welcome.

Philby spent some time in Paris before setting off. Nearly ten years later, walking through the streets of the liberated French capital with Malcolm Muggeridge, he would point out the corner flat at the top of a tall building 'where Litzi and I once lived for a while'. By a strange coincidence, Theodore Maly also arrived in Paris during the same spring of 1937 and called on his friends in the *apparat* of Ignace Reiss, announcing that he had completed his mission in London. It can reasonably be inferred that Philby was temporarily serving the interests of Krivitsky and Soviet military intelligence.[27]

Yet the early weeks of trial and error in and about Franco's headquarters at Seville were not wholly without hazard. His fairly flimsy credentials were never questioned. What fate befell the routine cables he despatched to the mythical London General Press agency need not detain us, but one or two of his more carefully written reports to *The Times* were favourably received and duly published. How, or through what underground channels, he was able to communicate with Krivitsky remained his own secret. In the ticket pocket of his trousers he carried with him, as he put it, 'a tiny piece of substance resembling rice paper'. This he had been given before leaving London 'for urgent communications'. It contained a code and several cover addresses outside Spain. In a moment of euphoria, Philby decided one April day in 1937 that he deserved some relaxation. He had noticed a colourful poster advertising a bullfight the following Sunday in Cordoba, some twenty-five miles to the east and close to the actual front line. At Franco's headquarters he was assured that no special pass would be required for the short rail journey to Cordoba. On the train he fell into conversation with some Italian infantry officers who politely refused his invitation to dinner that evening and, as later became evident, promptly reported him as a suspect alien to the local police.

In the small hours of the Sunday morning, Philby was rudely awakened by the sound of rifle butts on the door of his hotel room. Two civil guards pushed their way in, ordering him to dress and pack his bag. Then he was marched off to police headquarters. Philby's interrogator was a small, uniformed major who exuded unfriendliness. Seated opposite him beneath a single, naked light bulb and behind a long, polished table, the major fired his questions and listened sceptically to the answers: plainly, Philby's explanation sounded too simple and straightforward to be believed. The Spaniard scrutinized the British passport with distaste. It was quite in order, he agreed; but where was the visitor's official authorization for the journey to Cordoba, where was his ticket for the bullfight? Philby replied that he had arrived only the evening before and had intended to buy his ticket the next day:

> With every fresh outburst of scepticism, I became aware, with growing unease, that my interrogator was a confirmed Anglophobe. There were plenty of Anglophobes in those days in Spain, on both sides of the line. But by this time my brain was beginning to work normally, and I began to see possibilities in that wide expanse of gleaming table.

The major and two guards turned out Philby's suitcase, minutely fingering every article and every stitch of clothing. At length the suspect was ordered to turn out his pockets. He removed his wallet first, and, with a sudden flick of his wrist, spun it diagonally down the long table. As he had hoped, 'all three men made a dive for it, spreadeagling themselves across the table. Confronted by three pairs of buttocks, I scooped the scrap of paper out of my trousers, a crunch and a swallow, and it was gone.' Finding nothing incriminating on him, the disappointed major lectured Philby sternly on the iniquitous domination of the British Government by Communists, ordered him to leave Cordoba at daylight, and dismissed him.[27]

In his account of this alarming episode, Philby has acknowledged his luck as well as his presence of mind. Whether he would have fared so well at the hands of a Soviet interrogator is a question he wisely did not raise; as a true believer, Philby would doubtless reject any suggestion that in such circumstances he or anyone else would have been allowed to escape – 'almost literally by the skin of my teeth'. The unheroic incident did put him on his guard. The lesson also etched itself indelibly on his memory:

> The really risky operation is not usually the one which brings most danger, since real risks can be assessed in advance and precautions taken to obviate them. It is the almost meaningless incident, like the one described above, that often puts one at mortal hazard.[28]

Reflections apart, the misadventure had one or two awkward consequences. It obliged Philby to rearrange his immediate plans. An indirect SOS eventually reached Krivitsky's aides; and Guy Burgess, of all people, was alerted and sent across France to rendezvous with Philby at a safe meeting place, possibly in Saint-Jean-de-Luz. A freelance correspondent cannot hope to live on air and excitement alone, and Philby was running short of money. The two conspirators, the journalist and his emergency courier, seemed to have partly succeeded in earning the trust of their Soviet mentors; and it is not improbable that Burgess also handed over another 'scrap of paper' with coded instructions to replace the original which Philby had hastily gulped down. Many years later, as we shall see, the clear recollection of this clandestine meeting almost caused Philby to trip himself up in the course of a thorough cross-examination by a senior official of MI5. But how could a seriously committed Devil's Disciple be expected to learn the dark crafts of double-dealing without stumbling now and again? Living from day to day by their wits, the probationers had no care for the unforeseeable future.

5. THE TIME SERVERS

Like his demi-monde friend Brian Howard, a homosexual aesthete who went up to Oxford from Eton in 1922 at the same time as Harold Acton, Guy Burgess tended to put the best of himself into his vivid and stimulating conversation. Evelyn Waugh had already sensed the malign influence of Howard in their undergraduate days, applying to him the axiom of Lady Caroline Lamb that he was 'mad, bad and dangerous to know'. Allowing for the unhappily fragmented state of public, as against private, opinion from 1936 until Britain declared war on Germany in September 1939, it is not difficult to understand now the comparative ease with which the more versatile Burgess first obtained employment and subsequently earned the qualified praise of his astonished superiors in the Talks Department of the BBC. Colleagues on the studio floor were less enamoured of his glib tongue and marked aptitude for intrigue. 'Give him an inch,' complained Frank Gillard, later a war correspondent and then Managing Director, BBC Radio, 'and the man would grab a yard with every bit of official backing he could muster.'[1] Yet Burgess proved a baffling adversary. He could disarm critics at that and higher levels by acknowledging his abnormal sexual proclivities, while passing himself off as a political eunuch with discriminating right-wing undertones. As he also seemed to be on first-name terms with a formidable number of men and women prominent in British public life, seldom failing to persuade any of them to broadcast, he quickly established himself as one of the most awkward of the BBC's talented producers of promise.

How John Reith, that God-fearing Calvinist who still presided over an institution indelibly stamped with the imprint of his own rigid and powerful personality, would have reacted to a whisper from the Almighty that, in appointing Burgess to a recent vacancy at Bristol, his subordinates had installed a Soviet probationary agent, remains a question best left to the reader's imagination. True, the young man had not been selected without the highest recommendations. Had not the Regius Professor of Modern History at Cambridge, G. M. Trevelyan, personally endorsed the application in a note to Cecil Graves, Reith's number two at the pinnacle of the BBC hierarchy, who chanced to be a personal friend of the historian's? And did not the applicant's impeccable academic record suggest that the BBC was doing itself a positive favour in offering Guy Burgess a talks producer's job? As for Burgess himself, why should he have disdained the professional scope to bring to the microphone experts capable of clarifying and interpreting what was happening inside Britain and in the troubled world beyond? What did it matter if many listeners preferred the light music and commercials on Radio Luxembourg, shutting their ears to commentaries on the fate of Republican Spain or on the growing menace posed by Nazi Germany? Burgess could at least agree with the awesome Reith, whom he often mimicked, that the bounden duty of the BBC was to inform and educate as well as entertain its vast if often indifferent audience. Cyril Connolly recalled:

> During the Spanish War, I saw much less of Guy Burgess who had joined the BBC in Bristol. A terrible thing had happened – he had become a Fascist! Still sneering at the bourgeois intellectual, he now vaunted the intensely modern realism of the Nazi leaders: his admiration for economic ruthlessness and the short-cut to power had swung him to the opposite extreme. He claimed to have attended a Nuremberg Rally.[2]

Connolly would have had less reason to be astonished by the truth about Burgess than the self-righteous Reith, who had contrived to shape the BBC in his own high-minded image. If the Corporation usually echoed the cautious, muddled but well-meaning leaders of the Establishment, to which it adhered with the steadfastness of a limpet, this was the predictable fate of a monopoly licensed by Royal Charter. Evelyn Waugh had a contemptuous regard for BBC employees: he thought of them all as 'electricians'. With finer precision, the historian A. J. P. Taylor noted that the BBC, financed by licence fees from the owners of wireless sets and nominally under 'a board of distinguished governors nominated by the prime minister', became a cultural dictatorship under Reith's control,

> as though Milton and others had never made the case for unlicensed utterance. In no time at all, the monopolistic Corporation came to be regarded as an essential element in 'the British way of life'. Like all cultural dictatorships, the BBC was more important for what it silenced than for what it achieved. . . . The English people, if judged by the BBC, were uniformly devout and kept to the middle of the road.[3]

Born to caution out of Reith's conception of bureaucracy, the Corporation as Guy Burgess found it suited him down to the ground. He had no intention of staying. His life-long career lay elsewhere, in the shadows; but behind the sound-proofed studio doors, or chatting with colleagues at a table in the canteen, he played the part of a broadcasting professional without rousing suspicion. He had no difficulty, for instance, in extricating himself from the duty rota to keep that rendezvous with Philby in the late spring of 1937. Nor did anyone in authority query the occasional visits he paid to Paris for secret exchanges with Willy Muenzenberg and Otto Katz, the chief manipulators of the Comintern's propaganda apparatus in western Europe. If the private conduct of BBC officials did not concern their superiors as long as public scandals were avoided, the ways in which employees spent their holidays or filled their off-duty hours seldom gave rise to questioning. Despite a well-developed taste for exaggerating his own exploits, Burgess could be the soul of discretion whenever necessary; and nobody at BBC Bristol or later at Broadcasting House, London, regarded him as anything worse than a gay, witty, sometimes difficult egotist, with an appreciative eye for boys rather than girls.

During his two stints with the BBC, from 1936 until the end of 1938, and again from 1941 until he joined the press department of the Foreign Office in 1944, Burgess not only managed to restrain himself from pursuing males down the corridors but earned the reputation of being 'more of a talker than a do-er' in his homosexual interests.

It must be said here that his invisible links with the Comintern tended to lead back to those close intimates of Cambridge days who remained bound to him intellectually, emotionally and sometimes physically as active members of what has since been aptly nicknamed the 'Homintern'. 'Maurice' was still among the closest of them. Dobb, the most senior of the Communist gurus at Trinity College, had expressed puzzlement and disappointment at Burgess's histrionic break with the Communist Party. John Cornford, David Haden-Guest and other young Marxist militants had been sorely tempted to murder the renegade. 'Maurice' alone knew the reason for that rash and risky move on the part of his friend, Guy Burgess; but 'Maurice' chose to affect quiet amazement. Goronwy Rees, a heterosexual outsider, who had 'argued fiercely, then fallen out with Guy after his conversion to Nazism', began to see more of him about this time. For Rees had been appointed assistant editor of the *Spectator* in 1936; and Burgess kept a sharp eye not only on the articles written by Rees but on the more specialized contributions of the magazine's new art critic, Anthony Blunt. One evening an extraordinary dialogue with Burgess took place in Rees's Ebury Street flat. It stemmed directly from a sympathetic book review by the latter on the distressed areas of Britain and the wasted lives of the unemployed who lived there.

When Burgess, not for the first time, heaped inordinate praise on his friend, Rees finally cut him short. 'It was good,' he said 'but not all that good. So kindly drop the subject, Guy.' Not in the least put out, Burgess insisted that Rees 'had the heart of the matter' in him. The phrase puzzled Rees. 'What on earth do you mean?' he said. Burgess paused. 'There's something I ought to tell you,' he confided. 'I am a Comintern agent and have been one ever since I came down from Cambridge.' That was why he had deliberately hoodwinked all his old friends by pretending to embrace Fascism. The deception had been painful but unavoidable. When Rees riposted, 'I just don't believe you,' Burgess assured him that he was telling the truth. 'I want you to work with me, to help me,' he added. Rees hid his consternation by firing questions at him: What did he mean? What sort of help did he expect? Did anyone else know? Was he in it alone? It not, who were his friends?

'You ask too many questions,' retorted Burgess soothingly. 'But I'll give you one name only.' He then mentioned the real name of 'Maurice' and Rees said no more beyond muttering that he would have to 'think it over'. In fact, the very mention of the name stunned him. For Rees respected 'Maurice' as a likeable man of such erudition and integrity that 'I'd have been proud to follow him anywhere'. He promised Burgess there and then never to let 'Maurice' know how much he knew. The more Rees pondered this unsought disclosure, the greater his bewilderment grew. 'How could I be sure that Guy wasn't making me the victim of one of his elaborately cruel jokes? And even if he was sharing a secret, as he seemed to be doing, what trust could be placed in anything he said?' Rees's refusal to commit himself did not end their friendship, though it imposed a strain on it. Burgess, as if he had not been indiscreet enough, informed Donald Maclean, among others, what had happened. Rees, for his part, called on John Lehmann's sister, Rosamond whom he had sometimes visited with Burgess in the past, and told her how their mutual friend Guy had invited him to collaborate in his nefarious activities as a secret agent and why the unexpected offer had been turned down. Rosamond was inclined to dismiss the whole business as a typical Guy Burgess fantasy of wish-fulfilment; Goronwy, who prudently drew a veil over the alleged complicity of 'Maurice', confessed that he hardly knew what to believe.[4]

Rosamond Lehmann was the wife of Wogan Philipps, an old Etonian who had joined the Communist Party in its early days after graduating from Magdalen College, Oxford. The younger son of a peer, Philipps lived comfortably in the country with Rosamond and their two children, tilling his own land as a farmer and writing occasional verse. Many years would pass before he adopted the style and title of Lord Milford, with the

Party's approval and on the understanding that he took his seat in the Upper House in order to demand its abolition. Rosamond was herself a graduate of Girton College, Cambridge, which had partly inspired her first novel *Dusty Answer*, and her many friends on the Left relished the charm of her conversation, her beauty and her sagacity. Despite the political odds against her, she somehow managed to maintain a rare political detachment, reminding the romantic Cyril Connolly of 'the Alcazar of Toledo, an irreducible bastion of the bourgeoisie entirely surrounded by Communists'. Knowing how wilfully extravagant the imagination of Guy Burgess could be, Rosamond's intuition led her to a rational conclusion which only time would falsify: Guy was no Comintern agent, she insisted.

Thanks to the narrow, tightly enmeshed relationships which still characterized the structure of the British ruling class, whether at the centre of power or on the outer fringes, the gossip about Burgess did not spread beyond his intellectual friends of the Left. This alone does not explain why so intemperate a young man got away with living a triple life so easily for so long. Fortunately for himself, he had few friends in common with his BBC superiors and colleagues who, for the most part, inhabited a more prosaic and duller world than his. Yet he exploited his position at the BBC to seek out MPs, important civil servants and other leading lights whose influence or inside knowledge might come in useful at a later stage. If the BBC derived some immediate benefit from the exercise, the Soviet Union derived little: the use of Burgess to his secret mentors lay in the future, except when he could offer occasional items of invaluable inside information, on a par with details of that very close French Cabinet vote against unilateral military action to expel Hitler's troops from the newly reoccupied Rhineland in March 1936, or when he rose instantly to the challenge of rushing off as a courier to provide his fellow conspirator, Philby, with ready money.

The salary which Burgess earned at the BBC, less than £500 per annum, was not sufficient to keep him in the expensive style to which he had grown accustomed. The allowance from his father's estate would have been regarded by any young man of more abstemious habits as a bonus, making all the difference between modest and luxurious living. But Burgess needed plenty of ready cash to spend on his innumerable contacts; and where the niggardly BBC would not help him, his open-handed Soviet controller assuredly did. Goronwy Rees often noticed on one shelf of a large cupboard in the bedroom of his friend's top-floor flat in Chester Square an untidy file of letters and 'thick wads of banknotes'. The letters, so Burgess once declared with a wicked smile, had come, unsolicited, from love-sick boy friends: 'I never throw any away. One never knows, they might come in useful some day.' The bundles of currency, as Rees remarked, 'never seemed to shrink in size'.[5]

The flat itself was 'usually in a mess'. Its colour scheme was typically loud: bright red curtains, white walls and, to complete the patriotic toning, matching blue counterpane and cushions. When Rees called one Saturday morning, he found Burgess sitting up in his pyjamas, reading one of the newspapers that littered the counterpane. On the floor stood a large cooking pot containing a gluey mixture which he would sniff at and then fitfully stir with a spoon. It appeared that Burgess had decided to spend that weekend alone in solitary contemplation; and he explained that 'this gruel' would give him all the nourishment he required until Monday. He had rendered down kippers, garlic, cheese, wine and scraps of every kind from the kitchen into a nauseating but easily digestible porridge. Rees left feeling a little queasy and silently marvelling at the odd tastes of this wayward friend. At any rate Guy no longer pestered him for assistance in what Rosamond Lehmann had written off as an imaginary Red crusade. One uncertainty still nagged away at the back of Goronwy Rees's mind: Why had Guy deliberated so hard before disclosing the name of 'Maurice' as one of the conspirators? If Rees was ever tempted to confront this sage directly, he resisted the temptation resolutely for fear of making himself a laughing stock.

It is impossible to assess what value, if any, was placed by their

Soviet mentors on the information received orally or in documentary form from Burgess, Donald Maclean and Harold Philby. Gentlemanly wrangling among BBC controllers and departmental heads over abstruse technicalities and the fine hairs of policy no more interested the Kremlin than they interested Burgess, although it should never be forgotten that George Orwell would base his Ministry of Truth in *Nineteen Eighty-Four* on the BBC as he saw and experienced it during the Second World War. Burgess chiefly helped the Kremlin and himself by fostering useful contacts outside the office. He ingratiated himself, for instance, with members of British intelligence like Guy Liddell and David Footman, and with accommodating politicians like Harold Nicolson and Brendan Bracken who disliked the new Chamberlain Government's sleep-walking foreign policy. He reported confidently to his Soviet paymasters that Britain was in no mood and no fit state to get embroiled in European quarrels. As Burgess also saw Maclean from time to time, the Foreign Office view fortified his own judgement.

The mysteries of workaday diplomacy had long ceased to bother Maclean. Beneath his grave politeness, his conscientiousness, his ability to absorb and memorize complex policy issues, there lurked a feeling of contempt for most of his superiors. Yet most of these spoke well of him: Maclean had definite promise. They predicted a dazzling future for the prodigy who could see no future for himself in a country foredoomed to disaster by the very values those superiors embodied. Living a double life suited Maclean well in those bachelor days. When Anthony Rumbold, a Foreign Office colleague and the son of an eminent diplomat, became engaged to Felicity Bailey, one of the girl friends of whom Maclean had been particularly fond since Sir Donald's death, the couple were relieved at his reaction. 'Far from showing any jealousy or pique,' said Lady Felicity, 'he was best man at our wedding and even spent some time with us on our honeymoon in the South of France.'[6]

Only under the influence of drink would Maclean sometimes reveal glimpses of the dark, rebellious side of his mind. That was why, to a far greater extent than Burgess, he tried not to mix business with pleasure, seldom going out with his Foreign Office colleagues. Cyril Connolly and his circle saw more of him than Burgess, and Connolly noted how much he had improved:

> A strong supporter of the Spanish Republic, [he] seemed suddenly to have acquired a backbone, morally and physically. I remember some arguments with him. I had felt a strong sympathy for the Spanish anarchists, with whom he was extremely severe, as with other non-Communist factions, and I detected in his reproaches the familiar priggish tone of the Marxist, the resonance of the 'Father Found'. At the same time he could switch to a magisterial defence of Chamberlain's foreign policy and seemed able to hold the two self-righteous points of view simultaneously.... Unlike Burgess, he was without vanity. I think the simplest distinction between them is that if you had given Maclean a letter he would have posted it. Burgess would probably have forgotten it or opened it and then returned it to tell you what you should have said.[7]

Meanwhile, far away in Spain, Philby had consolidated himself as an official correspondent with Franco's army. *The Times* approved of the despatches sent 'on spec' by Jack Philby's son, a reporter with a good eye for essentials whom Deakin, the paper's foreign editor and an aquaintance of the father's, regarded genially as 'a chip off the old block'. When Philby returned briefly to London towards the end of May 1937, a few days after the Coronation of King George VI, he called on Deakin and left Printing House Square an accredited representative of a newspaper which many foreigners still wrongly thought of as the mouthpiece of the British Government. It was a pardonable error, especially in the middle and late thirties. Geoffrey Dawson, the *Times* editor, then produced something less than a journal of record. Lord Northcliffe had said long ago: 'Dawson is naturally pro-German. He just can't help it,' and for that reason had dismissed him in 1919. *The Times* had changed hands on Northcliffe's death in 1922, when Dawson was restored to favour by its new owner, the anglicized American millionaire Lord Astor, whose elder brother, the second Viscount Astor, happened also to be the proprietor of the *Observer*. Geoffrey Dawson 'wrote his own terms', securing complete freedom of expression.

'I do my utmost, night after night, to keep out of the paper anything that might hurt their [the Germans'] susceptibilities,' he informed his Geneva correspondent, H. G. Daniels, in May 1937.[8]

Philby, now one of Dawson's war correspondents in Franco Spain, probably owed that distinction to one of the better despatches he had filed as an industrious freelance after his narrow escape from the Civil Guard major in Cordoba and his subsequent meeting with Burgess. Entering Guernica with the victorious Nationalist forces on 28 April, he reported on the scenes of devastation. Two days earlier, the alleged destruction of the town by German aircraft had provoked cries of outrage all over the western world at the brutal and insensate slaughter of helpless civilians. The skilful propaganda machine handled by Willy Muenzenberg worked overtime, and the only contradictory voice heard above the din was the cool, calculating and contrary voice of Philby in *The Times*:

> It is feared that the conflagration destroyed much of the evidence of its origin, but it is felt here that enough remains to support the Nationalist contention that incendiaries on the Basque side had more to do with the razing of Guernica than General Franco's aircraft. . . . Few fragments of bombs have been recovered, the façades of buildings still standing are unmarked, and the few craters I inspected were larger than anything hitherto made by a bomb in Spain. From their positions it is a fair inference that these craters were caused by exploding mines which were unscientifically laid to cut roads. In view of these circumstances it is difficult to believe that Guernica was the target of bombardment of exceptional intensity by the Nationalists or an experiment with incendiary bombs, as it is alleged by the Basques. . . .

Philby had cause to feel jubilant. His pro-Franco, propagandist explanation of Guernica's destruction satisfied partisans of the Right until, some thirty years later, it was finally and authoritatively disposed of by Hugh Thomas's history of the Spanish Civil War. His controller had been right all along in urging him to strike a pro-German pose. What better protective camouflage could a probationer agent have wished to hide behind than a British national institution like *The Times*? Masking thoughts and feelings came easily to him, and as the tide of battle slowly turned in Franco's favour, so Philby's worth in the eyes of Dawson and Deakin increased. His reports from the front were often stilted and sometimes verbose, as if he felt obliged to adopt an old-fashioned style for an old-fashioned newspaper whose views he privately abhorred. Before the end of 1937 he had twice interviewed the Generalissimo himself. An expense account of £50 a month enabled him to live in comparative comfort, although he did not mind roughing it, or even risking his neck, whenever the prospect of getting a scoop presented itself. The dangers, of course, were relative. Perhaps the gravest was that of being caught by his Nationalist hosts in the act of passing on information to his Soviet friends. Circumstances had changed since Krivitsky's flight to Barcelona, early in November 1936, when Krivitsky's mission was

> to put my agents in Franco's territory under the orders of [Russian] staff officers in charge of [Republican] military operations which General Berzin [another Russian] was secretly directing. I thought that the information I was receiving from the rebel zones would be more useful in Madrid and Barcelona than in Moscow. General Akulov [Krivitsky's subordinate] had organized our secret intelligence service in the enemy's camp most efficiently. Our radio operatives there were working without interruption. . . .[9]

This secret network for transmitting military intelligence was, according to Krivitsky, remotely controlled from Lisbon and Hendaye. Some of Philby's English-speaking colleagues, including Sam Pope Brewer of the *New York Times* and Karl Robson of the *Daily Telegraph*, noticed how searching were the questions Philby asked at press briefings. Generalizations did not interest him; he wanted the names, numbers and strength of formations. And within the limits of security and censorship, he also appeared keen to prise out information about reinforcements and the direction of the next push forward. The Spanish press officers, notably Luis Bolen and Pablo Merry del Val, the son of the distinguished ambassador in London, did not resent the inquisitiveness of the man from *The Times* whose pro-

Nationalist sympathies they took for granted. Mildly anglophile themselves, they also liked him. Philby carried off his deception without stirring the least suspicion. His journalistic acquaintances ribaldly assumed that his eagerness to discover the minutiae of campaign planning was inspired by the heart rather than the head. For he had already acquired a glamorous mistress, Lady Frances Lindsay-Hogg, a divorcée who insisted on retaining her title and who looked on the Civil War as a theatrical spectacle arranged for her private benefit.

She had formerly starred on the London stage herself in light comedies by Noël Coward and Ivor Novello, and still exuded the frivolous, carefree spirit of England in the twenties. Her maiden name was Frances Dobie; as the spoiled daughter of a Canadian banker, she had found fulfilment in the wild social whirl of the Bright Young Things. On the strength of a former friendship with the exiled King of Spain, she claimed to be a wholehearted Royalist, hailing Franco as the champion who would restore Alfonso to his throne. Philby was too calculating ever to surrender his heart to such an impulsive and passionate woman. He merely pretended to do so and meanwhile extracted all the fun he could out of the *affaire*. She thus became a comma in the tangled tale of his life, never an emotional full stop. He derived extra satisfaction from showing off his lover to jealous or critical colleagues; and Frances, a stranger to self-conscious embarrassment, often occupied the passenger seat of his big, open car as he drove in state past the crowded cafés of whichever city the zigzag course of battle drew them towards.

During lulls in the fighting, they were often seen together in Salamanca. There Philby met Peter Kemp, a rare specimen among recent Cambridge graduates in that his Tory opinions caused him 'to view Communism and Fascism with equal loathing'. Kemp had volunteered to serve with Franco in November 1936, enlisting first with the Carlist cavalry as a trooper, then transferring to the Spanish Foreign Legion. Such chance encounters between acquaintances from the same college were usually much less civilized. In the fierce fighting on the Ebro front, for instance, 'two Trinity men, Malcolm Dunbar, Chief of Staff of the XV

International Brigade, and Peter Kemp were fighting each other on opposite sides . . .'.[10]

Regardless of differences in political outlook, the English-speaking journalists behind Franco's lines formed an outrageous little clique of their own. It was during that lull which brought him on leave to Salamanca that Kemp noticed the shocked looks of the earnest German military observers sitting at a large adjoining table in the dining room of the Grand Hotel:

At a smaller table near by sat the newspaper correspondents, among them Randolph Churchill, Pembroke Stevens, Reynold Packard and his wife, and Philby of *The Times*: Churchill's clear, vigorous voice could be heard deploring with well-turned phrase and varied vocabulary the inefficiency of the service, the quality of the food, and, above all, the proximity of the Germans at whom he would direct venomous glances throughout the meal. 'Surely,' he exclaimed loudly one night at dinner, 'there must be one Jew in Germany with enough guts to shoot that bastard Hitler.'[11]

If, as is not unlikely, any member of the British Secret Service was watching Philby at this time, no tentative approach was made to him. The Germans were less circumspect. One of their agents, introducing himself as Major von der Osten, spent a good deal of time and money entertaining the politely self-contained man from *The Times*, in the hope, as Philby put it, of recruiting 'a lady of my acquaintance' for personal and espionage services. However, though Philby eventually repaid the lavishness of his host by arranging an assignation, 'she turned him down indignantly on both counts and his manner to me became distant'. Apart from preferring her diffident but sincere Englishman, Frances drew the line at spying for Nazi Germany.[12]

After two quiet and satisfying months in her company at Burgos, Franco's administrative capital, Philby went forward again to cover one of the bloodiest battles of the war. It began in arctic temperatures round the walled town of Teruel on 15 December 1937. The place changed hands twice, the Republicans seizing it on 8 January and holding on until the Nationalists forced them out on 20 February. Peter Kemp thought himself lucky to come through unscathed:

All day we marched and fought under a hot sun. At night we lay down to sleep in the snow, often without blankets or even greatcoats, which we had to leave behind, and without fires, which would have betrayed our position to the enemy. Daylight would usually reveal the stiff corpses of two or three legionaries who had died of cold in the night.[13]

Philby missed death by inches on the last day of the old year of 1937, when he went to the front with a party of pressmen. The two cars in which they travelled were spotted by a Republican artillery outpost, and shells presently began to explode around them in the village of Caude. One shell hit the ground with a terrifying crash next to the second car in which Philby sat, smoking his pipe, with Edward Neil of Associated Press, Richard Sheepshanks of Reuters and a *Newsweek* photographer called Bradish Johnson. The fifth man in the party, Karl Robson, more prudent than his colleagues, had already got out to take cover behind a barn with some Nationalist soldiers. The shattered car stood barely visible through the billowing black smoke. Robson wrote:

Then Philby came running across the road. Blood trickled brightly from his forehead, down his face, on to his clothes. 'They're in there', he shouted, pointing to the second car. Sickeningly I saw three figures, with grotesquely blackened faces, lolling motionless in their seats. . . . When the door was opened, Johnson tumbled out dead. Sheepshanks, who had been sitting next to Johnson, was breathing in quick, deep snores, his temple torn open, and consciousness gone for ever. Neil was sprawling in the back. . . . Philby had been incredibly lucky. His head wounds were not serious.[14]

Next day, with a fresh bandage round his head, Philby celebrated his twenty-fifth birthday at Saragossa, where Frances fussed over him solicitously. The favourite son of the Nationalist press office was next recommended for a decoration; and Generalissimo Franco received him personally once more on 2 March, this time to confer on Harold Adrian Russell Philby the Red Cross of Military Merit.

Only a week before, on 23 February 1938, there had been

disapproving murmurs on the Labour benches of the House of Commons in London, when, on behalf of Communist MP Mr Willie Gallagher, a question was addressed to the Prime Minister. It implied that the British Government's attitude to this English war correspondent's award was ambivalent. Had not the ghoulish Franco offered it? And was it not true that the egregious 'Mr H. A. R. Philpot' had been only too happy to accept it? Had this Mr Philpot been authorized to do so? The reply by Mr R. A. Butler, the junior Foreign Office minister who spoke on Chamberlain's behalf, must have given sardonic satisfaction to the man from *The Times* and his Soviet superiors. 'I assume,' said Mr Butler, 'that the Hon. Member is referring to Mr H. A. R. Philby serving with General Franco's forces. I have seen in the press a report of the award of a medal by the Spanish Nationalist authorities to this gentleman. Mr Philby has not sought and has not been given any official authority to accept the distinction in question.'[15]

The last effective stand of the Republicans on the Ebro dragged on from July to November 1938, and readers of *The Times* could have inferred from the reports regularly filed by Philby, all unsigned in accordance with tradition, that it would be only a matter of time before Franco forced his Republican enemies to surrender. The Spanish Civil War had produced its expected crop of Trinity College martyrs among the dead of the International Brigade. John Cornford had fallen the day after his coming of age on 28 December 1936. Julian Bell, whose disillusion with Communist fraudulence prompted him to say in a farewell letter to the poet C. Day Lewis, 'revolution is the opium of the intellectuals – pseudo-revolution', had since been killed driving an ambulance. David Haden-Guest, who had served as a schoolteacher in Moscow out of disinterested Marxist zeal, also laid down his life, as did many thousands of others less well known and unknown. Philby may have secretly honoured his old comrades as fellow warriors who had made the supreme sacrifice, but how he viewed the confessions of the Bolshevik leaders marked down for liquidation by Stalin in the current purges is doubtful.

According to Krivitsky, who became the first senior Bolshevik spy to defect to the West in mid 1937, Stalin's intervention in Spain had one primary aim – 'and this was common knowledge among us who served him' – namely,

> to include Spain in the sphere of the Kremlin's influence. . . . The world believed that Stalin's actions were in some way connected with world revolution. But this is not true. The problem of world revolution had long before that ceased to be real to Stalin. . . . He was also moved, however, by the need of some answer to the foreign friends of the Soviet Union who would be disaffected by the great purge. . . . His failure to defend the Spanish Republic, combined with the shock of the great purge, might have lost him their support. . . .[16]

The last and most fruitful achievement of the Comintern before it was swallowed up by the increasingly powerful KGB had been to promote the revised Stalinist policy of the Popular Front. From 1935 onwards, Communists in the democratic nations obediently dropped their former opposition to elected governments and fell in line, most noticeably in the France of M. Léon Blum, with the non-Communist Radical parties. The Spanish conflict and the Comintern's strident anti-Fascist and pro-Popular Front campaigning diverted some attention, but by no means all, from the State Trials of Kamenev, Zinoviev, Yagoda, Bukharin, Radek, Tukhachevsky and the other Red Army generals, not to mention uncounted numbers of lesser 'Trotskyite' victims. Few escaped the reckoning. Krivitsky and Muenzenberg put off the hour, the former by escaping with French assistance to the United States, the latter by ignoring repeated summonses to Moscow. Both men were soon to die in suspicious circumstances, almost certainly at the hands of Stalin's execution squads abroad, Krivitsky on American soil and Muenzenberg in France after the military débâcle of 1940.

By a turn of misfortune, Arthur Koestler, an active member of Muenzenberg's 'inner circle', had been captured in Malaga on his second visit to Spain and instantly recognized by Luis Bolen, the Nationalist officer in whose esteem Philby ironically now stood so high. Koestler's period of confinement in a Spanish death cell imperceptibly sapped his faith in Communism; but Koestler's crisis of the spirit was of less relevance in 1937 than the well-orchestrated campaign of protest against the capital sentence pronounced by Franco on this almost unknown 'Liberal' journalist. The outcry, of which the condemned prisoner knew nothing, was particularly clamorous in Britain. It resulted in Koestler's release in exchange for a beautiful hostage held by the Republicans, Señora Haya, the wife of one of Franco's best fighter pilots. There now began a period of intense bewilderment for Koestler. It was enhanced by the contrast between his much-publicized escape from a firing squad and the silent liquidation of many friends in the Soviet Union without a single bleat of protest from the freedom-loving West. This paradox, which haunted Arthur Koestler, lay far beyond the experience or the comprehension of Philby, Maclean or Burgess. Compared with Koestler, they were wide-eyed, trusting neophytes and dupes for whom Stalin, their God, could do no wrong. Koestler has written:

> That the innocent victim happened to be a disguised Communist was, of course, not known to the public. But this ironical twist to the affair was equally characteristic of the days of the People's Front. . . . The men of goodwill of that era fought clearsightedly and devotedly against one type of totalitarian threat to civilization, and were blind or indifferent to the other. Such one-sidedness is perhaps unavoidable; it seems to be almost impossible to mobilize public emotions for an ideological two-front war. . . .[17]

The paradox etched itself more sharply still on Koestler's mind when he went back to London for several months and became acclimatized. He had good leftist friends on the Liberal *News Chronicle*, Norman Cliff, its foreign editor, and Philip Jordan and Willie Forrest, two of its correspondents, among them. He met and made others during his stay. The atmosphere was altogether different from the air of 'conspiratorial cunning' he had breathed for so long in continental Europe as an undercover agent of revolution:

By force of contrast, England appeared an island of innocence where plotting was confined to memories of Guy Fawkes and to Victorian melodramas, and where fair play was taken for granted even by members of the ridiculously small and provincial Communist Party. To be a Communist in disguise in Shepperton, Middlesex, with a retired naval officer for a neighbour whose daughters came over for tennis and tea on the lawn, seemed as grotesquely out of place as the proverbial Yankee at the Court of King Arthur. Fortunately I was never asked either in public or in private, except on one occasion, whether I was a Communist. . . . The exception was Katharine, Duchess of Atholl . . . President of the Spanish Relief Committee and dedicated to the cause of the Loyalists. . . . A Conservative by conviction, she often spoke for Spain on the same platform with Ellen Wilkinson, the Socialist, and Isabel Brown, the Communist. . . . At our first meeting she asked me whether I was a Communist . . . I had no choice but to answer 'No' out of a constricted throat; she said: 'your word is good enough for me'. . . . I was lunching with Katharine Atholl in their house in Chelsea when the Duke, a tall figure bent by age, shambled into the room, wagged a finger at me, remarked, 'You naughty boy, you are leading Katharine into bad ways,' and shambled out again.[18]

Like the Hungarian-born Koestler, the English author and radical, George Orwell, had meanwhile returned from Spain. Wounded while fighting in the ranks of the Catalonian workers' militia, the breakaway Marxist POUM, Orwell was vigorously denouncing its cold-blooded suppression by the Soviet secret police who controlled and ran Republican Spain virtually as a Russian colony. Unlike Koestler, Orwell lacked the synthetic crown of a near-martyr snatched from the jaws of death, so that his condemnation of Communist totalitarian savagery in and around Barcelona fell on disbelieving ears, whereas Koestler's milder criticism caused much embarrassment to the Party faithful in Britain. Not that this Marxist-turned-sceptic really cared: the more he saw of them, the firmer grew his belief that the majority of British Communists were 'cranks and eccentrics', closer to 'the Pickwick Club than the Comintern'.

Though Koestler cannot recall having met the ubiquitous Guy Burgess at this time, the latter certainly knew Otto Katz, a vividly audacious Czech whom the British Home Office had recently placed on their black list of undesirable aliens. Katz belonged to that small 'inner circle' round Muenzenberg from which Koestler was at last quietly disengaging himself; and it was Katz who acted as the link between Burgess, a fairly frequent visitor to Paris, and his influential homosexual friend Edouard Pfeiffer, who was again in a position to pass on useful information to Burgess about the restored Daladier Cabinet's mounting difficulties and anxieties. These Burgess would hand over to three different paymasters: the director of the Conservative Research Department, Sir Joseph Ball, who three years earlier had turned down Burgess's application for a job but was now finding him a source of useful intelligence from France; the British Secret Service; and, of course, Burgess's Soviet mentor.

Ball's involvement with Whitehall sprang directly from the Prime Minister's mistrust of the Foreign Office, and in particular of Vansittart, the permanent Under-Secretary, who was a tiresome yet unwearying advocate of resistance to the dictators. In addition, Sir Horace Wilson, nominally the Chief Industrial Adviser to the government, had by now become 'Chamberlain's closest adviser on practically everything, especially foreign affairs, and had more influence than many members of the Cabinet'. Ball was working behind the scenes for Wilson, Burgess for Ball, to bypass the usual Foreign Office channels in the interests of Chamberlain's policy of appeasement. Yet Wilson himself was no natural intriguer: 'he had enormous talents, a pure personality and a *sancta simplicitas* in foreign affairs', the ousted Vansittart later said of him. 'His winning ways captured S[tanley] B[aldwin] from me and spellbound Neville Chamberlain with whom he shared incomprehension of such ugly ideas as mine.'[19] Burgess, who dealt only with Ball, a man of coarser grain than the uncomplicated Wilson or the bleakly honest Chamberlain, took a cynical view of these pointless intrigues. He described to his journalist friend, Tom Driberg, the letters he carried from Daladier to the British Prime Minister as 'the communications of a confused and panic-stricken patriot to an ignorant provincial ironmonger'.[20] Nevertheless, he did not disdain the thirty pieces of silver, multiplied by three, which came from sharing out his services.

His superiors at the BBC were, of course, unaware of such extra-mural activities. They continued to regard him favourably as an energetic, creative producer, if one who tended openly to deride the Corporation's sacred rules of political balance and non-controversial utterance. When Reith, the founding father, suddenly departed from Broadcasting House in June 1938, Burgess was as unimpressed as the disgruntled Reith by the BBC Governors' inept choice of a successor. Recognizing that the new Director General, a University administrator called Sir Frederick Ogilvie, would not exactly set the Thames on fire, Burgess became increasingly restless. Austria had recently been annexed by Hitler; Czechoslovakia was already being threatened; yet, like a cobbler, the BBC stuck religiously to its last, seeking always to give the least offence to the greatest number. Konrad Henlein, the pro-German Czech leader, had visited London earlier in June; and Burgess, by wangling a temporary job for Jack Hewitt, one of his steady boy friends, as a telephone operator at the hotel where the visitor was staying, kept a check on all calls to and from Henlein and duly notified his various clandestine contacts.

With the exception of Churchill and his small band of followers, the bulk of the ruling Establishment supported Chamberlain's personal diplomacy at the height of the crisis over Czechoslovakia. The Prime Minister's adviser, Sir Horace Wilson, wrote a revealing note about the attitude of Montagu Norman, the long-serving Governor of the Bank of England and an admirer of Dr Hjalmar Schacht, the President of the Reichsbank:

> I did not see much of Mr Governor during the summer of 1938 but I remember that he was in sympathy with Neville Chamberlain's policy of trying to see whether Germany could be brought to reason, and he sent me a message of goodwill when it was learnt that I was to accompany the Prime Minister on his flight to Berchtesgaden to meet Hitler....[21]

Chamberlain correctly anticipated public apathy in Britain by contending that Czechoslovakia, 'a faraway country of which we know nothing', did not represent a genuine British interest, could not be defended, and therefore must be prepared to make concessions. Besides, the British armed forces lacked the weapons of war; rearmament, throttled back to the deliberately slow pace of economic recovery on the old, orthodox lines, was still in perilously low gear; and by mid September the nerve of the French Cabinet snapped. It was all very well for Daladier to advise that 'entry of German troops into Czechoslovakia must at all costs be prevented', when Chamberlain already knew (by courtesy of Ball and Burgess) that four out of ten French ministers favoured surrendering tamely to Hitler's demands.

The hapless mood of Chamberlain's political critics filled Harold Nicolson's diary entry for 19 September 1938. It read in part:

> Go to see Anthony Eden. I find him in the depths of despair. . . . We talk of what small comfort it is to have been proved right, and how terrible is the influence of the Cliveden set. As I leave him he says, 'Well, we shall not be able to avert war now'. . . . My heart is no lighter and my anger no way diminished as I make my way to the BBC. I am met by Guy Burgess and deliver my talk in a voice of ironic gloom. I then go to the Café Royal with Guy, where we meet James Pope-Hennessy [an author and homosexual friend of both] who is almost in tears over England's shame.[22]

The British people woke up with a start to the imminent perils of another unsought war. They followed the Prime Minister's next dramatic flight to Bad Godesberg, and then, after ten days of almost unbroken suspense, to Munich. Trenches were hastily dug in the London parks, sandbags propped against government buildings, the few available modern anti-aircraft guns trundled into the open. In more senses than one, Sudetenland was definitely Hitler's 'last territorial demand in Europe'. It looked as if the Führer had pushed Britain to the very brink of the abyss; and Chamberlain realized that the Führer knew how badly Britain lacked the strength and the will to repel him. Churchill, still excluded from office, implored the Prime Minister to mobilize the Fleet as a precaution; for once the Prime Minister responded positively. Harold Nicolson, the sole National Labour MP in the isolated Churchill group, accompanied Burgess to the BBC on 26 September to listen to a ranting speech by Hitler, then to broadcast his own desperately constructive commentary on the strength of its peaceful passages. In countless ordinary box-like homes throughout the land, British people sat with ears glued to their box-like radio sets. The calm BBC news kept them abreast of crisis developments; and Nicolson's commentaries, produced by Burgess, continued at intervals until the ecstatic hours of popular relief that marked the Prime Minister's return from Munich.

The acclamation of Chamberlain's statesmanship, though heartfelt, gave rise to doubtful second thoughts. Could the scrap of paper signed by the Prime Minister and the Führer be honestly regarded as a solid guarantee of 'peace for our time'? Until the end of that last year of precarious hope, an increasing number of Tory backbenchers and Labour and Liberal critics of the Munich settlement noticed that, whenever disputes occurred over the redrawing ot the new Czech frontiers, the disputes were invariably settled in Germany's favour. War had not been banished, merely postponed. At the BBC, Burgess was chafing under cautious restrictions imposed on producers and speakers alike. The relevant section of Nicolson's diary for 23 November ran:

> I go to the Reform to have a talk with Guy Burgess who is in a state about the BBC. He tells me that a technical talk by Admiral Richmond about our strategic position in the Mediterranean (which had been definitely announced) was cancelled as a result of a telephone message from Horace Wilson to the Director General. This has incensed him, and he wants to resign and publish why. I urge him to do nothing of the sort.[23]

It was the second time within a month that the BBC had tried to thwart Burgess. The first of his efforts to expose the limitations of British power in the face of Fascism almost succeeded against all the odds. The microphones of the BBC, a public service monopoly, were evidently less free from official pressure on its bureaucratic controllers than those self-important controllers liked to pretend. Burgess had recently gone down to Chartwell in the hope of persuading Winston Churchill not to cancel his contribution to the series on 'Aggression in the Mediterranean'. Having originally agreed to be the opening speaker, Churchill changed his mind after the Munich betrayal. Burgess swore that he would 'change it back', and he nearly succeeded. Driving down to the country home in Kent of the one British politician he still admired with the romantic half of his mind, Burgess found Churchill in the grounds, trowel in hand, carefully laying bricks on an orchard wall he was building.

They spent several hours together, discussing the Munich crisis and the darkening future ahead. The old warrior apparently warmed to the sympathetic and articulate conversation of his guest. For as Burgess prepared to leave, Churchill took down from his shelves a leather-bound edition of his recently published speeches, entitled *Arms and the Covenant*, inscribed the fly-leaf, handed the book to Burgess and said, 'If I ever return to a position of responsibility and you wish to help me, just bring this book along. I shall not forget.' It was not an offer that Burgess would ever be encouraged by his Soviet friends to follow up; but he would dine out on his one meeting with the disconsolate Churchill for the next ten years, silencing doubters who discerned his Walter Mitty streak by showing them the kindly, handwritten inscription in that book. It also gave him momentary pleasure to irritate his superiors at Broadcasting House with one of his rare memos, expressing wonder at Winston Churchill's charge that, virtually from its inception, the BBC had consistently 'muzzled' him.[24]

Burgess resigned from the BBC at the end of 1938, but it cannot yet be confirmed whether he left under a cloud. The Royal Archives at Windsor Castle can be scrutinized by *bona fide* researchers, just as most British Cabinet documents are open to inspection under the thirty-year rule; the BBC, however, adheres to peculiar regulations of its own. These were no doubt worked out after long, nervous deliberation and are still enforced with high-minded if somewhat anachronistic fairness. The rules prescribe that no first-hand evidence on the professional worth and personal qualities of any former servant can be divulged to outside historians.[25] Regardless of how the BBC judged the character of Guy Burgess, a London magistrate had to consider a case brought against him by the police shortly after the young man's triumphant visit to Churchill at Chartwell. The defendant was accused of having improperly solicited another man in a public lavatory. The plaintiff claimed that, while minding his own business, a suggestive note had been pushed under the partition of his compartment. Burgess denied this, asserting that the note had come the other way, disturbing him as he browsed over *Middlemarch*, one of his favourite George Eliot novels. The charge was dismissed on grounds of insufficient evidence, but the unpleasant publicity left the accused feeling momentarily ill-used.

Feigning outraged innocence came as naturally to Burgess as the kind of needless bravado he exhibited at this time to friends with whom he lunched one Sunday at a Chinese restaurant in the unfashionable East End of London. Suddenly excusing himself from the table, he walked out, crossed the street, stood for a second in front of a seedy seaman's outfitters that was closed, removed an envelope from his jacket, slipped it through the letterbox, returned, and resumed the conversation without turning a hair. Some twelve years later, when the same friends pointed out the place to an official of the security services, they learnt that the letterbox was one of several known 'drops' for Soviet agents.[26] In 1938, MI5 was unhappily less alert to such bare-faced transactions. Besides, whether or not the BBC was happy to see him go, Burgess had already been offered a job in the War Office as a propaganda expert. Sir Joseph Ball thus rewarded his freelance, who now prepared to fight Hitler with words. His Soviet mentor must have been delighted if mystified, especially in the aftermath of that recent court appearance.

Once again the 'old boy network' was heedlessly looking after its own. Burgess, as usual, did not conceal his homosexual appetites, returning from a winter break on the French Riviera with a handsome ex-public schoolboy who forthwith joined the domesticated Jack Hewitt at the Chester Square flat. Trust, the right academic and social background, and evidence of clubbability and good fellowship were criteria enough; so Burgess was enrolled without questioning. No positive vetting procedures then existed. Nothing was recorded against him. After all, one or two of his contacts in MI5 and MI6 had tipped him off about a colleague called Colonel Laurence Douglas Grand. This military engineer, who later reached the rank of Major-General in charge of Fortifications and Works, had recently been detailed to set up Section 'D' (for Destruction), an experimental War Office branch for training both propagandists and saboteurs to wreak havoc behind enemy lines, on the model of the fifth columns in Spain. The colonel gladly took on Burgess.

Donald Maclean, quietly reinforcing his reputation for soundness at the Foreign Office, had been posted to the British Embassy in Paris at the end of 1938. So far he had done little beyond discussing with Burgess such first-hand reports as came his way in the course of duty. Now his chance to serve the cause more adequately was beckoning. During the early months of 1939, Burgess visited Philby again at Saint-Jean-de-Luz. The war correspondent of *The Times* listened, doubtless with a touch of envy, to his collaborator's hilarious account of his entry into a new branch of the secret service. It was at least gratifying to learn that their Soviet controller expected him, the war-weary Kim, to worm his way in also as soon as possible. Since the Munich crisis, there had been signs that Stalin was cutting his losses in Spain. Two-thirds of the country had been occupied by Franco, whose government was formally recognized by Britain in February 1939. Contrary to the impression given elsewhere that Philby's increasingly frequent journeys to Hendaye and Saint-Jean-de-Luz were for the practical purpose of transmitting vital intelligence in safety, the fact was that Franco's victory had made Philby superfluous; and that victory could no longer be disguised in the fog of war.[27] Krivitsky's network, like Krivitsky himself, had gone scurrying out of business months before. In the Golf Hotel and the Bar Basque, Philby could merely seek confirmation of what he himself, Walter Duranty, Alan Moorehead, and other correspondents on both sides of the line already knew: Franco ruled. It was all over bar the mopping up.

Philby reluctantly stayed on in Spain for *The Times* to cover the mopping up and the unconditional surrender of the Republicans. Colonel Casado's *coup d'état* in Madrid against the Communist puppet régime of Negrin failed in its prime objective of paving the way for a negotiated peace with Franco. The Spanish Communist leaders moved out in the wake of the Soviet 'advisers'. The rank-and-file diehards, conveniently held in jail by Casado, were finally handed over to the victorious Franco and shot. The ruthless purges after the cease-fire sickened the man from *The Times*, but Philby never let down his guard until he left Spain in August 1939. His Spanish assignment over, he enjoyed the last three weeks before the outbreak of a bigger conflict among the fleshpots of Paris. His devoted Frances impatiently awaited his return to her father's villa on the outskirts of Saint-Jean-de-Luz. It is to be feared that she awaited him in vain. Not that Lady Frances, a creature of some resilience, proved inconsolable: she merely reproved him for thoughtlessness when they were briefly reunited some months later.

Philby's quandary was deep when he read in his newspaper on 22 August that Ribbentrop had accepted a sudden invitation to Moscow. British and French delegates, he knew, were still locked in negotiations with the Russians after weeks of inconclusive talking. What could that strange move signify – surely not some patched-up arrangement between Stalin and Hitler? The swift signing of the Nazi–Soviet Pact stunned him. Like a delayed-action bomb exploding beneath his feet, it seemed to make mincemeat of everything he had schemed and striven for since his probationary recruitment as a Cambridge undergraduate. Gradually he collected himself and shook off doubt. Perhaps his Soviet contacts in Paris succeeded in squaring the dialectical circle, explaining away the significance of this marriage of convenience between heaven and hell in appropriate Marxist terms, and possibly even reminding Philby that, for him, there could be no going back. If they did so, as is not unlikely, his compliance must have flattered them, although Malcolm Muggeridge hit the nail firmly on the head by commenting that 'Kim's allergy to nearly all things intellectual and spiritual almost certainly immunized him against deep worry. He was one of nature's original cavemen.'[28]

What can be affirmed is that the Soviet Union's pledge to stay neutral if Germany became involved in hostilities, as well as the

Nazi–Soviet agreement to carve up Poland along mutually acceptable lines, had a far less traumatic effect on Philby than on Burgess, who learnt the incredible news while sunning himself on a French Mediterranean beach. Driving northwards through the night like a man demented, Burgess was so confused on reaching Boulogne that he abandoned his car on the quayside, caught the boat train to London, took a needless taxi from Victoria to Ebury Street, a bare two minutes' walk away, and called on Goronwy Rees. 'You're lucky to find me in,' said Rees. 'I've volunteered for the Army and will be off shortly.' He had never seen Burgess looking so pale, dejected and agitated. They had a desultory discussion about the Soviet *volte-face*, and Rees could not resist taunting his friend for having backed a loser. 'Maurice', that fellow agent whom Guy had originally mentioned by name, seemed to have turned over a new leaf. At any rate he, too, had volunteered for military service and was on a special War Office intelligence course. Rees suspected that in his distress Burgess was sorely tempted to renounce Communism and whatever dark deeds of skulduggery he had performed for the cause in the past.[29]

6. THE CONFIDENCE TRICKSTERS

I must confess to the most profound distrust of Russia. I have no belief whatever in her ability to maintain an effective offensive, even if she wanted to. And I distrust her motives, which seem to me to have little connection with our ideas of liberty, and to be concerned only with setting everyone else by the ears. . . .[1]

So Chamberlain had privately noted on 26 March 1939, less than a week before announcing that Britain and France would guarantee to assist Poland against outside aggression. The duplicity of Molotov and his subordinates during the languid negotiations with the French and British delegates in Moscow had been of a high order, but the subsequent bombshell of the Molotov–Ribbentrop agreement shocked many thousands of left-wing intellectuals in the Western democracies. Resignations from the Communist Parties of Britain and France multiplied, especially after the declaration of war; and the anguish of an intelligent but volatile undercover agent like Burgess was understandable. Marxism, once so much in vogue, was suddenly out of favour. Patriotism, until recently something worse than Dr Johnson's 'last refuge of a scoundrel', had become a virtue again.

This swift transformation of mood did not make life easy for British Communists, overt or covert. Their morale crumbled at once. A nation at war could not tolerate enemies within the gates, even if the war had an unreal, trance-like quality which belied the public apprehensions that Hitler would at once deliver a knockout blow from the air. If that private note by Chamberlain, quoted in part above, had been published at the time he wrote it, there would have been loud and indignant protests from the Left. Indeed,

John Maynard Keynes had admitted in an interview with Kingsley Martin, the editor of the *New Statesman*, on 28 January 1939:

> There is no one in politics today worth sixpence outside the ranks of liberals except the post-war generation of intellectual Communists under thirty-five. Them, too, I like and respect. Perhaps in their feelings and instincts they are the nearest thing we now have to the typical nervous nonconformist English gentlemen who went to the Crusades, made the Reformation, fought the Great Rebellion, won us our civil and religious liberties and humanised the working classes last century.[2]

To do him justice, Keynes had always been critical of Marxism as such. It was the youthful Marxist intellectual who appealed to his romantic instincts. Yet, as T. E. B. Howarth has underlined, the Marxist economists at Cambridge – notably Pietro Sraffa, Richard Kahn and Joan Robinson – had earlier contributed to Keynes's revolutionary masterpiece, *The General Theory of Employment, Interest and Money*, by their regular dialogues with him at weekends, though the Keynesian recipe came too late to galvanize Britain's slowly reviving economy.[3] In any case, a house-keeper as old-fashioned as the then Chancellor of the Exchequer, Neville Chamberlain, would have spurned it. Now Keynes had taken on war-time duties at the Treasury as a special adviser, and was human enough to be flattered when that redoubtable pillar of financial orthodoxy, Montagu Norman, eventually invited him to become a director of the Bank of England.

Despite Churchill's belated presence in a government from which he had been excluded for so long, not even his aggressive spirit could alter the soporific character of the 'phoney war'. As First Lord of the Admiralty his hands were already full; only at sea did Britain sustain losses and have any serious fighting to do from September 1939 until the humiliating Norwegian campaign in April 1940, which precipitated Chamberlain's downfall and Churchill's rise to power. After the early rape of Poland by Hitler and Stalin in turn, an eerie and protracted lull settled over the western front. The British Expeditionary Force of two divisions had crossed the English Channel and lined up on the exposed north-eastern flank beyond the point where France's Maginot Line ended. The foreign editor of *The Times* had no hesitation in sending Philby, perhaps the most seasoned war correspondent on the staff, to cover a battle zone in which the two sides stood poised for months on end, watching, waiting and seldom opening fire in anger. It was an extremely tedious assignment, enlivened only by occasional visits to Paris, by hard drinking, and by the laborious efforts of imagination required to turn trivia into the more solid fare suitable for readers of the august newspaper he served.

Unlike Burgess, Philby had no qualms about Stalin's unexpected about-turn. If Soviet Russia had entered this pointless conflict as an ally of Britain and France, there might have been cause to question the sanity of his masters in the Kremlin; as far as Philby was concerned, they had behaved not cynically but realistically. He had expressed this view strongly and unhesitatingly to the badly shaken Guy Burgess on several occasions, imploring his friend to pull himself together and not swallow the soggy propaganda of the government. Philby did not care a rap how many pseudo-Marxists were running off to join the forces and do their bit for King and Country in what Stalin defined as 'an imperialist war'. People of that sort donned and doffed convictions like clothes. The cause would be better off without them. Nevertheless, Kim was more bothered about Guy than he appeared. He warned him in the end to close his mind to defeatist thinking. There could be no going back now on their joint commitment to serve the cause through bad times as well as good: that would merely expose them to something worse than passing doubts. They parted on good terms, Philby setting off for France with his fingers crossed.

Fortunately, Burgess adroitly glossed over his own unforgivable indiscretion in having blurted out the name of their fellow conspirator, 'Maurice', to Goronwy Rees. Nor did Philby realize that Guy had not stopped dropping broad hints to other intimates about his inner anxieties. The very idea of Burgess wrestling with his conscience reduced them to tears of laughter. Later, however, when Rosamond Lehmann heard that Guy had been driven to the stage of throwing in his hand as a Soviet agent, she could no more decide than could Rees whether he had ever *been* one. Was he not already in some hush-hush job at the War Office? Surely somebody there must have checked on his past, however murky, before recruiting him?[4]

The trouble with Burgess was that his doubts about Soviet policy became inextricably entangled with an almost manic anxiety not to lose the respect of his intellectual friends. Most of them had airily renounced their left-wing views without a struggle and seemed unable to comprehend why he did not automatically follow suit. They were strangers to that 'sanctity of doubt' which his favourite savant, E. M. Forster, preached. Equally they appeared to set less store than Forster or this muddled Marxist disciple of his on the importance of personal relations. Burgess had been so moved by Forster's revealing article in the *London Mercury* a few months previously that he would recite parts of it to anyone within earshot:

> One must be fond of people and trust them if one is not to make a mess of one's life, and it is therefore essential that they should not let one down. They often do. Personal relations are despised today. They are regarded as bourgeois luxuries, as products of a time of fair weather which is now past, and we are urged to get rid of them, and to dedicate ourselves to some movement or cause instead. I hate the idea of causes, and if I had to choose between betraying my country and betraying my friend, I hope I should have the guts to betray my country. Such a choice may scandalise the modern reader, and he may stretch out his patriotic hand to the telephone and ring up the police. It would not have shocked Dante, though. Dante placed Brutus and Cassius in the lowest circle of Hell because they had chosen to betray their friend Julius Caesar rather than their country Rome. . . .[5]

Philby, alas, would never understand the emotional tug-of-war that placed the Marxist Burgess at odds with the aspiring aesthete. Whether their Soviet mentors would have understood is even more questionable, though Ignace Reiss, whom Walter Krivitsky would not betray, preferring instead to defect to the West, was a Soviet agent opposed to the practice of blackmailing or coercing his informants: 'If for some reason a good source of information dried up, or a collaborator refused to work, Ludwik [Reiss's alias] used to quote an old saying, "The Lord giveth, the Lord taketh away, there is no use crying over spilt milk."'[6]

Burgess, no doubt wisely, did not take the risk of confessing to his Russian friends that he was tempted to apostatize. He learnt to live with his doubts, cultivated his friends in the spirit of Forster, and fed his mentor with any scraps of useful classified material he could lay hands on at work. Not that Section D had much to offer; Colonel Grand's experimental unit was still in embryonic form and growing slowly because it stood low in war-time priorities. Since his War Office duties were vaguely defined and unexacting, Burgess had ample opportunity to indulge his fetish for 'personal relations' under cover of the rigidly enforced nightly blackout. When John Strachey, perhaps the most potent of upper-middle-class Communist propagandists during the thirties, finally broke with the Party in 1940, he began to see more and more of Guy Burgess. According to Hugh Thomas, Strachey's biographer and the historian of the Spanish Civil War,

> for a time Strachey stayed with [his wife] Celia's mother who had always liked him and later, briefly, at the house of Lord Rothschild, 5 Bentinck Street, with, among others, Guy Burgess and Anthony Blunt. . . . With Burgess he had endless political discussions, though Burgess's espionage was concealed from him; nor did he join Burgess on his wild raids through the blackout of war-time London, in the company of Brian Howard, in search of delectable youth. Burgess did, however, leave Strachey one lasting benefit: a concern for music of which he had previously been ignorant: Burgess lived in a perpetual atmosphere of Mozart and late Beethoven quartets, and Strachey profited from that.[7]

This was the Britain, cautiously playing at warfare, which Evelyn Waugh immortalized in *Put Out More Flags*, with Brian Howard mincing his way in the character of Ambrose Silk through scenes of exquisite farce, reflecting the garish hollowness of this 'flashy amateur of modernism in all forms, including fashionable left-wing political opinions . . .'.[8] That Silk's political opinions had lately ceased to be fashionable detracted little from the realism of Waugh's caricature, since nearly every feature of Brian Howard himself was dated. Unlike Burgess, whom Waugh never encountered but would certainly have detested just as much had he done so, Howard had no other goal in life except self-indulgence;

and the nine uneventful months of what Churchill later described as 'the twilight war' enabled both men to indulge their appetites to the full.

There were few casualties on land or in the air during the monotonous period of the phoney war. The first British soldier to die on the open front, which ran along the French frontier skirting Belgium, fell in one of those limited reconnaissance 'pushes' that helped to relieve the tedium of waiting. Inactivity was the norm. The troops accepted it with stolid indifference, often wondering how long the waiting would last. Their commanders were just as much in the dark. Writing letters home, whiling time away at darts and football, or listening to popular programmes beamed by the BBC with their quota of repetitively escapist songs of good cheer like the one which promised

> We're gonna hang up the washing on the Siegfried Line,
> If the Siegfried Line's still there.

For Philby and other war correspondents, those nine months were fruitless and almost unbearably tedious. Their censored reports from the front were thin, unreal and trifling. In seeking to dispel malicious enemy propaganda that morale was suffering, the Allied High Command seemed to act as a mere extension of the British and French Information ministries, lulling everyone into a drowsy, false security.

Philby had no clear idea what would happen if and when the Germans attacked, but the inside information he had gleaned from Burgess suggested that the French lacked the equipment and the stomach for fighting. Donald Maclean, whom he met in Paris during a short leave from British General Headquarters at Arras, seemed to share the same low opinion of the French. Maclean was already justifying the confidence of his superiors by his customary willingness, acuteness of mind and thoroughness. The youngest of the dozen or so permanent members of staff at the British Embassy, he cut a dashing, Hussar-like figure at official receptions, in contrast to the raffishness of his dress and habits during off-duty hours. His bachelor flat was conveniently placed within walking distance of the Soviet Embassy, but it is most unlikely that any personal business he had to transact with inmates was ever transacted there. As a regular habitué of crowded haunts like the Café Flore and the Deux Magots in the Latin Quarter, he found it easier to arrange a rendezvous among the motley crowd of artists, students and voluble intellectuals. This 'general dogsbody' at the British Embassy, whose appetite for work enabled him to collect odd crumbs of intelligence dropped by trusting or condescending senior colleagues, passed on what little he could without fail. No doubt Soviet officials had access to a variety of French political and military secrets through experienced 'place-men' such as Burgess's associate, Edouard Pfeiffer; but their hunger for corroborative material seemed inexhaustible. Maclean responded dutifully by serving both masters with zest.

His private life became suddenly complicated in December 1939, some twelve months after his arrival in Paris, when an American drinking companion, a writer called Bob McAlmon, introduced him at the Café Flore one snowy evening to a girl who had already caught Maclean's eye several times before. Melinda Marling was her name; she was an American. She smiled prettily, talked well, and smoked big Havana cigars, an affectation which Donald found as touching as her shyness. His infatuation with this *petite*, waiflike creature, four years younger than himself, was instant and overwhelming. She lived next door to the Café Flore in the Hôtel Montana; and having monopolized her all one evening, he escorted her home that night. They were often seen together after that, a virtually inseparable couple who seemed quite carefree in their affection for one another. Melinda, who was spasmodically taking an external course in French literature and art at the Sorbonne, lived on an allowance from her mother and looked up to Donald as a paragon of learning and worldly wisdom. On the other hand, she gradually discovered his two most obvious weaknesses: the first, an urge to drink himself into a stupor when depressed; the second and more repelling, a desire, in that condition, to consort with homosexuals. This darker side of his otherwise attractive personality both scared and puzzled her. During the spring of 1940, Melinda went off alone for a holiday in the South of France and wrote to him: 'If you do feel an urge to have a drinking orgy, why don't you have it at home – so at least you'll be able to get safely to bed? Anyway, do try to keep young P. from completely demolishing your apartment.'[9]

To what extent Melinda was aware that Maclean's excesses might be connected with the mental strains of leading a double life on the official level remains a matter of conjecture. He seldom discussed politics, and then only in an offhand and rather cynical way. That he felt personally responsible for her future happiness she had no doubt; yet she lightly rejected his proposal that they must get married because of an underlying uncertainty about his motives. Though Melinda was now pregnant, she could not agree that this awkward fact alone sufficed to bind them together for a life of possible unhappiness. His strong sense of Calvinist propriety did not impress her. For the moment Melinda chose to leave Maclean in suspense.

The phoney war ended with cataclysmic abruptness on 10 May 1940, when the Germans attacked and rapidly advanced through neutral Holland, Luxembourg and Belgium, driving an armoured wedge between the unprepared Allied armies. The tactics of surprise and mobility, coupled with overwhelming air support, turned 'planned withdrawals' into creeping rout. 'Hitler has missed the bus,' Chamberlain had declared smugly on 4 April, a few days before Hitler's forces seized Denmark and Norway, frustrating the ill-coordinated British attempt to dislodge them. After a heated post-mortem at Westminster on the Norwegian débâcle, Chamberlain dithered for a little longer, then resigned.

The gravity of the hour demanded resolute and defiant leadership. Churchill, swept to power almost by acclamation, rallied his own nation but came too late to save France from the military disaster already engulfing her. The British Expeditionary Force in turn was effectively cut off. Most of its obsolete support aircraft had been destroyed; the race back to the Channel ports had begun. The ancient port of Dunkirk became the scene of an almost miraculous deliverance. Churchill ordered the rescue of 'the maximum force possible' from its exposed beaches, since Calais and Boulogne had fallen. An armada of little ships, braving the attentions of German dive-bombers, lifted nearly 340,000 men to safety, many of them French, between 27 May and 3 June.

An army had been saved to fight again, perhaps soon on English beaches; but stragglers and civilian refugees abandoned on French soil could expect no such brilliantly coordinated operation to save them. Floods of fugitives poured down the high-roads from Paris towards Bordeaux and the Spanish frontier. For most, the chances of escaping seemed very slender. Rumours of atrocities, fifth columnists and indiscriminate terror-bombing were rife. One can well appreciate the curious predicament of Donald Maclean, who stayed on in Paris with Melinda still anxiously trying to persuade her to accept his hand in marriage. She held out until it became plain that her own survival might depend on a positive answer. Only then did she relent. They went through the normal formalities, and on 10 June 1940, with the sound of distant gunfire drumming in their ears like approaching thunder, they walked together to the Mairie of the Palais Bourbon District, opposite the deserted Chamber of Deputies. They came out man and wife. Melinda hurriedly explained in a letter to her mother:

> We decided very suddenly because it seemed to be the only chance.... One is no longer allowed to travel without an impossible reason.... This was our last opportunity as God knows how long war will last.... darling, I am terribly in love with Donald and am sure there will never be anyone else.... We are not rushing blindly into it.

Quite naturally, Melinda did not mention her condition. Nor did she admit that Donald's constant harping on the pregnancy as a perfectly sound reason for going through with the wedding had almost prevented it. Instead, she hinted tactfully: 'My greatest desire is to have a baby while I am home as I am dying to have one and I couldn't bear to have it without you. Wouldn't it be wonderful, Mummy?'[10]

There was no time for celebrating. At once the Macleans set off in a friend's car heading for the south-west. They crawled slowly across the plain towards the spires of Chartres, spending the first night in a field by the road. The French Government had already moved to Bordeaux. The British Embassy had followed, and Maclean duly reported his arrival after what seemed an interminable journey. The couple even managed to spend two relatively peaceful days away from the chaos in an isolated village near Biarritz. When Donald returned to his desk in a makeshift office, he learnt of the French capitulation and turned his mind belatedly to the complex problems of arranging the emergency evacuation of many thousands of stranded British civilians.

Not until 23 June did the Macleans escape on a British destroyer. From its side they were transferred at sea, with other refugees, to the deck of an empty tramp steamer on its way back to Britain after delivering coal to Latin America. The home voyage lasted ten days, for the captain sailed north and west on a zigzag course to avoid the attentions of U-boats and long-range aircraft. Food and water aboard the overcrowded ship were scarce, but the Macleans' delight at escaping unscathed buoyed up their spirits. Realizing that the dilatory letter she had posted to her mother in Paris might never get through, Melinda's first act on their arrival in London was to send a cable with the news that she was now Mrs Donald Maclean.

It was not the most auspicious season for Nazi or Soviet agents, however well hidden, to go about their underhand business. The public mood in Britain, chastened by the recent military catastrophe, had been uplifted by the spirit of indomitable defiance that animated the Prime Minister. Throughout the ominously golden summer of 1940, while vapour trails were traced across the blue sky high over Kent, Sussex, Surrey and London, and the outnumbered Hurricane and Spitfire pilots of RAF Fighter Command took a steady toll of the German bombers, the British continued to hope for the best and to prepare for the worst. Apart from the Nazis, probably the least popular and most despised individuals in the land were members of the Communist Party. Churchill, with his long-held aversion to their creed, believed that 'Soviet-inspired Communism' had been largely responsible for the rapid deterioration of the French Army. He urged his Cabinet that 'very considerable numbers' of British Communists as well as Fascists and aliens 'should be put in protective or preventive internment, including the leaders'.[11] Though the Cabinet had compromised, ordinary citizens tended to regard all Communists as traitors. It was hardly surprising that Philby, Burgess and Maclean had little option but to lie low.

As 'sleepers' they could secretly console one another. They could also help to build for a better future by offering to help one another. This Burgess did with promptness when, still under the stimulus of Churchill's early enthusiasm for a bigger counter-terrorist effort, Colonel Grand was authorized to expand Section D. Philby received an unexpected telephone call one day in June 1940 from the War Office. Ignoring the well-intentioned advice of his foreign editor, Ralph Deakin, not to be so foolish as to leave *The Times* just yet, Philby went off to keep an urgent appointment in the foyer of a small hotel, the St Ermin's in Caxton Street, with a shrewd, middle-aged spinster called Marjorie Maxse. She sized him up thoroughly, asking questions, listening to his answers and generally assessing whether he measured up to her mysterious requirements. Once having got over the mild shock of encountering such an unexpected War Office intermediary, Philby felt at ease and acquitted himself to Miss Maxse's satisfaction. This authoritative lady commanded him to return to the same place at the same hour some days later. On the next occasion she did not arrive alone. Guy Burgess accompanied her. Like an honest broker, he had volunteered to come along and confirm or contest the good opinion Miss Maxse had independently formed of Philby's credentials:

I was put through my paces again. Encouraged by Guy's presence I began to show off, name-dropping shamelessly as one does at interviews. From time to time my interlocutors exchanged glances; Guy would nod gravely and approvingly. It turned out that I was wasting my time as a decision had already been taken. Before we parted, Miss Maxse informed me that, if I agreed, I should sever my connection with *The Times* and report for duty to Guy Burgess at an address in Caxton Street, in the same block as the St Ermin's Hotel. . . . I decided that it was my duty to profit from the experience of the only secret service man of my acquaintance. So I spent the weekend drinking with Guy Burgess. On the following Monday, I reported to him formally. We both had slight headaches.[12]

The suspicious ease of his entry into what proved to be a Cinderella branch of the Secret Intelligence Service made Philby wonder whether Burgess, to whom nothing was sacred, had lured him into the wrong organization as an elaborate practical joke. Guy, however, reassured him, introduced him to Colonel Grand and other colleagues, loosely described the history, aims and objects of Section D, but genially acknowledged that never since its birth in March 1938 had Section D carried out a single deed of derring-do, successful or otherwise. Their business must be to improve on that.

So uncoordinated and at variance were the overt and covert agencies of propaganda, before Churchill reformed them, that Burgess, with Colonel Grand's approval, had become a familiar figure at meetings of the mysterious Joint Broadcasting Committee, JBC, a Foreign Office-sponsored body which the BBC distrusted and tried hard to resist. 'I am sorry to appear persistent about the JBC problem,' J. B. Clark, a senior BBC executive had written as early as January 1940, 'but there is increasing evidence to show that their growing activities are bound to trespass on what we regard as the BBC monopoly.' Unable to keep his fingers out of this pie, Burgess used his technical knowledge of broadcasting to make life increasingly difficult for the prim men at the BBC. The JBC enjoyed ample funds, facilities and authority to produce its own recorded propaganda programmes in competition with the blander official output of the BBC. 'Sound pictures' of current happenings were sent to Hungary, Bulgaria and Yugoslavia; weekly 'news-flashes' to Argentina, talks on women at war to France.[13] All this was tame stuff, however, compared with some of the far-fetched schemes for frustrating Hitler at a stroke with which Burgess regaled staider colleagues at meetings, especially after the German military machine had overrun and conquered France.

Section D, the misbegotten child of a complacent secret service, designed to emulate Franco's 'fifth column' behind enemy lines, was expected to plan sabotage as well as propaganda. Regardless of the conflicts of interest between gathering intelligence and letting off bombs, between silent infiltration and noisy participation in a war of words, Section D carried on until it thoroughly discredited itself. Once, in the high summer of 1940, the opinionated Burgess was listened to in astonishment at a liaison session by a future star of the Special Operations Executive (which soon replaced Section D), Bickham Sweet-Escott:

> There was one boiling July afternoon when, with dogfights between the RAF and the Luftwaffe going on over our heads, Guy Burgess, who I believe was then employed by Electra House, nearly convinced the meeting that the way to end the war was to wait for a westerly wind and then send off large numbers of balloons in the direction of Central Europe, hoping that incendiary bombs attached to them would set the cornfields of the Hungarian Puszta on fire and starve the Germans out.[14]

In theory, there was much to be said for a policy of subversion in German-occupied Europe. In practice, the British Chiefs of Staff and the armed services could think of other and more pressing ways of spending public money, especially as Hitler's plans for mounting a full-scale invasion across the English Channel were being completed. Nothing daunted, Burgess, under whom Philby was now working, produced a draft scheme at the beginning of July 1940 for schooling agents not yet recruited in the techniques of underground sabotage. He argued that the plan warranted the setting up of a special training centre, named 'Guy Fawkes College' after the conspirator 'who had been foiled by the vigilance of the Elizabethan SIS'. Philby bent his mind to providing details of the training syllabus, the procedure for selecting trainees, the security aspect and the scale of equipment and accommodation required. Like a man who has seen a vision, Colonel Grand seized on the idea as if it were a marvellous strategic novelty. Committees were formed to discuss the pros and cons. Finally, to everyone's delight and amazement, the Chiefs of Staff approved the scheme and the Treasury grudgingly advanced the credits. Before the Battle of Britain reached its critical point, a former private school, Brickendonbury Hall, was commandeered. Standing in its own extensive grounds not far from the town of Hertford, this building became for the next few weeks the centre of Philby's closed world.

The commandant of the new establishment was an alert, kindly naval officer, Commander F. T. Peters. Somewhat to Philby's disbelief, he took a liking to Burgess, whose father he had apparently once known. The commandant repeatedly entertained both young men to dinner at his favourite restaurant in Soho. Soon the training staff was increased by the acquisition of explosive experts, foreign propaganda specialists, and Tommy Harris, an art dealer without military qualifications whom Burgess promptly signed on with the commandant's blessing 'as a sort of glorified house-keeper because he and his wife were inspired cooks'.[15] Caxton Street sent down a batch of Spanish, Belgian and Norwegian pupils as prospective guinea pigs, then lost heart or interest. Colonel Grand, it presently appeared, was already too busy fighting off bureaucratic attempts to bury him or take over his anomalous little empire to which, according to Whitehall purists, he had no title. Philby and Burgess bit by bit perceived that they were part of a very awkward squad.

When Churchill invited Dr Hugh Dalton, the Minister of Economic Warfare, to reorganize the sparse and diverse units then charged with planning sabotage and propaganda, the good doctor undertook to carry this extra burden without demur. Little did he foresee how furiously other ministers would squabble for equal rights to shoulder the blessed load. In Dalton's own words:

> This was a new instrument of war and I should be responsible for shaping it. . . . I accepted the Prime Minister's invitiation with great eagerness and satisfaction. 'And now,' he exhorted me, 'set Europe ablaze'. . . . I realized from the start that my relations with the Foreign Office would be both delicate and important. Halifax [the Foreign Secretary] consented – and I appointed Gladwyn Jebb [private secretary to Cadogan of the Foreign Office] to be my chief executive officer, and lodged him, with a very small headquarters staff for SOE in Berkeley Square House. . . .[16]

The new Special Operations Executive, SOE for short, was divided into two branches. Subversion and sabotage came under SO1; undercover propaganda under SO2. It looked simple enough on a diagram; it boded ill for the underworked, listless staff of 'Guy Fawkes College'. The laconic commandant enjoyed passing to Philby, for polishing, the drafts of queries, requisitions and so forth addressed to Colonel Grand; but Grand seldom favoured Peters with anything but evasive replies. In fact, the hapless colonel was increasingly uncertain of his own future as he watched the brickbats fly to and fro between the tetchy Dalton, the unctuous Lord Halifax at the Foreign Office, and the stubborn Duff Cooper at the Ministry of Information. This disunited Trinity could not agree on their respective areas of responsibility. 'Set Europe ablaze,' Churchill had told Dalton; but Duff Cooper claimed that half the box of matches belonged to him, while Halifax demurred at wanton acts of arson for arson's sake. Not only, he asserted, would such acts upset some of the London-based European governments-in-exile, but they might even disturb the post-war world by playing into the hands of extremists. Dalton afterwards confessed:

> There was inevitably a conflict of jurisdiction between myself and successive Ministers of Information. They were responsible for 'overt' propaganda, but there could be much argument as to where the dividing line should run. . . . My relations with Duff Cooper were sometimes rough . . . with Brendan Bracken [Cooper's successor] they were stormy.[17]

Not that this high-level wrangling deterred Dalton's new executive brooms from sweeping away deadwood within his undisputed area of control. The ominous silence of Grand, and the growing restiveness of Peters the commandant, gave sufficient warning. Characteristically, Burgess pooh-poohed the misgivings of Philby and continued to spark off exotic ideas. At their country retreat they saw little evidence of that other battle: the conflict in the skies to the south and east between Goering's Luftwaffe and the dwindling, exhausted pilots of RAF Fighter Command. The enemy's failure to knock out the radar stations and vital sector airfields forced Hitler to postpone the invasion attempt. Instead, the nightly blitz on London and other cities had begun. On an evening in the late summer one of the more imaginative inmates of 'Guy Fawkes College' let out a piercing yell. Others took up the cry in their various languages. The first witness clearly infected the rest with his eloquent powers of persuasion. For all swore that they had seen parachutes descending, though the exact number could not be vouched for. Peters, nursing an attack of eczema, ordered the Belgians to put on their uniforms and stand by a machine gun. The commandant then returned to bed, glumly informing a visiting instructor with whom he had been drinking: 'If the Germans have invaded, I'll get up.'

His one tactical error was to authorize Burgess to verify what had happened and ring up the duty officer in London. To quote Philby, 'Guy went about the business with a wicked conscientiousness.' Refusing to distinguish between the credibility of witnesses, he merely reiterated that parachutes had indeed been sighted. Exact numbers? The duty officer could take his pick – any number from eighty to nought. The excitement wore off as darkness fell. Next morning, however, Burgess resumed his telephoning to gauge how much dislocation and unfounded alarm had been caused by his firm evasiveness the night before. It appeared that Grand had been roused from sleep, Grand had alerted the War Office, the War Office had alerted Eastern Command, and the tanks of Eastern Command had rumbled uncertainly to their battle stations. At Brickendonbury a search party eventually found a single parachute. It was attached to an unexploded landmine, jettisoned from an enemy bomber, and it had been caught in the branches of a tree.

The incident would not have raised the stock of Guy Burgess in the much-tried colonel's eyes had Grand stayed long enough to conduct his own enquiries. But Grand came under the axe first, moving on in time to higher things; and tight-lipped visitors from Dalton's Special Operations Executive called more than once on Peters, asked curt questions, inspected the premises and facilities, and departed. The commandant composed a letter of resignation. Before long he would be back at sea; within eighteen months he would be dead. It is true, as Philby stated, that Peters was awarded a posthumous VC for outstanding valour in capturing Oran Harbour from Vichy France. Nonetheless Captain Peters VC did not die in that action but in an aircraft accident on the way home afterwards.[18]

The commandant remained at 'Guy Fawkes College' long enough to supervise the melancholy details of disbandment. Tommy Harris thought it all a shocking disgrace, then vanished for a while to reappear in MI5. The trainees dispersed to other units. Burgess and Philby reported to the headquarters of the firm that had taken them over, SOE, at 64 Baker Street, where nobody paid them any attention except for inquisitive members of the Marks and Spencer staff on the floors below. Then Burgess, who had recruited Philby in the first place, suffered the ignominy of being sent for and fired without explanation.

'One evening Guy dropped in for a drink in an unusually tongue-tied condition', his friend noted. 'Finally it came out; he had fallen "victim to a bureaucratic intrigue", by which I understood he had been sacked.'[19] Philby, virtually the sole survivor of the abortive venture at Brickendonbury, felt certain that he would be next. He was mistaken. Such are the improbabilities of fortune that the service kept paying him monthly, in cash, without troubling to provide either work or an office. Finally he was sent for by SOE's new and impressive director of training, Colin (later Major-General Sir Colin) Gubbins, who evidently did not believe in beating about the bush.

'Do you know anything about political propaganda?' he asked crisply.

'Yes, sir,' lied Philby.

'Right. Let's put you in the picture then.'

The picture was big and ambitious and in need only of the finishing touches. Its centrepiece, the main SOE training establishment at Beaulieu in Hampshire, was short of an instructor in underground propaganda techniques. From Beaulieu, recruits were hived off into one or other of a whole range of smaller, specialized units to become thoroughly proficient in the various black arts of subversion. Gubbins asked Philby to come back in a few days with a clear outline of a propaganda training syllabus.

'Make it short,' he said, showing Philby out of the office.

With some prompting from acquaintances in the advertising world, Philby produced a concise plan which Gubbins and a handful of colleagues looked over without a cheep of criticism. Beaulieu might be less attractive than London to a person with 'other interests'. SOE might not be the same thing as the secret service for which Burgess had recruited him with such high and misplaced hopes; but the calculating Philby still had a foot in the door.

Guy Burgess had meanwhile suffered another slight setback, though not without leaving some red faces behind at the Ministry of Information, the security services, and the higher reaches at the Foreign Office. His quixotic conduct also caused passing annoyance to Sir Stafford Cripps, the recently appointed British Ambassador to Moscow, to Harold Nicolson, and to Sir Isaiah Berlin, the Oxford savant whom Burgess tried to use as the mainspring of an ingenious confidence trick which very nearly succeeded. The decision to send Cripps, that high-minded left-wing Socialist of puritanical outlook and tastes, as his country's envoy to the Soviet Union was in itself a mistaken one.

'We did not at that time realize sufficiently,' Churchill later admitted, 'that Soviet Communists hate extreme Left-Wing politicians even more than they do Tories or Liberals. The nearer a man is to Communism in sentiment, the more obnoxious he is to the Soviet unless he joins the party.'[20]

The announcement of Sir Stafford's appointment not long after Churchill had formed his all-party war administration gave Burgess an idea. The Cripps mission would not be easy. No inexperienced ambassador could hope to achieve any success unless he had first-class, hand-picked aides. These men must have a sound working grasp of what the Soviet Union was up to, and their chief function would be to allay Russian hostility by convincingly interpreting Britain's war aims to the rulers in the Kremlin. Burgess eagerly unfolded this simple proposition to Harold Nicolson, whom Churchill had lately honoured with the minor post of Parliamentary Secretary to Duff Cooper, the overlord of the Ministry of Information. Nicolson mulled over the Burgess scheme. He confessed that it had merit; he liked it; and he promised to refer it upwards. Furthermore, he saw nothing wrong with the two names mentioned almost casually by Burgess for the two vacancies he had in mind: the first was Isaiah Berlin as press attaché; the second, of course, was Guy Burgess, who would be seconded from the War Office for 'special duties'.

Perhaps the breathtaking cheek of the proposal, reinforced by its author's high-pressure salesmanship, took in Harold Nicolson. At any rate, to the immense delight of Burgess, Duff Cooper raised no objections and Lord Perth professed to see much in its favour.

The hardest part was to overcome the suspicions of Isaiah Berlin, a forceful personality of perception who immediately smelled a rat. Burgess insisted that the scheme had the highest backing. He could think of nobody else in Britain with better qualifications for the role of press attaché to Cripps than Berlin, a native of Czarist Russia, a scholar versed in the muddy byways of politics and philosophy, and an acute student of human nature. But this Fellow of New College was also used to the flattering tongue of Guy Burgess, whom he had known fairly well for several years. The young Englishman could be amusing and companionable, yet his conversation had to be sampled in small doses because, in Berlin's judgement, it lacked the true flavour of originality. Moreover, when war had broken out the year before, Whitehall had refused Berlin's offer to help the country in any way he could. An unfeeling clerk had written to say that the country did not require the services of someone of alien birth. That slight had rankled.

At last, after much reflection, Isaiah Berlin swallowed the bait and agreed to accompany Guy to Moscow. Confirmatory letters were exchanged, the usual formalities completed. Then there followed one of those long, unaccountable silences beloved of administrators the world over; it lasted almost until the end of that fateful summer of 1940. Burgess himself was in no hurry to set off on a second wild goose chase while still enjoying with Philby and company the thrills and spills of a first. For though he did not believe that 'Guy Fawkes College' would survive the jealous scrutiny of its bigger rival, SOE, he clung on tenaciously, and revived the Berlin–Burgess–Cripps venture only when SOE let it be known that Brickendonbury would soon be closed.

Perhaps a measure of inspired desperation enabled Burgess to hoodwink Nicolson, Duff Cooper, Halifax (through Lord Perth) and his own War Office superiors, now that circumstances had freed him to fly to Moscow with Isaiah Berlin, via Washington, San Francisco, the Pacific and Vladivostok. He had a drink with Goronwy Rees and other incredulous outsiders about this time, swore them to secrecy and regaled them with hints of the next instalment of adventure opening up before him. The fact that Harold Nicolson had warned him weeks ago that there would be no call for Burgess to take on 'special duties' in Moscow was a petty obstacle hardly worth considering. Nicolson had noted in his diary on 29 June 1940: 'Guy Burgess comes to see me and I tell him there is no chance now of his being sent to Moscow.'[21]

By holding Isaiah Berlin as his trump card, and playing off one Ministry against another, persuading the War Office that the Foreign Office wanted *him* to go as well, dissembling to Nicolson, and committing nothing officially to paper, Burgess contrived to secure the cash and essential clearances without difficulty. He departed with his Oxford protégé on a VIP flight to the United States before the end of September.

The expedition did not get very far. The two men reported first to the British Embassy in Washington. A day or two later an urgent message arrived for them. The press counsellor, Stephen Childs, informed Burgess with regret that he would have to return home on the next available aircraft. The Foreign Office had belatedly heard from Sir Stafford Cripps, who strongly opposed Berlin's appointment. Sending him would be a waste of public money, since Cripps had never been consulted and sternly resented this attempt to foist unwanted people on him. He did not want Isaiah. As for the other person purportedly required to carry out 'special duties', Cripps wanted him still less. So a crestfallen Burgess flew back to London, leaving a somewhat peeved Berlin with the invidious choice of following at leisure or of staying on to help Stephen Childs with a specific task. After several weeks of sifting through American agency reports from London to detect any anti-British bias they might contain, Isaiah Berlin said his goodbyes and returned to Britain in late October. Nothing had been gained by the outing; but little had been lost either, some time and public money perhaps, but not that subtle spirit of empathy on which good fellowship is founded. Harold Nicolson invited the thwarted pair to a meal. He was anxious to smooth away any misunderstanding and to make up to Isaiah Berlin for Guy's shameless treatment of them both. 'Lunch with Guy Burgess and Isaiah Berlin who is just back from Washington,' ran Nicolson's diary entry for 28 October 1940. 'There is such a sense of suspense in the air that ordinary work seems hopeless.'[22]

Sir Stafford Cripps had to press on, unsupported, with what Churchill described as his 'bleak and unpromising task'. What Burgess imagined that he could have done in Moscow, if he had ever managed to get there, nobody knew, certainly not the impenitent wangler himself. The poseur in him surmised that Stalin needed him, even if Cripps did not. Such delusions of grandeur, mixed with some apprehensiveness about a German invasion of Britain, drove Burgess onwards just as much as his perverted sense of fun. Nor had he yet shaken off his doubts about the validity of working spasmodically as an agent for a Soviet Union in league with Nazi Germany. Perhaps in Moscow he might finally have shrugged off uncertainty by helping to teach Stalin the error of his ways. It would have greatly mortified him to learn that Cripps, of all unlikely people, had already gathered from the Soviet Leader's guarded lips that the USSR, while keeping out of trouble for as long as possible, expected a German attack on Russia some time in 1941.[23]

By another embarrassing twist of coincidence, the first Soviet master spy to defect to the West had recently paid a short visit to London, at the request of the Foreign Office and British security chiefs. Ex-Major-General Walter Krivitsky, the *soi-disant* former head of Soviet military intelligence in western Europe, had settled in the United States, after breaking with Stalin in France, before the end of 1938. The American authorities had interrogated him at length, primarily about espionage methods and procedures affecting them; but it was an American journalist, Isaac Don Levine, who took it on himself to draw the attention of the British Embassy in Washington to three points in Krivitsky's testimony of paramount concern to MI5. Levine by that stage was on close terms with the Russian, whose memoirs and articles for the *Saturday Evening Post* he had 'ghost-written'. Sir Victor Mallet, the counsellor at the embassy, listened carefully to Levine's astounding statement that, according to Krivitsky, there were two spies working for Soviet intelligence who had successfully penetrated the Foreign Office in London, the first of whom he could and did name. The second diplomat was unknown to him except by hearsay, but Krivitsky's general description provided some useful clues. All that could be said about a third British agent of the Soviet Union of whom Krivitsky had also heard was that the man concerned did not work at the Foreign Office. What Krivitsky knew was merely that this unnamed person had been a journalist employed by Soviet intelligence while covering the Spanish Civil War for a British newspaper.

Mallet reported Levine's story to his ambassador, Lord Lothian. To his credit, Lothian decided that it must be treated seriously. 'As a result,' said Mallet, 'we sent to London a very detailed and secret dossier.' There can be no doubt that MI5 independently checked and counter-checked Krivitsky's evidence. They kept a watch on the one named man, Captain John Henry King of the Foreign Office, who worked in the coding department; and presently they caught him red-handed on his way to deliver a top-secret message to his Soviet contact at a tea-room in the Strand. King's trial at the Old Bailey in October 1939 was held *in camera*, as befitted the first spy of British birth to be unmasked after the outbreak of war. The judge sentenced him to ten years' imprisonment.

MI5, having trapped one agent, now showed fitful keenness in trying to track down the other two; but amid the muddles and endless distractions of the period, their concentration faltered. When Krivitsky volunteered to come across personally and throw any further light he could on the problem, the Foreign Office welcomed the offer, and the security authorities cooperated in extracting as much as possible from him. Unfortunately, his evidence about the unnamed diplomat and the mysterious journalist was second-hand and far too general to provide immediate or sure leads. Krivitsky did say that the Foreign Office man was a 'Scotsman of good family, educated at Eton and Oxford, and an idealist who worked for the Russians without payment'. He 'occasionally wore a cape and dabbled in artistic circles'.[24] Gladwyn Jebb, since seconded to Dalton's headquarters staff at SOE, had interviewed Krivitsky at some length. Jane Archer, whom Philby praised many years afterwards as 'perhaps the ablest professional intelligence officer employed by MI5', conducted a second cross-examination.

The Krivitsky file was then put aside to gather dust. It is just conceivable that Guy Burgess may have heard whispers about it. If so, it is not improbable that this can be adduced as another reason for his improvised attempt to 'beat the system' and fetch up in Moscow with Isaiah Berlin. By now, the much-tried Oxford don was in no mood to be trifled with. Resisting Harold Nicolson's blandishments, Berlin retreated to Oxford until the Ministry of Information offered him a proper contract. This duly came in 1941 when, on the strength of his earlier copy-tasting, he went back to the United States as a much-valued 'specialist'.

Guy Burgess, at a loss where to turn next, hung about the War Office for a few more weeks, then decided that he could do worse than rejoin the BBC, with a helpful push from Harold Nicolson. Walter Krivitsky, for his part, had not much longer to live. A disillusioned man he may have been, but hardly someone bent on self-destruction. A suicide note was certainly found by his body in a Washington hotel on 10 February 1941. He had been fatally shot; but Arthur Koestler was by no means alone in his conviction that Krivitsky did not die by his own hand.[25]

Whether Donald Maclean had any inkling of this Soviet defector's vague but accusing testimony cannot be ascertained, though 'the darling of the Foreign Office', as Isaiah Berlin called him, probably came to hear indirectly of Krivitsky's visit and its disturbing purpose. Maclean had settled down with tight-lipped resignation to the rigours of married existence in a capital city made hideous by the nightly blitz. He and his wife were bombed out of two flats, narrowly escaping death or severe injury on each occasion. Yet the claustrophobic experience of one wakeful night in an overcrowded underground shelter convinced Melinda that she would be better off chancing a quick if violent end in their own bed. Donald felt that, if it could be arranged, she should cross the Atlantic and go back to her mother's home for the birth of their first child. She was homesick and lonely, he was overworked and oddly uncommunicative, and Melinda did not enjoy her own company. Donald certainly put in suspiciously long hours and would often creep back after midnight, quarrelsome and always the worse for drink. She had little in common with his colleagues, their wives, or his highbrow friends of old. The strains of this abrasive relationship under abnormal conditions gradually told on them both during that first winter together; and it was with mixed feelings that Melinda parted from Donald in November 1940. She sailed in a convoy and reached her mother's home at South Egremont, outside New York, in safety. Donald proved an irregular letter-writer, though he consoled her with emphatic assurances that he missed her and longed to make up for his past neglectfulness. When the news reached him at last that Melinda's baby had been born dead, Donald Maclean wept like an inconsolable child, to the alarm of his relatives and the mystification of gayer and more cynical friends outside the office.

These were lean and anxious days for all the conspirators. Their original commitment to the Soviet cause had been one of blind faith without compensating grace. Now their commitment had become irrevocable, as their Soviet controllers had no need to stress, owing to that treacherous blackguard Walter Krivitsky. The curtailment of Captain John Henry King's career at the Foreign Office and the stiff sentence passed on him served as a salutary reminder of what could easily happen to each of them. The subtle hint of Soviet blackmail may or may not have been uncalled for. At best it would remain a useful deterrent in the background to keep the allegiance of men whose eyes had been opened at last to one of the occupational hazards of spying.

7. THE DOUBLE PATRIOTS

The massive German onslaught on the Soviet Union did not descend without warning. It greatly vexed Churchill to discover that Cripps in Moscow had dallied before handing to Stalin the British war leader's cryptic personal note of warning. Yet the Soviet dictator continued to distrust all warnings from London, Washington and even from his own 'Red Orchestra' network of agents in Switzerland, until the first crushing hammerblow fell on 22 June 1941. Many hundreds of Soviet aircraft were destroyed at once on the ground; tens of thousands of Russian soldiers were killed. Well might Churchill ruefully ponder

the error and vanity of cold-blooded calculation of the Soviet Government and enormous Communist machine . . . war is mainly a catalogue of blunders, but it may be doubted whether any mistake in history has equalled that of which Stalin and the Communist chiefs were guilty. . . . We have hitherto rated them as selfish calculators. In this period they were proved simpletons as well. . . . Thus the ravings of hatred against Britain and the United States which the Soviet propaganda machine cast upon the midnight air were overwhelmed at dawn by the German cannonade. The wicked are not always clever, nor are dictators always right.[1]

Philby hid his own anxiety with characteristic sang-froid on hearing the news, brought with the morning tea by his batman, at the Beaulieu Training Centre. In the mess before lunch that bright Sunday morning, he listened without replying to the clipped comments, mostly unfriendly, of colleagues who were as unsure as himself whether Britain would lift a finger to prevent Germany from tearing the Soviet Union to pieces. The commandant, Colonel John Munn, hit the right conventional note by remarking: 'Russky's for the high jump, I'm afraid.' At nine o'clock the same evening, the Prime Minister settled the problem once and for all in a BBC broadcast. 'We shall give whatever help we can to Russia and the Russian people,' said Churchill. 'This is no class war, but a war in which the whole British Empire and Commonwealth of Nations is engaged, without distinction of race, creed or party.' Not that Churchill sought to disguise, still less recant, his pristine detestation of Communism. His single-minded aim was to destroy Hitler, so much so that, in the words he used beforehand to his private secretary, John Colville, 'if Hitler invaded Hell I would make at least a favourable reference to the Devil in the House of Commons'.[2]

Guy Burgess, whose distant and romantic admiration for Churchill had grown since 1938 by leaps and bounds, responded as incredulously as Philby to the ironic realization that the fortunes of war had transformed them overnight into 'double patriots'. Donald Maclean's relief was equally genuine. Melinda had returned to him from the United States after her mournful ordeal, and seemed to be adjusting herself with a better grace to living conditions which she had formerly found difficult and depressing. At a time when many British women were being conscripted to work in war factories or serve in the forces, Melinda decided to take on a part-time job as a bookshop assistant in the West End of London. The fixed routine and the sight of new customers each day created an interest of a kind and stifled tedium. In the process she grew less querulous about her husband's habitual serfdom at the Foreign Office where, if Donald could be believed, exorbitant demands were made on him morning, noon and even night in the recently created General Department handling shipping, contraband and other problems of economic warfare.[3] She had no wish to impose herself on his friends, whom he would sometimes meet at his club or elsewhere on the way home. Nor did she evince much curiosity in these comparative outsiders, mostly known to her only by name, who occasionally led him to drink far more than was good for him. If it had been brave of her to return and share with her husband the austerities of existence under a siege economy, she still hoped to find stability with this often secretive man of changeable moods whom she loved in a somewhat uneasy fashion. To Melinda, as to other Americans in London, the prospects of a British victory appeared remote. Indeed, until Hitler moved his armies into Russia, a German invasion of Britain had still been considered likely. So she could appreciate Donald's new-found cheerfulness as the natural response of a British patriot to better news; at least these long-suffering people, hers now by adoption, no longer stood alone against a seemingly invincible enemy.

Yet what if Russia failed to stop the advancing Germans? Donald Maclean refused to entertain the thought of a Soviet defeat. His insistence gave her pause, especially in the early days when every war communiqué spoke of swift enemy successes and enormous Russian losses. His faith struck her as touching but unusually stubborn in face of the facts. At the BBC, meanwhile, colleagues of Guy Burgess were remarking on the same phenomenon in his glibly sophisticated appraisals of Soviet powers of resistance. 'To hell with expert opinion,' he would declaim. 'I KNOW that Hitler can't win'.[4] Maclean was an occasional visitor to the flat in Bentinck Street where Burgess stayed and almost perpetually held court. Philby was seen there also on his visits to London for official consultations. What particularly enraged Burgess was the hesitancy of the BBC as an institution to acknowledge Britain's latest ally. Burgess had been nominally reinstated as a producer in the Talks Department, where, it was remembered by contemporaries, he had shown enterprise and not a little originality during the pre-war years of Chamberlain's grey premiership. With his passion for intellectual debate, he now joined in earnest, official deliberations over such tremendous trifles as whether or not the BBC should play the *Internationale* on the air. As the historian Asa Briggs has justly commented:

> An element of farce crept into discussions inside the BBC and the Ministry [of Information] about Russia. . . . Many months of war were to pass before the *Internationale* was played. The controversy, absurd though it was, reflected the uneasiness with which many people in high places viewed the entry of Russia into the war.

On the other hand, when Sir Stafford Cripps and the best military opinion would give the Soviet Union only a few weeks' grace before being knocked out, traditional BBC caution was perhaps justifiable.

Inevitably, this policy of prudence was taken too far. As summer lengthened and faded into autumn, with Russian resistance stiffening, the Foreign Office tried to sharpen BBC sensibilities; so did the less certain Solomons at the Ministry of Information; so did Burgess with individualistic persistence. How should the BBC project the Soviet ally to its millions of listeners at home? Asa Briggs has recounted that Sir Richard Maconachie, the head of Talks, favoured material on Russian cultural achievements as against political or historical items, reaching this conclusion after consulting Lady Violet Bonham Carter, a new BBC Governor and one of Maclean's long-standing Liberal patrons, who had just been to the Soviet Embassy for a long talk with Maisky. 'Guy Burgess, also in the Talks Department, supported this view. So did Maisky, the Soviet Ambassador.'[5]

There was much inside information to which Burgess had access. He got it through his personal contacts with Harold Nicolson, who left the Ministry to join Lady Violet on the BBC board in July, and from well-placed officials in other government services, including security. This obviously strengthened his professional influence. The inclination of BBC executives, then as now, was to look nervously over their shoulders and calculate long and hard before deciding anything. But their circumstances in 1941 happened to be unpleasantly precarious. Churchill had never cared for Reith, the BBC's founding father, nor for the attitude he called 'pontifical mugwumpery', which it had inherited from Reith. In the Prime Minister's jaundiced view, Reith remained 'that Wuthering Height', a despotic and self-righteous Scot whom he had since cut down to size by offering him second-grade ministerial posts on the fringes of real power. So, in July 1941, Churchill appointed as Minister of Information his elusive friend and shadow Brendan Bracken, a versatile Irishman who had 'risen without trace', mischievously encouraging rumours that he was Winston's natural son and hailed from Australia, not Ireland.

Bracken always moved with the surefooted grace of a cat. Since the benefits of American Lend–Lease had not yet begun to work through into Britain's economic bloodstream, the mid-1941 period was one of severe financial stringency; and both the Treasury and the Public Accounts Committee were strongly critical of the BBC's combination of high spending and poor book-keeping with unchanged Reithian delusions of grandeur. The new Minister of Information set about reform.[6]

Bracken's first step was to send to the BBC a financial and administrative specialist called Robert Foot to straighten out the accounts and reorganize the executive machine. Foot forsook with some reluctance the boardroom of the Gas, Coke and Light Company, and Bracken's initial teasing was pointed: 'Your sentence shouldn't last more than three months, Foot. After that you can go back, if you wish, to your bloody gas.' Naturally, the old guard at the BBC, including Reith's honourable if faint-hearted successor, Ogilvie, tended to look askance at this interloper from the world of industry. Foot did not mind being cold-shouldered. He did mind, and skilfully resisted, attempts to obstruct him in a difficult fight against time. 'Before our appointment,' he noted, 'there is little doubt that whatever Ogilvie's personal hopes and ideas may have been, the BBC was drifting nearer and nearer to control by the government. . . .' Bracken wept no crocodile tears when Ogilvie saw the red light and departed: he wanted brisk, businesslike leadership. Yet he had little sympathy for Churchill's vindictive desire to pull down the house that Reith had built. For Bracken's underlying aim was constructive: to use a reinvigorated, better-run Corporation as a bludgeon in his political struggle to outdo Dalton. By this same means he would get a tighter grip on the so-called Political Warfare Executive (PWE), the tripartite propaganda machine which Dalton, in Bracken's view, already regarded as his own property. In theory, PWE was managed by a consortium of co-equals; but Eden, now at the Foreign Office, had neither time nor taste for in-fighting, while Bracken and Dalton could seldom agree about anything.

The disputed territory between the two ministerial adversaries offered Guy Burgess, despite his nominally lowly position in the

BBC hierarchy, ideal cover for promoting his private and professional objectives. Dalton encouraged his own 'black specialists' at Woburn Abbey in asserting their right to supervise the policy content of all broadcasts to Europe; and Burgess became one of their linkmen inside. These propagandists operated several secret broadcasting stations, using the lie as a war weapon, sometimes with remarkable effectiveness. The BBC in its transmissions to Europe scrupulously eschewed the lie and concentrated exclusively on 'white' propaganda. Bracken's main watchdog, the tough, soldierly Ivone Kirkpatrick, an ex-diplomat, rarely yielded an inch of ground to the Woburn Abbey intruders. So the bad blood between 'black' and 'white' propagandists persisted until Bracken won his way.

As often happened at moments of national crisis, the squabbling for scraps of power inside the Churchill Government reached such a pitch early in 1942 that the Prime Minister had no option but to reshuffle his ministerial team. Beaverbrook resigned in high dudgeon, after his efforts to bully Churchill into demoting Attlee had failed. The Socialist leader became deputy Premier, regardless of Beaverbrook's claim that Attlee was 'the symbol of opposition to a policy of friendship with Soviet Russia'.[7]

An indignant Reith was dismissed from his minor post of Minister of Works and Building, and Dalton was transferred from Economic Warfare to the Board of Trade, leaving the propaganda field and the spoils clear at last for the jubilant Bracken. Yet the latter's jubilation appeared premature and misplaced. There had been a litany of military disaster throughout the second half of 1941, from the Libyan Desert to Greece, Crete, the Russian steppes and all the way back to the Libyan Desert. True, the Germans had been held at the gates of Moscow by the battered and harassed Soviet forces; and the United States had finally been forced into the conflict as an ally by the Japanese attack on Pearl Harbour. On balance, however, the outlook in the Far East could hardly have been gloomier for Britain, whose two latest and most powerful battleships had recently been sunk off Malaya, a catastrophic prelude to the over-running of the Malayan Peninsula and the humiliating surrender of the army at Singapore where British naval guns, pointing the wrong way, were seized by the Japanese without firing a single shot. Compared with these demoralizing reverses, the success of Bracken's scheming to oust his main rival for the unenviable post of Britain's arch-propagandist, and set himself up as Churchill's answer to Dr Goebbels, seemed rather pointless.

The Political Warfare Executive, however, had become Bracken's political plaything. To do him justice, the minister handled it with increasing dexterity. Bracken's success in saving the BBC, first from itself and its worst defects, then from Dalton and the 'black' propagandists, persuaded Burgess to stay put. Harman Grisewood, the assistant to Ivone Kirkpatrick, was one of several senior officials of the BBC who could not make out the exact role of the insatiably curious and ubiquitous Burgess: 'We met, of course, but I can recall only one of his monologues. It was about the Vatican, and it left me with an impression of fanaticism. I remember also George Barnes' unreserved admiration for him, and Harold Nicolson's unfailing expressions of affection.'[8]

Cripps had returned from Moscow, without authorization, on 23 January 1942. His public reputation stood high, though based on a somewhat exaggerated assessment of what he had achieved; so Churchill appointed him Leader of the Commons after Cripps had refused Beaverbrook's job. Beaverbrook felt free to revert to his puckish outsider's role and backed the Communist-inspired clamour for opening a second front. Burgess took a lively interest in these political developments, as befitted a good double patriot.

One instance, described at length by Nicolson, perfectly illustrated the inspired rumour-mongering techniques on which Burgess thrived. The diarist's entry for 9 September 1942, stated:

Guy Burgess has heard from his friends who are in close touch with Cripps that the latter is so discontented with the conduct of the war that he proposes to resign. He has already sounded *The Times*, and possibly Kemsley's papers, to see if they will give him press support. Guy and I agreed that Cripps' attitude was probably wholly disinterested and sincere. He really believes that Winston is incapable of dealing with the home front and that his handling of the minor problems of production and strategy is fumbling and imprecise. We agreed also that Cripps would find the atmosphere of Downing Street (with its late hours, casual talk, cigar smoke and endless whisky) unpalatable, while Winston never regards with affection a man of such inhuman austerity as Cripps, and cannot work easily with people unless his sentiment as well as his respect is aroused.

We also agree that Cripps, who in his way is a man of great innocence and narrow vision, might be seriously unaware that his resignation would shake Winston severely, that around him would gather all the elements of opposition, and that in the end he would create 'an alternative Government' and take Winston's place. . . . [I] suggested to Guy that we should visit Violet [Bonham Carter] and tell her the whole story. She is the only outside person I know who is on terms of intimate friendship with Winston and also has the confidence of Stafford and Lady Cripps. We told her the story. She said she was in an awkward position, as Lady Cripps had taken her into her confidence and told her much the same. She could not betray this confidence, much as she agreed with our point of view. We arranged therefore that Violet would see Cripps or his wife, and ask whether she might say a word to Winston – a word of warning. Failing this, I should see Brendan Bracken.[9]

As it happened, neither Churchill nor Cripps had need of intermediaries. The two men were quite capable of dealing directly with one another, and the process had already started. Cripps tendered his resignation, Churchill persuaded him to defer it until after the Allied landings in North Africa, and in November 1942 the austere Sir Stafford left the War Cabinet and settled for the job of Minister of Aircraft Production.

In his routine duties of radio production, Burgess made practical use of his better-placed political friends to get his own way in promoting pro-Soviet causes. Nor did he shrink from playing off the Ministry of Information against his nominal BBC superiors whenever he thought it necessary. Thus he arranged a series of talks by Brian Howard, a reject freelance of the old, unreconstructed MI5, and now a uniformed aircraftman-clerk. Howard was a fairly regular visitor to the flat in Bentinck Street, where John Strachey still called, though less frequently, to pay his respects. In the words of one of his current friends, Patricia (later

Lady) Llewelyn-Davies, Strachey was 'a person *en fleur*', once he shook off his Marxist shackles. His reverence for the prowess of the RAF and its commanders at least equalled his former devotion to the Communist Party and its gurus. Yet Burgess clung to Squadron Leader Strachey for two sound reasons: first, Strachey was a fine broadcaster; and, second, Strachey not only had access to classified information on the war in the air but could usually be coaxed or goaded into talking openly about it. By 1944, Strachey's 'Air Commentaries', originally produced and inspired by Burgess, 'made Strachey's a familiar voice all over Britain.'[10] Again, on such programmes as *The Week in Westminster*, Burgess became personally acquainted with many MPs, and extremely friendly with a few who promised to be of further value to him in his role as double patriot. The Labour MP Hector McNeil, whom he had known at the BBC in pre-war days as a young journalist newly arrived from a Glasgow newspaper, instantly fell for his flattering attentiveness. So did Tom Driberg, an influential columnist and a man of much the same background, views and tastes as his own. The BBC had no secrets worth passing on to a Soviet controller; but through the contacts and friendships forged in its London studios and in the corridors of the Ministry of Information, Burgess acquired a surprising amount of incidental political and military intelligence. Moreover, as a result of his close personal relationship with such members of the security services as Anthony Blunt and Guy Liddell, his working knowledge of 'The Firm', of its plans, its preoccupations, its personnel, its strength and its weaknesses was, and remained, up to date.

Before the end of 1943, the last of Brendan Bracken's 'trouble-shooters' was brought into the BBC, to the impotent fury of Harold Nicolson. The new 'placeman' was Willian Haley, a future editor of *The Times*, who had already attained high managerial positions on the boards of Reuters and the *Manchester Guardian*. Haley, with the designation of BBC Editor-in-Chief, was expected to add a touch of breadth, courage, common sense and professionalism to programmes. Not unnaturally, the BBC Governors resented Bracken's high-handedness in failing to consult them first about the appointment. 'You may soon hear that Violet

[Bonham Carter] and I have resigned,' Nicolson informed his wife, the novelist Victoria Sackville-West. He acknowledged that Haley was 'a clever man but not at all suited to the cultural job we had in mind. To my horror the chairman of the Board informed us that he had already obtained Brendan Bracken's consent . . . and that he had got Haley to agree to take it.'[11] There were no resignations; and when Bracken's original 'placeman', Foot, gave up his post and returned to industry, Haley replaced him at Bracken's prompting, as Director General of the BBC. It was now or never for Guy Burgess to intrigue for a permanent position commensurate with the high estimate he put on his own creative talents. That Burgess did not succeed must be ascribed to the dogged independence of the shy but tough Haley:

> I was subject to repeated pressures, from inside and outside the BBC, to promote this fellow, Burgess, to a senior position in the inner council of my controllers and advisers. Being a peasant at heart, I withstood the pressures, for I took a fixed and strong dislike to the man himself. The whole business seemed to me peculiar, and I had a hunch that I was doing the right thing in standing up for myself. Eventually I was relieved to hear that Burgess had departed to better himself at the Foreign Office.[12]

Fear of Communism had been set aside in Britain for the duration, but the logic of British strategy ruled out any early prospect of that second front which Stalin started to demand during his first exchanges with Churchill in 1941, after the German failure to over-run Soviet Russia. The Prime Minister knew that no 'war of words' alone would destroy the common enemy: Hitler and his Axis allies would be toppled by force, not propaganda. On that at least he agreed with Stalin. Meanwhile, the restructured BBC was transmitting acceptable programmes to the world in forty-three languages. Its news broadcasts were reliable, helping to foster the spirit of resistance in conquered Europe and the continents beyond. Many RAF aircraft were risked, many lives lost, in supplying active, underground movements of resistance. These provided in return much useful intelligence. The hour of liberation was not yet. Apart from the costly night offensive of RAF Bomber Command, whose brief as developed by its latest Chief, the fiery Arthur Harris, with general public approval, was to carry the war to the civilian population as well as the factories of the Third Reich and thus shorten the war, no large-scale land operations could be contemplated from the beleaguered British Isles until the manpower and resources of the United States were fully available.

Roosevelt and his military advisers, as suspicious in their way as Stalin and his ideologues of any tactical diversions to prop up tottering British imperial interests, at first disliked the concept of deploying American troops in the Mediterranean theatre, then yielded reluctantly to the inexorable pressure of events. The plans for a second front were systematically prepared. Their execution had to be delayed, despite American querulousness and the well-orchestrated popular clamour in Britain for bold and instant action to help Stalin.

The bulk of Britain's fighting services, it should be remembered, were based at home from the time of Dunkirk onwards. They became an accepted part of the community; soldiers, sailors, airmen and women in uniform were a sight as familiar as firemen or civil defence workers. Convoyed troopships were sent out, of course, with necessary reinforcements for North Africa and the Far East, while ships of the Royal Navy and cargo vessels continuously ran the gauntlet of the enemy submarine campaign to keep the nation and the war machine fed. Under the leadership of Churchill, the much-tried British people had settled willy-nilly for an unavoidable form of Socialism by consent. This was dictated by the vital demands of total warfare, though the presence in Churchill's Government of able Labour ministers like Clement Attlee, Ernest Bevin, Herbert Morrison, Hugh Dalton and Stafford Cripps encouraged left-wing patriots to believe that the values of the old, class-ridden Britain were vanishing.

Recurring criticisms of Churchill for committing too many strategic blunders detracted little from his massive personal standing, for no other man could have adequately taken his place. Yet among the minority of double patriots – not only Burgess,

Maclean and Philby but hundreds of covert and overt Communists whom Stalin's revived public esteem had encouraged to reassert their Marxist faith – deeper and darker forces of discontent were already stirring. Far from allaying class antagonisms, these forces helped to stimulate and sharpen them. In the political judgement of these double patriots, Churchill and his circle were staking everything on the ultimate triumph of the Anglo-American partnership at the expense of Stalin and the Soviet Union. This 'tug of loyalties between the United States and Soviet Russia',[13] as A. J. P. Taylor has neatly described it, played right into the hands of the relatively few committed Marxists, overt and covert, who had never ceased plotting and working for a Soviet Britain.

The Communist Party boasted of tripling its open membership after 22 June 1942. Communist shop stewards in the factories followed the Party line and became strike-breakers instead of trouble-makers. Ordinary people, affected by what they heard and read, put aside their mistrust of Russian and Marxist ways. Stalin assumed a jovial, friendly image. The press called him 'Uncle Joe'. The admiration for Russian courage was genuine and widespread. Only on rare occasions did open Communists let their zeal run away with their judgement. Ironically, this happened to Douglas Springhall, by now the Communist Party's National Organizer, who was arrested, tried for espionage and sentenced to seven years' imprisonment in October 1941. This sharp reminder to all double patriots that the security authorities in Britain had not fallen totally asleep appeared to affect Maclean more acutely than anyone else. Burgess despised and mocked him for it. Worse still, just to demonstrate that blackmail could be an unpleasantly two-sided affair, he invited his Foreign Office friend to a stage-managed orgy at Bentinck Street and warned him later that he, Guy, had added to his own private collection some choice erotic photographs of Donald, taken while the latter had been lying naked and oblivious in the arms of another man.[14]

Springhall's folly baffled his comrades. They saw nothing wrong in his persuading a naïve and lonely young Air Ministry clerk, Mrs Oliver Sheehan, to hand over technical secrets on jet engines so that Britain's brave but neglected ally, Soviet Russia, might improve its chances of survival. Indeed, the only crime committed by Douglas Frank Springhall, former commissar of the International Brigade and 'cut-out' man in the talent-spotting of potential recruits at Cambridge, was to get caught. Mrs Sheehan had poured out everything when counter-espionage agents questioned her. At the subsequent court-martial of a less innocent accomplice of Springhall's, Captain Ormond Leyton Uren, this officer admitted that he had gladly passed secret military plans to his friend out of Marxist conviction.

As soon as Springhall was found guilty, the Communist Party expelled him. He had twice denied to senior colleagues that he was visiting the Soviet Embassy with material acquired by spying; yet, as Douglas Hyde, the then news editor of the *Daily Worker*, has recounted:

> He was expelled, not because the Party disapproved of his activities as such, but for two quite different reasons: first because we had no desire, least of all at that moment of growing popularity, to get the public reputation for condoning spying by our members (for this reason his wife, who worked on the *Daily Worker*, was sacked at once); second, because, viewed from any angle, it was a major indiscretion for the National Organizer, of all people, to take such risks at such a moment....

Nevertheless, Springhall's disgrace had no deterrent effect whatever on the Party faithful. As Hyde put it:

> The reaction of the average member was: 'If they won't supply the information to Russia, we will.' The spying which had gone on during the 'Imperialist' war was nothing to that which followed. The information came from factories and the Forces, from civil servants and scientists. And the significant thing to recognize is that those who did it were not professional spies, they took big risks in most cases, received no payment whatsoever, and, this is doubly important, did not see themselves as spies, and still less as traitors. As Party members they would have felt that they were being untrue to themselves and unworthy of the name of Communist if they had not done it.[15]

Guy Burgess had been known to suffer from panic but never from scruples. His Bentinck Street flat was at one and the same time a den for intellectual and social revellers and a handy centre for picking up and sorting out information of potential value to the Russians. Malcolm Muggeridge had visited the place only once, while the London blitz was raging; for, in his own words, 'once was more than enough for me'. Muggeridge was taken there by Andreas, the son of Beatrice Mayor, a cousin of Kitty Muggeridge. Tessa Mayor, Andreas's sister, who later married Lord Rothschild, happened to be a resident. Malcolm Muggeridge found the place full of the most bizarre contrasts: 'Above was the office of the *Practitioner*, in whose boardroom we lingered, seated, lordly on leather chairs, and staring at the magazine's splendidly bound volumes, before venturing below.' On the evening of this solitary visit, Muggeridge noticed among 'the displaced intellectuals' drinking in the basement,

> John Strachey, J. D. Bernal, Anthony Blunt, Guy Burgess, a whole revolutionary *Who's Who*. It was the only time I ever met Burgess; and he gave me a feeling, such as I have never had from anyone else, of being morally afflicted in some way . . . the impression fitted in well enough with his subsequent adventures; as did this millionaire's nest altogether, so well set up, providing, among other amenities, special rubber bones to bite on if the stress of the blitz became too hard to bear. Sheltering so distinguished a company – Cabinet Minister-to-be, honoured Guru of the Extreme Left-to-be, Connoisseur Extraordinary-to-be, and other notabilities, all in a sense grouped round Burgess; Etonian mudlark and sick toast of a sick society. . . . There was not so much a conspiracy gathered round him as just decay and dissolution. It was the end of a class, of a way of life; something that would be written in history books, like Gibbons or Heliogabalus, with wonder and perhaps hilarity, but still tinged with sadness, as all endings are.[16]

Muggeridge overlooked just one thing. To the outside wall of the house adjoining this 'millionaire's nest', leased for the duration by Victor Rothschild to Burgess, was fastened a blue ornamental plaque. Its legend in white lettering stated: 'Edward Gibbon, the historian, lived here.' That symbolic detail did not escape the malignant eye of Burgess, whose complicity in the British Empire's decline and fall was coming along nicely.

It would have shocked Guy Liddell, if not the impassive 'Maurice', to discover that for every sparing titbit of intelligence Burgess occasionally fed to MI5, he collected a dozen items for his friends, the Russians. Behind the façades of the numerous and expanding Soviet purchasing, supply and liaison missions that sprang up in and after 1941, Britain's Soviet ally strengthened its espionage links in London and elsewhere. It is certain that Burgess worked directly for Filip Kislytsin, one of the successors of Simon Kremer, who became the controller of the atom spy Klaus Fuchs. Nor can it be seriously disputed that Kislytsin, among others, greatly prized the contributions of Burgess. In fact, as the Russian agent was to tell a future colleague, Vladimir Petrov, shortly before the latter's defection in Australia some years later:

> The volume of material Burgess supplied was so colossal that the cipher clerks of the Soviet Embassy were at times almost fully employed in enciphering it so that it could be radioed to Moscow, while other urgent messages had to be dispatched in diplomatic bags by couriers.[17]

Having a tidier mind and a stronger will than Burgess, Philby was able to move quietly from the SOE Training Centre at Beaulieu into the secret service proper by the late summer of 1941. He could not have managed this without help; and help was generally forthcoming when he most needed it, because usually people either liked him for himself or respected him for being the son of Harry St John Philby. The fact that the father had fallen foul of the Churchill Government in its uncertain early days was certainly not held against Kim, though Kim conceived, but never showed, a deep and lasting loathing of the authorities for locking up a man whose only offence had been to tell the truth as he saw it. Since Harry St John Philby had spent his whole adult life disagreeing with the policies of his superiors, nobody had the right to be surprised, still less vindictive, at his defeatist remarks about Britain's nonexistent prospects of victory in the summer of 1940.

Philby senior's long association with the Middle East, which had begun in Iraq where he served as a political officer during the First World War, vigorously opposing the Arab solutions of T. E.

Lawrence, had ended abruptly if temporarily when the King of Saudi Arabia, Ibn Saud, took exception to his personal adviser's anti-British strictures after the outbreak of the Second World War. Earlier in 1939 this friend and consultant to the Arab ruler had tried to break into British politics, standing first as a Labour candidate at Epping, then as a 'People's Party', anti-war independent at Hythe. In both by-elections he forfeited his deposit. Smarting under these setbacks, he returned to Saudi Arabia and at once incurred the renewed displeasure of Ibn Saud by the bitterness of his attacks on the British war effort. Philby senior, who, like Mussolini, claimed to be 'always right', maintained that Ibn Saud did not banish him but that he left of his own free will. At Karachi he boarded a ship bound for the United States. However, security men moved in, arrested him and deported him to Britain. Tried under Section 18B of the Defence of the Realm regulations, he was held in detention for four months; his release came about the time his son had begun to look around for some alternative to working half-heartedly as a propaganda instructor of SOE trainees in a rural backwater.

The release of his father, far from hampering him, reinforced Kim's hopes of a speedy transfer. It was Tommy Harris, the art-connoisseur-turned-chef of 'Guy Fawkes College' days, who originally suggested that he ought to consider joining MI6. The most promising area for a keen and personable newcomer was its undermanned counter-espionage section. This was headed by an ex-Indian police official, Felix Cowgill by name, who had apparently become the *bête-noire* of MI5, the internal counter-espionage or security service to which Harris now belonged. If the absurd overlapping of propaganda efforts between the Foreign Office, the Ministry of Economic Warfare and the Ministry of Information had given rise to interminable bickering and unedifying jockeying for position at every level, the rivalries inside the closed world of intelligence were possibly even less savoury. Between the two world wars an aura of mystery and glamour had persistently clung to the British Secret Service, not only in the public mind but in the minds of Comintern and KGB agents. Since it did not officially exist, its structure and strength and title to respect could never be measured or openly challenged. This obviously protected the service; but equally it blinded ministerial overseers to any inherent or acquired weaknesses. Still, the veil of secrecy did cause Krivitsky, Ignace Reiss and other Soviet agents between the two world wars grossly to overrate its capacity. As Elizabeth Poretsky puts it:

> Unlike their British counterparts, the Soviets found [in the late twenties] they could not carry on effective intelligence work through military attachés, and were forced to build up elaborate covers; this contributed to the gradual separation between legal and illegal apparatuses, and to an increase in efficiency and security. The high repute of the British intelligence service and the fact that members of the 'best families' in Britain did not hesitate to serve it out of pure patriotism also had a tonic effect on Soviet agents. What a British patriot could do for his country – so went the reasoning – a Communist could do for the Soviet Union, only better. Soviet agents were convinced that their historic role gave them an innate advantage in dealing with world politics, that, in Bukharin's words, 'We Communists can hear the grass grow under our feet.' British intelligence agents did not reciprocate the high opinion the Soviets had of them. They appeared to consider the Soviets mere rabble.[18]

Imitation being the sincerest form of flattery, the Soviet spy network had since surpassed itself by recruiting agents from among the disillusioned sons of the British ruling class. The once envied British model had also contracted in size and scope during the inter-war years, thanks to Whitehall's tight-fistedness. Its most striking feature was amateurism. From 'C', the Chief, downwards, the Secret Intelligence Service acted on the cardinal principle that gentlemen were preferable to players in the underground world of espionage, because gentlemen could be trusted. This mystique of class superiority came as naturally to its members as breathing; that it might be a false mystique which had dangerously outlived its validity simply did not occur to anyone. Gentlemen from good, well-connected families, with the right school and military background, could be relied on to 'play the game', irrespective of the Churchillian epitaph on one of his past political colleagues: 'He always played the game – and always lost it.' The upper-crust,

Edwardian tone of SIS survived virtually intact until the eve of the Second World War, partly because of its élitist and somewhat haphazard recruiting methods, but mainly because of the long reigns of its first Chief, Captain Mansfield Cumming, and of his successor, Admiral Hugh Sinclair. Cumming held office throughout the First World War and retired only in 1929; Sinclair followed and died in harness just before the Second World War. An entry in the diary of Robert Bruce Lockhart for 16 July 1929, stated:

> Dined with Fletcher [an official in the service, a former naval officer and later a Labour MP] at the St James. He gave me a lot of information about our secret service. The head of it is now Admiral Sinclair, a terrific anti-Bolshevik, who has succeeded the old 'C', Mansfield Cumming. The new 'C' is hard up for men for Russia....[19]

The third 'C', unlike his predecessors, was a forty-nine-year-old Army officer. Lieutenant-Colonel (afterwards Major-General Sir Stewart) Menzies could rightly claim more impressive social connections than Cumming or Sinclair. An old Etonian, related through his mother to some of the oldest families in the kingdom, Menzies's first wife was a daughter of the eighth Earl de la Warr, his second the daughter of the Honourable Rupert Beckett, a banker and the proprietor of the *Yorkshire Post*. According to one of his war-time secretaries:

> Rumour had it that 'C' was himself an illegitimate child of King Edward VII. Though Menzies knew this, he made no attempt to confirm or deny it. He looked every inch the nobleman, especially when he wore ceremonial uniform or the required dress for Royal Ascot.[20]

Nevertheless, Menzies worked hard. He could astound subordinates of superior mental ability by the accuracy of his 'hunches' about problems and people. This was the man who became Kim Philby's overall boss in late 1941, thanks to the initial prodding of Tommy Harris and of a member of MI6 called Dick Brooman-White. The intervention of Harry St John Philby, whose recent release from detention had in no way diminished either his bridling self-confidence or the tolerance with which his friends of the old days in India still viewed him, also proved helpful. Had not E. M. Forster, John Maynard Keynes and Dennis

Robertson, other allies of his, protested against the sentence passed on him? And had not the authorities repented by revoking unconditionally the detention order on Harry St John Philby?

The wheels had been set in motion by Harris. Then Dick Brooman-White, the head of MI6's Iberian Section, had moved in. Another Dick White, a career official of MI5 who later began to suspect the integrity and loyalty of Kim Philby, mentioned his name to Felix Cowgill, the head of Section Five and a former senior intelligence officer in the Indian police, then on the look-out for talented and willing recruits. But the final decision was made by someone who had known the candidate's father for well over thirty years. Over an informal lunch with Menzies's deputy, Colonel Valentine Vivian, another ex-servant of the Raj who remained on good terms with 'Jack Philby', the matter was clinched by the father in his son's favour. When Vivian happened to remark that he understood the boy had been 'a bit of a Red at Cambridge', Philby senior pooh-poohed the implications. 'Oh, that was all schoolboy nonsense,' he retorted impatiently. 'He's a reformed character now.' Vivian, the deputy Chief of SIS, thereupon took it on himself casually to approve the recruitment of Kim Philby without more ado.

Cowgill talked at length to the recruit about the work of SIS, its relationship with MI5 and other interested clients, and the special difficulties of Section Five, the counter-intelligence department, whose headquarters were not in London but in a large country house outside St Albans in Hertfordshire. Between September 1941 and the beginning of 1942, Philby absorbed the atmosphere and routines of Brooman-White's Iberian unit, discovering the hard way that all the violent criticisms he had heard of Cowgill's needlessly excessive secrecy from Harris, Brooman-White, Blunt and other officials of MI5 were well founded in view of the almost paranoid obstructiveness of his new superior. As Philby afterwards put it himself:

> His intellectual endowment was slender. As an intelligence officer, he was inhibited by lack of imagination, inattention to detail and sheer ignorance of the world we were fighting in. . . . Cowgill revelled in his

isolation. He was one of those pure souls who denounced all opponents as 'politicians.'[21]

Philby's first and most important task was to mend fences, ingratiate himself with Cowgill's opponents in MI5 and elsewhere, and at the same time master his own job while learning it. With his trained memory, his quick eye for the salient facts, his refined skill at dissembling, his adaptability and easy charm, Philby quietly made himself 'the best asset ever to fall into the hands of the unappreciative Cowgill', to quote one of his own future subordinates. Unlike other departments of SIS, Section Five had men in the field both to protect the secret intelligence agents and to warn MI5 of impending enemy moves in or against Britain.

Domestic counter-espionage, the prime function of MI5, had originally been a police responsibility. The Special Branch of Scotland Yard was set up in 1887 to track down Fenian plotters and sympathizers, including the real father of Brendan Bracken, who remained on the 'Wanted' list for several years. Then, with the overhaul of the War Office by Lord Haldane in 1905 and the creation of a General Staff and a Committee of Imperial Defence, military intelligence gradually came into its own. Increasing jealousy between the Army and the Navy induced the authorities to intervene and stop wasteful inter-service competition. Positive or secret espionage was then taken out of Admiralty and War Office control; in future, their needs would be supplied by a single organization called MI6, independent of both and nominally under the Foreign Office. This new intelligence arm would also control the counter-espionage activities of MI5 for the best part of the next thirty years. While MI6 was ruled in turn by Captain Mansfield Cumming and Admiral Hugh Sinclair, MI5 had only one man at its head, the steady, dependable, but far from creative Major-General Sir Vernon Kell. It was Kell's sad misfortune to fall foul of Churchill during the phoney war. Several costly mishaps, including the failure to check the alleged activities of a mythical German spy whose information led to the sinking of the *Royal Oak* by a U-boat in Scapa Flow, and to the equally annoying blowing up of a munitions plant at Waltham Abbey in Essex, were unfairly blamed on MI5 and its long-serving head.

However, what put the final nail in Kell's coffin was the indisputable evidence of muddle and ineptitude at Wormwood Scrubs, the ugly Victorian Gothic prison in West London where the files and staff of MI5 were temporarily housed. In response to wartime needs, there had been a hasty recruiting drive for secretaries and clerical assistants, as well as agents. The egregious Brian Howard was among several wholly unsuitable 'catches' at the intermediate level, while an assortment of débutantes, chosen for their physical attractiveness and social connections rather than anything else, idled the hours away in vapid chatter.[22] Without proper supervision, these untrained handmaids of the service neglected the registry and paid scant respect to security. In case of enemy air attacks, the card indexes of MI5 had been microfilmed, and the microfilms were kept in a separate, safer place. Unfortunately, when German aircraft dropped incendiary bombs on the district, a big proportion of the original untidy filing system went up in smoke. It may be questioned whether the mounds of charred ashes greatly mattered in view of the microfilmed records; but panic ensued when it was discovered that some of these proved indecipherable. Kell did not survive the subsequent inquest. The National Security Executive, under Lord Swinton, recommended sweeping changes in the direction, recruitment and working routine of MI5, and the days of freebooting officials like Brian Howard were numbered.

In the subsequent reshaping of the two-tiered intelligence structure, MI5 inevitably emerged as the poor relation. Sir David Petrie, the new head of MI5, was kept firmly under the thumb of the new 'C', Stewart Menzies, whose two principals, Colonel Valentine Vivian and Colonel Claude Dansey, embodied the deep-seated enmities which had existed between the rival intelligence branches for years.

Vivian, the recruiter of Philby, was Director of Security for SIS and technically in charge of all counter-espionage operations. His bitter antagonist, Dansey, disapproved of counter-espionage as such, and pressed hard always for the expansion of the overseas networks of secret agents he theoretically controlled. Cowgill's section of SIS had a foot in both camps. The division of responsibility in SIS lay between two groups: the G Sections, which administered and ran the overseas networks; and the Circulating Sections, which scrutinized and evaluated the intelligence thus produced. The G Sections were subdivided according to the geographical location of networks; the Circulating Sections according to the political, military or miscellaneous subject matter produced. Alas, the subject matter of Cowgill's small empire was counter-espionage; and as his main client happened to be another secret organization, the old enemy MI5, it would have required an abler diplomat than Cowgill to preserve the peace. Personal antipathies were aggravated by unavoidable disputes over lines of demarcation. MI5 maintained that they had the right to every particle of intelligence that crossed Cowgill's desk. The latter insisted that his sources and their products were sacrosanct, and that only such information as might affect the security of the realm was MI5's entitlement. He had been sticking tenaciously to this view for months before Philby's arrival, to the vague embarrassment of Menzies, to the sardonic amusement of Dansey, and to the growing despair of Vivian.

The arrival of Philby as one of Cowgill's brighter young men was greeted with as much curiosity as relief by the troublesome Cowgill's staff at St Albans. One person in particular, himself a recent and accidental recruit to the specialist research unit of Section Five, wondered whether the new Daniel would tame the lions or be pitilessly devoured in the attempt. This articulate witness, the historian Hugh Trevor-Roper, noted:

As an undergraduate at Oxford I had heard admiring accounts of him from a friend who often travelled with him in vacations. And, sure enough, while we were still waiting for Philby, my old Oxford friend himself appeared in Section Five as a herald of the coming Messiah. . . . I admit that Philby's appointment astonished me at the time, for my old Oxford friend had told me, years before, that his travelling companion was a Communist. By now, of course, I assumed that he was an ex-Communist, but even so I was surprised, for no one was more fanatically anti-Communist, at that time, than the regular members of the two security services, MI6 and MI5. . . . And of all the anti-Communists, none seemed more resolute than the ex-Indian policemen, like Colonel

Vivian and Major Cowgill, whose earlier years had been spent in waging war on 'subversion' in the irritant climate of the Far East. That these men should have suspended their deepest convictions in favour of the ex-Communist, Philby, was indeed remarkable. Since it never occurred to me that they could be ignorant of the facts (which were widely known), I assumed that Philby had particular virtues which made him, in their eyes, indispensable. I hasten to add that, although I myself knew of Philby's Communist past, it would never have occurred to me, at that time, to hold it against him. . . . My own view, like that of most of my contemporaries, was that our superiors were lunatic in their anti-Communism. . . . We were therefore pleased that at least one ex-Communist should have broken through the net and that the social prejudices of our superiors had, on this one occasion, triumphed over their political prejudices. . . .[23]

Trevor-Roper, in admitting that his main mistake lay in misunderstanding the nature of Communism as a fanatical religious faith, was still more perplexed by Philby's elusive character. The man's guard never slipped; his reluctance to be drawn freely into any intellectual discussion was marked, despite his 'casual, convivial conversation I found so congenial'. Malcolm Muggeridge, whom Trevor-Roper dismisses as 'that agile nihilist', formed a less charitable impression of Philby at St Albans. As a former Communist who had lost his faith in Moscow, Muggeridge suspected that the newcomer's unwillingness to engage in political discussion was something more than a blind:

He rarely spoke about politics, though one assumed he took the vaguely Leftist position fashionable among the bourgeois intelligentsia of his generation. Far stronger in him than anything of this kind, as it seemed to me, was his romantic veneration for buccaneers and buccaneering, whatever the ideological basis, if any, might be. Boozers, womanizers, violence in all its manifestations, recklessness however directed, he found irresistible. Hence his, and many others', otherwise unaccountable love for Burgess, and tolerance of his preposterous and unlovely ways. On this showing he would have been more at home among Nazi bully-boys than the pedantic terrorists of the USSR. He actually said to me once that Goebbels was someone he felt he could have worked with. . . .[24]

Right: *Guy Burgess, aged 23, as an undergraduate at Trinity College, Cambridge, posing for a studio portrait which gave him a soulful look unfamiliar to most of his contemporaries. A relatively late convert to the Communist movement in the University, Burgess exerted his influence through 'The Apostles' and incessant socialising.*

Below left: *Donald Maclean, photographed in 1934 when he was already a committed Marxist. Like his colleague, Burgess, with whom he enjoyed a curious love-hate relationship, he delayed in joining the Communist movement until after the death of his father, Sir Donald Maclean, one of the Liberal Cabinet Ministers in the 1931 National Government.*

Below right: *Harold Philby, pictured here about the same time, was a quieter and less flamboyant figure at Cambridge. Unlike Maclean and Burgess, he took no part in Communist activities, remained outwardly loyal to the University Socialist Society, but was on terms of guarded friendship with many Communist undergraduates, including his future fellow-agents.*

Above: *A group of 'The Apostles' during the early thirties. Anthony Blunt (centre, wearing an open-necked shirt) was a young fellow of Trinity College, a close companion of Burgess and an ardent Marxist. The future knight and keeper of the Queen's Pictures is seen here with (left to right) Richard (later Lord) Llewellyn-Davies, now a famous architect; poet Hugh Sykes Davies; Alistair Watson; Julian Bell who was killed in the Spanish Civil War; Andrew Cohen (later knighted), distinguished diplomat.*

Left: *Victor Rothschild, member of the famous banking family, photographed during his undergraduate days at Trinity College where he first met Guy Burgess. Rothschild, while professing left-wing views, was more interested in entertaining and driving fast sports cars than in propagating, or listening to, his friend's Marxist convictions.*

Above: *Donald Maclean, First Secretary at the British Embassy in Washington, wearing bow-tie and light suit as he sits on the edge of Sir John Balfour's desk. Balfour, the Minister at the Embassy, regarded Maclean as 'arrogant but efficient'. Neither he nor Lord Inverchapel, the then ambassador, suspected him of being an active Soviet agent. On Balfour's right, the present ambassador, Sir Nicholas Henderson, who was Second Secretary in 1946. The fourth diplomat is W. D. Allen* (Head of Chancery).

Right: *Melinda Maclean, the defector's wife, seen boarding a plane at London Airport for an undisclosed destination in Europe a year after her husband fled to the Soviet Union with Guy Burgess. Settling in Switzerland with her two children, she was spirited away to Moscow in 1953.*

WANTED

Donald D. Maclean

Date of birth: 25 May 1913

Home: Beacon Shaw Tatsfield, Kent. England

PP Nr. Br. C 36575, Issued in Rome, 20 July 1949

Discription:

6'3", normal built, short hair, brushed back, part on left side, slight stoop, thin tight lips, long thin legs, slpopy dressed, chain smoker, heavy drinker.

WANTED

Guy Francis Be Money Burgess

Date of birth: 6 April 1911

Home: Unknown

PP.Nr. 1674591, Issued in London, 20 July 1950

Discription:

5'9", slender built, dark complexions, dark curly hair, tinged with gray, chubby face, clean shaven, slightly Pidgeon toed.

Call in case apprehended:
Vohenstrauss 112
Munich Civ. 481688
Munich Military 7401
Herford 2297
Herford 2172

"Maybe using forged pass-ports"

These FBI pictures of Burgess and Maclean as men 'MISSING AND WANTED' were posted in American military bases in Europe after they vanished in May 1951.

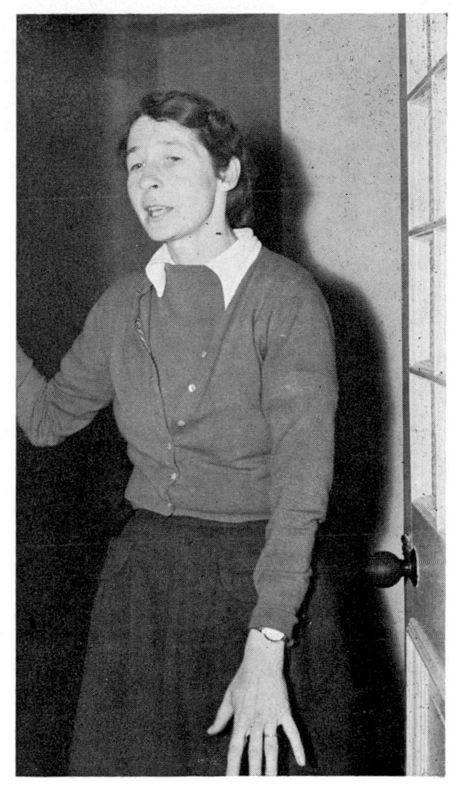

Above left: *Harold ('Kim') Philby caught momentarily offguard by a flashlight during the press conference held in his mother's London flat shortly after Harold Macmillan, Britain's Foreign Secretary, had prematurely cleared him as the so-called 'Third Man'.*

Above right: *Aileen (the second Mrs) Philby, pictured at the door of her home in Crowborough, Sussex, on the night a Labour MP, Marcus Lipton, had named her husband as the 'Third Man'.*

Left: *Eleanor (the third Mrs) Philby about to enter her car below the apartment in Beirut where she lived with 'Kim' until his mysterious disappearance in January 1963.*

hope you had a good
alther has been vile in Moscow
sh I was still on the Black Sea

Above opposite: *Guy Burgess sunning himself on a Black Sea beach during the summer of 1956, the year in which he and Maclean officially 'reappeared' in Moscow. A fragment of the note to his mother, written after his Crimean holiday, appears as an inset in the lower left of the photograph.*

Below opposite: *Kim Philby (centre) and George Blake enjoying an outdoor lunch at the Philby dacha outside Moscow. The fifth Mrs Philby (a Russian) and Mrs Blake are also in the picture.*

Above: *Mr and Mrs Donald Maclean, accompanied by Georgi Stetsenko, who had worked with Burgess at the Foreign Language Publishing House, after the cremation of Guy Burgess in Moscow. Maclean spoke the funeral oration.*

Right: *Sir Stewart Menzies, head of the Secret Service, universally known as 'C', who thought highly of Philby and whose relatively early death may have been brought on by the later and irrefutable evidence of Philby's treachery.*

Below left: *William Skardon, the quietly incisive MI5 interrogator who was mainly responsible for making Dr Klaus Fuchs, the atomic scientist, confess his betrayal to the Russians of nuclear secrets, had much less luck with the unflappable Kim Philby.*

Below right: *Sir Helenus Milmo, the prosecuting counsel used by MI5 in the first serious attempt to secure a confession from Kim Philby after the flight of Burgess and Maclean.*

Whatever may be said for or against Philby's character in the light of hindsight, he sought to create a favourable impression as Cowgill's most promising recruit and prospective deputy. It did not take him long to grasp the fact that spies in the classic tradition of John Buchan's virtuous hero Richard Hannay were outmoded. The exploits of adventurous individualists in the past like the anti-Bolshevik agent Sidney Reilly were just as irrelevant. Not only Section Five but the whole of SIS depended far more than its leaders cared to admit on intelligence derived from enemy signals, intercepted and deciphered by the 'backroom boys' of the Radio Security Service and the so-called Government Code and Cypher School (GCCS) at Bletchley Park. Unlike SIS, with its unique authorization to collect information by illegal means which none could question, GCCS (irreverently known to its inmates as the Golf Club and Chess Society) simply plucked messages out of the air without infringing any law. Once Alfred Dillwyn Knox, the veteran code-breaker – assisted by outstanding mathematicians like Alan Turing, Gordon Welchman and others – had succeeded in unravelling the complex mysteries of the Enigma cipher machine used by the German armed forces and the *Abwehr*, this vital source of secret intelligence rapidly outweighed all the rest in value and importance.

Dilly Knox had started out (during the First World War) in the Admiralty's famous Room 40. Among his fellow cryptographers then were his brother Ronald (the future writer and Catholic scholar Monsignor R. A. Knox), Oliver Strachey, the elder brother of Lytton Strachey, F. Fetterlein, a Czarist Russian expert, and Frank Adcock, a Fellow of King's College, Cambridge. Perhaps their two greatest coups were the intercepting of a German naval signal which led to the arrest in 1916 of the Anglo-Irish rebel Sir Roger Casement; and then of the notorious Zimmermann message in January 1917, offering Mexico an offensive alliance against the United States, which led to the American entry into that earlier conflict.

Somehow, but more by individual foresight and thrifty house-keeping than by deliberate policy, the nucleus of this secret code-breaking unit was preserved. Few government ministers even realized that it had been kept alive; none made proper use of it in peace-time, though a little timely expenditure during the thirties might have enabled Brigadier Alastair Denniston, the school's director, to eavesdrop on Hitler's and Stalin's political intentions.

On the outbreak of war, Denniston and his originally small staff left SIS headquarters at 54 Broadway for Bletchley Park,* some forty miles north of London, and presided over the rapid expansion of resources in specialists and equipment from then onwards. The first rudimentary computer, vital for the intricate task of stripping numerical additives from enciphered codes, had already been installed some two years previously. Sir Frank Adcock returned from Cambridge, recruiting from that university the brains of more than twenty brilliant dons, including F. L. and D. W. Lucas, Geoffrey Barraclough, Max Newman, Leonard Forster (the undergraduate contemporary at Trinity Hall of Donald Maclean), F. H. Hinsley, J. H. Plumb, H. O. Evennett, Alan Turing, of course, as well as Frank Birch. (Philby, before following Burgess into Colonel Grand's unreconstructed Section D in 1940, had tentatively approached Birch in the hope of finding a suitable opening in codes and ciphers. That field, however, was largely reserved for the talented academic specialists of Oxbridge.) Oxford also contributed a number of its most gifted men, among them Denys Page and Leonard Palmer, as well as the radio security team of Gilbert Ryle, Stuart Hampshire, Charles Stuart and Hugh Trevor-Roper. Thus Denniston's once puny unit grew apace into a big centre of secret and extremely effective intelligence-gathering and sifting, with an overcrowded establishment of nearly 7000 people.

In the judgement of Ronald Lewin, the most recent and best-informed British historian of Bletchley and its extraordinary war-time achievements,

Just as the City of London and Balliol College, Oxford (manipulators of two of the most efficient Old Boy Networks in the country) became

* The premises and estate were purchased privately by Admiral Sir Hugh Sinclair before the outbreak of war, a shrewd investment which the Chamberlain Government eventually underwrote.

mainstays of SOE, so Cambridge fed Bletchley. . . . The mathematical strength of Cambridge made the University an obvious hunting ground. . . . It is no coincidence that when in 1943 the Americans were faced with the problem of recruiting at speed the right sort of men to serve in Special Branch as handlers of Ultra, precisely the same system of personal and covert selection was used.[25]

To a large extent, the counter-espionage activities of MI6 were a hollow pretence. Turing, Welchman, Knox and the small army of code-breaking fellow academics had rendered them partly redundant. Yet the pretence was necessarily kept up to 'preserve the security of the source'. MI5 obviously wanted all the information they could wheedle or prise out of Cowgill. Since Menzies, the Chief of SIS and as ardent a believer as Churchill himself in the war-winning potential of 'Ultra' intelligence,* had put him in control also of material extracted from radio intercepts, the excessive secretiveness of Philby's immediate boss naturally gave rise to almost incessant feuding and wrangling. Some critics maintained that Cowgill was obstructing the war effort by insisting on his right to be the sole judge of what could or could not be handed on from St Albans to his rivals in MI5. Philby, who loved rows and intrigues, soon began to enjoy himself. He could not understand how Cowgill could seek to take on, single-handed, the rest of the secret service, however pure and disinterested his motives. For 'C' did not wish to be disturbed, while Dansey and Vivian preferred to ignore the wrangles and difficulties for selfish reasons of their own. As Trevor-Roper wrote,

Colonel Dansey and Colonel Vivian – what old frustrations they recall to mind! All through the war these were the grandees of our service, the Aaron and Hur who, from right and left (but with eyes steadily averted from each other), held up the labouring hands of our Moses, CSS or 'C', Sir Stewart Menzies. How we used to sympathize with Menzies! He held a most invidious position, responsible to an exacting Prime Minister. And yet where could he lean for support? At the beginning of the war, Colonel Dansey's 'agents' in Europe were mopped up and swept away, and in a public speech (of which the text was kept

* Menzies, accompanied by Denniston and Knox, had visited Poland with French representatives a few weeks before the German invasion in September 1939 and secured a perfect replica of the Enigma military machine.

secret even within SIS), Himmler named all the chief officers of SIS, from 'C' downwards. As the progress of the war left it further and further behind, 'C's' whole empire was racked by internal tensions. . . . When I looked coolly at the world in which I found myself, I sometimes thought that, if this was our intelligence system, we were doomed to defeat. . . .[26]

What prevented any likelihood of defeat, and ironically enhanced the reputation of Menzies and SIS in Churchill's eyes, was the unending flow of priceless, first-hand intelligence from Denniston's team of experts at Bletchley. Cowgill might still go through the motions of supplementing this source by manoeuvring his agents on the ground in neutral Spain, Portugal, or North, East and West Africa and elsewhere; but without the intercepts, all the manoeuvring would have proved futile. The calculating mind of Philby fastened on this central fact and exploited it. Grateful as he was to Cowgill for giving him houseroom in effective charge of the Iberian subsection, his gratitude did not run to blind loyalty. He went out of his way to make allies of Cowgill's sworn adversaries in MI5. He called personally on Vivian and Dansey. The latter, of course, had no patience with counter-espionage, still less with the isolated and suspicious Cowgill, proclaiming his own romantic faith in the role of the traditional spy networks which no longer existed as if he had never heard of Knox, Turing or Denniston. Claude Dansey, who had worked in intelligence during the First World War, had since acquired a pronounced taste for the high life. An incurable snob, he emulated Menzies's quite natural bias in favour of upper-class recruits, some of whom undoubtedly joined the service from the bars of White's, Boodle's, the Turf and other exclusive clubs. Philby's sectarian contempt for Dansey was controlled and well masked:

Dansey was a man who preferred to scatter his venom at long range, by telephone or on paper. The only way to deal with him was to beard him in his office; a personal confrontation lowered the temperature and made it possible to talk common sense. As soon as I grasped this, I had little difficulty with him, except to keep a straight face when he started to make cracks about Vivian, my boss's boss. . . .[27]

For Colonel Valentine Vivian, Dansey's pet hate, Philby had an even deeper contempt. He exorcized it carefully on his regular visits to the Assistant Chief of SIS, conceding that 'he probably had a better mind than either Cowgill or Dansey, both of whom, in any case, avoided the timorous Vivian like the plague'. Another useful and highly placed contact was Peter Koch de Gooreynd, a boon companion of Menzies and a distant kinsman of Montagu Norman, the ageing governor of the Bank of England. Of this foppish personage, Philby has written acidly:

> I was prepared to dislike him thoroughly as I had heard appalling reports of him: his nickname was 'Creeping Jesus'. . . . Yet he had a capacity to ingratiate himself with senior members of the Foreign Office which, much to my surprise, I came to admire. Furthermore, I was increasingly drawn to him for his inability to assess the intelligence that passed through his hands. . . .[28]

Going the rounds of SIS and MI5, 'sucking up' to impressionable superiors, and generally demonstrating his keenness, awareness and efficiency, Philby discovered as much about the inner workings of the intelligence organization in six months as others less committed to an over-riding cause would have discovered in six years. The knowledge was grist to the voracious mills of his Soviet masters; yet at this stage their agent had little enough to offer them regularly. Philby's Iberian subsection, to which Malcolm Muggeridge and Graham Greene were later attached as operation agents in Mozambique and Sierra Leone respectively, was fully preoccupied with moves and counter-moves against the *Abwehr* on Spanish and Portuguese territory. The constant queries and requirements of the fighting services, the Allies in their London exile, as well as the Foreign Office, had to be dealt with; the MI5 complaints of less-favoured-nation treatment had to be sympathetically handled. The routine variations absorbed Philby's attention. He took a manifest professional pride in solving problems. Increasingly Cowgill, too, came to rely on his judgement; for their part, Vivian, Dansey and even the implausible Koch de Goorcynd seemed relieved to learn the latest developments from Philby instead of from Cowgill.

Perhaps the only positive and worthwhile information Philby passed on to his Soviet mentors, at any rate until the tide of war started to turn in the Allies' favour in 1943, was his own selection of important background material drawn from the central archives of SIS then stored at St Albans. Obviously, a breakdown of the SIS 'order of battle', with code-names, wavelengths, and identification of networks and agents in all parts of the world, would not have been unwelcome – and this, in all probability, was systematically provided by him. Indeed, Philby has said as much. His lighthearted account of an incident which nearly landed him in 'serious trouble' with the normally friendly and accommodating Bill Woodfield, the archivist of the SIS central registry, deserves examination. Having worked his way through the sourcebooks of SIS activity relating to Spain and Portugal, his rightful field, the eager student borrowed the two volumes relating to the Soviet Union and duly returned them. Then Woodfield complained that one volume was still missing, refusing to accept his best customer's sincere protestations that he, Philby, could not be held responsible as both volumes had already been re-entered and signed for.

After further fruitless searching, the understaffed archivist remained puzzled and unconvinced. He indicated somewhat peevishly that the matter would have to be reported at once to no less a person than Menzies. The mystery unexpectedly solved itself when one of Woodfield's assistants came back from sick leave and artlessly owned up. She, it turned out, had been guilty only of excessive tidiness. In order to save shelf space, the girl had neatly bound the two volumes together into one. So Philby could go out cheerfully and drown his secret guilt and relief in alcohol, with the apologetic Woodfield as his thirsty guest. It is extremely doubtful if a formal interview with 'C' to explain away his unwarranted zeal as a student of SIS activity in the Soviet Union would have done Philby much good so early in his career. The lesson taught by this minor accident was sharp and should have been salutary; but Philby forgot its significance. The self-assured adventurer could never resist taking chances on the spur of the moment when the odds appeared to be in his favour. Inside the rabbit warren of SIS headquarters at Broadway, as at St Albans, the bustle and confusion tended to play into his hands, though inside MI5's orderly offices in St James Street such opportunism would have been more easily thwarted had he been working for them instead.

A few of MI5's war-time recruits, Victor Rothschild and Anthony Blunt for instance, had long been known to him. Philby's business mostly lay not with them but with Guy Liddell, the head of B Division, and Dick White, his deputy. This important unit assessed all incoming intelligence reports and authorized action on the home front. The informal personal approach, as Philby had come to realize, paid higher dividends as a rule than the thoughtless rude minute or brusque barking down a telephone. Liddell, whom Philby recognized as a courtier of Guy Burgess's in off-duty hours, was not only likeable but impressively professional during office hours, 'an ideal senior officer for a young man to learn from, always ready to put aside his work to listen and worry at a new problem'. Dick White, no doubt because he proved to be the only British intelligence officer who persisted in his later suspicions of Philby as the so-called 'Third Man', naturally rated less highly than Liddell in the Third Man's retrospective narrative, which, of course, had to receive an *imprimatur* from the Kremlin equivalent of the Holy Office. White, wrote the spiteful author, 'would have been the first to admit that he lacked outstanding qualities'; besides that, White's 'most obvious fault was a tendency to agree with the last person he spoke to'; and just to suggest a degree of impartiality, White, 'with his usual good sense, was content to delegate a lot of work to his subordinates and to exercise his gifts for chairmanship. . . .' The inescapable fact is that Dick White did collaborate closely at this time with Philby; each respected the other's thoroughness, and White undoubtedly saw at least as much of Cowgill's obliging aide as did the frequently distracted Liddell. Both of these MI5 men tacitly understood why he cultivated them. Their gratitude for small mercies both flattered and pleased him: 'I formed the habit,' as he put it, 'of slipping my friends information off the record – that is to say, without Cowgill's knowledge. The rewards of such unorthodoxy were often generous.'[29]

Yet Philby also kept Cowgill sweet by spending many off-duty hours in his company, discussing tactics, plans, and the bitter nuances of office politics. He had rapidly made himself an indispensable flywheel; and when a hand-picked group of Americans from the Office of Strategic Services, the newly formed US intelligence organization, descended on St Albans and Broadway in the early months of 1942, Philby's powers of adaptability were extended to the full. The Americans might be raw, self-deprecating, even naïve; but their determination to learn and their speed on the uptake appealed to him. Their arrival opened up a new and wider horizon of opportunity for this venturesome opportunist who loved risk like a mistress. As will be shown, the American involvement gradually added another dimension of intricacy to the already tangled rivalries within the SIS. Philby could not have wished for anything better, given his Soviet controller's assurances that he was definitely in the right place at the right time.

Only one minor inconvenience threatened to spoil everything. Because the sexual companionship of women was as necessary to him as liquor, Philby had recently acquired, by deed poll, a substitute wife for the discarded Litzi, to whom he was still legally married. Patricia Lindsay-Hogg and another girl of similar type, who had briefly consoled him in France before the military débâcle of 1940, had long since faded out of the domestic picture; but Litzi, now also living with someone else, could not be erased so easily. In the slapdash and half-hearted security check on his background, the circumstances of his marriage in Vienna had been ignored when he joined Cowgill. Sooner or later he would have to resurrect them himself, especially if he rose higher in the service and had to regularize his present liaison with Aileen Furse.

He had first set eyes on Aileen in the spring of 1940. They grew closer during his short sojourn at 64 Baker Street, the headquarters of SOE and of Marks and Spencer, the firm which really owned the premises and occupied the lower floors of the building. Aileen, a lively and quite alluring brunette, was one of the daughters of a rich and old-established family from the English West Country. She worked for a while with the Bletchley code-breakers. It may well be true, as the author and journalist Patrick Seale has contended, that Aileen's medical history of emotional unbalance was then a closed book to Philby, who 'did not realize the true position'.[30] She certainly betrayed no nervous instability during the early, ecstatic months of their relationship; and it would have been out of keeping with his self-centredness to enquire too closely into the mysteries of her past. If Aileen ever became an encumbrance, he would have no compunction in discarding her like the others, though with the advent of their first child he was human enough to feel both proud and possessive in the isolated, rural cottage they rented outside St Albans.[31]

8. THE ENEMIES WITHIN

The turning point of the war came in 1943. In that year, imperceptibly but surely, world leadership passed from Britain to the United States. When the church bells rang out on 15 November 1942, the peals marked the victory of El Alamein, not the successful Anglo-American landings in French North Africa. Yet those bells also tolled the death of British strategic independence. Few people outside the government yet realized this fact; probably few would have cared. Among the informed minority who did, for their own perverse reasons, were Philby, Maclean and Burgess. Now that the Soviet Union had survived the danger of a knockout blow and was forcing the Germans to give ground, the double patriots in Britain pledged themselves to work harder for a total Russian victory. Philby's Iberian subsection of SIS had been a critical nerve centre while the Mediterranean was closed to Allied shipping, and the risk of an enemy invasion of Spain could not be wholly discounted. The loss of Gibraltar would have been a disaster, and counter-plans had been drawn up to seize the Canary Islands for protecting the Atlantic convoys. There were fears that the neutrality of Vichy France might so favour the Germans that the *Abwehr* agents of Admiral Canaris would endanger British shipping and rule out all prospects of Allied operations in the Mediterranean.[1] Yet even before Hitler had finally abandoned the plan to invade Britain, Churchill was reasonably confident that Franco would not move, and that the Germans would not try to overrun Spain. The Prime Minister had minuted his Chiefs of Staff as early as 6 January 1941:

> According to Captain Hillgarth (our Naval Attaché in Madrid), who has lived long in Spain and is fresh from contact with our Ambassador,

it is becoming increasingly unlikely that the Spanish Government will give Hitler passage or join the war against us.[2]

Captain Alan Hillgarth enjoyed a special relationship with Churchill and through him, with Stewart Menzies and SIS. Despite the slightly sour note Philby sounded in evaluating Hillgarth's role, there can be no questioning the accuracy and reliability of this naval officer's political and military sources. By 1942, when SIS had its own undercover agents on the ground in Lisbon, Gibraltar, Tangier as well as Madrid, and when the code-breakers at Bletchley were producing first-hand intelligence of inestimable importance, the Iberian subsection naturally knew far more than Hillgarth about day-to-day developments. One day, somewhat to his astonishment, Philby was summoned by 'C' himself. Cowgill advised his subordinate that Menzies wished to discuss an important message that had just arrived from Hillgarth; he was no less curious than Philby, who found the shy Menzies 'in a playful mood', almost gleefully anxious to prove that 'he had been poaching on my preserves, doing a bit of counter-espionage in Spain'. It appeared that 'C' had authorized 'Armada', Hillgarth's cover-name, to purchase 'for a very large sum' details of the leading *Abwehr* agents. Now those details had come in, and Menzies passed the message to Philby. When the latter remarked that the information was sound as far as it went, 'C' looked surprised. 'Accurate. How do you know?' Philby explained that his Iberian subsection already had this and much more information about enemy counter-intelligence, a remark which caused Menzies to ask pointedly why he had been kept in the dark. 'But, sir, we send you a copy every month about the progress of our investigations.' To which 'C' retorted amiably: 'My dear Philby, you don't expect me to read everything that's put on my desk.'

The interview with Menzies irked the rising young bureaucrat of SIS. Why, he fumed, should money be lavished on Hillgarth for stale information, while he, the Iberian subsection leader, 'had to fight to get an extra £5 a month for agents who produced regular, if less spectacular, intelligence'? Not that Philby would have dreamed of saying so to Menzies or even to Cowgill, but the

Hillgarth episode was a symptom of the muddled working of the system. For Philby correctly deduced from what he knew the official Spanish source of Hillgarth's material; and, knowing the person bribed to be particularly greedy, he privately mocked the naïveté of Hillgarth and the gullibility of 'C'. Apart from recurring irritants of this kind, Philby on the whole relished the painstaking work of fitting together the minute and disconnected pieces of a huge jigsaw. He had the memory, the concentration and the intuition for it. Only too often the over-caution of Cowgill in fumbling for conclusions that stared him in the face demanded some patience. Philby was inclined to agree with Trevor-Roper that Section Five badly needed a central 'German desk' for the systematic analysis of enemy intentions, so that appropriate action could be coordinated promptly. In the end Trevor-Roper, stung beyond endurance by Cowgill's withholding from his own staff information necessary for evaluating enemy intentions, virtually accused the man of sabotage, and brought on himself the threat of a court-martial. He had to back down by writing a letter of apology for insulting a lawful superior. But only then was anything constructive done. Only then did Menzies, for the sake of peace, let Trevor-Roper stay and set up his own little empire for the precise purpose this caustic critic of the system had originally proposed. 'Indeed,' the intended victim confessed, 'the organization was adjusted to separate me from Section Five in which I had been an indigestible part. This separation certainly made things much easier all round.'[3]

However, Philby had excellent reasons, quite unconnected with his stammer, for keeping his own temper and never antagonizing Cowgill. Instead, he tried to win him over by mixing flattery with persuasion, giving his secretive boss credit for ideas which sometimes came from other people and watching him bask in the reflected glory of success afterwards. That, broadly, was what happened when Philby's bold suggestion for countering the *Abwehr*'s so-called 'Bodden Operation' in Spain won Cowgill's belated interest and unqualified support. The name 'Bodden' itself had roused early suspicions. For Bodden happened to be a strip of water in the Baltic, separating the island of Rugen from the German coast, not far from the research station of Peenemünde. Additional evidence from the Bletchley code-breakers showed that experts from Bodden were concentrating in and around Algeciras.

Their purpose was sufficiently plain; and Dr R. V. Jones, the scientific expert whom Section Five at once consulted, confirmed that the Bodden specialists evidently had designs on shipping passing through the Straits of Gibraltar at night: their infra-red detection system posed an immediate and grave threat. Armed with the conclusive opinion of the 'formidable Dr Jones', Philby thought out his next move thoroughly, then went to see Cowgill. As he had foreseen, his boss's obsessive concern to safeguard the 'security of sources' needed deft handling; but Cowgill liked the strongly worded draft protest which Philby had prepared for presentation to General Franco. It demonstrated in damning detail that the British Government knew precisely what Gustav Lenz, the Chief of the *Abwehr* in Spain, was up to, even if General Franco did not. Yet the draft gave nothing at all away about the source of the information. So Cowgill approved, taking Philby's paper to Menzies, who also approved. The Foreign Office agreed in turn that a firm, diplomatic line would be in order this time, and not long afterwards the British Ambassador in Madrid, Sir Samuel Hoare, called formally on Franco to deliver a vigorous protest, backing it up with a copy of the document. The results, which the Iberian subsection could follow day by day through the intercepts provided by the Bletchley code-breakers, were swift and heartening. Panic overtook Lenz and his agents when the Spanish Government condemned their flagrant abuse of Franco's friendly neutrality. In due course the German Bodden Operation was called off, and Allied planners could prepare for the invasion of French North Africa with easier minds. By common-sense tactics this minor triumph sent up the personal stock of Philby, who had indisputably combined initiative with restraint.

Then Cowgill did himself a characteristic disservice by contriving, with inadequate finesse, to establish his claims as the overlord of all Allied counter-intelligence, American as well as British. Between early 1942 and mid 1943, the Cowgill campaign moved unsteadily forward, hampered at every turn by the determination of individuals in the US Office of Strategic Services (OSS) not to be patronized. Philby regarded the average American performance in the field of intelligence as raw and counter-productive, since William Donovan's agents often appeared clumsy and naïve in trying to outwit experienced *Abwehr* agents, especially on Spanish, Portuguese and Swiss territory. The details of the numerous difficulties created by Anglo-American differences of approach need not detain us. The evidence does indicate, however, that Colonels Dansey and Vivian backed Cowgill, at any rate to start with, and that the diplomatic 'C' himself did not demur. Indeed, when Cowgill proposed that joint Special Counter-Intelligence Units should be attached to the Allied army staffs for the French North African landings, the scheme was approved at the highest level. Extra resources were allocated to Section Five from the secret fund, and a gratified Philby accepted Cowgill's offer to add French affairs to his Iberian commitment.

By trial and error, Cowgill's system of safeguarding the security of sources while deceiving the enemy in the field was soon working reasonably well. The military tide was slowly turning at last, and with it the professional fortunes of Philby seemed to be rising swiftly as well. Yet he craved for greater powers. Except for information from the St Albans files on all British agents operating in eastern Europe and Soviet Russia, and a few random items extracted from the logbooks on occasional turns as night-duty officer at the Broadway centre, he had not been able to pass on anything of real value to his fastidious but extraordinarily patient Russian controller. To be assured that his true value was long term, that it lay in his position as a strategically placed secret agent, taxed his credulity at times, though he could hardly dispute the fact: plainly, Stalin and his underlings were dealing relatively openly with their Allied counterparts, and were being told nearly everything they required to know at first hand.

The invasion of Sicily and Italy rapidly followed the collapse of German resistance in North Africa, and during the summer months of 1943 the responsibilities of the work-hungry Philby increased. On paper at least, he was now in charge of Italian counter-espionage as well as African, French and Iberian. Section

Five had meanwhile moved back to London, bag and baggage, setting up shop in Ryder Street, conveniently close to its American and British clients. Cowgill still looked upon the latter with an almost pathological mistrust. It was a measure of his boss's isolation that Philby alone received Cowgill's unreserved confidence; and gradually he took advantage of it to outmanoeuvre him. In this, of course, the ambitious younger man could count on the support of Cowgill's critics in SIS and of his unforgiving enemies in MI5. American students of the arts of in-fighting watched developments, though nobody considered the outcome a certainty for either side, unevenly matched as they were.

It has been well said that when a man lives a fantasy, as Philby had schooled himself to do over the past decade, the appetites of his dominant self may inadvertently give him away. Philby had a marked hunger for power. Nor did he succeed in wholly disguising it from sharp-eyed colleagues like Muggeridge or Trevor-Roper who, having no reasons to question his ulterior motives, ascribed it simply to ambition. In Muggeridge's view, anyone who seriously wanted a place at the top of the secret service 'needed to have his head examined'. For the service was riddled with deficiencies. Only its secret nature and war-time exigencies prevented the kind of searching enquiry which would have led to its being forced to reform itself or put up the shutters. By now Muggeridge had left for Lourenço Marques in Portuguese Mozambique to counteract the spying activities of local enemy agents, German and Italian, against Allied shipping. Few were surprised when Cowgill nominated Philby as his official deputy, before leaving London for a month's visit to the United States. Trying his boss's desk for size, Philby noticed the untidy array of memoranda and pending files in the in-tray.

One particular file, which Cowgill's stand-in dug out and memorized, concerned a fresh source of German Foreign Office material recently opened up in Switzerland by the Americans, after the British resident agent in Berne, aware of the political form at home, had rejected it out of hand as spurious. It was the last quarter of 1943. Defeat already stared Germany in the face. Defectors in growing numbers were seeking asylum, usually with tempting offers of help which, in Philby's phrase, 'had to be treated with care for a number of good reasons', not excluding the reason closest to his heart, namely, the danger of creating any avoidable rift between Soviet Russia and its Western Allies. For, as he revealingly put it, 'the air was opaque with mutual suspicions of separate peace feelers'. What happened in this instance was that the German official, whom the British had already rebuffed, presented himself to Allen Dulles of OSS. Dulles, on looking at his impressive caseful of documents, welcomed him with open arms. Next he examined these in detail and pronounced them genuine.

Colonel Dansey duly got courtesy copies. Without troubling to cross-check them for possible authenticity, Dansey pronounced them to be planted fakes. Like Cowgill, Dansey abhorred the interfering presence of OSS on Swiss soil. As Philby noted Dansey's intemperate comments, he suddenly recalled Cowgill's oblique references before departing to an important case on which he was collaborating with Dansey. At once the penny dropped. Here, thought Philby, was a golden opportunity for treating something strictly on its objective merits, always provided that he did not incur Dansey's lasting enmity in the process. His first move was to send a dozen samples out of the Allen Dulles batch, all messages from the German military attaché in Tokyo, to Commander Alastair Denniston and the code-breakers at Bletchley. Enthusiastic requests for more material came from Denniston, and Philby complied instantly. The code-breakers had independently intercepted a few of these messages already. Comparisons with the originals, it seemed, had increased their appetite for further examples. They hoped to 'crack' next the German diplomatic code. Philby decided now to circulate the Dulles material, without designating its OSS origin, to the armed services and the Foreign Office. At once these customers started yelling for more. Before humouring them, Cowgill's nimble-minded deputy asked for appreciations from the receiving departments, including Denniston's, and only then made arrangements to see a disgruntled and suspicious Colonel Dansey. The latter's fury simmered down once he took in the fact that this material, which he swore would give OSS *carte blanche* to 'go on the rampage' and 'undo the good work of SIS', had not been distributed as OSS material, so that any credit accruing would be Dansey's. 'You're not such a fool as I thought,' he said to Philby.

Allen Dulles, whom Dansey and Cowgill unwisely deprecated as a raw and potentially reckless bungler, was, in fact, no stranger to counter-espionage. Nor was he unfamiliar with Switzerland, where he had worked as a young American agent against Germany and the Austro-Hungarian Empire towards the end of the First World War. By the autumn of 1942 Dulles, far from blundering in the dark, could claim to have acquired a working knowledge of the *Schwarze Kapelle*, the German underground military opposition to Hitler and the Nazi Party, cleverly orchestrated by Admiral Canaris through his own chosen agents in the *Abwehr*. By a coincidence, Hugh Trevor-Roper and his small team of German specialists were, at the same time, piecing together a similar picture from their own separate sources at Bletchley.

The personal assistant of Dulles was Gero van Schulze Gaevernitz, the son of a leading Berlin economist, close to Canaris, who had lived in Switzerland since 1939. When Gaevernitz introduced his American Chief to an immensely tall Prussian ex-Gestapo official, Hans Bernd Gisevius, Dulles was at first suspicious. For SIS, on the advice of the sceptical British resident, regarded Gisevius as a 'deception agent'. Nevertheless, Dulles decided to take a chance. With Gisevius he worked out a means of communication that would cut out Gestapo surveillance, and arranged with his control in Washington a highly restricted distribution system for his messages about the *Schwarze Kapelle*. On the list were the experts in the White House map room, Secretary of State Cordell Hull, the intelligence centre of the US Chiefs of Staff, and the executive assistant to Hull's number two, Fletcher Warren. The British were not, however, excluded. Dulles forwarded to Washington a considerable amount of original material from early 1943 to May 1944, including the lengthy history, compiled by Gisevius, of the *Schwarze Kapelle*, none of which ever appeared in the records of the Joint Chiefs of Staff. But if Philby, the secret penetration agent of the Soviet, made it his business to 'sit on' all such political material as firmly as possible, there were no 'moles' at large in Washington: 'Indifference, not treachery, was at the root of America's attitude to the [German] conspiracy.'[4]

The SIS handling of the 'Berne Papers', which largely contributed to Philby's success in ascending the SIS promotion ladder, was markedly different because Philby handled it differently, no doubt at the prompting of his Soviet controller. Again, as had originally happened to Gisevius, a second *Schwarze Kapelle* emissary was refused a hearing by the British resident, Count Vanden Huyvel. Again Dulles took a chance and received the caller, Fritz Kolbe by name, 'a short, wiry man with a halo of blond hair around a bald pate'. He was forty-two; and he claimed to be the special assistant to Ambassador Karl Ritter, an envoy who undertook important diplomatic missions on behalf of the Wehrmacht. Kolbe, it appeared, personally handled and 'screened' all secret information which reached Ritter's desk. To demonstrate what he meant, Kolbe produced there and then from his suitcase a remarkably large and varied collection of documents. The operational items were distributed by Philby; the political items concerning the *Schwarze Kapelle* and the opposition to Hitler were suppressed.

It is interesting to note how Philby's own amusingly irreverent account of his part in the affair tails off abruptly enough to leave the impression of a Kremlin censor's hand. Beyond the admission that 'our German friend proved to be an intrepid operator, and paid several more visits with his useful suitcase', Philby could not go. Operational material was one thing, political background on *Schwarze Kapelle* quite another. Lisbon and Madrid were other key junctions in Admiral Canaris's lines of communication to the West. The icy reception awaiting Otto John, one of the Lufthansa's lawyers, when he met a woman agent of SIS by arrangement, could hardly have surprised Philby. This lady, according to Otto John, 'told me that strict instructions had been received from London forbidding any further contact with emissaries of the German opposition. [She said] the war would now be decided by force of arms.' The fruitless encounter took place in August

1943, in the same month in which the 'Berne Papers' came to light.

The contrariness of Philby's attitude had been irritating and perplexing the industrious Trevor-Roper for a long time, ever since Cowgill had put him in charge of the Iberian subsection:

> Late in 1942 my office had come to certain conclusions – which time proved to be correct – about the struggle between the Nazi Party and the German General Staff, as it was being fought out in the field of secret intelligence. The German Secret Service (the *Abwehr*) and its leader, Admiral Canaris, were suspected by the Party not only of inefficiency but of disloyalty, and attempts were being made by Himmler to oust the Admiral and to take over his whole organization. Admiral Canaris himself, at that time, was making repeated journeys to Spain and indicated a willingness to treat with us: he would even welcome a meeting with his opposite number, 'C'. These conclusions were duly formulated and the final document was submitted for security clearance to Philby. Philby absolutely forbade its circulation, insisting that it was 'mere speculation'.
>
> He afterwards similarly suppressed, as 'unreliable', a report from an important German defector, Otto John, who informed us, in Lisbon, that a conspiracy was being hatched against Hitler. This also was perfectly true. The conspiracy was the Plot of 20 July 1944, and Canaris, for his contribution to it, afterwards suffered a traitor's death in Germany.
>
> At the time we were baffled by Philby's intransigence, which would yield to no argument and which no argument was used to defend. From some members of Section Five, mere mindless blocking of intelligence was to be expected. But Philby, we said to ourselves, was an intelligent man: how could he behave thus in a matter so important? Had he too yielded to the genius of the place? . . .[5]

Menzies, as it turned out, was not interested in meeting Canaris. The Foreign Secretary, Anthony Eden, a stickler for correct procedure, had counselled against replying directly to such overtures. It would be unwise needlessly to antagonize Stalin, as Maisky kept reminding him. Besides, even Churchill had lost his earlier enthusiasm for manipulating the *Schwarze Kapelle*. When he raised the question with Roosevelt at the White House in May 1943, the President commented sharply and adversely. After all, was not the policy of 'unconditional surrender' the only doctrine acceptable to all the Allies? As far as the President was concerned, Canaris had nothing to offer. 'There is no doubt,' stressed Robert E. Sherwood, 'that Roosevelt never took the possibility very seriously as a solution to the problem of achieving total victory.'[6]

Conditioned to think and act in Stalin's interests whenever possible, Philby was lucky enough also to find support for his anti-Canaris moves at the highest levels in London and Washington.

The code-name for the Teheran Conference of November 1943 was 'Eureka', but what Churchill found there did not altogether please him. Roosevelt and Stalin made common cause against him; and for the first time since 1940, Britain's war leader felt distinctly uneasy about the prospective shape of the post-war world. This was the unhappy prelude to victory; and the still more ominous outcome of the Yalta talks in February 1945 deepened the Prime Minister's uneasiness. The American President had no brief, no personal or political desire, to restore the British Empire. Stalin had given only a slight hint of his vindictive intentions. 'I have pointed out to the Cabinet that the actual terms contemplated for Germany are not of a character to reassure them at all, if stated in retail,' Churchill minuted on 19 April 1944:

> Both President Roosevelt and Marshal Stalin at Teheran wished to cut Germany into smaller pieces than I had in mind. Stalin spoke of very large executions of over 50,000 of the staffs and military experts. Whether he was joking or not could not be ascertained. The atmosphere was jovial, but also grim. He certainly said that he would require 4,000,000 German males to work for an indefinite period to rebuild Russia.... There are a lot of other terms implying the German ruin and indefinite prevention of their rising again as an armed power....[7]

Churchill, the veteran foe of Bolshevism among British politicians, preserved a veneer of comradely respect for Stalin, but meanwhile took belated steps at home to counter Communist infiltration. 'We are purging all our secret establishments of Communists,' he noted, 'because we know they owe no allegiance to us or to our cause and will always betray secrets to the Soviet, even while we are working together. . . .'[8]

That minute, written on 13 April 1944, was an implicit confession of frustration. By then most dedicated Communists, and the handful of covert agents of the Soviet Union, had wormed their way so effectively into positions of trust that they could not be so easily dislodged. They had not been idle, even while basking in the reflected warmth of 'Uncle Joe's' popularity as a folk hero; and though Stalin's popularity had begun to wane, no programme for rooting out 'moles' could have been launched in the spring of 1944 without dislocating the intense preparations for D-Day.

MI5 watched the known Communists, wired Party headquarters and eavesdropped, but completely failed to uncover the important 'moles'. London, of course, remained the Communists' focal point, as the war-time seat of the various European governments-in-exile. Party members in each of them 'were planning for the post-war Communist world, and all were using their governments for that purpose', commented Douglas Hyde, at that time an active and deeply entrenched militant of the British Communist Party.

Coordinating their activities and pooling their experiences was a hush-hush body in London which came near to being a little Communist International in itself. Its administration was the responsibility of an old and trusted one-time political Bureau member, Tommy Bell, who kept me informed of all that was going on in the various foreign parties. Had MI5 kept itself sufficiently aware of their activities too, it is probable that the Fuchs case would never have occurred. The Communist émigrés saw themselves as the rulers of tomorrow and were confident that they could deal with their respective Coalition governments when the day came. All were closely in touch with London Soviet circles, who saw their importance at a time when others thought that they counted for little.[9]

The Czech diplomat Otto Katz (for this was the respectable disguise under which the former Comintern colleague of Willy Muenzenberg and Arthur Koestler now moved) could usually be found after dark, holding forth in the Bentinck Street flat of Guy Burgess, mingling with the displaced intellectuals, a few *louche* representatives of MI5 and SIS, and the usual hangers-on and boy friends of the host. One night during this period, Goronwy Rees looked in after a busy day at his War Office desk, carrying a heavy briefcase. The nightmare thought crossed his mind afterwards that some of those present might have cheerfully throttled him, had they guessed that his bulging briefcase contained top secret papers on the military plans for D-Day. Philby, who was then on the look-out for a suitable town house, could often be seen in the company of Burgess, either at Bentinck Street or in the more elegant surroundings of Tommy Harris's home in Chesterfield Gardens, Mayfair, where good food and wine never seemed to run out.

Donald Maclean appeared less frequently at these gatherings, and never with Melinda, his wife. The couple had clearly grown closer and fonder of each other, despite Donald's recurring and spectacular lapses. Naturally, when Melinda learnt in March 1944 that her husband's hard work had at last been rewarded with the offer of a posting as First Secretary to the British Embassy in Washington, she was so overjoyed that she could not begin to understand his immediate doubts and hesitations.

Churchill himself, for quite different reasons, snapped hard at the Foreign Office for its aimless reshuffling of the diplomatic pack, after assenting to the transfer from Rio to Rome of the British Ambassador Sir Noel Charles. 'I certainly did not expect it would lead to a kind of "general post",' he complained to Anthony Eden. But the departmental machinery, once set in motion, could not be smoothly reversed. Donald Maclean, the 'golden boy' of the service, had added to his laurels by the 'consistent high quality of his work'. Left to himself, he would have gladly welcomed the Washington posting as an honourable reward, but did not relish being bullied and flagrantly blackmailed into going by the insufferable Guy Burgess solely because it suited their Russian friends. In fact, the D-Day files inside Goronwy Rees's briefcase were as stale chickenfeed compared with the secrets inside the heads of the Anglo-American atomic scientists of the Manhattan Project.

Philby had been among the first to appreciate how much was

at stake. He had told Burgess how greatly their Soviet friends counted on obtaining by clandestine means as much information as possible about this secret enterprise which the Western leaders would never divulge openly to Stalin of their own free will. So Burgess had just enough background to illuminate with his fierce imagination as he strove to bring Maclean to heel. Burgess's self-indulgent excesses had caused him visibly to deteriorate in the months since Malcolm Muggeridge had caught his first and last glimpse of him at Bentinck Street. Cyril Connolly, the editor of *Horizon* – a magazine on which Burgess often poured scorn as a symbol of bourgeois decadence – was one of several observers who recognized the change for the worse:

> He had become much more insulting and destructive when he drank – he seemed to hit on the unforgivable thing to say to everyone. His mental sadism, which sometimes led to his getting knocked out, did not exclude great kindness to those in trouble. Above all, he disliked anyone to escape his clutches, he was an affectionate bully, capable of acts of generosity, like a magnate of the Dark Ages.[10]

Despite the many competing war-time claims on scientists and basic resources, Britain had decided in 1939 that research into releasing energy by atomic fission must continue. Whether nuclear bombs could be fashioned for use before the conflict ended was then very doubtful. Nevertheless, the fact that German scientists were as alert to the possibilities as their British, French, American and Russian colleagues had prompted the British Government to carry on with the project, which 'at this stage was carried out mainly in our universities, principally Oxford, Cambridge, London (Imperial College), Liverpool and Birmingham,' wrote Churchill. 'Such progress was made that by the summer of 1941 Sir George Thomson's committee was able to report that in their view there was a reasonable chance that an atomic bomb could be produced before the end of the war. . . .'[11]

Churchill's abridged account glossed over the somewhat lukewarm initial attitude of most British physicists to the practical prospect of manufacturing a nuclear bomb in war-time, an attitude which their absorption with 'immediately urgent problems' after September 1939 served only to increase. 'Scepticism was almost universal and profound,' has declared the historian of the United Kingdom Atomic Energy Authority.[12] Both in Britain and in the United States, émigré scientists alone had the leisure to concentrate on the theoretical possibilities. For these men were at first debarred by stringent security regulations 'from participating in radar and other high-priority research'.[13] By April 1940, the two most distinguished émigré scientists in Britain, Dr Rudolf Peierls from Berlin, and Dr Otto Frisch from Bohr's Institute at Copenhagen, had managed not merely to outline a method for developing an atomic weapon but to suggest a means for detonating it, quite apart from explaining how the isotope Uranium 235 might be separated from Uranium 238. Nor was it altogether surprising that President Roosevelt's active and continuing interest in the beginnings of U S nuclear research had been originally roused by a personal letter to himself signed by Albert Einstein and actually written by the Hungarian-born physicist Leo Szilard, both of whom feared that German scientists, having been the first to split the uranium atom in December 1938, might again be the first to produce a war-winning weapon for Hitler's use.

The 'Directorate of Tube Alloys' was set up in Britain as a special division in the Department of Scientific and Industrial Research; and in October 1941, even before the Americans declared war, Roosevelt had suggested to Churchill that the venture should be 'jointly conducted', preferably in the United States, with advantage to both sides. The pooling of information followed; and in June 1942 the decision to concentrate an intensive programme of experiment in Canada and the United States was informally agreed by Churchill and Roosevelt at the President's Hyde Park home by the Hudson River. By then a German refugee from Hitler, the young and brilliant mathematical physicist Dr Klaus Fuchs, had settled down in England to work on the Manhattan Project. Fuchs had recently emerged from internment in a Canadian compound, where he had been sent from Britain as an 'enemy alien' during the invasion scare of 1940. His spell behind barbed wire had merely hardened Fuchs's secret Communist faith, a process not reversed by the German attack on the

Soviet Union. In his youth he had studied at Kiel and Leipzig, before Hitler's accession to power. Arriving in England as a fugitive, he had resumed his academic studies in Bristol and Edinburgh. Though the Canadian interlude had soured Fuchs and he professed vaguely left-wing views, he responded gladly when a professor at Birmingham University, the eminent émigré physicist Dr (now Sir Rudolf) Peierls, offered to recruit him for work on the atomic project. Sir Rudolf has written:

In 1940, when it was clear that an atomic weapon was a serious possibility, and that it was urgent to do experimental and theoretical work, I wanted someone to help me with the theoretical side. Most competent theoreticians were already doing something important, and when I heard that Fuchs, whom I knew and respected as a physicist from his work at Bristol, was back in the UK, temporarily in Edinburgh, it seemed a good idea to try to get him to come to Birmingham. There was at first some difficulty about security clearance, and I was told I could not tell him what it was all about.... I explained that in the kind of work that had to be done he could be of no use to me unless he knew exactly what one was trying to do, and that there was no half-way house. In the end he was cleared.[14]

On 18 June 1942, Fuchs signed the Official Secrets Act. Not long afterwards he applied for and was granted naturalization as a British subject. Nobody in the British security services took the trouble even to screen him. Fuchs would later confess:

When I learnt of the purpose of the work, I decided to inform Russia, and I established contact with another member of the Communist Party. Since that time I have had continuous contact with persons who were completely unknown to me, except that I knew they would give whatever information they had to the Soviet authorities. At this time I had complete confidence in Russian policy and believed that the Western Allies deliberately allowed Germany and Russia to fight each other to death.[15]

The laxness of MI5, first, in failing to uncover the fact that Fuchs was a Communist, and second, in failing to maintain a check on his movements, seems both unintelligible and inexcusable in retrospect, even allowing for war-time pressures and the embarrassing lack of pre-war records. The department similarly overlooked the known political sympathies of Alan Nunn May, the English physicist, who had made no secret of them since graduating from Trinity Hall, Cambridge, at the same time as his friend and contemporary Donald Maclean. Despite Nunn May's public protests from Communist platforms against the 'imperialist war' many months before the German attack on the Soviet Union, no serious security screening took place, no restraint was placed on him, when 'Tube Alloys' sought his services. Like Philby's entry into SIS, the enlistment of these two scientists was a formality, unaccompanied by questioning or routine surveillance. Perhaps the signing of the Official Secrets Act was thought sufficient deterrent during the darkest period of the war, especially as the security services were relatively undermanned and therefore fully stretched. The mood of the British people in 1942, as Cyril Connolly has stressed, certainly induced less concentration on Marxists and their liability as security risks than at any time before or since: 'The position of Russia as an ally made things easier for Communists. Waverers returned to their allegiance, and those who had never wavered were respected.'[16]

In 1944, Donald Maclean eventually succumbed, though not without a few qualms, to the blackmail of Burgess.[17] Philby was happy to leave the details to the dependable Guy. Like Fuchs and Nunn May, Philby had signed the Official Secrets Act; unlike them, he thrived on the double life he led. Deception was more than his hidden trade-mark; it had become his *raison d'être*. His duty during the final victorious phase of a destructive war, a war in which the Soviet Union had suffered far heavier losses than its nominal allies, was to ensure that the British and Americans did not outstrip the Russians in the development of nuclear weapons. Burgess, his middle-man, was as determined as Philby that their stubborn and less than cooperative fellow conspirator, Maclean, 'should not renege and let the side down'. Through his own classified knowledge of the daring and successful British raids on the German heavy-water installations at Rjukan, in Norway, not long after his arrival in SIS, Philby had stumbled on a clue which gradually elucidated the whole eerie subject. Positive evidence about the sinister nature of 'Tube Alloys' had meanwhile been provided to the Russians by the quiet, obliging Klaus Fuchs. Clearly, Maclean's presence in the Washington Embassy, as a purveyor of whatever secret information he could lay hands on, was not merely desirable but imperative. The Soviet spy networks in Canada and the United States were already in place and beginning to gather technical information, thanks to Nunn May, Fuchs and others, but an unsuspected diplomatic colleague, enjoying complete immunity from surveillance, might add to the store of vital knowledge.

In his free confession afterwards to his MI5 investigator, William Skardon, whose gentle but deadly questioning wore down Fuchs's resistance, the lonely but self-sufficient Fuchs would describe himself as 'a controlled schizophrenic'. There could be no doubting the spiritual loneliness of Donald Maclean, the ex-Presbyterian turned Marxist. His residual Calvinist conscience, which never ceased to torment him at inopportune moments, brought on recurring bouts of almost uncontrollable schizophrenia. Melinda noticed with alarm acute symptoms of this old complaint in the spring of 1944, though she merely told friends: 'Something's worrying Donald to death, and he won't say what it is.' For the best part of six weeks her husband seldom came straight home at night. Several times unknown companions helped him into the flat, blind drunk, with his clothes badly stained and reeking of whisky. Yet while these orgies were wearing him out, congratulatory letters on Donald's deserved promotion were arriving from such distinguished people as Lord Halifax, then British Ambassador in Washington, and from Ronald Campbell, the minister under whom Donald had formerly served in Paris. Melinda managed to reassure the anxious Lady Maclean and others in the family circle. Donald, she suggested, was suffering from overwork; there had possibly been more celebration and farewell parties than his nervous stamina could stand.

If Melinda, who was again pregnant, had been able to meet Burgess or Philby, her intuition might have warned her that Donald, against his better judgement, was being drawn into a conspiracy as an only half-willing accomplice. She would also have realized that the constant rehearsing of his part in trying to wrest diplomatic and atomic secrets from the Western Allies forced him to drown his conscience in alcohol. Whether Burgess would ever have used the pornographic pictures in his possession to destroy Maclean's career, had the victim persevered in his first refusal to cooperate, remains a tantalizing question. It did not, however, arise. Veiled threats of exposure, coupled with persuasive arguments about the unjust Anglo-American treatment of their staunch Soviet ally, and the rights of that ally to any war-winning weapons that might be going, proved sufficient. Maclean, the waverer, had to be driven into line under the lashing tongue of Burgess. The treatment worked.

Before the end of April 1944 the new First Secretary to the British Embassy in Washington reached New York with his wife, installed her safely at her mother's home, and kept his first secret appointment with a member of the Soviet Consulate, in accordance with instructions. Then he completed his journey to the American capital and reported for duty. On the voyage across he had time to collect his thoughts and persuade himself that, on balance, the unspeakable Burgess was probably right. History certainly appeared to favour the Soviet side.

Meanwhile, Guy Burgess was preparing to move from the BBC to be closer to its political masters. Since 20 January 1941, his nominal work as a Talks assistant had not greatly extended him. George Barnes, the overall head of the group, had run him on a very loose rein, letting him roam freely around the fringes of Bracken's Ministry of Information and Robert Bruce Lockhart's Political Warfare Executive in order to keep Barnes fully posted on the activities of the 'black propagandists' and the latest Ministry gossip. Barnes, who wrote glowingly of Burgess's gifts in his annual reports about the young man, was mystified and sorry to receive notice of his resignation about the time Maclean left for the United States. Apart from understandably adverse comments on Guy's 'untidy office administration', Barnes could think of no other man or woman in broadcasting of comparable flair and adaptability. If this suggested that Barnes was a rather poor judge of character, it should also be said that he was snobbish enough to be influenced by the good opinions of public celebrities like Harold Nicolson, Lady Violet Bonham Carter, Desmond MacCarthy, Cyril Connolly and Lord Elton. George Barnes, as it happened, was among the senior BBC executives who vainly tried to persuade the new Director General, William Haley, that Burgess deserved a higher position on the permanent staff, one appropriate to his talents. Fortunately, perhaps, for the Corporation, the aloof Haley 'smelled a rat', resisted 'the pressures from inside and outside', and quite indifferently let Burgess go.

Through the numerous contacts he had already made at the Foreign Office, Burgess heard of a temporary opening in its press department, applied for it, and was promptly accepted. On 4 June 1944, two days before the Allied invasion of Normandy, he left the dead-end of Broadcasting House to deploy his gifts in the corridors of Whitehall. Philby agreed with him that the move was sensible and could well become significant. The rising star of SIS confided that he himself had hopes of soon rising higher in the closed world of counter-espionage. The minds of his superiors were beginning to focus on the future. An experimental department called Section Nine, headed by an improbable, superannuated fugitive from MI5 sporting a hearing aid, was beginning to scratch the surface of an ambitious, long-term enterprise: the post-war penetration of the Soviet's worldwide espionage network. J. C. Currie was the name of the unfortunate man whom 'C' had already commissioned, on a temporary and purely makeshift basis, to organize the new section; and, by all accounts Currie was running into many local and man-made obstacles.

Felix Cowgill, for one, felt that if anyone in SIS had the necessary expertise, seniority and authority to undertake this task permanently, it was himself. Had he not been originally recruited by 'C's' predecessor, Sinclair, in 1938, for that very purpose? While denying Currie full access to the pre-war files (the contents of which had, of course, been sifted by Philby and passed on to the Russians), the security-conscious Cowgill still sounded confident that Section Nine would fall into his hands in the fullness of time. Without one serious competitor in sight, he applied himself steadfastly to the job in hand: 'Let's beat the Germans first,' he often said; 'then we can get down to the Communists together.' When Philby mentioned these developments to his Soviet controller, he was slightly taken aback by indelicate suggestions that the new job ought not to become another Cowgill sinecure. It would help, of course, if Philby found employment there under his present boss; but why should he not start intriguing himself to succeed Currie and supplant Cowgill?

The Soviet controller attached such weight to the dangerous plan that his English 'mole' obliged by writing 'several memoranda on the subject which we analysed in exhaustive detail'. The Centre in Moscow was next consulted. Their instructions were that 'I must do everything, but *everything*, to ensure that I became head of Section Nine, whether or not it merged with [Cowgill's] Section Five.' Strong as was Philby's appetite for power, he had little stomach for in-fighting, and said so. He owed a great deal to Cowgill; and despite the latter's faults, Philby retained some faint liking and respect for him. According to Philby's account, his Soviet mentors enjoined him to work against the promotion of his boss with the utmost guile and discretion, preferably using Cowgill's enemies within. By so doing he would be able to show that 'the position had been thrust on me', particularly if 'things went wrong'. So began the tortuous and nasty business of allying himself with Cowgill's critics to dish Cowgill's chances.[18]

Looking back on the episode, Philby had the grace to admit that it made 'sour reading, just as it makes sour writing'. The interest of Moscow in every stage of the subsequent manoeuvres was understandable. It buoyed up Philby, who employed cunning and cold judgement, with no shred of compunction, from March to October 1944. First, he sowed an idea in the receptive mind of Colonel Valentine Vivian; since others seemed to share Vivian's reservations about 'the obstructive Cowgill', should he not try to get their assistance? To take an obvious example: Commander Christopher Arnold-Foster, the former Assistant Director of Naval Intelligence who had become principal staff officer to Menzies, would draw the right conclusions, provided that he received the necessary evidence. Perhaps Colonel Vivian could arrange a meeting between Arnold-Foster and Guy Liddell of MI5? Then at least the reasons for needless friction between rivals who should be close collaborators would at last be brought into the open. The Deputy Chief of the secret service, a weak character who had long smarted under Cowgill's self-righteous scorn, was grateful to Philby for this crafty advice. Vivian, knowing that Cowgill was then busily travelling abroad, acted on it. When Arnold-Foster rang up Philby unexpectedly and invited him to drop in for a talk, it became apparent that Vivian had already set the wheels in motion. 'He was obviously appraising me,' wrote Philby of his frank exchanges with Arnold-Foster, 'and I tried to be as sensible and straightforward as possible. Cowgill's name was not mentioned.' Vivian, anxious to push forward while Cowgill was away, found ready support from the Foreign Office whose representative with SIS, Patrick Reilly, had little regard for Cowgill's political discernment. As for the Bletchley code-breakers, their hostility to the obstructiveness of Philby's chief proved uncompromising.

Having prepared the ground, Vivian completed with deliberate care his function as the unwitting Cowgill's executioner. Not until October 1944, when his intended victim had returned from lengthy visits to centres, units and agents in the Middle East and Europe, did Vivian finally send for Philby. Vivian's face shone with pleasure as he passed across the desk a long, flowing note he had just composed for the approval of 'C'. This dwelt on the unsatisfactory conditions of friction throughout the service, imputed these to Cowgill's poor leadership, proposed radical changes for peace-time improvement and mentioned Philby by name as the most suitable candidate to run Section Nine. In due course, Menzies summoned the candidate, addressed him for the first time as 'Kim', let him see Vivian's minute, which Philby pretended to read out of politeness, and waited for his comments.[19] Only one point of substance occurred to the hesitant, deferential Chief-designate of Section Nine: the need to protect his flanks against possible future attacks by MI5. Naturally, he did not put it so crudely, merely hinting that he would feel happier if, in view of past difficulties, SIS could be officially assured of MI5's approval of the new appointment. Menzies took the tactical point at once, promising to write to Sir David Petrie, the head of MI5, without more ado. 'I left him in the hope that he would claim, and perhaps more than half believe, that the whole credit for the idea was his own,' commented Philby. Yet it is exceedingly doubtful if Petrie, who remained on friendly terms with Cowgill until he died, would have written and signed anything so critical of the past record of the ousted head of Section Five as Philby and his Soviet censors have implied. Petrie, in fact, privately disapproved of the underhand scheming which eventually forced Cowgill to swallow his pride and resign from the secret service.[20]

Naturally, and correctly, the mortified Cowgill suspected Vivian both of plotting his downfall and of twisting the knife in his back. If it was bad enough to come back and find that a 'palace revolution' had been fomented in his absence, it was far worse to learn, too late, that he had been unceremoniously supplanted by Philby, one of his own underlings to whom he had always shown kindness and consideration, largely for Vivian's sake. However, Cowgill did not take the humiliation lying down. He twice explained forcibly to Menzies why he felt exceedingly hard done by. The records also confirmed that he had sacrificed excellent prospects in India six years earlier to join SIS and organize its anti-Communist section, a point which Vivian had carefully left out of his indictment. The war against Germany had caused the original plan to be shelved. Did 'C' seriously contend that Cowgill's hard work as head of Section Five merited such a cruel recompense as this? Alas, Menzies listened quite unmoved. The decision had already been taken, he said, with the future welfare of the service in mind. Nothing else mattered. He would, of course, fit Cowgill in somewhere else; but Philby was his personal choice as Chief of Section Nine. Cowgill declined the offer and tendered his resignation, more concerned about his own prospects than his dignity allowed him to admit. Apart from a chief constable's appointment in a provincial police force, which Cowgill also declined, Menzies and his staff had nothing concrete to suggest.

Philby avoided his former boss like the plague. Yet Cowgill never dreamed, until he read his supplanter's somewhat overdramatized version of these events in *My Silent War*, how easily Valentine Vivian had been manipulated by Kim and his Soviet controller. Mary Cowgill, his wife, was equally hoodwinked by the charming, oddly diffident Kim, not realizing at the time that Kim's 'sweet and attractive' Aileen herself had also been deceived from the start to finish by the husband she adored. Perhaps the consistency of the Cowgills' unforgiving attitude to Valentine Vivian was best reflected in the bewildered question once asked by one of their children, and overheard in the home: 'Who is this great friend Daddy used to have – and Mummy would like to kill?'[21]

Few people in Section Five, at Broadway headquarters, at Ryder Street or at Bletchley deeply regretted the departure of Felix Cowgill, though several OSS observers did so.[22] It was generally agreed that Philby deserved his preferment and would be an improvement on his unlamented predecessor. The sole critic of a régime short-sighted enough to admit such an unpredictable character as Kim to its higher ranks was the unrelenting Malcolm Muggeridge. Like his friend and SIS colleague Graham Greene, Muggeridge had by now returned to London after completing his counter-espionage work in Africa. Tours of duty with French intelligence in Algeria and Italy had followed, then an unquiet interlude at Ryder Street until he was despatched to liberated Paris in mid August 1944. Muggeridge knew nothing of Philby's subtle machinations to replace Cowgill. What he did notice with a fresh and dispassionate eye was that 'Kim set the tone and the pace of Section Five', in Cowgill's absence. Graham Greene, who 'appeared to feel as out of place there as I did, and like myself enjoyed Kim only in small doses', certainly took strong exception to 'a blatant attempt by Philby to foist promotion on him as an inducement to stay on permanently in the service'. Greene responded decisively by handing in his notice.[23] It was a period of change and restiveness. The temporary staff longed for the war to end; and the more caustic spirits among them marvelled at the folly of the small handful of ambitious men and women eager to remain in permanently airtight boxes as members of SIS.

Many weeks before the Cowgill issue came to a head, the acting

Personnel Chief, Commander Kenneth Cohen, took it on himself to invite comments from the 'temporaries' on the would-be post-war 'regulars'. Cohen seemed interested in receiving frank, uninhibited assessments of their personal and professional qualities. Inevitably, he asked Muggeridge one day to give his honest opinion of Philby, remarking that anyone so able and energetic as Kim would almost certainly be found a permanent post.

'You can't be serious, Kenneth,' Muggeridge expostulated. 'I like the man as well as you do, but I wouldn't give him house room.'

'Why not?'

'For one good reason. Kim simply can't be trusted. He happens to be one of nature's *farouches*, a wild man capable of turning the place upside down for his own ends.'

Cohen made a sceptical note of this unexpectedly vigorous opinion, but events overtook any formal use he might have made of it, even had he felt so disposed. Philby emerged with unruffled smoothness as head of SIS Soviet counter-intelligence with the unanimous support of Menzies, Petrie, Dansey and Vivian. All that Muggeridge could find to say in retrospect was this: 'If Kenneth Cohen had believed me, and forced his superiors to listen, the secret service would have saved itself and Britain an awful lot of trouble.' Yet Muggeridge had not the heart or the spirit to harbour personal animosities. As has emerged with clarity elsewhere, he bore Philby no grudge for deceiving and wholly outmanoeuvring his superiors in SIS:

> It would be equally untrue for me now to say Philby's double-cross fills me with abhorrence. If I were to run into him, I should, I am sure, pass as agreeable an evening with him as I ever did in the days when we were both in Section Five. I have never been able to relate my feelings about people as individuals to my reactions to their public attitudes and behaviour, whether approving or disapproving. . . .[24]

With the novelist's feeling for human motivation, Graham Greene long afterwards would say of Philby:

> I liked him. I've often asked myself what I would have done if I'd discovered he was a secret agent at that time. . . . I think, perhaps, if in a

drunken moment he had slipped a hint, I would have given him twenty-four hours to get clear and then reported him.[25]

It was in Paris during the bleak winter of 1944–5, when Philby was busily forming his new Soviet counter-espionage section, that Muggeridge met him again. They were staying at the Rothschild mansion in the Avenue Marigny, which had been thoughtfully put at the disposal of Victor, the scion of the liberating English branch of the international banking dynasty, and which had since become the large, sombre billet of several members of the secret intelligence fraternity. 'Hitlers come and go,' said the concierge, 'but Rothschilds go on for ever.' Two small incidents imprinted themselves indelibly on Muggeridge's mind. Each concerned Philby. The first was a heated discussion at table about the rights and wrongs of withholding important Bletchley intercepts from the Soviet Union. It was Victor Rothschild who raised the matter, startling Muggeridge by his vehemence in criticizing this standard practice. Intelligence relating to the German order of battle and operational plans, Rothschild argued, would be invaluable to the Russians. The British and the Americans were supposed to be fighting on the same side as the Soviets. To deny such vital information was worse than an unfriendly act. Muggeridge contradicted him:

> Such caution was legitimate, especially in view of the way the Russians had passed on to the Germans everything they knew about us and our intentions during the period of the Nazi–Soviet Pact. Another similar occasion for treachery might arise, and we were right to guard against it....

The debate waxed hotter, and, for once, Philby joined in:

> He spluttered and shouted that we were in duty bound to do everything within our power, whatever it might be, to support the Red Army, including risking – if there was a risk – the security of the Bletchley material.

Muggeridge suddenly felt like the skeleton at the feast. He had never seen Philby so angrily sure of himself. In retrospect, but incorrectly, he dated Philby's treachery from this moment. For

Philby had long known through his Soviet controller that the Bletchley material was reaching the Russians through the 'Lucy' network in Switzerland.

The second incident, recounted by Muggeridge at length, was altogether stranger. By late October 1944, Muggeridge had received a secret directive from headquarters about the formation of Philby's new department for handling Soviet intelligence, including sabotage and subversion. Any queries should be passed through Jacques Soustelle's Services Spéciales, to which Muggeridge was then attached. Apart from asking two token questions, so simple that Soustelle and his colleagues dismissed them as a bluff, Philby remained curiously uninterested in Soviet clandestine activities in France. When Muggeridge was independently approached by Colonel Arnould, the war-time head of the SIS network in Paris, and given precise details of Communist infiltration of the French Government, the administrative machine, and the security services, he naturally informed Philby.

> From Philby I got back a contemptuous dismissal of the Colonel's allegations as so much poppycock, and a recommendation to put any further offerings from this source straight into the w.p.b. (I particularly remember the newspaper-style use of initials, as scrawled editorially on some proffered news item or syndicated feature).

Muggeridge did not pursue this hare. For one thing, Jacques Soustelle and his associates insisted that poor old Arnould was slightly deranged, a possibility which had already struck the sympathetic but case-hardened Muggeridge; for another, Philby had already decided to call on his own agent both to explain the teething problems of Section Nine and to sound him out on 'a certain proposition he had in mind' – a proposition which concerned Malcolm Muggeridge and nobody else.

Philby's brief visit to Paris, which had begun with that sharp altercation at the Rothschild mansion about the propriety of withholding the Bletchley intercepts from the Russians, ended in an apocalyptic glow of alcoholic absurdity late one night outside the Soviet Embassy. Over an expensive dinner earlier, Muggeridge had waited patiently to hear what Kim's personal proposition amounted to. I was disappointed, though not altogether surprised, at his inability to broach a difficult subject. I knew that he had lately fired Steptoe, a splendid character, straight out of the pages of P. G. Wodehouse, who'd worked for a while with me in Mozambique and then temporarily succeeded Currie in charge of Section Nine before Philby's permanent appointment was promulgated. Kim hadn't come across to fire me because I wasn't on his strength, officially. The wild thought did cross my mind that he might be on the point of inveigling me, a well-known anti-Communist, into joining his expanding empire. Yet that seemed too egotistical a fancy, so I just held on expectantly. I believe now that this is what he may have wanted to bring up, but Kim, perhaps remembering how Graham Greene had brushed him off, and fearing a repetition, decided not to raise it at all.[26]

In his corrosively individualistic way, Muggeridge loathed the pettiness of SIS office politics, and his foreign assignments had served to increase the loathing. Had he been more familiar with the intrigues behind recent reforms carried out at headquarters, he would certainly have been still more suspicious of a horizontal system of gathering Soviet intelligence which concentrated excessive powers into one pair of hands, whether Philby's or anyone else's. And if he felt sorry for the luckless Steptoe, it would have infuriated him to discover, as the discarded Cowgill would soon discover, that Philby, for reasons of prudence, intended to rid Section Nine of Jane Archer, its one specialist on Russian affairs, who had interrogated the ill-fated Walter Krivitsky in the early days of the war, and who might have proved a bigger thorn in her boss's flesh than the awkwardly angular Muggeridge himself. To this day Malcolm Muggeridge has retained an exceptionally clear impression of that convivial evening with Philby, who dwelt so obsessively on the appalling task of trying to penetrate the hidden and ultra-efficient Soviet intelligence organization that his puzzled colleague 'hardly knew whether to laugh or to cry'. The monologue started in earnest after they left the expensive restaurant where they had drunk more than their fill:

Instead of returning to the Avenue Marigny, we strolled by the river, and Kim pointed up to a block of flats, saying that he had lived there with his first wife.... Quite suddenly Kim said: 'Let's go to the Rue de Grenelle!' I didn't know then (though I should have) that this was where the Soviet Embassy was situated, and supposed he might have in his mind some favourite café or night-spot. Anyway, I was in a mood to go anywhere, so we set off. Kim now began at last to talk about his new responsibilities, and I realized, at the time without any particular amazement, that we were making for the Soviet Embassy. How are we going to get in there? Kim kept saying, and went on to expatiate upon the special difficulties of penetrating a Soviet embassy as compared with others – no chance of planting a servant when all the staff, down to the lowliest kitchen-maids and porters and chauffeurs, are imported from the USSR and sometimes in reality hold quite senior posts in the intelligence *apparat*. Tremendous obstacles, too, in the way of bugging the place; they never let foreign electricians or builders, anyone like that, into the embassy. Listening devices, observation posts, inside agents, all ruled out; the staff themselves, high and low, rigidly controlled, only certain picked members allowed to circulate freely, and even they are often kept under surveillance. Look at it! – by this time we were in the Rue de Grenelle – every blind drawn, every door locked, every window with its iron grating, the very fire escape contained steel netting; even so, behind the doors and windows, round-the-clock guards, burglar alarms, every imaginable and unimaginable security precaution.

He carried on like this in an almost demented way; not exactly shaking his fists, but gesticulating and shouting at the hermetically sealed embassy, standing so insulated and isolated in a Paris street, as though it had just been dropped there out of the sky, to be removed, intact, when its purpose had been served. While all this was going on, we were in full sight of the embassy, and of the two *flics* posted at its main entrance. Despite my fuddled state, I had my wits sufficiently about me to register in my mind that this was most irregular, if not reprehensible, behaviour on the part of a senior MI6 officer, to whom we were not allowed to refer to by name, but only by symbol, even in a coded message. When I awoke the following morning, I saw it as, not only irregular or reprehensible, but inconceivable. Had it really happened? I was forced to conclude that it had. I had neither dreamed nor imagined it – the two of us in the Rue de Grenelle, loitering there in so noticeable a way, and Kim behaving so strangely and uncharacteristically....[27]

When Muggeridge wrote down that vivid description of his last outing with Philby, he could find no wholly convincing explanation of the latter's histrionic elation. Content to believe then that 'the magnetic field' of Philby's mind was momentarily disturbed, enabling him to catch a glimpse of 'Kim's other self', he has since been driven to conclude that the weird charade staged for his benefit was

> Kim's roundabout method of suggesting that I'd be doing him and the Secret Service a favour by volunteering for a job under him. He had that trick of letting others assume that they understood quite well what he thought or intended. His Soviet friends possibly persuaded him to try it on me, reasoning that a recruit whose name was down in the Kremlin's black books would strengthen rather than weaken Kim's position in the eyes of his superiors. He was, I'm afraid, out of luck. I couldn't get out of SIS fast enough, and Philby possibly knew that, too.[28]

As the end of the war approached, political disillusionment spread like a thundercloud, darkening the once dazzling prospect of final victory. Few were unaffected by the contrast. Churchill had recently complained, not without justification, that 'the Russians treat us like dogs'. A majority of representative British and Americans knew from experience that the churlish Russian habit of taking everything for granted, behaving as if their exertions on the battlefields entitled them to dictate the entire post-war settlement, created deepening mistrust as the German armies fell back on all fronts. There were, of course, still the wishful thinkers like Anthony Eden, brimming over with good will, who contended against all the evidence that Stalin had so far kept his pledged word, even to the point of insisting that all Russian prisoners in the West should be herded back to the Soviet Union like cattle to the slaughter house. The British Ambassador in Moscow, Sir Archibald Clark Kerr (later Lord Inverchapel), tried at first to console his gloomier friends with his assertion that the Soviet Union aspired to join the 'Concert of Europe' and genuinely wanted to 'belong to the Club'. What particularly irked

Churchill was the cool ambivalence of Roosevelt, who had fewer doubts than himself about Stalin's ulterior motives. With the Russians advancing more rapidly in the East than the Anglo-American forces, the Communist system was being systematically imposed on the countries thus over-run and 'liberated'.

The Yalta Conference of February 1945 marked the end of the war-time alliance of nominal equals. Harsh controversies followed the agreed decision of Roosevelt, Churchill and Stalin to abandon Poland, whose freedom to live in peace had led an unprepared Britain to take up arms in the first place, to Moscow and its Lublin Committee puppets. Roosevelt, already ailing, had 'ganged up', in a sense, with Stalin, clearly in the naïve belief that he had already gained and could keep the Soviet dictator's confidence. Just as it was no part of the American President's purpose to accept the futile Churchillian dream of a renovated British Empire, so he sidetracked the Prime Minister's attempts to drive a harder political bargain with the Soviet Union in Europe. Poland, Rumania and Bulgaria were already under Soviet control; Hungary was occupied during the month of March, nor could Hitler's broken military machine halt the Red Army's advance through East Prussia towards Berlin. Only the Communists in the West rejoiced; only those few, covert and privileged Soviet agents who appreciated the high stakes they were playing for looked forward to seeing Stalin fully confirm, by fresh advances, their revolutionary faith. Guy Burgess gave his friends and acquaintances the gloating impression that 'right had finally triumphed' at the conference table as well as on the battlefield.

In the news department of the Foreign Office he prided himself on his flair for instantly interpreting the political nuances of the Yalta agreement. His handling of the press was skilful. On occasion, as when he wished to influence the minds of MPs, he would produce chapter and verse to support his thesis that all was sweetness and light. One of his easier victims was Harold Nicolson, who noted in his diary on 26 February 1945:

I dine with Guy Burgess who shows me the telegrams exchanged with Moscow. It is clear that the Ambassador's Commission (consisting of Molotov, Clark Kerr and the American Ambassador, and empowered to settle the composition of the new Provisional Polish Government) is not to be a farce in the least. They insist on Mikolajazyk being included in the Provisional Government. Archie [Clark Kerr] seems to be handling the thing well.[29]

Burgess succeeded not only in enjoying himself but in persuading his new superiors that he was well worth considering for a permanent post in the service. He duly applied, appeared before a selection board, and was accepted.

Philby too was beginning to move more frequently out of his closed box in Broadway. After France, he visited his agents in Germany, Italy and Greece. He enjoyed getting away from the administrative routine, the paper work, the meetings. For the general mood of war-weariness permeated SIS headquarters also. Nobody could foretell how long it would take to defeat Japan; the popularity, if not the prestige, of Churchill had noticeably declined; and there were disturbing signs that the National Coalition administration would not last much longer. The emergency which had brought it into existence was a thing of the past. Regardless of the vaguely menacing problems posed by the spectacular progress of the Red Army and the inscrutable intentions of Stalin, the old-fashioned political axes were being sharpened again at Westminster. The Labour colleagues of Churchill were restless, some determined to go their own way. Had not the Prime Minister already admitted that 'it would be wrong to continue this Parliament beyond the period of the German war'? But who then could have foreseen that Roosevelt would die suddenly on 12 April 1945, less than a month before Germany surrendered?

Harry S. Truman, the unknown and untried Vice-President, entered the White House; and there followed an uneasy, protracted deadlock between the Western Allies and the Soviet Union over the Polish question. As far as Stalin was concerned, Britain and the United States had no more right to interfere in Poland than the Soviet Union had in Belgium or Greece. Both sides stood firm. Churchill failed to rouse Truman to the dangers:

'Before we halted, or still more withdrew, our troops, we ought to seek a meeting with Stalin face to face and make sure that an agreement was reached about the whole front.' There had been a foretaste of future difficulties in Austria, where a Provisional Government, again under Soviet auspices, now controlled the country. Representatives of the Western Allies had actually been debarred from entering Vienna. The military elimination of Germany had become the Soviet Union's political opportunity, and Stalin was seizing it with alacrity. Churchill warned Truman on 12 May, immediately after the Victory celebrations:

> An iron curtain is drawn down upon their front. We do not know what is going on behind. There seems little doubt that the whole of the region Lubeck–Trieste–Corfu will soon be completely in their hands. To this must be added the further enormous area between Eisenach and the Elbe, which will, I suppose, in a few weeks be occupied, when the Americans retreat, by the Russian power . . . and then the curtain will descend again to a very large extent, if not entirely. . . . Meanwhile, the attention of our peoples will be occupied in inflicting severities upon Germany, which is ruined and prostrate, and it would be open to the Russians in a very short time to advance if they chose to the waters of the North Sea and the Atlantic. . . .[30]

Truman remained unruffled. Leaning on his advisers, he refused to meet Churchill before conferring with Stalin. That, he said, would be tantamount to 'ganging up' on the suspicious Soviet leader. A date was fixed, highly inconvenient to Britain's Prime Minister, for another Three-Power Conference at Potsdam in mid July. The National Government had ceased to exist in London on 23 May; Churchill himself was now only the caretaker Premier; a General Election had been arranged for 5 July. To allow the votes of men and women in the British armed services to be registered and sent home, the result would be held back until 26 July. Meanwhile, as if casually throwing away a bargaining counter, Truman ordered back the American forces, three million strong, from the heartland of Germany to the Zone of Occupation decided on long ago at Quebec by Roosevelt and Churchill. The President saw no point whatever in provoking Stalin; on the contrary. Churchill had to accept another accomplished fact. Then, when the votes were at last counted at polling stations throughout Britain, the Labour Party gained an overwhelming popular victory. The bewilderment and disarray of Winston Churchill was complete. He failed to understand how the people's admiration and gratitude could co-exist with a refusal to trust him a little longer as their peace-time Prime Minister, regardless of the fresh perils that suddenly faced the Western world as a whole and a tired, weakened and impoverished Britain in particular. As A. J. P. Taylor put it,

> The Conservatives relied chiefly on the glory of Churchill's name, and he, egged on by Beaverbrook, zestfully turned against Labour the talent for political vituperation which he had previously reserved for Hitler. . . . The electors cheered Churchill and voted against him. . . . Folk memory counted for much. Many electors remembered the unemployment of the thirties. Some remembered how they had been cheated, or supposed they had been cheated, after the General Election of 1918. Lloyd George brought ruin to Churchill from the grave.[31]

Everything seemed to be falling neatly into place, at home and abroad. The prospects were better than Burgess and Philby could have hoped or expected. The new Prime Minister was the brisk but uninspiring Clement Attlee. He had attended the first session of the Potsdam Conference merely as an adviser. Now he replaced Churchill at the side of Truman and Stalin for the closing stages. The outcome was predictable: continuing deadlock on every subject. Stalin disallowed interference with the political régimes in territories freed by the Red Army. Apart from Truman's private advice to Stalin, which the Soviet dictator appeared not to take in, that the Anglo-Americans had successfully developed their own atomic weapons and that these might be used shortly against Japan, the meeting settled nothing. In the correct assessment of A. J. P. Taylor, 'Potsdam indeed marked the beginning of "the cold war" and therefore of post-war history.' Attlee had invited the tough ex-trade unionist, Ernest Bevin, to serve as his Foreign Secretary; Bevin selected as his right-hand man the bright young Scottish MP and ex-journalist Hector McNeil, who lost no time in persuading his friend Guy Burgess to join him in the role of personal assistant. Slightly peeved at this flouting of the finer points of departmental protocol, the Foreign Office moved in their own nominee, Frederick Warner, thus giving the new Minister of State two aides for the price of one. Luck continued to smile on Burgess. Warner, as it happened, liked him. They struck up a superficial comradeship which would endure.

Philby had, by now, reorganized Section Nine, the crucial Soviet intelligence unit of SIS, largely to his own specifications. Only once since the previous autumn, after that strange encounter with Muggeridge who had, in the meantime, abruptly quit the secret service for a job on the *Daily Telegraph*, was Philby almost unmasked. The incident had occurred during the Anglo-American advance into Germany. As a result of it, James Jesus Angleton, the assistant to Jim Murphy – the administrative head of OSS whom Philby had often chaffed and teased at Ryder Street in Cowgill's day – began to harbour vague personal doubts about the efficiency, if not the reliability, of Section Nine's new Chief. The trouble arose over a German called Schmidt, whom the Gestapo had executed as a British agent. The case came to the attention of Angleton when Frau Schmidt, the dead man's mother, wrote directly to the British. Her letter seeking compensation was passed on to a Special Counter-Intelligence Unit which, in turn, brought the facts to the notice of Philby in London. No action followed. Unfortunately, the message – or so it was later claimed – either got lost in transit or mislaid at headquarters, nobody ever found out which. The excuse itself sounded thin to Angleton. Nevertheless, no record could be traced on the files. Subsequently, when the captured *Abwehr* archives were examined in Washington, it emerged that Schmidt had been working for the Russians as well as the British. In fact, Schmidt proved to be the chief informant of the *Rote Kapelle* inside the Luftwaffe High Command.

Faint American suspicions of Philby's competence, though not yet of his loyalty, were stirred by this small but significant oversight or deliberate act of negligence. Yet something potentially more damaging happened in August 1945, within the jurisdiction of SIS and of 'C' himself. A summons to Menzies's office came one morning. 'C' pushed some papers across the desk for Philby to study. A startling message from the British minister in Istanbul disclosed that Konstantin Volkov, the KGB representative at the Soviet Consulate, was seeking political asylum in Britain for himself and his wife in return for important information. Menzies watched impassively as Philby took in the details of the preliminary exchanges between Volkov and Page, the local British Consul whom the Russian had sought out. On Volkov's 'shopping list' was an offer to reveal the names of three British spies working for the Soviet Union, two in the Foreign Office, the other in a key branch of the secret service. It was again Philby's turn to be lucky, at least for a while. Volkov was adamant that the Russians could read certain British ciphers. He therefore insisted that all communications with 'C' should be conducted by diplomatic bag. The inevitable delays played right into Philby's hands, ensuring the luckless Volkov's removal to Moscow for a traitor's summary liquidation. Naturally, Philby had at once warned the Moscow Centre through his own controller. Not for the first nor the last time, the head of Section Nine exulted in a murder he had arranged for others to commit. His own cold-blooded account of his blithe scheming to outwit both Volkov and Menzies reeks of the smug amorality characterizing the schoolboy ringleaders in William Golding's *Lord of the Flies*. The argument that 'it was either Volkov's head or mine' no doubt appealed as much to Burgess as it did to the impenitent Philby. Yet it doubtless dawned on him at the same time that the risk of detection would probably increase, not diminish, whenever Russians of the calibre of Kritivsky and Volkov chose to defect to the West. Volkov slipped the noose round his own neck by time-wasting. Menzies had humoured the security-crazed Russian, forbidding all radio communication with Istanbul. From start to finish, nearly three weeks had passed before Philby set foot on Turkish soil himself in the reasonable expectation that the would-be defector had already been satisfactorily dealt with. On the other hand, nobody in SIS, least of all Philby, liked handling delicate rescue operations that failed:

During the homeward journey, I roughed out a report which I would present to the Chief, describing in detail the failure of my mission. Necessarily, it contained my theory of Volkov's disappearance. The essence of the theory was that Volkov's own insistence on bag communications had brought about his downfall. . . . Doubtless both his office and his living quarters were bugged. Both he and his wife were reported to be nervous. Perhaps his manner had given him away; perhaps he had got drunk and talked too much; perhaps even he had changed his mind and confessed to his colleagues. Of course, I admitted, this was all speculation; the truth might never be known. Another theory – that the Russians had been tipped off about Volkov's approach to the British – had no solid evidence to support it. It was not worth including in my report.[32]

Menzies was disappointed and somewhat displeased, all the more so when it later turned out that there had been some loose talking about the case on the telephone, and that the two British diplomats concerned might have unwittingly alerted the Russians. Philby could begin to breathe more easily again, though it hurt his pride to pretend that even he might have off-days. The conspiratorial half of him rejoiced in another secret triumph. The Japanese cities of Hiroshima and Nagasaki had been destroyed by atomic bombs at the beginning of August. As a result, the war in the Far East had come to an abrupt end during the troublesome Volkov affair. If the enigmatic Stalin had appeared indifferent at Potsdam to Truman's mention of these new weapons, Philby could appreciate his reasons. He already knew that his fellow-agents and their accomplices across the Atlantic had not been idle, and that the Soviet Union now possessed most of the scientific secrets which the British and the Americans had been at such pains to withhold. He was glad that Donald Maclean had proved, and was continuing to prove, an invaluable link in the underground chain.

Philby's delight would have yielded to great anxiety if he had also realized that, as a result of careless ciphering by a minion at the Soviet Consulate at New York, a succession of damaging messages had recently been intercepted by American and British cipher experts. In the immediate post-war confusion, nobody attempted to decipher them. In any case, messages sent on the so-called 'one-time-pad' principle were deemed almost impossible to break down. This batch turned out to be different, as the crypto-analysts eventually discovered. Furthermore, their contents would prove that there was someone spying for the Soviet Union under the hallowed roof of the British Embassy in Washington, and while Maclean was serving there. Secret agents invariably have to live in boxes, surviving from one day to the next on tiny morsels of knowledge. It may have been just as well for the sanity of Burgess, Philby and Maclean that this was so, though it must be admitted that the astonishing trustfulness of their superiors in the Foreign Office and the British Secret Service helped them not only to survive, but to keep sane and stay 'in place' as Soviet agents for the next six turbulent years of phoney peace.

9. ENTER THE FIFTH MAN

Clement Attlee was no better prepared for the burdens unexpectedly thrust upon him by the votes of the British people towards the end of July 1945 than Harry S. Truman had been in mid April, after Roosevelt's sudden death. Returning to Potsdam for the closing stages of this meeting of deadlocked minds, Britain's new Prime Minister and his tough but raw Foreign Secretary, Ernest Bevin, had little to contribute but good will. The unbroken impasse between the two main protagonists, Stalin and Truman, boded ill. Even before his recent electoral eclipse, Churchill had remarked favourably, if with some puzzlement, on the new-found vigour of the President, a vigour which Truman had singularly failed to assert during earlier sessions of the conference. 'He stood up to the Russians in a most emphatic and decisive manner,' Churchill noted, 'telling them as to certain demands that they absolutely could not have and that the United States was entirely against them.' The explanation came indirectly the following day, 17 July, when Britain's war leader was shown the full and detailed report from General Leslie R. Groves in Washington on the successful testing of an atomic weapon at Alamorgordo in the New Mexican desert. 'Now I know what happened to Truman yesterday,' said Churchill. 'When he got to the meeting after having read the report he was a changed man. He told the Russians just where they got on and off and generally bossed the whole meeting.'[1]

Stalin showed no emotion on 24 July on learning casually from the President that 'we had a new weapon of unusual destructive force'. Inscrutable as ever, the Soviet leader said 'he was glad to hear it and hoped we would make "good use of it against the

Japanese"'.[2] However, that same evening, a few hours before Churchill's departure for Downing Street and the bitter blow awaiting him at the hands of his own electorate, Stalin did not attempt to disguise his true feelings from Molotov and Marshal Zhukov: 'They simply want to raise the price,' he told them. 'We've got to work on Kurchatov [the director of Soviet energy research] and hurry things up.'[3] So, although Truman had desisted from provocatively using the American nuclear monopoly, from which Britain herself had been effectively excluded, as a direct bargaining counter against Stalin at the conference table, the Russians already suspected the worst. The diplomatic cold war had thus begun; and the unassuming Clement Attlee, while regretting this fact, lacked the power and the authority to prevent the steady escalation of tension.

Tory diehards were not alone in their fears that Attlee's rise to the highest office spelled the end of an era: the old world, which Britain had once shaped and largely controlled as a great imperial power, no longer existed and would never return. Few doubted, or had any reason to doubt, that the dry, colourless but able Socialist Prime Minister, a person of highly respectable middle-class origins, a product of Haileybury and Oxford, and an ex-major who had survived the First World War, would hesitate to carry out his Party's pledges and introduce his own quiet kind of social revolution, despite the darkening international outlook.

Churchill had taken defeat magnanimously. He bore Attlee no ill will. What probably hurt him most in the hour of rejection was the thought of being separated from his beloved red despatch boxes: 'It will be strange tomorrow,' he said, 'not to be consulted upon the great affairs of State.' He even felt a twinge of pity for his opponents: 'The new Government face terrible tasks. Terrible tasks. We must do all we can to help them.'[4]

Some of Churchill's most seasoned lieutenants had lost their parliamentary seats. His son-in-law Duncan Sandys, Leopold Amery, Walter Elliot, Harold Macmillan and Brendan Bracken were among them. The elusive and beguiling Bracken proved less than magnanimous in his verdict on the electorate. They reminded this pugnacious ex-minister of his own war-time censors; they were 'like mules [with] no pride of ancestry, and no hope of posterity'.[5]

In contrast to Bracken, the more practical Harold Macmillan began to consider at once how best to pave the way for his own political comeback. The odds were stacked high against the new Labour Government from the outset. Churchill himself would have been hard-pressed now to tilt back the Anglo-American partnership in Britain's favour. Even in the last stages of the war, that partnership of nominal equals had come to resemble an unbalanced arrangement between patron and client. Truman's decision at Potsdam to use atom bombs against Japan had been taken without bothering to seek British consent, as had been formally agreed at Quebec. This was a precedent for harsher decisions in store. The President was returning from Europe, aboard the cruiser *Augusta*, when he was informed of the atomic attack on Hiroshima. The American termination of Lend–Lease was abruptly announced in Washington on 17 August 1945, Victory Day in the joint struggle against Japan. The President's decree served notice on Britain that she would have to fend for herself economically from that day forward, or answer for the consequences herself. The business-like address of Truman brought it home to Whitehall and the British public that Attlee's social experiments would certainly not be subsidized by the American taxpayer.

Undismayed, the Labour Government refused to be diverted from its targets. Attlee and his Cabinet had a short-list of State-ownership schemes to carry out, and carry them out they would, regardless of the omens. In the words of A. J. P. Taylor:

> The legacy of war seemed almost beyond bearing. Great Britain had drawn on the rest of the world to the extent of £4198 million. . . . The British mercantile marine was 30 per cent smaller in June 1945 than it had been at the beginning of the war. Exports were little more than 40 per cent of the pre-war figure. On top of this, government expenditure abroad – partly for relief, mainly for the armed forces – remained five times as great as pre-war. In 1946, it was calculated, Great Britain would spend abroad £750 million more than she earned.[6]

The slogan was coined and officially approved that 'We must

export – or die.' Yet Attlee clung to his ideals. Nothing Truman did would shift him from his plans to inaugurate a Welfare State, to nationalize the Bank of England, the coal, gas, electricity and steel industries, as well as the country's transport system, as first steps towards the rebuilding of a fairer and happier, if poorer, society.

In a moment of euphoria, Hugh Dalton, the new Chancellor of the Exchequer, had declared, once Labour's landslide triumph at the polls was a certainty: 'After the long storm of war . . . we saw the sunrise.'[7] The sun's rays had been since obscured by accumulating thunderclouds. Even so, the verdict of the electorate could not be easily set aside or reversed. Bemused and uncertain the British people might be, but their innate sense of fair play demanded that Attlee's Government should at least be given a chance.

Guy Burgess and Harold Philby had every reason to be pleased. The colourless Attlee was a safer bet than the impenitent old warhorse Churchill; and though Bevin at the Foreign Office might prove a stumbling block, Burgess was well placed in the inner sanctum of his friend Hector McNeil, the Minister of State for Foreign Affairs, to anticipate trouble and keep the Kremlin informed. Philby's Soviet Affairs section of the reconstructed secret service was certainly its largest and most important department; he, too, would not fail to furnish his Soviet masters with up-to-date details of Britain's intended moves in the undeclared and unending secret war. Neither man thought highly of the Prime Minister's tepid Socialist prescriptions. They did see considerable advantage to the Soviet Union in the bitterly divisive controversies which the Government's proposals were already causing in a country that lacked the capital resources to ensure a quick and steady recovery from war-weariness and insolvency. The Americans, they realized, had played into Stalin's hands by cutting off Lend–Lease without warning. The Soviet Union had lost the benefits as well; possibly Truman's prime purpose had been to deprive the Russians, but the British could afford it less. The public seldom took kindly to any political gestures which promised to prolong the hardships of war-time survival. Truman had been unwise to sign the order with such indecent haste.

Two men of Marxist sentiment had been brought into the Cabinet: John Strachey, the ex-Communist, as Minister of Food, and the Welsh ex-miner Aneurin Bevan, as Minister of Health and Housing. Their deep misgivings about the terms on which Britain should borrow money from the United States were shared by other more moderate ministers. The predominant figure in the Cabinet and Attlee's constant counsellor was the Foreign Secretary, Ernest Bevin, who feared that the Americans were withdrawing into isolation again as in 1918; American support, he maintained, would be essential to hold an aggressive Soviet Union in check. There was little love lost between Bevin and 'Nye' Bevan, as the fiery Welshman was nicknamed. 'Nye is his own worst enemy,' one critic is said to have told Bevin. 'Not while I'm alive, he ain't,' was Bevin's blunt retort.[8] Yet every member of the Cabinet felt obliged to keep quiet while the financial expert John Maynard Keynes tried to obtain the best terms possible from the United States.

From late August until December 1945, the loan negotiations weighed heavily on the Attlee Cabinet. Truman's 'body blow', as the Prime Minister afterwards described the cutting off of Lend-Lease, had demonstrated that the US administration was in anything but a generous mood. Keynes, who claimed to understand the American mind, hoped to get £1500 million, either as a gift or as an interest-free subsidy, which would keep Britain solvent until 1949. Lucidly and persuasively though Keynes argued his case, the 'strings' attached by the American negotiators to the disbursing of any large sum were drawn tighter and tighter, causing Keynes more than once 'to hit the ceiling' in protest.[9] One particular condition on which the Americans insisted was that Britain's war-time sterling balances should be made convertible within a year of the signing of any loan agreement. For the United States disliked the sterling area, regarding it as a gigantic underworld of discriminatory practice which, like the crumbling British Empire, deserved only to be dismantled.

Few middle-class Labour supporters shared the perverse faith of Burgess and Philby in Marxism and in the ultimate triumph of the Soviet Union. For few yet realized that the Cold War had already begun, still less that Stalin was determined to win it by fair means or foul. At the same time, these same middle-class Labour supporters could not comprehend the feckless outlook and conduct of many British workers, who were already behaving, and would continue to behave, as if the free world owed them a living. Harold Nicolson, who belonged to an older and more privileged generation, unquestionably voiced a widely held middle-class grievance when he wrote to his wife, Victoria Sackville-West, early in December 1945:

I do not pretend to enjoy a socialist system, but I think it right and am prepared to make personal sacrifices for it. But what I do loathe and fear is the decline in spiritual values. Truthfulness is giving place to bigotry. Cruelty is replacing tolerance. And the sanctity of the individual is being blurred by mass emotions. I fear I have not got a communal mind.[10]

Perhaps the passage from total war to uneasy peace, from the regimentation of life accepted in the interests of national survival to an apparently inopportune Socialist experiment begun under the conditions of a siege economy, had been altogether too swift. Only clandestine Soviet agents had any real cause for gratification. Members of the British Communist Party naturally supported the Soviet Union through thick and thin, but felt frustrated by the defiant individualism and self-interest of their fellow citizens, fellow travellers included. Douglas Hyde, then news editor of the *Daily Worker*, noted that

among the Labour men returned [to Parliament] were a number of our own Party members who had slipped in almost unnoticed, as it were.... By the time the list was complete we knew that we had at least eight or nine 'cryptos' in the House of Commons, in addition to our own [two] publicly acknowledged MPs. It was not long, however, before some of them were finding reasons for quietly dropping the Party, explaining that they felt they could do more good for the cause by doing so.... Some of them may genuinely have come to feel that the parliamentary way to socialism was the best or the only way in Britain, others became attracted by a political and parliamentary career which they felt would not be helped by a secret association with the Communist Party. Others who were returned as Labour men were subsequently among those 'purged' by the Labour Party itself and who, in the 1950 election, all lost their seats in Parliament.[11]

It was not the best of times for Attlee's quiet revolution. The new Cold War, as Burgess and Philby well knew, might last for years; and despite Ernest Bevin's refusal to be browbeaten or intimidated by Molotov or any other Soviet leader, many of his compatriots wondered at times whether confrontation with the Russians was necessary. Churchillian jokes at the Prime Minister's expense were, to say the least, uncomplimentary as the months dragged by. In seeking to account for Attlee's alleged reluctance to fly to Moscow and speak plainly to Stalin, the Leader of the Opposition mused: 'It's probably a case of – when the mouse is away, the cats will play.'[12]

Fred Warner, the other occupant of Hector McNeil's outer office, found out before long that Guy Burgess was 'an acquired taste', both socially and professionally. Warner had first set disbelieving eyes on him at a Foreign Office press briefing towards the end of the war: 'Who in God's name can *that* be?' he had asked one of his colleagues. 'Ah,' said the latter with an air of resignation. 'You mean Guy Burgess, I suppose. Well, don't go too much by appearances. He looks slovenly and disreputable, but he's quite a character.' Burgess had handled the journalists with ease and impressive skill on that occasion; and a few mornings later, while Warner, an extremely tall ex-naval officer, was striding across St James's Park towards the Foreign Office, he heard hurrying footsteps behind him. Burgess had caught up with him, greeted him like an old friend, and at once sounded off about 'some perfectly futile decision' just taken by Anthony Eden and briefly reported in that day's *Times*. Tearing Eden and his decision to shreds in loud, indignant tones, Burgess proceeded to draw a neat parallel with the bold foreign policy of Castlereagh: 'He'd never have messed it up like Anthony. Here's what Castlereagh would have done. . . .' And he was still immersed in his animated reconstruction of events when they reached the main door of the building together, showed their passes, and parted.[13]

Warner had since grown to like this unaccountably weird young colleague, though the appointment of Burgess as supernumerary personal assistant to Hector McNeil, the new Minister of State, had smacked of downright favouritism. 'Most irregular' was the common verdict. A good-natured, shrewd, ambitious Scot, with a good journalist's nose for 'the inside story', McNeil had needed little persuasion (from Burgess, among others) to take aboard the former BBC producer whose formidable range of contacts and originality of mind outweighed his general air of eccentricity. The fact that senior men in the Foreign Office still pursed their lips in disapproval at such an improper appointment had merely served to steel McNeil's resolve. He dug his heels in. He insisted on having the speech-writer and 'political dogsbody' of his choice, and eventually senior officials yielded. When David Footman of SIS first heard of this improbable happening, he was polite enough to wish Guy the best of luck, then went off brooding on the 'vanity of politicians'.[14] He doubted whether Burgess would last long inside the private office. For this self-possessed executive in the political section of SIS surmised correctly that Labour ministers would not readily subscribe to procedures which had always suited the Tories. They prided themselves on being defiant, even brash, in their experimenting. Sometimes in the past, Footman had watched Burgess climb the steps and dive gracefully from the top of the high board into the swimming pool at the Royal Automobile Club in Pall Mall. Guy's *joie de vivre* could be dangerously infectious, he realized; it might tempt an innocent but cocky junior minister, however intelligent, to jump, fully clothed, into the political deep end and risk his neck, if not his career, just for a 'dare'.

In fact, neither the Foreign Office nor Hector McNeil could find any fault with Burgess at the outset. He brimmed over with enthusiasm and bright ideas. No matter how little time he allowed himself for sleeping off a long night's revelry, he always arrived punctually at work. He seldom missed appointments. He also flattered McNeil by fawning on him. His carelessness about dress and appearances constituted the only consistent black mark against him. He had a particular horror, for instance, of keeping a tidy desk. Confidential papers were strewn over it like confetti, yet he could easily retrieve anything wanted urgently by burrowing like a squirrel beneath the daily newspapers and his drawing pad, on which he would sketch libellous caricatures of any subject that momentarily took his fancy. Outside friends occasionally dropped in to pass the time of day. Goronwy Rees, for one, noticed amidst the unsorted debris on the desk a half-gnawed clove of garlic, the powerful smell of which seemed to cling permanently to the crumpled suit and entire persona of Burgess. He chewed the clove intermittently, as footballers chew gum, causing visitors to wince and draw back, and eventually inducing one of his irate superiors to send a stiff memo urging him to desist from the disgusting practice, at least during office hours. Burgess, of course, ignored the advice. More than once when Rees was present, the minister would sound the buzzer peremptorily, an unmistakable summons to one or other assistant to drop everything and answer McNeil's bidding. Instead, an argument often broke out between Warner and Burgess as to whether the buzzer had sounded at all, and as to which of them should respond, if indeed it had:

'Oh Lord, there's Hector again.'

'What on earth can he want?'

'I can't think.'

'Perhaps you'd better go in, Guy.'

'Oh no, he can't possibly want me. I've been in *twice* today already. You go, it's your turn.'

The amicable bickering would continue until Burgess produced an acceptable solution: 'We're doing Hector a kindness by leaving him to get on with his own important business. Let's forget him. If he wants us, he'll buzz again.'[15]

Harold Nicolson, one of many former MPs swept away in the Labour landslide, visited Athens to give a lecture towards the end of October 1945. At the prompting of Burgess, he saw McNeil at the Foreign Office on his return. British troops were still in

Greece. The Labour Government, uneasily aware of Soviet machinations in the Balkans and inside Greece herself, would not shirk their responsibilities. Nicolson learnt that Hector McNeil 'is being sent out to Athens to examine the situation and to assist Greece in her efforts for reconstruction'. Nicolson's advice to the Minister of State was brief and pointed: choose the best government team possible, send out good financial advisers, and hope for the best. 'Rather to my surprise,' noted Nicolson, 'he absolutely agrees with this. He says that Ernest Bevin absolutely refuses to impose a Government on Greece. He adds that British troops will remain there for many years.' One of Nicolson's private ambitions was to become a peer of the realm, though he did not belong to the Labour Party, and naturally, in the circumstances, had reservations about joining it too hastily. Burgess, in whom Nicolson had foolishly confided, invited him to dinner at the Reform Club early in December, as the guest glumly confided to his diary that night:

> He tells me (on what authority I don't know, but I suspect Hector McNeil) that Bevin has turned me down for Chairman of the British Council, and that in some way my peerage was involved in that appointment, so that this has also disappeared.[16]

Burgess increasingly enjoyed the vicarious sense of power which his position gave him, using protocol and established practices entirely for his own convenience. He had no illusions about the vigorous anti-Soviet line followed by Bevin, the Foreign Secretary, and McNeil, the junior minister. Nor could he do anything to impede or alter it. Yet his very presence in the office of Hector McNeil, and the latter's easy and trusting friendship, enabled Burgess to supply his Soviet mentor with a steady stream of gossipy but accurate assessments on every twist and turn in departmental thinking and policy planning. The documents that he removed, photocopied, and returned no doubt helped the Russians. This fact has been disputed by Warner who, without any suspicions at the time about the true allegiance of his colleague, contends to this day that his own relaxed vigilance excluded the possibility of classified papers falling into the wrong hands:

I had the keys to the Minister's boxes, and Guy hadn't. It was a point of professional honour with me not to part with those keys to anyone. Except when I was sick or otherwise absent, the boxes were safe. Besides, Burgess never showed the least interest in the contents, though I now realize that this may have been bluff on his part.[17]

Burgess was too wily, too experienced in the furtive techniques of smuggling out documents and passing them on, ever to run risks with a colleague as observant as Warner. It was simpler to bypass the normal channels, exploiting his confidential position with Hector McNeil. Because McNeil liked him, humoured and pampered him, accepted his undergraduate wit and flashes of erudition in the mistaken notion that the department, the government, and the public were the beneficiaries of his own astuteness in selecting this exceptional personal assistant, Burgess had the complete run of the inner sanctum. If he needed the minister's keys, he asked for them. If *he* wanted access to classified files, he secured the necessary authorization without question by saying that *his minister* wanted such-and-such at once. Since, to the increasing chagrin of such ministerial colleagues as Aneurin Bevan, the Foreign Secretary and his junior minister seemed obsessed with the growing Soviet threat to the Western world, much of the material on the files was of considerable interest to the Soviet masters of Burgess in London. A sidelight on his casual flouting of internal rules and conventions was offered on another occasion to Goronwy Rees. Burgess led the visitor out of McNeil's office and into a large, ornately furnished room where the Foreign Secretary presided on formal occasions. At one end of the room stood a bookcase of reference books, among which was one precious volume which Burgess kept there 'out of harm's way', so that nobody – not even Bevin – would borrow it and then 'fail to return it'. It was a copy of the recently published Kinsey Report on the sexual activities of the human male, then unobtainable in Britain, which Burgess had promised to lend him. 'I had to hide it somewhere safe,' he said. 'Everyone's trying to get hold of it.'[18]

The day did come when even the long-suffering McNeil began to wonder whether, by defending Burgess against his many inside critics, he might not be standing in his own light. The minister, after reading a particularly testy complaint about his personal assistant's disregard for regulations, sent for Warner.

'Really,' he said. 'Guy's becoming quite impossible. What's to be done about him, Fred?'

'I don't know, Minister. But he's your man. You took him on, and you'll have to talk sternly to him.'[19]

McNeil did occasionally try to remonstrate with Burgess, but to little or no effect. Contrition came as readily to the capricious lips of his personal assistant as insouciant devilry. Yet if Hector McNeil felt at times that he was being let down by Guy, his friend, then Burgess could only say how deeply upset he was to hear it; and he would solemnly promise to behave in future like an adult.

Warner and Burgess sometimes discussed politics and the uncertain drift of democracy in hard-pressed Britain and the liberated lands of western Europe; Warner said:

> I can't recall that Guy automatically followed the Stalinist line. In fact, I doubt very much whether he cared a rap for the teachings of Marx or Lenin. In those days he sought to convey the impression of being a radical Social Democrat who believed firmly in Tawney. But the only writer he idolized personally was the novelist E. M. Forster, who still seemed to exert a powerful spell on him. That overworked maxim of Forster's about hoping he'd betray his country rather than his friend(s) was one Guy enjoyed quoting *ad nauseam*. I'm quite convinced he meant it. Friendship mattered a lot to him.[20]

Before the end of 1946, a recently appointed official had begun to harbour doubts about the honesty and reliability of Burgess. George Carey-Foster, a former group captain in the RAF, did not underestimate the difficulties of his new task in charge of the embryonic security branch of the Foreign Office; apart from his secretary, he had as yet no permanent members of staff. He succeeded in gradually recruiting a small nucleus of officers from the armed services for security requirements in overseas embassies; and, in response to his repeated pleas, one or two young men from MI6 were loaned to him temporarily for internal needs. Burgess first came to Carey-Foster's notice when McNeil's personal assistant complained that a departmental messenger was behaving suspiciously and deserved watching as a security risk. When the charged proved totally unfounded, the plaintiff naturally came under the hard scrutiny of a mildly disgruntled Carey-Foster, who subsequently made the ironical discovery that Burgess had been taking home official telegrams to study at leisure. Far from pleading guilty to a serious breach of basic security, the culprit defended himself vigorously as a zealous martyr to duty.[21]

By now Burgess had moved from Bentinck Street to a first-floor flat in Lower Bond Street where, on many an evening, he would entertain his peculiar assortment of friends. Goronwy Rees and the writer James Pope-Hennessy were among the few familiars who recognized that the host's lavish life-style had not changed for the worse in the dreary post-war era of rationing, controls, shortages, black marketeers and spivs. Late one night, after a bottle party at the flat had broken up in a flurry of violence, Pope-Hennessy left with one of the young working men whom Burgess had casually invited as a guest, only to discover on waking up next morning that his wallet had been stolen. Fortunately for Burgess, the 'honour system', under which officials were expected to perform their duties on trust, remained standard practice at the Foreign Office. Hector McNeil's misplaced good will merely provided his personal assistant with extra cover, regardless of Carey-Foster's growing doubts about Burgess. Philby kept a watchful eye on his old friend and fellow agent from a discreet distance, seldom attending the rowdy Bond Street parties, at which he might have been noticed. The two of them had every confidence in the future. After all, they were on the winning side. For poor old Britain, led by the pallid and palsied Attlee, the belligerent but clumsy Bevin, and the clever but powerless Dalton, seemed to be slithering downhill fast towards political as well as financial ruin. The chances of the country 'going Communist' could not be wholly discounted. In any case, whether that happened quickly or not, the spies could comfort themselves with the certainty that Stalin and history were with them. They would never lose, come what may.

Philby had looked on, passively and always without a qualm, while the necessary pruning down of the war-time secret service had been debated and eventually agreed upon. Allergic though he was to committee work, he had served gladly enough in late 1945 on the reconstruction panel which Menzies formed to consider and determine methods of rendering a smaller service, more flexible and professional in the discharge of its post-war duties. Not every recommendation had been to 'C's' liking; but he had approved and accepted most of them, including an ironical solution for harmonizing the evaluation of Communist and Soviet data by concentrating overall responsibility for counter-intelligence operations in the safe hands of Philby himself. This battle of principle had taken some winning. For, as Philby has since admitted, 'my interest was heavily engaged'. The argument had raged round the old conundrum: should service branches be divided along vertical or horizontal lines? Ought each branch to be answerable for processing as well as assessing what it produced? Or ought the dividing line to fall between production and assessment, so that Philby would have access to the raw material he needed from each of the regional branches of SIS? As it happened, David Footman, an articulate member of the committee, firmly supported Philby's stand on grounds of practicality. So, in the end, did Menzies himself: 'C' agreed that there was more to be said for studying subjects on a global rather than a local basis.

By a fortunate chance, partly induced through financial stringency, Attlee himself decided to curb the former free-ranging operations abroad of Britain's secret agents. The decision reduced the direct damage Philby would otherwise have been able to inflict on the service during this first uncertain period of the Cold War. Even so, largely restricted though SIS was to counter-espionage, the head of its Soviet section, who had recently been awarded the Order of the British Empire for his war-time work, kept Moscow abreast of every move he was making. No doubt a number of British agents still in the field were compromised as a result. How many suffered death, injury or imprisonment through Philby's studied duplicity remains to this day a matter of guesswork; perhaps three dozen casualties would be a conservative estimate for the years 1945 to

1947. As Burgess was only too happy to fill in gaps with his detailed knowledge of Labour foreign policy, Philby served his masters in the Kremlin only too well. Such crucial matters as Britain's determination to arm herself with nuclear weapons – a decision taken by Attlee and Bevin without proper endorsement by the full Cabinet – were wormed out of Burgess and duly passed on. By way of reassuring Menzies that he had not lost his touch, Philby was almost certainly fed by his Soviet mentor with crumbs of accurate but out-of-date items of 'disinformation' about active Soviet agents and likely Soviet targets. The vital factor was that of maintaining a reassuring front of pretence that British secrets could not be in better or sounder hands.

Since 1944, Philby had been living with Aileen in a large, pleasant house in Carlyle Square, Chelsea. He told early visitors, one of them Malcolm Muggeridge, that Aileen's mother had generously put up the money for a twenty-year lease. To the sceptical mind of Muggeridge, that just passed as an explanation of the way in which their home had been acquired at a time when market values were low, and on the point of sinking lower still, once the German buzz-bombs and rockets started to fall indiscriminately on London. It did not, however, explain the generous hospitality dispensed to stray guests, let alone the family's typically informal but noticeably higher standard of living. Only when Philby vanished from Beirut in 1963 did Muggeridge appreciate at last 'the true source of Philby's ready funds for the out-of-pocket expenditure needed to drink hard and drug what may have remained of his conscience'.[22] By late 1946 Aileen had officially become the second Mrs Philby. The marriage took place at Chelsea Registry Office on 25 September that year. Tommy Harris, the art dealer whom Muggeridge had never wholly trusted, was the only male witness. Aileen, who had already given birth to three children, attended the informal ceremony in an advanced state of pregnancy. Her fourth child was born less than two months later, in November 1946. Philby had pondered long and hard before deciding to make an honest woman of her. He had notified Colonel Vivian earlier in the year of his previous unsuccessful marriage of convenience to Litzi (Alice Friedman). Braving the risk that her Communist past would now emerge, he had asked Vivian for special leave to visit Litzi in Paris and request a divorce. As a matter of routine, Vivian asked MI5 for a trace on Litzi's past. In due course, MI5 informed Vivian that Alice Friedman, then living with Georg Honigmann in East Berlin, was a Soviet agent. As Patrick Seale and Maureen McConville disarmingly comment: 'It is a measure of the confidence and affection in which Philby was held by his colleagues that this revelation should seem to add nothing to what he had already confessed to Vivian.'[23]

Nevertheless, the unsuspected evidence Philby had thus volunteered against himself was studiously filed away in the mind of Dick White, the rising star of MI5 and a discerning judge of human nature. While willing to acknowledge that Felix Cowgill, in his day, could sometimes be 'an awkward bugger', White had not liked the way Cowgill was supplanted by Philby with the connivance of Vivian. Nor was he yet entirely convinced that the unconventional head of the SIS Soviet Section deserved to be treated with kid gloves, in accordance with Valentine Vivian's overkindly suggestion.

In the English-speaking nations at large, pro-Soviet sentiment was rapidly cooling. On 5 September 1945, more than a year before Philby's marriage to Aileen, a cipher clerk at the Soviet Embassy in Ottawa had walked out to freedom, carrying a briefcase full of startling and incriminating evidence. At first, the Canadian police had been slow to recognize the authenticity of the documents, relating to an effective espionage ring which had been busily passing on to Moscow the technical secrets of the atomic bomb. After studying and checking the incredible evidence brought to them by Igor Gouzenko, the absconder, the Canadian security authorities acted and pounced on most of the ringleaders. At secret service headquarters in London, Philby composed his anxieties as best he could. To him this was far more dangerous in some ways than the Volkov case. Then he had managed to intervene personally, and time as well as luck had favoured him. Now he could only wait and hide his uneasiness. He knew that the key person in the Canadian spy ring, Alan Nunn May, the British scientist without whose cooperation the entire operation could not have succeeded, was due back in Britain shortly, seemingly either quite uninterested in, or wholly oblivious of, his fate. Yet Philby's other source, his Soviet mentor and control, had nothing constructive to suggest, apart from counselling the Englishman to be patient and never to lose heart.

If ever Philby can be said to have considered throwing in his hand, this was probably the most tempting occasion. The implicated British scientist, Dr Nunn May, had been a friend and contemporary of Donald Maclean's at Trinity Hall, Cambridge; Philby knew as well as his Soviet mentor that the unravelling of the Ottawa network might lead to revelations nearer home. When Nunn May set foot in Britain again, he was at once arrested. Only when his trial began *in camera* did the general public begin to get a faint glimmer of the treacherous lengths to which the Soviet Union and its hidden accomplices were prepared to go. Nunn May had not only given the Russians reasonably complete details of the structure of the nuclear bomb dropped on Hiroshima, within days of the event, but had even smuggled out of his laboratory specimens of enriched Uranium 233 and 235, the lethal core of the weapon. These samples had been immediately flown to Moscow. In addition, Nunn May had picked up from fellow scientists, who proved 'as talkative as soldiers', further information about the American proximity fuse which had helped to destroy the Japanese Air Force in the Pacific skies. Nunn May's defence at his trial was simply that, as a Communist, he could see no reason why the Soviet Union should be deprived of new inventions discovered by its so-called friends and allies. He was found guilty of espionage and sentenced to ten years' penal servitude.

If the British public was mildly shocked at the plain evidence of slackness on the part of the security services in overlooking this known Communist scientist, who had been automatically cleared for secret work, opinion in the United States began to harden quickly and perceptibly. Could Britain ever be fully relied on again? A once-great nation, which had now taken to dabbling with Socialism, despite its manifest poverty, appeared to have forfeited the lasting trust and sympathy of its powerful but distracted American ally. Shortly after the surrender of Japan,

Senator Brian McMahon of Connecticut had urged instant restrictions on the future control and uses of atomic energy. The McMahon Act had been duly passed by Congress; now the Nunn May disclosures had the unhappy side effect of stirring ancient and deep antipathies and doubts in Washington. This at least consoled the uneasy Philby. Like his friend Burgess, he detested the hypocritical self-righteousness of the Americans, glorying in their strength and in the ostentatious materialism of their way of life, as much as he despised the masochism of the British, striving to heal the wounds of war under the care of an unqualified Socialist quack called Attlee.

What possibly deterred Philby from 'ratting' on his Soviet friends was not the staunchness of his faith in Stalinist Marxism but the chilling memory of Krivitsky's premature end. The thought of dying violently in mysterious circumstances, the fate apparently reserved for most defecting Soviet agents, may well have repelled yet steadied him. To the Russians, Philby had long been '*Nash*' – 'ours'. His double life had penalties as well as compensations. The price of deception as a vocation was the blurring of the moral faculties. Cynicism had become a habit of mind with him. Lacking the intellectual pretensions of Burgess, Philby took what pride he could in his gifts as an adventurous craftsman 'in place', believing that he could still speed the decline and downfall of democracy in Britain. Orwell had written as long before as 1941:

> England is a family with the wrong members in control. Almost entirely we are governed by the rich, and by people who stay in positions of command by right of birth. Few if any of these people are consciously treacherous, some of them are not even fools.... The shock of disaster brought a few able men like Bevin to the front, but in general we are commanded by people who managed to live through the years 1931–9 without even discovering that Hitler was dangerous. A generation of the unteachable is hanging upon us like a necklace of corpses.[24]

In Philby's revolutionary Britain, there could be no safe place for pseudo-prophets like Orwell who rejected the ultimate, Marxist solution. Such men were far more dangerous than those effete Establishment leaders of Left and Right who complacently accepted Philby as one of themselves, if on a somewhat lower plane of eminence.

Donald Maclean was not directly affected or personally shaken by the implications of the Nunn May affair. He felt sorry for the shy, almost insipid, Communist acquaintance whom he had befriended at Cambridge, wondered idly at first whether Gouzenko's disclosures might lead the hunters into the United States and thus endanger him, but settled for his Soviet control's assurance that there was no cause whatever for alarm. Maclean had the twin roles of an accomplished British diplomat above suspicion and a wholesale purveyor of classified information to the Soviet Union. At the British Embassy in Washington, his star had been in the ascendant since his appearance in late April 1944. He had arrived then alone, leaving Melinda at her mother's farmhouse in South Egremont, and explaining to colleagues that she would join him shortly after the birth of her baby. Maclean at first shared a large apartment with a younger man on the embassy staff, who noticed how often Donald took papers home in the evening to spend hours alone finishing work which, he would snap, 'could not wait'. A testy martyr to duty, a somewhat supercilious model of efficiency, the First Secretary made no bones about his acquired taste for drudgery. He led a quiet social life, attending the formal receptions and dinner parties which he was expected to attend, but accepting few personal invitations because, as he confessed, 'I'm not all that keen on cultivating our American friends.'[25] In fact, beneath the prickly-charming veneer, Donald Maclean proved himself more anti-American than seemed fitting in a British career diplomat based in the capital of the United States at such a time.

A few observant colleagues sometimes wondered whether Maclean's marriage was on the rocks. He rarely spoke of his wife. He appeared studiously vague about his plans for bringing her south and setting up a home of his own after Melinda produced their first child. Occasionally he would melt a little and exhibit distant affection by letting others see photographs of her which he had taken himself. The prints were excellent. Clearly, this reluctant husband was an able amateur photographer, who, as in everything else he did, ensured the best results by developing his own snapshots. During his first eight or nine months of enforced bachelorhood, Maclean adopted the routine of travelling twice a week from Washington to his mother-in-law's house to visit Melinda.

Nobody in authority raised an eyebrow. Nobody troubled to check or question his movements. Nobody really noticed. What a diplomat of his seniority chose to do outside the office was strictly his own business; in any case, Lord Halifax, the ambassador no less, understood and sympathized with the domestic predicament of the energetic and conscientious First Secretary, whose father he had liked and admired, and whose own adaptibility and willingness to shoulder extra work persuaded the minister at the embassy, Sir Ronald Campbell, under whom Maclean had served in pre-war Paris, to let him deputize for Michael Wright as Head of Chancery. This strategic position suited Maclean to perfection. It enabled him to remove and evaluate every message of importance that crossed the ambassador's desk. There was no difficulty in taking away papers whenever he knew he would have the apartment to himself, making microfilm copies, and handing these over to his mentor as a matter of routine on his next compassionate journey to the family outside New York. Donald Maclean's preference for spending his evenings alone with official documents in front of him, and a consoling bottle of whisky to hand, had quickly become accepted by colleagues as one of his more endearing oddities.

Sir Isaiah Berlin, whom Burgess had inveigled into that abortive wild goose chase to Moscow nearly three years earlier, was employed as a specialist attaché at the Washington Embassy when Maclean first arrived. The recluse-like habits of the newcomer suggested anti-social traits which Berlin considered abnormal and unhealthy in a young and presumably ambitious diplomat. Berlin, never noted for reticence, taxed Maclean on the subject, only to learn how utterly tedious the First Secretary found the same old conservative faces and hard-line opinions which greeted him at every cocktail party and dinner he had to attend. Partly to prove that there were still Liberals and New Dealers left in the United States, Berlin thoughtfully arranged a small dinner party to which he asked only friends of his whose views might be more to Maclean's fastidious taste. The evening was a social disaster. Everyone made an effort to draw out the tall, handsome young colleague of Berlin's, quite without success. Maclean said little, drank hard, gradually came out of his shell and grew more morose and combative as the night wore on. Finally, on overhearing Berlin recounting one of the latest witticisms of Alice Longworth, the daughter of Theodore Roosevelt who enjoyed a legendary reputation as a wickedly outspoken society hostess, Maclean created an unpleasant scene.

Towering over his short, stocky British colleague, Maclean berated him in slurred tones for being so crass as to repeat the words of the stupid and reactionary Alice on such an occasion. When Berlin bridled, advising him to curb his temper and act like an adult, Maclean reached down and grabbed his host by the lapels of his jacket. Douglas Fairbanks Junior interposed himself and held the pair apart. Next day Berlin received a short letter of apology which a now contrite Maclean followed up by calling on his colleague. Within a few minutes the younger man's basic anti-American prejudice betrayed itself again in another tantrum. As if desperately trying to make amends, Maclean said enigmatically: 'Why don't you join *us*?' and left the room. After this incident Berlin decided to give a wide berth to this dangerously unpredictable 'darling of the Foreign Office'. Bores he could seldom tolerate: bores who were also prigs he could never abide.[26]

Melinda eventually joined her husband in a rented house complete with nursery and a small den which Donald used as a combined study and photographic darkroom. She was soon equally taken aback by his pronounced antipathy for Americans. He could not disguise his contempt for what he regarded as their naïve ways of thinking, their inability to converse as adults, their instinctive vulgarity, their undiscriminating eating and their drinking habits. As for American women, their inane chattering and pathetic desire to please drove him nearly mad. Not unnaturally, Melinda resented his intolerance and rebuked him for it. She already knew of his irrational devotion to all things Russian; and it is impossible now to believe that she did not suspect, if she did not yet fully comprehend, the extent of Donald's commitment to the Soviet cause. Nevertheless, the childish way he condemned all things American she found personally offensive. It was also risky, especially in view of his excessive drinking. His uncontrollably bad manners under the influence of liquor would put the worst-behaved Americans to shame, she reminded him. His brooding silences and recurring bouts of depression were worthy of a spoilt schoolboy.[27]

It says much for Maclean's efforts to keep the private and public halves of his life stringently apart that no formal complaints were ever laid against him at the embassy. Isaiah Berlin was not the only colleague to disapprove of his scorn for 'our bloody Yankee friends', as he called them. Yet, in the presence of superiors, Maclean's natural deference bridled his tongue. Not once did he betray his private feelings to Halifax or to Campbell. They continued to see him as an urbane and exceptionally talented young professional, who would almost certainly reach the top of the service. Neither the ambassador nor minister appeared to realize that Maclean continued to travel regularly to New York as if Melinda, whom both had met, was still living at her mother's home. Because they trusted him without reserve, his right to go where he wanted when he wanted, whether for pleasure or on official business, went unquestioned.

The only person who reproached him for his repeated absences was Melinda herself. She had become a kind of outsize wastepaper basket for her husband's emotional outbursts. His tense manner before and after each journey, the late hours he usually kept in his study, the solace he constantly found in the whisky bottle, irritated and upset her constantly.

Just as he would invariably gloss over the reasons for his impassioned hatred of America and Americans, so he refused to discuss with her the nature of his mysterious excursions. Two or three of the more observant officials at the embassy were convinced by now that the Macleans' marriage had all but broken up. They supposed that Donald must be keeping 'a fancy woman' in New York. Melinda knew better. If she had not already surmised how deeply he was involved in spying for the Soviet Union, the homeland and cradle of his beloved Communist faith, she tolerated with difficulty his brusqueness, his morose teasing, his secretiveness, because she still loved him and longed to protect him in spite of everything. Even with daily hired helps in the nursery and kitchen, she would have chosen to stay with the baby rather than accompany him on his journeys, had he bothered to invite her. Donald Maclean, to do him justice, seemed equally anxious to spare her the burden of his guilt, forgetting in his self-centred way that no misdeed he committed could surprise or shock Melinda any more. What possibly hurt her most was his reluctance to confide in her and share his crippling load.

The stream of first-hand documentary evidence which passed through Maclean to the Kremlin from 1944 onwards undoubtedly affected world events by influencing the shifts in Soviet foreign policy. The quality of the material he supplied probably surpassed much of what his London-based confederates, Philby and Burgess, managed to provide between them. If the Bletchley code-breakers had put a war-winning weapon into the hands of the Western Allies, enabling them to read the minds of the enemy and anticipate their every move, the sensitive information divulged by Maclean on, and immediately after, the eve of final victory may well have strengthened Stalin's resolve to turn that victory to the Soviet Union's lasting advantage.

Before, during and after the Yalta Conference, the growing doubts and frustrations of Churchill about the thrust of Soviet intentions, expressed in personal messages to the ailing Roosevelt, could be studied and construed without delay by the policy-makers in Moscow. On occasion, Maclean was requested to offer his own assessment of the implications, a welcome sign in itself of the Kremlin's confidence in his expertise and judgement.

Up to this point, the high summer of 1945, Maclean had acted alone. In the familiar realm of Allied politics and diplomacy, he required no direction, no accomplices. Had his Soviet control been content to leave it at that, it is likely that the First Secretary of the British Embassy in Washington would have carried on his successful espionage activities undetected and unsuspected by American counter-intelligence, until his tour of duty ended in

1948. But when Maclean told his control one day that Roger Makins had arrived as a minister in charge of 'Economic Affairs' – a comprehensive post that embraced not only the British loan negotiations, United Nations' Relief, Food and Agriculture but most significantly the problems of atomic development – and that the British Ambassador had nominated Maclean himself to serve as joint secretary of the Western Allies' new combined policy committee on atomic development, he was advised by his Soviet mentor that specialist guidance would now be necessary; it would be immediately arranged. So, not long after the surrender of Japan, when the manifest intention of the Truman administration was 'to bring the boys home' and disengage from all war-time commitments, the Fifth Man entered. He proceeded to complicate the already involved and troubled life of Donald Maclean. 'Basil' was a pleasant Englishman of homosexual bent, a gifted physicist some six years older than Maclean and a covert Marxist, who had studied in London, as well as the feet of one of the Western world's leading nuclear physicists, and now held several positions of trust as an official coordinator between the teams of scientists engaged in producing the first nuclear bombs.[28]

Thus Maclean was also able to turn over to the Soviet Union an equally impressive array of detailed and carefully selected material on the nuclear thinking, planning and stockpiling of the Americans and their Allies. No Fifth Man had been needed to interpret the bare, plain announcement that reached the British Embassy in July 1945 that the Western scientific team had successfully tested an experimental device in the stony desert of New Mexico; but the Fifth Man's specialized knowledge and direction became increasingly important a little later when Maclean started to keep the minutes of the Combined Policy Committee on the intricacies of future nuclear development. Without the prompt and systematic supervision of this agreeably self-effacing fellow agent, whom he welcomed as a vast improvement on Burgess or on Philby, Maclean would have floundered hopelessly out of his depth. Fuchs and Nunn May, by their separate endeavours, were meanwhile providing the Russians with technical secrets which greatly speeded the development of the first Soviet nuclear weapons, in accordance with Stalin's wishes; but Maclean's first-hand evidence on arrangements in the United States for stockpiling and controlling both the vital raw materials and the completed weapons was no less important as a pointer to the future. Roger Makins (now Lord Sherfield) was happy enough to delegate routine business 'on the atomic energy side' to Maclean, 'an efficient officer [who] did his work conscientiously, carefully and intelligently. And if he sometimes seemed reserved and hesitant, that was readily ascribed to Scottish caution.' No whisper of intemperance or abnormal conduct of any kind in this subordinate's private life ever reached the ears of Makins: 'There was no occasion for me to question what he did in his spare time, and no reason why he should not go to New York as and when he had the opportunity.'[29]

So much importance was attached to Maclean's role that George Carey-Foster, the Foreign Office Security Chief, supervised the installation of a safe with a special combination for storing the highly sensitive paperwork which the First Secretary at the British Embassy was handling. Carey-Foster, then on a visit of inspection, did not like the determined questioning about his job to which Melinda Maclean subjected him afterwards at an informal dinner party. He wondered why she was so interested, fenced her off politely but firmly, and jumped to the unfair though correct conclusion that 'her husband must have put her up to it'. Since everyone spoke of Donald Maclean's competence and trustworthiness with respect, Carey-Foster merely made a mental note of that little incident for future reference.[30]

'The atomic bomb,' declared President Truman in August 1945, immediately after the devastating attacks on Hiroshima and Nagasaki, 'is too dangerous to be loose in a lawless world. That is why Great Britain and the United States, who have the secret of its production, do not intend to reveal the secret until means have been found to control the bomb so as to protect ourselves and the rest of the world from total destruction.' Truman insisted that the United States' virtual monopoly of atomic weapons and production techniques should be controlled by civilians rather than the military; but the President's plans for future international regulation of nuclear development were opposed by the Soviet Union and Poland in 1946 before the newly established United Nations Commission on Atomic Energy. The Kremlin counter-proposed, in effect, that 'we should destroy our atomic bombs'. Only then would 'the Russians be willing to discuss arrangements for the exchange of scientific information and the formation of international controls. . . . If we accepted the Russian position we would be deprived of everything except their promise', so that in the event of a Kremlin-instigated atomic arms race, 'our present advantage and security gained by our discovery and initiative would be wiped out.'[31]

Unfortunately for Truman, Britain took no more kindly to his assumptions about the exclusive American monopoly in the domestic field than the Soviet Union did in the international. Attlee disliked the McMahon Bill that had been placed before Congress. Not only would it force Britain to start developing atomic energy 'on her own', but it would rule out the sharing of nuclear secrets with any nation until UN controls became effective. A bitter wrangle ensued between London and Washington. As Truman himself admitted, 'the Combined Policy Committee, which was the British-American body that handled such questions, came to a complete deadlock . . .'. Attlee's indignation at Truman's alleged breach of trust led Britain's Prime Minister to decide, almost alone and without seeking approval from his divided Cabinet, to authorize the production of British nuclear weapons. Donald Maclean was equally indignant on behalf of the Russians.

Having gathered from his Soviet control that the Russians had already obtained basic atomic secrets from agents inside the Manhattan Project, he applied himself zealously to his continuing task as a specialist informer, under the Fifth Man's clandestine tutelage. Not until 1948, a year after Makins's departure and shortly before Maclean left Washington himself at the end of his long assignment with glowing reports on his total reliability and professional skill from both sets of his masters, did Lewis L. Strauss of the recently established US Atomic Energy Commission wake up to an uncomfortable discovery:

I learnt that an alien was the holder of a permanent pass to the Commissioner's headquarters, a pass, moreover, which was of a character that did not require him to be accompanied while in the building. It developed from the record maintained by the guards that this particular alien was a frequent visitor in the evenings after the usual work hours. Being concerned, I took the matter up with my colleagues and found that none of them had been aware of the situation. The pass was withdrawn at once. The name of the alien was Donald Maclean, an attaché of the British Embassy. . . .[32]

The volume of traffic from the Soviet Consulate in New York to Moscow had been noticeably heavier during the summer of 1945. It was not the British code-breakers at Bletchley but their more numerous American counterparts in Washington who remarked on this fact, logged it, then slowly but systematically set about the painstaking, thankless business of trying to decipher the batches of intercepted messages. One day many months later, a sharp-eyed American cryptoanalyst with a good memory noticed something unusual and exciting. The old intercepts he was studying had been enciphered in a manner which looked vaguely familiar. Cross-checking proved that the code had been used before for transmitting low-grade intelligence on Allied shipping movements in and out of New York. For some unaccountable reason, a Soviet cipher clerk had blundered.

With unfeigned delight the Washington code-breakers fastened on this unexpected clue. Gradually they succeeded in breaking down sufficient groups in these out-of-date top secret Soviet signals to ascertain that the Russians appeared to have had their own source inside the British Embassy in Washington. Only then did they inform the British. There were still indecipherable gaps throughout; but the code-breakers found, among other items, carefully copied personal telegrams that had passed between Churchill and Truman. The inside source bore the code-name 'Homer', and internal evidence suggested that the mysterious agent had been in the habit of visiting his Soviet control twice a week. In a sense, the blundering cipher clerk at the Soviet Consulate in New York had unwittingly outdone Igor Gouzenko, the defector who had absconded from the Soviet Embassy in Ottawa taking with him incontrovertible evidence that trapped the British physicist,

Nunn May, and his associates in the Canadian atom spy ring. Of course, Maclean's control was too seasoned a campaigner to offer the slightest hint that the security services in Washington and possibly London had been inadvertently given these veiled but potentially ruinous clues which, if followed up and identified, would eventually expose the First Secretary, Donald Maclean, as the source of these leaks from the Washington Embassy. Since a little blackmail had been required to persuade this touchy diplomat to undertake, in the first place, the job of espionage he was now doing so satisfactorily, even the mildest warning to tread warily might have been taken the wrong way by Maclean, to the detriment of his zeal.[33] Besides, the voracious appetite of the Centre in Moscow appeared to grow by what it fed on: the Director was impatient for more and more classified secrets of the same high quality, so Maclean's control said nothing to him or to 'Basil', the Fifth Man, about the earlier and regrettable lapse of the careless Soviet cipher clerk in New York. The British diplomat, in any event, had troubles enough already. Possibly as a result of strain and overwork, he looked nervous and by now was far from well.

Maclean had resumed the old habit of drinking himself into a tipsy stupor on free evenings, staggering out occasionally in search of homosexual consolation. Melinda could do nothing to dissuade him; and there were times when she must have feared for his sanity. Whether she realized the fact or not, her highly strung husband, in contrast with Burgess or Philby, had to contend with the still small voice of a residual Calvinist conscience. No Marxist rationalizations, no cynical outrages against the accepted rules of decent behaviour, could shut out that still small voice for long. How the First Secretary managed to avoid causing a public scandal remains a mystery. Through sheer good luck rather than through cunning, he was never seen in the throes of his excesses by any superior at the British Embassy. The FBI naturally proved somewhat more vigilant. The local office was bound to take an interest in his nocturnal prowlings. Agents particularly noted his association with 'Basil', the English physicist. The FBI, however, had no evidence whatever which led them to suspect that either man was engaged in spying for the Soviet Union. Such evidence might have been forthcoming from the few remaining specialists in the shrunken rump of the OSS; but the activities of that moribund and demoralized service were restricted, its days already numbered, thanks to the foolish advice, on which Truman soon afterwards acted, 'of an old drinking crony and playboy companion, George Allen, a myopic individual who saw no point whatever in letting the United States retain a full-scale, post-war intelligence organization of its own'.[34]

Before the close of 1945, Sir John Balfour had replaced Campbell as senior minister at the British Embassy and remained in Washington for the next three years. A calm, witty, yet dignified envoy of the old school, Balfour was not inclined by temperament to accept without questioning the very flattering opinion of Maclean passed on to him by his predecessor:

> There were two Ronald Campbells, you know. The older man of that name had been our ambassador in Paris just before the fall of France in 1940. He commented unfavourably on Maclean's surprising dilatoriness and neglect of his duties during the last critical days. He thought of him, perhaps a bit harshly, as something of a weakling. I hadn't forgotten that personal verdict.

Yet Balfour was also ready to let bygones be bygones. Soon, like everyone else, he could find only praise for Donald Maclean's manifest competence, especially 'when acting as Head of Chancery, though I didn't altogether care for a certain cold haughtiness of manner which showed through at times'.[35]

Balfour's wife noticed this as well. One morning not long after their arrival, she fell into conversation with Maclean, to whom she had been introduced at the office. Having just spent two hard and gloomy years in Moscow, she confessed how much she preferred the civility of people in the United States: 'At least Americans will talk and smile on trains, even if you're a complete stranger. Not like those damned, unfriendly Russians.' Maclean stared hard at her. He seemed to be making an intense effort 'to suppress some cutting reference to my naïveté and ignorance. The cross look directed at me was sufficient. It betrayed how strongly he felt.' The Balfours had little to do socially with the Macleans in the months that followed, though when the minister's wife called at Melinda's home one day she could not help noticing the crates of empty liquor bottles stacked at the side of the building. She remarked later to her husband: 'Either they've been celebrating with the whole of Washington society or else Donald must have a very big thirst.'[36]

By and large, Sir John Balfour shared his predecessor's respect for the First Secretary's professional finesse and all-round thoroughness. He continued to detect a 'touch of conceit which could be off-putting'; and he was quite at a loss to account for Maclean's prim disapproval on catching a first glimpse of the Russian valet whom Archibald Clark Kerr (Lord Inverchapel), the new ambassador, brought with him, unannounced, from the Soviet Union in the spring of 1946, after the departure of Lord Halifax. It appeared that when Clark Kerr had gone to bid farewell to Stalin, the Soviet leader graciously invited him to choose any parting gift he cared to name as a token of esteem. 'I don't suppose you'd permit me to take my Russian valet with me to Washington?' ventured Clark Kerr. 'Why not?' countered the mischievous Stalin. And so it was arranged. To be fair, Maclean was by no means the only member of the British Embassy staff to look askance at the grotesque apparition which met his eyes at the airport. This incongruous little body servant from the steppes, who followed his master like a shadow and dressed up like a poor itinerant Cossack, astonished nearly everyone. Maclean found it harder than others to disguise his air of disdain, especially as the valet took to installing himself inconveniently in the ambassador's office and insisted on poking his nose into every corner of the building, including the Registry. Perhaps the First Secretary's main concern was the curiosity of the FBI and American officialdom in general about a newcomer who seemed as out of place in the British Embassy as an emissary from Mars.

Months passed before Clark Kerr reluctantly acceded to hints that 'Stalin's parting gift' might be causing more trouble and scabrous rumour than the little valet was worth, so he arranged with the Soviet Embassy for the unfortunate Russian to be flown home.

An indispensable link at the embassy between past and present, Maclean went out of his way to ease in his new masters. They responded by deferring to his local experience, by relying on his judgement, and by agreeing to let him run on as free and loose a rein as Halifax and Campbell had sanctioned before them. In March 1946, two months before Clark Kerr's arrival, Churchill had served notice to the free world at Fulton, Missouri, that the Soviet Union was already waging the Cold War, whether its late allies yet recognized the fact or not. The warning was soothing music in Maclean's ears. With one half of his being he exulted in his secret handiwork to advance the revolutionary cause; with the other, he laboured away scrupulously in his embassy office, unobtrusively currying favour with his elders and seniors like any keen young diplomat determined to reach the top of the tree. Walter Bell, who accompanied Lord Inverchapel (Clark Kerr) to Washington as a special assistant, recalled:

> No trouble was too much for him. He spent a lot of time putting us in the picture. Donald certainly knew his way around, and his pleasant if reserved manner suggested that he'd be quite happy to go on elucidating problems all night if necessary. The Macleans weren't greatly interested in entertaining. Donald was obsessed with his work. No trouble was too much for him. Whenever Philip Jordan, the Embassy press attaché, arranged special background briefings for foreign correspondents, Maclean invariably enjoyed the business of parrying tough questions and giving as far as possible the reasons behind new policy decisions.[37]

One journalist who attended several of Maclean's illuminating press briefings was Malcolm Muggeridge, the Washington correspondent of the London *Daily Telegraph* between 1946 and 1947, when the first phase of the Cold War appeared to be going the Russians' way. Muggeridge remembered:

> There's no doubt that Maclean knew his stuff. I found him a dull, humourless and rather pompous young man who tried a bit too hard to appear agreeable and relaxed. Philip Jordan, who happened to be an

old professional sparring partner of mine, seemed to be on exceptionally close terms with him, and I couldn't help wondering what Philip saw in him. Later, Jordan applied for – and got – the more prestigious post of press officer to Attlee at 10 Downing Street, succeeding Francis Williams. I can't say I ever warmed to Maclean. He was far too much of a cold fish beneath the polished surface charm. Nevertheless, during a bad period when the Americans were obviously determined to carry on in their own semi-isolationist way – Cold War or no Cold War – I couldn't but admire Maclean's astute appreciation of day-to-day diplomatic difficulties. He never struck a wrong note in public. He never lowered his guard.[38]

Moscow also relied on Maclean's assessments of the latest turns in American and British policy. Their repeated requests for his expert opinions on material he gave them may have inflated the fine conceit he already had of himself. In the end these Soviet requests enabled the infinitely painstaking Western code-breakers, and in due course the British Security Service, to eliminate all minor suspects from their search for the hidden source inside the Washington Embassy.

In the view of Sir Robert Mackenzie, a shrewd old Etonian who had formerly served with Philby in the Iberian subsection and arrived in Washington as regional security officer in 1948, shortly after Maclean's departure:

It must have vexed him to learn that the cryptoanalysts, without whom we'd probably have lost the war, had eliminated from their enquiries all the Embassy cleaners, cooks, chauffeurs, bottle-washers and minor officials because of the Russian's eagerness to get informed opinions from their inside source. If they'd failed to come up with that clue, it would have been impossible to decide where to start looking for the leak. On the other hand, the relatively small number of senior Embassy officials who'd had access to secrets and were capable of giving expert guidance proved an easier matter to cope with. The whittling down took far longer than it should have done partly because the Americans and the British were exchanging progress reports. What slowed down the process wasn't anything Kim Philby did or could have done later to put them off the scent. I fear we put ourselves off. The simple fact was that everybody at the Foreign Office believed Donald Maclean to be clean above suspicion. He was utterly trustworthy, and as such the Foreign Office would protect him tooth-and-nail to the last.[39]

For the remainder of their time in Washington, the Macleans as a couple continued to stay out of the social limelight. Now and then Melinda would put on a brave face and stand in as hostess at the embassy receptions. Only when driven to it did she entertain guests at home. As the late Geoffrey Hoare accurately noted: 'If Donald invited only two friends to dinner, he could not tell Melinda until they were actually there.'[40] Melinda knew too much to be able to sit back, switch off, and innocently enjoy herself like other embassy wives. Her one desire was to shake the dust of Washington off her feet, especially after the birth of her second son on 27 July 1946. Despite her loyal efforts to cover up for Donald, notably when the stresses and strains of his mysterious double life reduced him to a ranting, sodden wreck who would come stumbling home in the small hours, she feared with good reason that eventually he might be cornered and compromised by the American police, if not by the FBI. She was less worried by his easy-going British colleagues. Those drunken forays and assignations of Donald after dark, usually with men she presumed to be his lovers, must by now have registered with the local security authorities; and his diplomatic immunity might be no defence if they once decided to pounce.

Melinda's intuition was not far wrong. As the records show, the FBI had been keeping him under surveillance. His depraved tastes concerned the agency less than the identity of the companions with whom he most frequently consorted. One of these increasingly perplexed and puzzled the FBI: 'Basil', the busy and distinguished British nuclear scientist, with access to many secrets of the atomic energy project. Ever since the Gouzenko disclosures which had led to the uncovering of Nunn May and the Canadian spy ring, J. Edgar Hoover's agents had been on the alert for possible links with the nuclear teams still working in the United States. The fact that nothing was known against 'Basil' was inconvenient; the fact that 'Basil' was British proved sufficient incentive in itself for Hoover to suspect his seemingly impeccable credentials; and the additional fact that 'Basil' held regular meetings, invariably alone, with the First Secretary of the British Embassy, a person of obvious instability, induced the FBI to redouble its vigilance from late 1947 onwards.

By that late date, more than two years after the capitulation of Japan, the United States still lacked a permanent and effective intelligence organization. By executive order, Truman had scrapped the war-time Office of Strategic Services in 1946. That the President acted with unseemly haste and without any coherent idea of what should replace the OSS there can be no possible room for doubt. Owing to his personal antipathy towards William J. Donovan, one of Roosevelt's favourites whom Truman disliked as someone 'altogether too big for his boots', the blueprint prepared by Donovan and his right-hand man, James R. Murphy, was rejected out of hand:

> It was a disgraceful and irresponsible business. Truman summarily dismissed his only intelligence chief and did not even trouble to observe the customary ritual of sending for him personally. I remember in those dogdays, before I packed up and returned to my law business, receiving an order from the joint Chiefs of Staff to wind up the large network of secret agents we'd established in all four zones of Germany. I had to obey. I found ways of maintaining the people we'd managed to place inside Czechoslovakia, and very useful they proved to the United States in due course. At a time when most of the old, experienced hands were resigning or being asked to resign, I also managed to persuade one of the best of them, Jim Angleton, not to give up but to stay on and finish the important assignment he was on in Italy.[41]

James Jesus Angleton, as has been related, had joined Murphy's staff at St Albans in 1942 with the lowly rank of an enlisted man, when the OSS advance party was settling down to learn the rudiments of counter-intelligence work under Felix Cowgill, head of Section Five of the British Secret Service. There the youthful Angleton, a tall, angular, taciturn young man who possessed a retentive memory and a very sharp brain, had first met Kim Philby and other SIS recruits, including Malcolm Muggeridge and Hugh Trevor-Roper. A graduate of Yale, Angleton liked the British and felt very much at home in their country. He had spent part of his boyhood there. His father had been a senior executive in Europe of a giant adding-machine company with international interests, and the son was educated at Malvern, one of the smaller English public schools. James R. Murphy was quick to recognize that young Angleton had a rare aptitude for the finer points of counter-intelligence work. Enigmatic, exceptionally intelligent, but also subtle, patient and endlessly persistent, he possessed the keen trout-fisherman's controlled enthusiasm for holding on until an elusive catch had been 'elicited' from the water. As has also been indicated earlier, Angleton had certain instinctive reservations about Kim Philby's marked absence of opinions on anything serious, political or otherwise. For that reason he had been greatly taken aback at the end of 1945 to hear the Englishman remark unexpectedly, after receiving the Order of the British Empire at Buckingham Palace from King George VI: 'This country could do with a really stiff dose of proper Socialism.' Taking that chance remark in conjunction with other stray bits of adverse evidence that had since come his way, Angleton felt that Philby, if 'played' long enough, might well prove a more sinister character than an urbane casualness and impeccable reputation for proficiency suggested. He filed the problem away. But he did not forget it.

With customary care and dexterity, Angleton went on casting tentative lines in various unexpected streams after 1945; quite characteristically, he kept his own counsel. He would have been foolish not to do so, in view of the uncertainty he and other OSS veterans felt about the precarious independence enjoyed by the fledgling CIA. Hoover of the FBI had not yet given up hope of quietly absorbing the CIA into his empire. Nor was the Pentagon any more willing than the State Department to relinquish the temporary grip they had secured on this prize before President Truman's belated decision to 'unify and coordinate' in one agency the various departmental sources of secret intelligence from overseas. During Angleton's tour of duty in troubled Italy, he lost no time in renewing his war-time association with undercover agents of Haganah and the Jewish Agency, by now at bitter odds with a British Government stubbornly if ineffectually trying to enforce on Jews and Arabs alike the terms of its pre-war Palestine Mandate. In the words of one CIA colleague with inside knowledge of Angleton's deep game:

It's true that the CIA really came into being only in 1948, following its chartering the year before, [but] the predecessor organization in the War Department [SSU and later SSO] had been up to its hips in the overseas and domestic intelligence world from October 1945 on. This fact is very important because key FBI personnel made the shift to the SSU/SSO with Hoover's blessing, and became his eyes and ears during the period when the question of a post-war central intelligence set-up was being hotly debated. . . . There was a close liaison until 1947 between Hoover's FBI and agents like Bill Harvey and Angleton who were in the SSU/SSO organization. Once the United States recognized Israel on the formal level, this began to change. Although informal FBI/CIA relationships remained much the same, Hoover, because of his own problems in trying to extend the FBI's international writ, placed himself at official arm's length from the Israelis. Into this gap flowed Angleton. . . .[42]

It was in war-time London that Arthur Goldberg, James J. Angleton and other officers of OSS had first encountered a few undercover agents of the shadowy, peripatetic yet extremely resourceful Jewish Intelligence Service, the very existence of which MI5 prudently chose to ignore. The headquarters of the Jewish Agency and Zionist Federation were conveniently situated at 77 Great Russell Street in Bloomsbury, where Dr Chaim Weizmann and his councillors conducted their day-to-day business. Under the terms of the Mandate, the Agency had its own recognized advisory role to play in the affairs of Palestine; and such was its influence among Zionist and non-Zionist Jews, notably in the United States, that this increasingly complex Agency had virtually become 'a state within a state'. Weizmann's enormous prestige gave him personal access to most leading politicians in Britain, and no more vivid impression has been drawn of the Agency's constancy in striving for the peaceful establishment of a Jewish homeland than the account left by Blanche Dugdale, the niece of the author of the famous Balfour Declaration and the sole Gentile to serve for many years in its inner councils. As the editor of the Dugdale Diaries points out:

> In many ways, the years the diaries cover (1936 to 1947) were the most momentous in the history of Zionism. They saw the first, fateful Arab uprising in Palestine against Zionist aims and British policy; they witnessed the first suggestion, however faint and ambiguous it then appeared, to establish a Jewish state; they noted the effects of appeasement upon the fortunes of the Jewish people. Above all else, these were the years of the Second World War and the holocaust. The traumatic impact of this tragedy gave an added bite to the movement's struggle against the Labour Government during the postwar years, and determined both psychologically and politically the necessity for a Jewish state and its unceasing, even obsessive preoccupation with security problems in after years. . . .[43]

Blanche Dugdale's Diaries provide sufficient random evidence to indicate that the intelligence arm of Haganah was active before, during, and particularly after the Second World War. Moreover, according to CIA sources:

> James Angleton, along with Arthur Goldberg and other OSS members in London, had developed a relationship outside the nominal US/British relationship with what might be termed the shadow government of Israel.

Exactly how London-based Jewish intelligence dug out the original information, which eluded MI5, that at least one important British nuclear scientist in addition to Nunn May had undertaken to spy for the Soviet Union is still a mystery. It seems more than likely that the information came through one of their numerous private channels into the British scientific community. As became sound undercover agents, they sat on their secret until Angleton renewed his relationship with two key members of Haganah's intelligence section in post-war Rome. To quote the same CIA source:

> As part of the price for uninterrupted but informal cooperation with US intelligence, a crucial necessity to the Jews by 1946–7 owing to the intransigent policy of Britain, these two agents passed on to Angleton the name of the British nuclear scientist whom they had unearthed as an important Soviet agent.[44]

This important spy was 'Basil', the code-name of the Fifth Man. After Angleton's recall to Washington from Rome, it so happened that his Jewish informants soon followed on official business. One of the pair, incidentally, still occupies a prominent and respected position in Israeli public life today.

The British were not told of this significant and dramatic disclosure which, in a sense, concerned them primarily. However, Angleton had his reasons. He did not, indeed could not, take into his immediate confidence more than half a dozen of his American colleagues, and then only on the strict understanding of their professional 'need to know'. The process of cornering and 'turning' the Fifth Man made such limited sharing of the secret almost inevitable; yet temperamentally and politically, Angleton was more than content to

> run the operation out of his hip pocket for at least a couple of years. My further understanding is that, besides Angleton and Bedell Smith [who became Director of the CIA in 1950], only Scotty Miler and Jim Rocca were aware of the full game. Whether Hoover himself was fully informed is questionable. What can be said is that the FBI did learn eventually that 'Basil' was working under CIA control as a double agent. It is impossible to be more precise than this because no complete chronological record of the operation was kept: next to nothing was committed to paper – or to the supposed hierarchical order of the US intelligence community.

And no hint of the operation involving 'Basil' can be found in the files declassified under the Freedom of Information Act. Neither Allen Dulles nor Frank Wisner, for instance, were aware of Angleton's coup before the sudden escape of Burgess and Maclean in May 1951. Determined to protect his sources at all costs, especially when the British and the Israelis were at each other's throats, Angleton would not share the secret with his old colleagues in SIS while Donald Maclean remained in Washington. 'Basil' had to be kept in play after that, and at the same time watched incessantly, in case his Soviet mentors tumbled to his double game. No doubt Angleton intended to pass on to SIS everything he knew when he judged the moment ripe; but what saved him the trouble of doing so in late 1948 was that quite separate discovery by American cryptoanalysis of the Russians' source inside the British Embassy in Washington, a source which had passed on vital classified information during the last stages of the war. The British were told of this at once; and from January 1949 onwards, both American and British cryptoanalysts worked hard in unison – a slow, protracted effort to identify the source of the war-time leaks from the embassy.

It had not surprised the counter-intelligence interrogators that 'Basil' broke down quickly and easily, confessing that he had become a covert Communist in his student days and a secret agent for the Soviet not long afterwards. They had offered him a calculated choice: either to continue serving his Russian masters under their orders, or to refuse and take whatever penalties were visited on him by American law. 'Basil' agreed to change sides as directed, gratefully accepting guarantees of protection and the promise of American citizenship when his work was done. According to another informant:

> This British scientist was turned with ease, and on practical rather than ideological grounds. He was not a strong character. He proved cooperative because he knew which side his bread was buttered on. The agency kept tabs on him. Jim Angleton couldn't have let the British in by the back door at that early stage. So the cryptoanalysts' separate discovery and their warning to London came as a relief. A little later, when the CIA learnt of Menzies's plan to send Kim Philby across as the next SIS liaison officer in Washington, Angleton must have felt justified in his reticence.[45]

For 'Basil' had indicated plainly that the Soviet spymasters also had their own man inside the British Secret Service, and Angleton intended to use 'Basil' next to test the slight suspicions he had long nursed about Philby. Had British intelligence been offered even a hint of Angleton's success in manipulating this unsuspected scientist for his own subtle purposes, it is more than probable that MI5 would not have groped about in darkness for the next three years, eventually letting Maclean as well as Burgess slip through their fingers, and finally failing to establish Philby's deeper complicity in the ring of spies.

Angleton, nevertheless, held back for many reasons, political and otherwise. Nor could he ever have been expected to allow his natural anglophile sentiments to sway his cold professional judgement. The work of 'Basil' more than vindicated that judgement, once 'Basil' had been 'turned'. Until October 1948 the British scientist continued to see Donald Maclean as regularly as ever, advising him which nuclear programme files, and which items on those files, should be extracted from the US Atomic Energy Commission's headquarters whenever the First Secretary used his special unauthorized pass to gain entry, unattended. The information thus obtained was carefully monitored by the Americans before 'Basil' handed it to Maclean, for transmission to the Russians.

The relationship between the turned British scientist and the unsuspecting British diplomat remained harmonious and unruffled until the autumn of 1948. By then Melinda Maclean felt that she could begin to breathe more easily again. The news that Donald would shortly be recalled to London, prior to taking up a new post as Head of Chancery at the British Embassy in Cairo, came as an immense relief. Her husband's treacherous conduct, if not his fanatical beliefs, his split personality and a conscience as undependable as an overwound alarm clock, had cleverly been brought under remote control by the redoubtable James Jesus Angleton. It was now up to British security to play this Scottish trout and hook him. Angleton could not and would not yet help MI5 directly. He knew that, in time, the Soviet signal intercepts, on which the American and British experts would doubtless be working in tandem, should point unerringly towards Maclean, the suspect whose guilt he had already discovered thanks to 'Basil' and the 'Israeli connection' that had been forged in war and satisfactorily tested since in peace. With a double agent of his own in place, he was already angling for bigger fish.

10. THE RUNAWAY AGENTS

'If there are any lights amid the encircling gloom,' Brendan Bracken wrote to his 'beloved enemy' and war-time fellow minister, Lord Beaverbrook, in March 1947, 'they are carefully concealed from me. Conditions here are worse than any we knew in the darkest days of war. . . . The Government, while putting out fires in our hearths, is even more determined to quench fires in our bellies. And that is what we need to save us in these sad times.'[1]

The nation had too few financial reserves to honour existing commitments. Nor could she pay her crippling war debts, and this at a time when the aggressive designs of the Soviet Union were rousing Truman's administration in Washington to belated recognition of the physical and moral prostration of western Europe as a whole. Thanks to the alertness of Burgess in McNeil's inner sanctum, and to Donald Maclean's complementary reports from the British Embassy in Washington, the Russians were often ahead of developments. Molotov knew even sooner than the Secretary of State George Marshall, for instance, that the British had reached the end of their tether and were about to warn the State Department of their intention to withdraw from Greece, since they could no longer afford to maintain 40,000 troops there to prevent a Communist takeover. Nor did it seem likely that Britain could prolong her Mandate in Palestine, where Jewish terrorists were systematically defying and twisting the arm of the protective power. The bad blood between London and Washington on this issue had long been an open secret. In Truman's sharp judgement: 'Not only are the British highly successful in muddling the situation as completely as it could possibly be muddled, but the Jews themselves are making it almost impossible to do anything for them.'[2]

The full measure of Britain's plight became plainer that summer. Adhering to the letter and spirit of the stringent American Loan Agreement negotiated by Keynes in 1945, the British Treasury made sterling freely convertible. Within six weeks, tens of millions of borrowed dollars had melted away, forcing Britain to abandon the attempt to walk when she could scarcely crawl. One gleam of promise flickered on the overcast horizon. This was a broad hint dropped by George Marshall that the United States might help Europe up the steep road to economic recovery, provided that European nations themselves took the initiative and agreed on a joint programme. Fortunately, Sir John Balfour had anticipated this move and informed London, while Maclean was conscientiously informing Moscow. The Marshall Plan evoked an instant and positive response. Bevin, prepared, gratefully seized the offer 'with both hands'. The Soviet Union, equally well primed, played a waiting game. Molotov even joined Bevin and Bidault of France in preliminary talks on the drafting of a recovery agenda. This was a propaganda ploy on Moscow's part. In Bidault's words, 'Molotov clearly does not wish this business to succeed, but on the other hand his hungry satellites are smacking their lips in expectation of getting some of your money. He is obviously embarrassed.'[3]

In due course, sixteen nations, including Greece and Turkey but excluding West Germany, attended a plenary conference to determine how they could best cooperate and what they would require by way of technical and monetary aid. Czechoslovakia and Poland had originally expressed the wish to take part but were ordered by the Kremlin to stay away, Molotov departing from Paris 'with a blast against capitalism and the United States'.[4] The 17,000,000,000-dollar recovery programme authorized by Truman and approved by the US Congress was hailed in the West as an enlightened and generous act of statesmanship. It probably prevented France and Italy from going Communist, just as it indubitably saved Britain from going broke, before the close of 1947. The funds earmarked for the rebuilding of Europe were large; yet, as Truman noted, they represented 'only 5 per cent of the sums we expended to defeat the Axis' and 'less than 3 per cent of our total national income' during the estimated four years of the programme.

These were suddenly cheerless times indeed for Burgess. The sombre evidence of the British Empire's accelerating decline and fall alternately infuriated and depressed him. His contrariness seemed to grow with age. Until the Americans stirred from their isolationist slumbers, and rose to lift Europe out of its post-war ruin and decrepitude, nearly everything had been running smoothly for the Russians. Burgess had believed that nothing could stop Soviet expansion: soon Communist régimes would be installed in most of western Europe, with or without bloodshed. Now thanks to the promise of American aid, the hopes of the old ruling class in Britain had begun to revive. Fair-weather Communists were again going to ground. Anthony Blunt had been appointed Surveyor of the King's Pictures; and much of his time was spent cataloguing the Royal art treasures at Windsor. Blunt thus held a position of trust which, willy-nilly, was turning him into a creature of the noblest, oldest and most sensitive branch of the Establishment: the Crown itself. Burgess felt increasingly out of touch, however, now that his closest confederate, the cool and practical Philby, had handed over the Soviet counter-espionage section of SIS to Brigadier Douglas Maxwell. In January 1947 Philby went to Turkey on his first tour of active duty in the field. It further annoyed Burgess to discover that even Hector McNeil was catching a dose of that blustering spirit of defiance with which Bevin, his boss and private idol, had always been cursed. And 'Cold War fever' appeared to be spreading across the land like an epidemic.

McNeil no longer saw only the black side of things. Nor would he swallow so easily his personal assistant's cynical arguments. The Burgess thesis that Marshall Aid was an ingenious dollar trap for Britain and her European neighbours did not amuse Hector. 'Wait and see' was Guy's repetitive refrain: 'We'll all end up as Yankee vassals. Then you'll be obliged to agree that I told you so.' Nevertheless, he retained a sneaking admiration for the toughness and stubborn common sense of Bevin. These qualities enlivened the Foreign Secretary's off-the-cuff account to Harold Nicolson of a private conversation he had with his intransigent Soviet opposite number. The one-sided exchanges took place in Bevin's flat towards the end of 1947, and the contrary Burgess revelled in them.

'Now, Mr Molotov, what is it that you want? What are you after? Do you want to get Austria behind your Iron Curtain? You can't do that. Do you want Turkey and the Straits? You can't have them. Do you want Korea? You can't have that. You are putting your neck out too far, and one day you will have it chopped off. . . . You cannot look on me as an enemy of Russia. Why, when our Government was trying to stamp out your Revolution, who was it that stopped it? It was I, Ernest Bevin. I called out the transport workers and they refused to load the ships. Now again I am speaking to you as a friend. . . . If war comes between you and America in the East, then we may be able to remain neutral. But if war comes between you and America in the West, then we shall be on America's side. Make no mistake about that. That would be the end of Russia and of your Revolution. So please stop sticking out your neck in this way and tell me what you are after. What do you want?'

'I want a unified Germany,' said Molotov.

'Why do you want that? Do you really believe that a unified Germany would go Communist? They pretend to. They would say all the right things and repeat all the correct formulas. But in their hearts they would be longing for the day when they would revenge their defeat at Stalingrad. You know that as well as I do.'

'Yes,' said Molotov, 'I know that. But I still want a unified Germany.'

And that was all he could get out of him.[5]

Caught off guard by western Europe's prompt acceptance of the Marshall Plan, the Soviet Union redoubled its efforts to regain the upper hand. A permanently weakened Germany, as Molotov had implied, could still become a Kremlin pawn: and a Germany gradually unified from within by Soviet manipulation became Stalin's prime objective in the West towards the end of 1947. For propaganda purposes, an Eastern counterpart to the Marshall Plan was launched for the benefit of the Soviet satellites. A secondary aim was to cut off the trickle of trade which had started to flow between the two halves of divided Europe. Then, taking the calculated risk of a military confrontation with the Western powers in Berlin, the Soviet Union tested as never before the patience and resolution of its former allies.

Allied control of Berlin and of Germany as a whole had been hampered since the Potsdam agreement by the Soviet policy of treating their zone and city sector as if these were exclusively Russian territory. The anti-German feelings of the French proved a minor complication. When the Russian representatives finally walked out of the Allied Control Council on 20 March 1948, their Western colleagues needed no reminding of the underlying reason. Plans for reforming the debased German currency were by then well advanced; but the Russians stolidly refused to endorse any measure which would deprive them of an inflationary monopoly they had accidentally enjoyed since the armistice. The printing plates of the German Mint had fallen into their hands at that time, and they had no interest whatever in helping to create a stable Deutschemark. Instead, they retaliated by announcing that, from 1 April 1948, all freight traffic entering or leaving Berlin would be stopped and checked.

'The Russians opposed our currency reform,' President Truman noted, 'because it exposed the basic unsoundness of their own currency. And it became one of the major points of contention during the discussions on the Berlin blockade.'[6]

General Lucius Clay, the American military governor, advised the President that, short of trying to force the Russians to withdraw, it would be essential to fly in supplies, though Clay was at first somewhat doubtful about sustaining an airlift. The Americans, the British, and to a more moderate extent the French, stood firm, however, and responded to the Soviet blockade with vigour. Every serviceable aircraft was mobilized for the non-stop delivery of food, fuel and raw materials to the people of the city and their defenders. Public opinion throughout the West generally supported Truman and Attlee in accepting this unsought and perilous challenge. Not that the Western powers neglected the task of talking and trying to negotiate with Soviet representatives in Berlin, Moscow, at United Nations headquarters and wherever else opportunity offered, while unarmed aircraft went on flying above the empty highways and the guarded Russian checkpoints, landing their cargoes, refuelling and taking off again for more. The stockpiling of coal and foodstuffs ensured that Berliners did not starve or freeze during the bitter winter of 1947–8. The perceptive Harold Nicolson, in the course of a brief visit to the city at the end of September, contrasted his own subjective impression of 'helplessness' amid the endless ruins of war with the businesslike bustle of senior Allied organizers intent on averting another and greater conflict through hesitancy or infirmity of purpose.

'He is a formidable man – Napoleonic,' Nicolson recorded of Lucius Clay. . . . 'He says the chances of war are only one in ten. "The Russians know they would be licked. If they cut our air route, they know it is an act of war. They won't cut our air route." . . .'[7]

Guy Burgess found it hard to hide from friends like Nicolson the welter of frustration and annoyance he felt. To be a passive witness of this latest, bloodless battle between East and West seemed to revive perverse echoes of schoolboy patriotism, which would not have edified Philby, still less his own Soviet control. When, eventually, Stalin drew back from the precipice, and the Russians declared their willingness to raise all restrictions on traffic to and from the city, Burgess was just as downcast. The blockade ended at last on 12 May 1949, after fourteen months of dangerous deadlock. Such classified information as Burgess had passed to Moscow actually benefited the Russians little. The Berlin crisis, from start to finish, had been conducted in the light of common day. Millions of ordinary people could and did judge the merits of the case for themselves. Nothing from the files or in-trays of Hector McNeil could have provided comfort to Stalin. The moral reverse suffered by the Soviet leader may have been deserved. It did nothing to buoy up Burgess, who suddenly appeared 'to go to pieces', causing some of his colleagues to wonder how much longer his chequered career at the Foreign Office could conceivably last.

Like Maclean, whom he had privately conferred with in September 1948, when the diplomat returned from New York on leave before taking up his next post in Cairo, Guy Burgess found solace in hard and indiscriminate drinking. His first-floor flat stood not far from the Piccadilly end of Bond Street. It was still a haunt for the same inner circle of oddly assorted friends who had frequented that Bentinck Street basement in which Maclean had been compromised more than four years previously. Hector McNeil was an occasional caller now. So, too, as before, was Guy Liddell of MI5. The presence of the minister and this senior security man lent a plausible respectability. Burgess could no longer tolerate his own company; and the number of boon companions who could tolerate him seemed to be dwindling. In the small hours of one morning his Foreign Office colleague, Fred Warner, knowing Burgess would be there, looked in at a Soho nightclub patronized by homosexuals 'to make sure that Guy got home safely, without creating a public mischief on the way'. Apart from a bad-tempered manager and the prone form of a man in a crumpled suit lying still and insensible on the floor, the dimly lit club was deserted. Warner recognized his friend, knelt over him, and vainly tried to rouse him. There was congealed blood on the side of his face and head. 'How long's he been lying here like this?' Warner asked the manager sharply. Mumbling something inaudible but obviously uncivil, the manager conveyed that he neither knew nor cared what precisely had happened, as if stray casualties of the kind were all in the night's work. 'In that case,' snapped Warner, 'kindly ring for an ambulance. This person needs treatment.' Still the manager would not budge, shrugging apathetically and implying that the victim had probably been 'asking for trouble'. When Warner repeated his request, the manager replied firmly: 'Nobody's going to send for an ambulance. I've got my licence to consider. And look at the mess he's made of my carpet.'

Tiring of this pointless discussion, Warner stooped and slowly lifted the deadweight of the injured Burgess across his shoulders like a sack of flour. Bidding the manager good morning, he staggered down the long staircase, one step at a time, until he reached the door and the street outside. Pausing for breath at intervals, he called at an all-night chemist's shop without being stopped and questioned. He waited while Burgess was patched up and bandaged, then bundled him into a taxi and saw him safely home. Reconstructing the incident later from the victim's somewhat hazy recollection of a drunken argument, which had led to a quarrel, a brawl and a long blackout, Warner surmised that the assailant must have knocked Burgess out before bouncing him down the stairs, where a waiter had picked him up, carried him back and laid him reverently, face down, in a corner. The Irish poet Brendan Behan may well have been involved in this unseemly fracas. According to the wryly perceptive David Footman, who heard 'slightly divergent though complementary versions of the incident' from Warner and Burgess in turn, this was by no means the only occasion on which 'Guy came to grief at the hands of someone he'd provoked beyond endurance.' It amused Footman to reflect in after years how heavily embroidered such tales grew in the telling and retelling. People seemed to prefer legends in recounting the misadventures of Burgess. The idea of his being kicked down the steps of his own respectable club, the Reform, by an irate Foreign Office colleague had a more sensational ring than the strange truth of his being carried bodily out of the notorious Boeuf sur le Toit by a friend-in-need called Warner. But then in almost every department of his contradictory and disorderly existence the facts about Guy Burgess were less credible than the fictions on which others often based their judgements. Some of these incidents were reported to George Carey-Foster, who duly noted them in the debit column of this 'Bad Hat's' catalogue of misdeeds.[8]

Goronwy Rees, who probably knew him best, continued to see Burgess now and then. Rees noticed two changes in his friend's pattern of behaviour. The first was a reluctance to talk politics; the second a startling increase in his dependence on drugs as well as alcohol:

> He was now perpetually taking sedatives to calm his nerves, and immediately followed them with stimulants in order to counteract their effect; and since he always did everything to excess, he munched whatever tablets he had on hand as a child will munch its way through a bag of dolly mixtures until the supply has given out. Combined with a

large and steady intake of alcohol, this consumption of drugs, narcotics, sedatives, stimulants, barbiturates, sleeping pills, or *anything*, it seemed, so long as it would modify whatever he happened to be feeling at any particular moment, produced an extraordinary and incalculable alteration of mood, so that one could not possibly tell what condition he would be in from one moment to the next. On the whole, however, it was fair to assume that sooner or later he would lapse into one of those moods of morose silence to which he was more and more frequently liable.[9]

When Rees tried to draw Burgess out on politics, 'he simply drank more and faster of whatever he happened to be drinking', eventually lapsing into a glum stupor. With Rees he consistently refused to discuss issues which would revive painful memories. Communism and Soviet intentions were taboo topics. Only three subjects ever led Burgess, in Rees's hearing, to launch forth into lucid denunciations of Western policies. These were the civil war in Greece, the American trial of Alger Hiss, and the precipitate withdrawal of the British from India. 'If one ventured to defend Anglo-American intervention on the ground that it was the only alternative to a Communist dictatorship in Greece,' Rees noted, 'he would sink into a gloomy silence which put an end to any argument.' As to Alger Hiss, while acknowledging the illiberal campaign of persecution of which Hiss seemed to be just another scapegoat, Burgess firmly contended that Hiss

was precisely the kind of person who was capable of carrying out the systematic programme of espionage of which Whittaker Chambers, so improbably as it seemed, had accused him: and only a Communist could be capable of such a feat.... The Hiss case fascinated Guy; he saw it as a battle of good and evil in which all the good was on the side of Hiss and all the evil on the side of Chambers.

Britain's withdrawal from India he vilified as the betrayal of a great historic mission because of the crude political partitioning of the subcontinent and the appalling loss of life which accompanied it.

It occasionally crossed Goronwy Rees's mind that his friend's fits of depression, his compulsive need for drugs and drink, might be explained by his continuing role as the spy he had once claimed to be when seeking to enlist the services of Rees himself. But this still appeared too fantastic a proposition to merit serious consideration. So Rees rejected it once more because 'it argued a degree of self-control, and a depth of dissimulation, which would be quite extraordinary in anyone, but in Guy seemed entirely out of the question'.[10]

Herbert Morrison, Lord President of the Council and Leader of the House of Commons, one of Attlee's less favoured rivals for the premiership, and the man who eventually but briefly held the post of Foreign Secretary when terminal cancer forced Ernest Bevin to relinquish it, was among the few public men never to have set eyes on Guy Burgess. He had heard of him, of course:

> I gathered that he was an intelligent and bumptious young man and a typical career diplomat. As a personal assistant to the Minister of State, Hector McNeil, he had access to the most secret documents. McNeil liked him, regarded him as a live wire, with a pleasant manner and considerable intelligence; indeed he had pressed for Burgess as his personal assistant. It is strange, therefore, that the security authorities regarded Maclean as the principal suspect. . . .[11]

What must surely be regarded as far stranger was the sublime ignorance or the faulty memory of Herbert Morrison. His dismissal of Donald Maclean as a relatively unimportant link in the conspiracy still reflects poorly on Morrison's evaluation of men and events.

By Christmas 1947 Hector McNeil had decided that it would be best for everyone to let Burgess deploy his talents somewhere else in the Foreign Office. Fred Warner had already grown so bored of hearing the minister's rhetorical question: 'What's to be done about Guy?' that he could hardly believe his ears at the unexpected news.[12] It appeared that a suitable vacancy was to be found for the miscreant in a new, hush-hush section directed by Christopher Mayhew, the Parliamentary Under-Secretary. Mayhew belonged to the large intake of Labour Party intellectuals who had won seats in 1945. A staunch anti-Communist since his schooldays at Haileybury, he had once joined a students' excursion to Moscow and Leningrad – 'more out of curiosity than anything else' – and was amazed to observe the impressive turnout of 'Cambridge pilgrims' among the tourists. Anthony Blunt had been a prominent member of the group; and Mayhew had sometimes wondered since whether Blunt had yet renounced his Marxist faith. Like Herbert Morrison, Mayhew had not encountered Guy Burgess. Hector McNeil invariably spoke with such warmth of his assistant's capabilities and flair that Mayhew was shocked by the young official's off-hand manner and dissolute appearance at their first formal meeting. Dismissing as unworthy the fleeting suspicion that 'Hector might be offloading a dud on me,' the Parliamentary Under-Secretary explained to the scruffy and fidgety Burgess what he hoped to achieve for Britain through the work of the new Information Research Department, IRD.

IRD was, in a sense, Mayhew's baby. He had conceived the idea and sold it to an enthusiastic Bevin. He had next been summoned by Attlee to Chequers for a talk about it. In his dry, prosaic way, the Prime Minister had said to Mayhew: 'Go ahead, with my blessing, but keep it dark.' Since the launching of the Marshall Plan, more money had become available for an agency which would counteract by positive means the endless outpourings of the Soviet propaganda machine; IRD was authorized to do just that. The recently founded Central Intelligence Agency in Washington would shortly embark on similar fringe operations, though on a bigger and much more lavish scale. A staff of writers, including émigrés to Britain from countries now behind the Iron Curtain, was being recruited. They would be briefed and supervised by Foreign Office organizers, turning out books, pamphlets and an array of background material for distribution, through British embassies abroad, to the media and the opinion-formers of the free world. Burgess began to show more animation as Mayhew's description of the new project continued. Yes, he understood and liked the whole concept. With his war-time experience of propagandist techniques, he felt certain that he would not only enjoy the work but make it prosper. Mayhew again stressed the paramount need for discretion. If the Russians got wind of this concerted propaganda exercise, its cutting edge would be blunted. Some sixth sense warned him that Burgess was untrustworthy; but Mayhew had promised McNeil to give this 'reject' a fair trial, and that promise he meant to honour.

The trial period lasted barely three months. Then, one spring day in 1948, Mayhew sent for Burgess again. He said bluntly that he had no alternative but to get rid of him at once. He had already reported the reasons to Foreign Office Personnel. 'From all I've heard and observed myself,' he told Burgess, 'you are nothing but a dirty, disreputable and idle good-for-nothing. I've no room for the likes of you in IRD.' Nevertheless, Guy Burgess had been less than idle on behalf of his Soviet control. He had passed on documentary evidence showing what the new department did, how it functioned and who worked for it. In addition, he had travelled to the Middle East on holiday in January 1948, making detours to brief officials at various British embassies about the special needs of IRD's listed clients and potential customers. The main purpose, however, was to escape the rigours of the English winter and to confer with his accomplice, Kim Philby, in Istanbul. As an exercise in diplomacy and salesmanship, the trip was not exactly a success. Wherever Burgess moved, sultry clouds of recrimination seemed to follow. Normally placid diplomats took exception to the visitor's misconduct off duty and to the studied insolence invariably directed at them by this improbable representative of the new propaganda section of the Foreign Office. Nor did the handful of secret servicemen whom Burgess managed to winkle out respond favourably to his embarrassing ribaldry at their expense. The chorus of official protests eventually reached Mayhew through the usual channels. This proved to be the clinching factor in the Parliamentary Under-Secretary's decision to dispense with an impossible underling.[13]

Nevertheless, in the strange underworld of Soviet espionage, Guy Burgess had reason to be satisfied with the useful talks he had in Turkey with Philby, with whom he stayed as a guest, much to the disgruntlement of Aileen. She had never pretended to like him and deplored his disruptive and unwholesome influence on her husband. The pair sometimes went for long walks together in the woods and countryside near Philby's remote home on the Asiatic shore. Almost inevitably, after heavy evenings out celebrating, they would return boisterously tipsy. Aileen could not fathom what Kim admired in the unspeakable Guy; and, according to friends, her nerves and odd behaviour gradually 'got the better of her'.[14] On paper at any rate, Philby was now a First Secretary attached to the British Embassy in Turkey, 'with no known Embassy duties', as he put it, but with a small staff of five people, including a secretary, to assist in his intelligence-gathering activities. What these two confederates found to discuss, apart from the usual exchange of gossip between friends, may seem quite irrelevant today. Yet the fact that Philby omitted any mention of their meeting in his own selective account of his career could be a paradoxical pointer to its importance.

The fortunes of two other men were undoubtedly of interest and mild concern to Philby: Donald Maclean, for one, and George Blake, for another. Burgess was well informed enough to be able to reassure Philby that no progress had yet been made by the Americans or the British in tracing the source of the leakages from the British Embassy in Washington. The hounds were apparently still concentrating their efforts on the atomic scientists, a fairly natural reaction in the wake of hostile American criticism of slapdash British security since Nunn May. If it disappointed Philby to learn that Burgess no longer had the run of Hector McNeil's secret files, he could console himself that George Blake, a Royal Navy lieutenant whom he had 'talent-spotted' as a possible SIS recruit for counter-espionage work in Germany, was now taking a crash course in Russian at Downing College, Cambridge. The Foreign Office had conveniently endorsed the good opinions formed about Blake, outwardly a withdrawn but keenly ambitious young man, who lacked the usual social and educational qualifications, being partly Dutch and partly Arab and never having studied at university. In a department run by Bevin, a tough ex-trade union leader who dropped his aitches and had no false sentiments about class differences, the recruitment of Blake had not been unduly difficult.

Perhaps it was just another coincidence. Perhaps Burgess wished to prove that he could still pull a string or two of his own. For certainly, not long after returning to London in disgrace to brave Mayhew's withering gibes, Guy Burgess was unceremoniously shunted to the Far Eastern Department of the Foreign Office, where George Blake duly arrived on attachment in the early summer of 1948. There is no contemporary evidence that these two remarkably dissimilar birds of passage became close, at any rate during office hours. Blake was as disappointed at being earmarked for notional consular service in the Far East as was Burgess at his latest demotion, or even Philby at having to go through the motions of gratitude for small mercies in distant Istanbul. Possibly suspecting that Blake might be malleable material and that he might do worse than sound him, Burgess seized the opportunity of befriending a friendless colleague. Blake's appointment as temporary Vice-Consul was promulgated on 1 September 1948. In advising him that he would shortly be posted to Seoul, the capital of South Korea, Counsellor R. H. Scott, the head of the Far Eastern Department, begged him to discount any idea that he was being sidetracked to an obscure little country far away where nothing ever happened. By then Korea's future, like Germany's, had become another bone of contention in the worldwide Cold War between the Soviet Union and the West. Split into two halves by the 38th Parallel, a Communist puppet régime held power in the North and was beginning to provoke the loosely democratic government in the South. The bitter civil war in China between the advancing armies of Chou En-lai and the forces of Chiang Kai-shek was an awesome complication in the background. The dangers of another East–West confrontation were not immediate, but the Foreign Office did not discount them altogether. And by far the loudest critic in the Far Eastern Department of British subservience to American policy was naturally Guy Burgess.[15]

Within two or three weeks of Blake's first junior appointment, a more seasoned but less self-possessed diplomat returned to London and the plaudits of his Whitehall superiors. Donald Maclean had been absent in Washington for nearly four and a half years. He spent his leave visiting relatives, renewing old friendships and being briefed on current difficulties between Egypt and Britain. He looked paler, older and plumper; but he had lost none of the coolly dismissive style of conversation which admirers remembered. Cyril Connolly, who had always sensed a strong streak of ambition in him, considered that nothing now could stop him evolving into 'Sir Donald', the shining paragon of His Britannic Majesty's Diplomatic Service:

> He gave a dinner party. It was a delightful evening; he had become a good host; his charm was based not on vanity but on sincerity, and he would discuss foreign affairs as a student, not as an expert. He incidentally enjoyed the magazine that I then edited [*Horizon*], which was a blue rag to Burgess, a weak injection of culture into a society already dead.[16]

Two other witnesses who met Melinda and Donald Maclean quite independently during this interlude were Malcolm Muggeridge and Geoffrey Hoare. An old 'Cairo hand' himself, Hoare was invited with his wife, Clare Hollingworth, to the home of Bernard Burroughs, head of the Southern Department and technically Maclean's future boss. Melinda sat next to Geoffrey, who found her

> thrilled at the thought of going to Cairo. [So] I told her all I could about that large, dusty, perversely attractive city. . . . Although Donald, a tall, rather remote but by no means unfriendly figure, showed no marked enthusiasm, I felt that he too was pleased with his new appointment. . . . Our farewell to them had been, 'See you soon in Cairo.'[17]

Neither Malcolm nor Kitty Muggeridge could grasp the motives that prompted Philip Jordan, Attlee's press officer and a reasonably close friend of theirs, to press them into dining alone with the Macleans at an elegant private flat in Long Acre. Years earlier Muggeridge had wasted valuable time trying to introduce Egyptian students at Cairo University to the beauties of English literature, but that seemed too far-fetched a reason for arranging this meeting, since Muggeridge's slight acquaintanceship with Maclean derived merely from the occasional background briefings he had attended recently in the First Secretary's office at Washington. If, as Muggeridge half-suspected, the prospective head of

Chancery in Cairo wished to sound him out on ideological grounds, then Maclean's courage must have failed him. Yet the wary Muggeridge had the odd feeling that at any moment, struggling through the polite banalities, there might be detected 'some faint hint of an offer or even a faint cry for help'. As they left Long Acre towards midnight, the mystified Malcolm asked his wife whether she could fathom the purpose of Philip Jordan's arrangement. The equally perplexed Kitty confessed that she had no notion at all.[18]

There was much more venom in the clandestine exchanges between Maclean and his fellow conspirator, Burgess, at this time. The indirect knowledge which Burgess had gleaned about the likely result of any thorough Anglo-American enquiry into the war-time leaks from the Washington Embassy was too rich a morsel to keep to himself. He could not let slip the chance of telling Maclean to his face of the risk of eventual exposure. The bully in Burgess doubtless drew malicious satisfaction from observing the effect of his words on this 'darling of the Service' whom he envied and despised. If Melinda noticed her husband's subsequent depressed condition, she probably put it down to a recurrence of the ungovernable problem which had marred domestic peace throughout their stay in the United States. She was looking forward to a spell of comparative tranquillity in Egypt. The thought that such local inconveniences as the undeclared 'war of liberation', which the Arab countries were ineffectually waging against the new and beleaguered State of Israel, might somehow affect the relaxed tempo of life in Cairo's diplomatic enclave hardly troubled her. The best was yet to be.

In fact, when Geoffrey Hoare next saw them about six months later, the Macleans still seemed to be enjoying the novelty of change. Their commodious, three-storeyed house in Sharia Ibn Zanki stood in its own large, well-tended and shady garden. They had a governess for the two young children and four Berber servants to cook, clean and attend to their wants. Hoare noted:

> I found Melinda on top of the world. She still adored Cairo, had made dozens of friends, and had probably for the first time in her married life

emerged from her protective shell. Donald was also doing exceptionally well at the Embassy and he too appeared at this time to be enjoying his new post.

Soon afterwards Clare Hollingworth, Hoare's journalist wife, arrived in Egypt. The couple were loaned a house almost opposite the Macleans' front door. Apart from linking up 'at the endless round of Cairo parties', the Hoares and the Macleans often visited each other's homes on free evenings to 'dine together and play family bridge'. Maclean lowered his guard only now and then. From chance remarks he made, both Geoffrey and his wife understood that Maclean had conceived an intense dislike for Egypt and her corrupt ways. He felt like a castaway, cut off from the real world by a sea of suffering around him: 'The contrast between the quite shocking poverty of the population and the arrogant, ostentatious wealth of the small ruling class minority outraged his liberal principles,' concluded the Hoares. King Farouk was still in power. Maclean, the radical diplomat, condemned this obnoxious ruler's blatant zest for 'playing the British off against the Wafd, the Nationalist Party'. He equally deplored the traditional and wholly contemptible British policy of 'wait and see':

> He felt that as we could not escape from the predominant position in Egypt which our previous status had given us, we should accept our responsibilities and try to persuade the rulers of Egypt to institute the reforms which alone, in his opinion, could save the country from Communism. And, except to stress its dangers, that was all I ever heard Donald say about Communism.[19]

Needless to say, the Head of Chancery was never imprudent enough to voice such opinions in the hearing of his embassy superiors, though it can safely be presumed that he continued to pass on surreptitiously to the Russians any positive evidence about current changes in British Middle East policy. Sir Ronald Campbell, the younger of the two otherwise unrelated British ambassadors to bear that name, had known Maclean since the latter's arrival in Paris after the Munich crisis as an inexperienced Third Secretary. Unlike the elder Campbell, who had organized the evacuation of the Paris Embassy in 1940 and had complained of Maclean's negligence at that time as the mark of 'a weakly character', the younger Sir Ronald tended to spoil this gifted Counsellor at his embassy. For this Campbell treated Donald Maclean as his protégé, and Maclean naturally sought to please and impress the Ambassador. In the eyes of Campbell, his Head of Chancery could do no wrong professionally. Being in the 'Grade A' category, Cairo was on the distribution list for every secret document and cable that passed between the Foreign Office and other nerve centres, not excluding Washington. So Maclean had as complete a picture as before of the whole diplomatic game, and this was of considerable value to the Soviet Union. By a curious mischance, the security officer, Major Sansom, was a stickler for regulations. Sansom suspected with reason that 'it would have been hard to find a man less fitted for such a responsible position' as the Head of Chancery, who brusquely refused permission for 'spot checks' on the briefcases of staff entering or leaving the embassy. The suspicions of Sansom, disregarded by the Ambassador, were nevertheless reported back to George Carey-Foster at the Foreign Office and carefully noted.[20]

The demands of Geoffrey Hoare's foreign editor now led to another lengthy absence from Cairo; by the time Hoare returned, in February 1950, he at once noticed a marked deterioration in the off-duty behaviour of his diplomatic neighbour. Maclean was drinking heavily. His loathing of Egypt and her false values predominated in his conversation. His temper was quicker and hotter than Hoare remembered. Melinda had become understandably worried, though 'there had so far been no scandal, and, at any rate officially, the Embassy knew nothing about it'. In fact, Sir Ronald Campbell could no longer ignore the consequences of several riotous incidents which caused either physical injury or deep offence to members of his staff, and the Foreign Office was thus forewarned, however mildly, of Maclean's Jekyll-and-Hyde tendencies as early as the spring of 1950. The first in a series of lurid episodes occurred before the end of March when Melinda's sister, Harriet, arrived in Cairo on holiday. It involved a hapless embassy colleague of Maclean's and a felucca, hired for an evening's outing down the River Nile, which was unexpectedly becalmed.

The plan to sail along for dinner with some friends living at Helouan some twelve miles away went sadly awry. The wind suddenly dropped; the felucca crept sluggishly forward; there was no food, only crates of alcohol, aboard. Then darkness fell and an ill-tempered Donald became drunk, abusive and uncontrollably violent. When his wife tried to silence him, he seized her by the throat and had to be restrained. By the time the party reached Helouan, nearly eight hours had dragged by; their intended hosts had long since given up waiting and retired to bed. Suddenly a night watchman, armed with a primitive rifle and alarmed by the babel of foreign voices, approached to challenge the intruders. Maclean jumped on him, wrenched the rifle from his grasp, and swung it like a club as if determined to smash the man's skull. An embassy colleague again intervened, but Maclean would no longer be denied. Grappling with this interloper, Maclean lost his footing and fell heavily on top of him. The rifle cracked down hard, Maclean's colleague screamed with pain. His leg was badly broken. Not until breakfast time the following morning did the dishevelled and weary guests escort the injured official to hospital in a borrowed car.

This bizarre episode was officially played down as a regrettable accident. Worse was to follow, however; and two other visitors, Walter Bell, who had served with Maclean under Clark Kerr (Lord Inverchapel) in Washington, and Bell's wife, Tanya, the daughter of US Air General Karl Spaatz, witnessed the swathe of damage and distress cut by their friend in the course of his final and most spectacular binge of all. Such previous peccadilloes as urinating publicly at a formal diplomatic reception were not comparable. When Philip Toynbee, a correspondent of the *Observer* and an old left-wing acquaintance of Maclean's, arrived from England early in May 1950, the self-restraint of the Counsellor at the British Embassy appeared to go straight out of the window. Toynbee stayed at the Macleans' house, to the annoyance of Melinda who, not having been consulted, considered him 'an uninvited guest'.

The Bells had come to Cairo in response to Donald's warm and repeated invitations, only to find that 'Philip Toynbee had beaten us to it', and was lodging with the Macleans. For Toynbee's amusing, iconoclastic views were music in Donald's ears, and the two men seemed to vie with one another in trying to shock people. On 8 May they escorted Melinda and her sister Harriet to a cocktail party and later to a reception. Maclean was separated from his journalist friend in the throng. Returning home alone in the small hours, he roused Toynbee and persuaded him to get up. They then stole out in search of further amusement, knocked up a junior member of the British Embassy staff, were admitted to the flat and demanded whisky. Their reluctant host found them a bottle, left them to it, and went back to bed. Toynbee and Maclean were still on the premises when the resident left for work. The Bells presently received repeated telephone calls 'from an exalted Donald Maclean: "Come over for a dram," he urged them. "I'm at this other friend's place."' The Bells wisely declined. Having drained the whisky in one flat, Maclean next forced his way into a second on another floor of the same block. The tenant was an American girl who had already gone off to her job in the library of the United States Embassy. While helping himself to her alcohol, Maclean decided to renew his invitation to the Bells. Tanya noticed that Donald 'sounded really angry' at her sharp refusal to join the revelry. The next destructive move he made was to smash the furniture, break up the bathroom, and, as a final gesture of contempt, to throw articles of underwear into the pan of the lavatory. Melinda and Harriet eventually came, surveyed the damage, and dragged off the miscreant, who by then was utterly incapable of resistance. Naturally the American girl-tenant was outraged; and the US Ambassador at once lodged a formal complaint with his British opposite number.

The next morning, 10 May 1950, Melinda braced herself and called on Sir Ronald Campbell. She pleaded that her husband had been far from well for weeks past. She believed that he was suffering from severe mental stress and needed specialist medical attention. The Ambassador accepted her plea and immediately arranged for Donald to fly back to London. Campbell's report was sympathetic to this victim of circumstance. A slightly obstreperous Philip Toynbee turned up with Melinda to see Maclean off, alongside two solemn-faced officials from the embassy; and Geoffrey Hoare, once more recalled by his London office, sat opposite Maclean on the flight from Cairo. 'Melinda may have looked soft and frail and helpless,' said Tanya Bell. 'Underneath, she was tough and adaptable and very shrewd.'[21]

When, on 23 September 1949, President Truman had announced: 'We have evidence that within recent weeks an atomic explosion occurred in the USSR,' the sense of gratification shared by Maclean, Burgess and Philby had gradually yielded to uncertainty. True, the West had lost its vaunted nuclear monopoly sooner than expected; the long lead supposedly held by the Americans over the Russians had disappeared; separate British efforts to build their own nuclear stockpile mattered less. The Cold War had entered a fresh and altogether more evenly balanced phase which the Kremlin might yet turn to permanent advantage, and that was a blessing. But would the consummation come soon enough to save the three spies? They had each personal reasons to doubt it. Time was running out for Maclean, and well he knew it. In his growing apprehensiveness he could confide in nobody, not even in the knowing Melinda. She lived as always from day to day, sampling and genuinely enjoying the round of pleasures offered by Cairo society. Once again the bottle had become for the Counsellor and Head of Chancery an indispensable drug, until his manic misconduct, resulting from over-indulgence in this medicine against despair, led to Melinda's single-handed intervention on his behalf. An ambassador, over-lenient to the point of laxity, had readily accepted her story. Sympathetic Foreign Office superiors considered the case in the light of the evidence to hand and recommended that Maclean should go for treatment to a psychiatrist of his own choosing. Only Carey-Foster, the Head of Security, counselled caution.[22]

In addition to his collaboration with 'Basil' as a purveyor to the Soviet Union of first-hand information on the West's atomic energy policy, stockpiling and supplies, this outwardly smooth but inwardly deranged diplomat had also warned Moscow in good time about imminent plans to create the North Atlantic Treaty Organization. After Hungary, democratic Czechoslovakia had been captured from within by the militant Communist minority in 1948. Ernest Bevin had responded to what looked dangerously like the expected Russian 'big push' by establishing Western Union, a loose defensive alliance between Britain, France and the Benelux nations. This Brussels Pact had been a beginning; but a firm American commitment alone would stiffen western Europe's will to resist Soviet aggressive designs. In the delicate negotiations in Washington between the Brussels Pact delegates, Canadian representatives and the State Department, Maclean had missed no point of substance: everything noteworthy inevitably reached Moscow.[23] Nevertheless, it had disturbed Maclean when the NATO security agreement was signed and quickly ratified by the United States Congress. The rebuff to his frenzied dreams of speeding a 'peaceful' Soviet takeover in western Europe was severe. The subsequent news that Soviet scientists had successfully detonated their first nuclear weapon, at least two years before the most pessimistic of Western experts expected it, brought him in Cairo only a momentary sense of exhilaration. More sombre thoughts oppressed him as the months dragged past in the exotic hot-house of his diplomatic enclave. For Maclean knew that sooner or later American, if not British, intelligence might trace the leaks from the Washington Embassy to himself, just as Burgess had suggested. The Russians were hard taskmasters, taking the risks Maclean ran quite for granted.

The colleagues who worked with Burgess in the Far Eastern Department held him in continued respect for the ingenuity and force of his arguments in favour of the new Communist régime in China. To what extent his advocacy influenced, at least indirectly, the decision of Britain to recognize the new Marxist dictatorship in Peking is hard to say. Naturally, the idea has been pooh-poohed by senior diplomats. No official of such humble status could have prevailed over the complex policy-making machinery of the Foreign Office. In view of the Labour Government's favourable attitude towards the new People's Republic in Peking, there was probably no need for Burgess to preach to the converted. Yet nobody disputed the fact that Burgess's expertise did persuade his superiors to let him deliver formal lectures to senior diplomats and secret service officials on the historical background and development of Britain's policy towards China. He was proud of this small achievement, as he freely admitted to his friend Goronwy Rees:

> His interest in China was an old one which had begun as far back as the days when he was a Communist at Cambridge; he was a particular admirer of the Indian revolutionary, M. N. Roy, who from 1926 to 1927 had been the Comintern's representative in China. Guy had the kind of mind which is extremely tenacious of the knowledge and ideas acquired in youth; in some respects, indeed, he might be said to have never advanced beyond them, but he was extremely able and ingenious in adapting them to changed circumstances. . . . In those days, professional theorists of the Chinese Revolution were hard to find, more especially if their theories appeared to coincide with British interests, so much so that when, in the summer of 1949, the Foreign Office held a summer school at Oxford, it was Guy who was chosen to lecture Britain's representatives, who included members both of MI5 and MI6, on *Red China*. And no doubt it was because of his renewed interest in the Chinese Revolution, in explaining which Marxist arguments could be ingeniously used to justify British recognition of the People's Republic, that Guy's virulent anti-Americanism became increasingly acute. . . .[24]

Burgess, by all accounts, had reached a curious plateau of contentment with his otherwise undistinguished lot. But he descended to sea-level abruptly in private whenever he fell to analysing the latest American 'outrage' that affronted his Marxist prescription for creating a brave new world. Then he would 'go quite berserk'. Goronwy Rees wondered at intervals whether Burgess might not be settling at last for respectability of sorts. He even talked of getting married and once startled his friend by claiming that he had a particular girl in mind. Nothing came of these wistful, improbable dreams of becoming wholly conventional. His old Etonian acquaintance, Michael Berry (today Lord

Hartwell, the newspaper proprietor), had also been sceptically awaiting the publication of the banns for months. One Monday morning, alighting at Paddington from the train he usually took from the station near his country home, Berry had come upon Burgess walking along the platform towards the ticket barrier, accompanied by a plain, rather mousy young lady. The two men exchanged greetings. It seemed that Guy and his companion had travelled to London in another compartment of the same train. Then, quite unabashed, Burgess introduced the girl: 'She's my fiancée,' he explained, adding lightly, 'It's simply an experiment, of course.' All three shared a taxi as far as Burgess's flat towards the Piccadilly end of Bond Street, where Burgess and his mysterious friend got out and said goodbye. The 'experiment' was eventually abandoned. Berry neither saw nor heard of her again.[25]

A fiancée would have scarcely fitted into the chaotic style of life which Burgess had adopted too long ago to alter at whim. His self-indulgences, whether homosexual or alcoholic, followed capriciously steady lines. He would always be a creature of habit. The décor of his flat was still picked out in stridently patriotic tones of red, white and blue. An enormous double bed was the centrepiece, among the bookshelves and some good period furniture. Special friends, not necessarily or always male lovers, enjoyed looking in for involved, hilarious conversations about politics and the latest social scandal. Rees noticed that Guy now possessed a record player as well as an antique miniature harmonium, retrieved during the war from a bomb-damaged house: 'In the evenings, when the noise of the Bond Street traffic had died down, he would seat himself at this precious acquisition and pick out pieces of Mozart and Handel with one finger.'[26]

The craving for what was familiar governed his leisured routine. For instance, on Monday nights, accompanied by two women and two men friends, the latter being senior officials of MI5 and MI6 respectively, Burgess would revel in the sketches and songs of artistes at the Chelsea Palace music hall in King's Road. In those pre-television days he adored the slapstick comedy and would join in the choruses of sentimental ballads that were the legacy of a more spacious age before Britain lost her way. Of Burgess's companions on these ritual evenings of old-fashioned relaxation, Rees commented: 'Even to me, who knew them well, they always used to seem a strangely constituted quartet. There was something *queer* about them, not in the homosexual sense, but in the sense which applies to members of the security services when they are off duty.'[27] It looked occasionally as if Guy Burgess himself had joined their club *honoris causa*, so completely was he accepted at face value.

By this stage Rees had convinced himself that his eccentric friend was no longer the self-professed Comintern agent of yester-year. So, one evening while they were chatting together, Rees asked Burgess to his face to describe how and when he decided to drop the Soviet Union. Burgess refused point blank to discuss the matter. Instead he 'relapsed into a sullen silence'. Partly to tease, partly to coax the truth out of him, Rees recalled the original occasion in the mid thirties when Burgess had vainly solicited his cooperation as a fellow spy: 'I have a complete record of our exchanges that night,' said Rees. 'I wrote it down at the time. I decided then that the safest thing to do would be to lodge a sealed copy with my lawyer.' Burgess stared at him in horror, then became agitated and very annoyed. He implored Rees to destroy the document: 'If it ever gets out, it will ruin me and my career at the Foreign Office.' He stormed round the room, interrupting his progress every few steps to beg Rees again and again not to betray him. For a long time he would not listen to Rees's repeated assurances: 'But Guy I was only joking. There's no such written record. That's something I invented for your benefit.' Slowly Burgess calmed down. Yet the undisguised terror on his face revived the suspicion that had been lurking at the back of Rees's mind for over fourteen years. He departed feeling more upset than Burgess, a man who 'knew the composition and routines of Britain's security services like the back of his hand through his highly placed friends within'.[28]

Before the end of 1949, Burgess fell from grace again at the Foreign Office as a result of another bacchanalian holiday trip to Tangier, via Gibraltar and Spain. Goronwy Rees believed that nothing now could save his friend from the consequences of his latest indiscretions. Wherever he had moved, Burgess called on British diplomats and secret service officials, earning their censures with

a record of drinking bouts and brawls which would have done credit to Dimitri Karamazov. He had also, at each stage of his travels, insisted on visiting the local representatives of MI6 and on discussing their characters, habits, opinions and professional inadequacies with anyone who chose to listen to him in any bar in which he happened to be drinking.

As if that were not enough, Burgess added insult to injury by vilifying British policy and castigating the said MI6 officials for being craven enough to obey it. The ensuing protests were at least as vehement as those earlier recriminations which had led to his demotion at the hands of Christopher Mayhew. 'The sooner we get rid of this appalling man,' minuted the assistant from MI6 currently attached to Foreign Office security, 'the better for all of us.' To which Carey-Foster added laconically: 'I agree.'[29] Burgess abjectly told Rees that he was 'finished'. Then he handed him a lengthy and elaborate defence of his indefensible behaviour which, he said, would be submitted in a final endeavour to placate his unforgiving superiors.

At Rees's prompting, Burgess tore it up and rewrote a shorter, simpler memorandum. This made no attempt to answer specific charges, stressing that the writer reserved the right to 'seek a board of enquiry' if he were threatened with anything sterner than a reprimand. The episode also served to push Goronwy Rees's renewed suspicions of treachery into the background, and merely seemed to re-emphasize how accident-prone Burgess had become. The likelihood that any self-respecting foreign intelligence service like the KGB could ever have stooped to recruit him was utterly preposterous.

The Honourable Mrs Miriam Lane, whom Burgess had known since youth as Miriam Rothschild, the sister of his former Trinity friend Victor, concealed her astonishment when the Foreign Office telephoned one morning and the irrepressible Guy came on the line. He announced breezily that he wanted some professional advice from the best entomologist in the world. Wondering how this comparative stranger had found her unlisted number, she listened to his ludicrous queries about the life cycle of worms.

Lunching one day recently at a fashionable restaurant, Burgess to his disgust and annoyance had noticed maggots crawling about the fish. He made a furious scene, he said, and about three weeks afterwards had suddenly developed a tape worm. Was there a direct connection, he asked me, between his tape worm and the maggoty fish, since he wished to sue the restaurant for damages? I offered him a factual account of the worm's life-cycle and explained that there could be no connection. . . . He expressed deep disappointment but, after giving vent to his irritation, he paused and added: 'Oh, well, I will sue them all the same – I expect they'd pay up rather than face the publicity.'[30]

Burgess had this sudden way of surprising people whom he had not met for years. He also possessed an incomparable knack of saddening others who admired the better side of his wayward character. Harold Nicolson noted on 25 January 1950:

I dined with Guy Burgess. Oh my dear, what a sad, sad thing this constant drinking is! Guy used to have one of the most rapid and acute minds I knew. Now he is just an imitation (and a pretty bad one) of what he once was. Not that he was actually drunk yesterday. He was just soaked and silly. I felt angry about it.[31]

That tempestuous holiday excursion of Burgess to Tangier had occurred just after Philby's return to London from Istanbul. The latter, after being briefed for his next assignment as secret service liaison chief in the United States, told Burgess that the British security net was being drawn tighter round a small group of Foreign Office suspects, all of whom had served at one time or another during the war in the Washington Embassy. When whispers of Maclean's misdemeanours in Cairo began to reach him, Burgess could well appreciate why this predestined victim of circumstances had fallen. But railing against fate and condemning the lunacy of the Western powers' anti-Soviet policies would achieve nothing. So Burgess swallowed his pride. He meekly accepted the severe reprimand administered by his Foreign Office superiors, realizing that he had got off lightly. Then he waited as patiently as possible for Maclean to reappear. In mid May 1950 Burgess took himself and the downcast fugitive from Cairo in hand. Putting the best face possible on the darkening prospects, he went out of his way to persuade Maclean that if he brazened it out, all might yet be well. The unexpected leniency of the Foreign Office in his own case was proof enough of this.

Outside witnesses did not pierce the malingerer's contrite mask. They could not reach the tortured spirit cowering behind it. At the Garrick Club one lunchtime towards the end of May 1950, Malcolm Muggeridge caught a glimpse of Maclean's handsome profile by the crowded bar. Asking his companion, the novelist Anthony Powell, to guard their drinks, he moved across to greet the diplomat. Muggeridge noticed that one of the diplomat's legs appeared to be encased in plaster. 'Nice to see you back, Donald', said Muggeridge, 'but you've been in the wars, haven't you?' Maclean hastily attributed his fractured limb to a fall. They chatted amiably and parted. Muggeridge could only suppose that current rumours of Maclean's difficulties in Egypt had possibly been exaggerated.[32] One of the new MPs in the general election of 1950, the near-deadlocked results of which reflected the state of the public mind, was the future Liberal Party leader Jo Grimond, who had married Laura Bonham Carter in the year of Munich. Aware of the family's concern about Donald Maclean's recent excesses and their detrimental effect on the diplomat's mental balance, Grimond took him to lunch but could not break down his guest's studious evasiveness.

> There was nothing wrong with his memory, nor with his grasp of the international situation. He made light of his own troubles too, even suggesting that soon he might be going back to rejoin the Embassy staff in Cairo. I said firmly that I didn't think that at all a sound idea in view of all that had happened. Then we changed the subject.[33]

The Foreign Office handled Maclean as gently and considerately as his medical advisers did, notably the accommodating woman psychiatrist in Wimpole Street whom he chose in preference to anyone else. She probed unsuccessfully to elicit the underlying causes of her patient's black depression, which had again led to compulsive drinking and homosexual lapses. The specialist also humoured him, not probing too hard. Sir Ronald Campbell's report from Egypt had dwelt favourably on the splendid quality of Maclean's work, indicating plainly enough that his Head of Chancery's misconduct during off-duty hours could best be explained by overwork and strain. It appeared that, apart from those recent and wholly regrettable incidents in Cairo, which could not of course be overlooked, nothing similar had ever been recorded officially against Maclean: his past conduct and character wore a wholly impeccable look. 'Almost too good to be true,' mused Sir William (later Lord) Strang, the Under-Secretary of State, a sharp yet fair judge of human nature. No witnesses were summoned by the 'three wise men' who dealt with the case. If there had been a partial cover-up in Egypt, the *esprit de corps* which doubtless promoted it seemed once more quite appropriate. Friendly outsiders like Cyril Connolly and Philip Toynbee frequently addressed themselves with mock-solemnity to 'Sir Donald', anticipating the knighthood to come for this paragon of the service. The future Sir Henry Ashley Clark, then Chief Clerk at the Foreign Office, and Sir George Middleton, the head of personnel, were among the members of the judicial panel; they entertained no such jocular thought as they gravely scrutinized and weighed the evidence. The majority verdict proved to be predictably favourable. Donald Maclean was clearly guilty of unbecoming conduct. Just as clearly, his judges drew the line at compromising, still less terminating, a career of merit and enormous promise; so they entered a mere question mark against his name. The mitigating circumstances of excessive nervous strain told heavily in his favour. It would be for the doctors finally to decide when, rather than if, Maclean would be fit enough to resume work.

This is why misbehaviour which, for others, would have meant dismissal, resulted in his being given sick leave and sent for medical treatment. You may ask why we did not spot a traitor in him sooner than we did. I think, looking back, the explanation was quite a simple one. It was not just his background. Nor was it solely the *esprit de corps* which was indeed strong in the Foreign Service until he let it down. It was the fact that he was to all appearances an extremely able operator: just like Philby.[34]

So Burgess got off with a reprimand and Maclean without one, while Philby, now settling down in Washington but ever on the alert, kept his fingers nervously crossed. The interlude in Turkey from early 1947 to the summer of 1949 had been interesting but relatively unproductive, a rest cure of sorts after all the excitement and unremitting toil of the war years. The risks Philby had run then, as a punctilious agent working for both sides, had never seriously troubled him. Yet since his calculated mishandling of the dangerous Volkov case, Philby had become more keenly conscious of the invisible minefields around him. Surefooted as a mountain goat himself, he knew that the clumsiness of Maclean or the exhibitionism of Burgess could destroy him still. Nor could he do anything to anticipate the consequences of further defections from Soviet Russia, leading to the unmasking of further Nunn Mays or Fuchses.

At his office desk in the British Embassy, where the cool, business-like Sir Oliver Franks had replaced the florid and erratic Lord Inverchapel as Ambassador, Philby enjoyed sifting the high-grade messages from the dross, passing on to his Russian friends the intentions and proposals of their Western opponents. He felt useful again in Washington.

If he had accomplished little in Istanbul and Ankara, at least he had been glad of the respite. He had managed also to hoodwink the good-natured but watchful Stewart Menzies on several occasions. The Turkish security directorate was no better and no worse than Stewart Menzies or Philby had any right to expect. Its senior officers, with whom he usually dealt personally, would not budge before receiving regular bribes in the convenient form of 'subsidies for information received'. Philby's liaison with them had yielded little fruit worth picking. Yet if his low opinion of their efficiency was justified, his lofty dismissal of his Turkish colleagues for making what he later described as a 'sorry mess of the only operation I ever entrusted to them' is surely reminiscent of Satan rebuking sin. For the detailed plan was Philby's, originally fathered on him by 'C' and his arm-chair experts, and Philby had ensured that the plan foundered. It was Philby who guided a trio of hapless émigré Armenian infiltrators to a remote and inhospitable crossing point on the border of the Soviet Union – and to certain death. His Turkish collaborators did not warn the Soviet frontier guards. Philby had naturally taken that precaution.[35]

One of Philby's pet aversions in Istanbul was the ring of amateur spies, mostly refugees from Bulgaria, Rumania and Yugoslavia, who had sought to pass off bogus information. His impatience with their pretensions was so thinly veiled that it caused one long-serving member of his staff of five people, including a devoted secretary, to wonder 'whatever had got into him to make him so sore about a lot of fugitives from Communism'.[36] By a grim coincidence, the State trial of Traicho Kostov and other old-guard defendants of the Bulgarian Communist leadership took place in Sofia before Philby's tour of duty in Turkey ended. There is no reference to it in his own account of his life, and this would appear to be another careful omission. For the predictable outcome of that elaborately staged peep-show of Marxist justice must have given him personal satisfaction. His own study of the intercepts at Bletchley had indicated that Kostov and other captured Communists were probably 'turned' in prison by the war-time internal security chief, Nikolai Geshev. A former Fascist double agent, Geshev had won them over by combining torture with blandishments. The information was duly transmitted to Moscow via Philby. Later, from a safe distance, he involved himself in the arrangements by which Kostov was lured into admitting to a British agent his earlier collaboration with the unsavoury Geshev. This ploy within a ploy doubtless appealed as much to Philby's taste for good, rounded melodrama as to his inverted Marxist sense of fair play.

Kostov confessed to his accusers in open court:

> I found myself hard pressed. It became clear to me that the dossiers

were at the disposal of British intelligence, of which it is known that, let it only once take hold of a man's finger and it can always pull out the man's arm and after that the whole man himself. Because of this I did not even think of resisting. . . .[37]

Shortly before Philby was recalled to London for the protracted briefing on his delicate new assignment in Washington, Kostov and his co-defendants had been executed. Their 'rehabilitation' came only after Stalin's death in 1953. Had the head of the British Secret Service station in Istanbul exerted himself as willingly for Britain as for the Soviet Union, he would have produced something far more tangible than a topographical survey of the Anatolian hinterland or an unfinished photographic atlas of the trackless Russo-Turkish frontier which he code-named 'Operation Spyglass'. Both were his own suggestions. He presented them so well on paper that the defence advisers in London had encouraged him eagerly. It was an excellent excuse for spending the summer months far away from prying embassy superiors, the dusty routine of his own office, and tiresome details of the interminable administrative paperchase. He could breathe more freely in the open air. The results of these arduous, lengthy reconnaisances were unavoidably sketchy. The Americans, equipped with modern weapons and sophisticated electronic eyes in high-flying machines like the U2, had not yet moved into Turkey; Philby's laborious, virtually single-handed excursions by truck, complete with heavy hand-held gear, belonged to a period in which aerial mapping from the stratosphere had not yet become a commonplace.

This was basically an escapist's experiment on which his father, still the peppery personal adviser to a desert monarch, might well have complimented him. The one visit Philby paid to Ibn Saud's arid kingdom, on the second-to-last leg of the flight out from London to Istanbul in 1947, turned out to be a rather disenchanting experience. Despite Harry St John's pride in the featureless landscape, and his manifest delight in the noble inhabitants, his son could detect little nobility in the latter, no obvious beauty in the former. Worse still, liquor had been unobtainable. He could never complain of a whisky shortage in Istanbul, nor in the expensive, secluded villa which he rented on the unfashionable Asiatic shore, commuting by ferry each day to his office in the city.

He had selected this isolated home for its devious professional advantages, though Aileen had been quick to point out the countervailing domestic disadvantages when she eventually joined him with the children. As one perceptively critical colleague expressed it: 'Kim was always good at putting his own wants before anyone else's, Aileen's especially. He was so self-centred that it seldom even crossed his mind how badly he neglected her in that lonely place.' A severe nervous ailment which had afflicted her, on and off, since childhood suddenly began to assert itself again; after one mysterious outbreak, which appeared to be self-inflicted, Philby felt so helpless that he rang up his erstwhile colleague, Nicholas Elliot, in Berne and had her temporarily removed to a private Swiss clinic. There it was found that the ugly rash or boils disfiguring most of Aileen's body had been caused by injections of urine and insulin.[38]

'I never did the second half of Spyglass,' he noted. 'In the summer of 1949 I received a telegram from headquarters [offering] me the SIS representation in the United States where I would be working in liaison with both the CIA and the FBI.'[39]

Aileen rapidly became her old high-spirited self in the bustling and friendly atmosphere of post-war Washington. Her husband again kept reasonably regular hours at the British Embassy; and his cheerful presence at home blotted out the sense of alienation and self-pity which had upset her emotional balance towards the end of their stay in Turkey. The first house they rented in Washington was somewhat too small. With four young children to feed and shelter, and a fifth already on the way, Aileen decided that they ought to find a larger home. Kim agreed. His original impulse to 'camp at the mouth of the lion's den' and live opposite the sardonic Johnny Boyd, then Assistant Director of the FBI in charge of security, had been a little inconvenient as well as socially unwise. Soon they found a roomier place on Nebraska Avenue; and professional visitors were drawn to it as if by radar. Callers seemed to enjoy dropping in nightly until all hours, thirsty colleagues from the embassy, sparring partners from the newly expanding CIA or the long-established FBI, even odd journalistic acquaintances who invariably claimed to remember Philby from his younger days. He was a popular host, disarmingly agreeable and quietly irreverent. Better still, he always seemed to be available. A studious listener, he might now and then cap someone else's anecdote 'with a wisecrack or a spontaneous guffaw', but rarely did guests hear him express a provocative opinion of his own.

His wariest American associate was, of course, the enigmatic James Jesus Angleton. Under Truman's post-war national security reforms, the future Central Intelligence Agency had been set up in 1947 as an embryonic, untried but well-funded successor to 'Wild Bill' Donovan's disbanded OSS; now it was slowly beginning to assert itself. The armed forces were still jealous of it; so, of course, was J. Edgar Hoover. Yet most of the staff lacked training and operational experience in the field, since many of Donovan's war-time associates had long returned to their former jobs and the newcomers were still somewhat unsure of themselves. Only Angleton, the effective head of counter-intelligence, bridged the gap between past and present. So Philby instinctively turned to Angleton and tried hard to win the esteem and trust of this astute but introspective personality whose mind proved extremely difficult to read. Philby noted:

> Our close association was, I am sure, inspired by genuine friendliness on both sides. But we both had ulterior motives. Angleton wanted to place the burden of exchanges between CIA and SIS on the CIA office in London – which was about ten times as big as mine. By doing so, he would exert the maximum pressure on SIS's headquarters while minimizing SIS intrusions into his own. . . . By cultivating me to the full, he could better keep me under wraps. For my part, I was more than content to string him along. The greater the trust between us overtly, the less he would suspect covert action. Who gained more from this complex game I cannot say. . . .[40]

The game which Philby had been officially briefed to play in Washington was decidedly tricky in itself. His predecessor, Peter Dwyer, had been obliged to cultivate Hoover and the all-powerful FBI before the breach-birth of the CIA and in the precarious period of its infancy. Stewart Menzies now wanted closer ties between the British Secret Service and its natural, though relatively inexperienced, American counterpart. Ironically, he had selected Philby, already marked down by Angleton as a suspect who must be handled with kid gloves, at least until he betrayed himself. For 'C' was not in Angleton's confidence; and 'C' regarded Philby as the most suitable person to establish good working relations with the CIA, and to do so without needlessly ruffling the feathers of the hypersensitive Hoover. The 'turned' Fifth Man, 'Basil', whom Angleton had discreetly used since Maclean's departure to continue passing on doctored atomic information to the Russians, received a fresh commission as soon as Philby began to ingratiate himself with the inscrutably polite and attentive counter-intelligence specialist of the CIA. 'Basil's' final task was to keep a vigilant eye on Philby. Thus was the stage set.

The unsuspecting Philby saw the problems facing him in narrower but no less complicated terms. He realized that the rivalries between the CIA and the FBI were at least as acute as those which still bedevilled relations between MI6 and MI5 in Britain. Hoover looked askance at the activities of the reinaugurated United States' Secret Intelligence Service. So long as the CIA did not trespass on his expansive preserves, Hoover would probably let it make its own mistakes. However, being something of an anglophobe with delusions of Napoleonic grandeur, the Director of the FBI would be sure to turn against Philby, once he understood that the purpose of the Englishmen's assignment was to 'tilt the balance of cooperation' in favour of the upstart CIA. This prospect did not unduly disturb Angleton, whose personal relations with Hoover were reasonably cordial, at any rate on the surface. The fact that FBI agents were encouraged to discount British agents generally as security risks suited Angleton's book. So Philby's mission was beset from the start by deep pitfalls. Some sixth sense warned him to walk warily in case he fell headlong into one. Nevertheless, the Russians expected much of him, and the interests of the Soviets had always to come first.

During his London briefing in September 1949, Philby had been incidentally told by Maurice Oldfield at SIS headquarters of the progress so far made by Anglo-American counter-intelligence to trace two disturbing leaks: the first from the British Embassy in Washington, the second from the atomic energy establishment at Los Alamos. The Americans had divulged only a little of what their separate enquiries had so far yielded. Since Philby had learnt about both leaks at least four years earlier, we must disregard his bland assertion that Oldfield's information came as a shock to him. This deserves to be treated as a disingenuous fiction. Except for appearances' sake, he had no need to carry out 'a quick check of the Foreign Office list' which 'left me in little doubt about the identity of the source of the British Embassy'. Equally, Philby had no cause whatever to seek confirmation of something he already knew from his Russian friends. As a senior KGB agent in place, he would have been advised in confidence of the potentially dangerous consequences arising from the errors of a negligent cipher clerk at the Soviet Consulate in New York in 1945. Even Guy Burgess had found that out; and Burgess, unable to keep a secret, had foolishly forewarned the wretched Maclean. To some extent, Philby had already lost control of a case that had been gathering dust for too long. Only well-timed preventive measures could now save the war-time British Embassy spy. Another warning to Maclean would be like crying wolf. Maclean was in any event too unstable to be trusted. Besides, Philby swiftly recognized that his own anomalous official status in Washington exposed him uncomfortably, like a practice target, to Hoover's sniping and Angleton's smoother range-finding.

The FBI not merely snubbed him but kept him gingerly at arm's length. He got little change out of Hoover's sleuths. His relations with his ex-neighbour, Johnny Boyd, for instance, did not improve, however hard he tried to soothe him. Boyd looked on anyone outside his firm as a potential crook, a natural enough reaction in an early G-man who had formerly helped to cleanse Chicago of its gangsters. So while Philby gained nothing by flattering the uncooperative Boyd, Boyd scored by playing MI5 and SIS 'off against one another so as to exploit any differences between us'. Philby's frustration was genuine. Only self-control enabled him to curb it. Afterwards he gave vent to his feelings in this Kremlin-inspired outburst against the FBI, and Hoover in particular:

> I had a great deal to do with its counter-espionage work, and its record in that field was more conspicuous for failure than for success. Hoover did not catch Maclean or Burgess; he did not catch Fuchs, and he would not have caught the rest if the British had not caught Fuchs and worked brilliantly on his tangled emotions; he did not catch Lonsdale; he did not catch Abel for years . . . he did not even catch me. If ever there was a bubble reputation, it is Hoover's.[41]

The extra sneer reserved for Hoover's wasteful combing through the backgrounds of past non-British servants on the British Embassy payroll was unwarranted. Since a Jamaican maid who had once worked part-time for the Macleans turned out to be a Communist, and Lord Inverchapel himself had arrived from Moscow accompanied by the Russian valet, the determination of Hoover to leave no pebble unturned was reasonable enough. After all, Hoover did not share Philby's inside knowledge. He had to eliminate, one by one, suspects of low and high degree. That MI5 finally let Maclean slip through their fingers certainly cannot be blamed on the FBI. Here the Foreign Office and the British security authorities blundered, as we shall see. Had Hoover known fully about 'Basil', whom Angleton had trapped and moulded to his own uses as a double agent working for the United States, the FBI would certainly have been less industrious in pursuing the small fry. But then Philby did not know yet that 'Basil' had been turned; and though 'Basil' himself had confirmed what Angleton learnt from the Israelis about Philby's suspected role as a Soviet agent, the wily American counter-espionage expert still would not pounce prematurely. He chose to wait patiently in the over-ambitious hope that Philby might lose his concentration or his nerve, allowing others besides himself to be hooked and caught.

Peter Dwyer, the retiring SIS officer, had already ensured that Philby would not delay the isolating and trapping of Fuchs. Dwyer's final service to SIS, which Philby could retrospectively applaud as one professional acclaiming another, was to supplement FBI evidence and demonstrate that only Fuchs could have been in the right places at the appropriate times to betray atomic secrets to the Russians. It did not comfort Philby to learn from his Soviet friends that the stubborn Fuchs had refused point blank to go on working as a spy and indeed appeared content to confess everything when arrested, meekly knotting the noose round his own neck. The fear that Maclean might do the same must have plagued Philby when full reports of Fuchs's voluntary confession to Skardon, the MI5 investigator, reached him at the embassy. Fuchs had talked so freely that he helped to uncover Harry Gold and others in the American nuclear espionage network. Apart from Philby himself, only two other members of the British Embassy staff had access to the files on the now intensive Anglo-American search for the unidentified diplomatic spy: Geoffrey Patterson, MI5's representative in Washington; and Sir Robert Mackenzie, the regional security officer. Both of them thought they knew Philby well enough not to be surprised by his dry, professional appraisal of the open-and-shut case against the penitent Fuchs. 'Only a man so long hardened to Soviet discipline could have stood up so well to the strain,' commented one of Philby's senior colleagues, who would soon have reason to question the smoothness of the Philby façade. 'It's amazing how he managed to run such an uphill course without once stumbling.'

If Philby had a weakness, it was his increasing dependence on excessive intakes of whisky. One night he drank so much that he passed out and slumped down in a heap on his own sitting-room floor. Angleton and Mackenzie eventually agreed that they could do worse than carry their host upstairs to bed. They did so, undressing him roughly and lowering him between the sheets. What astonished Mackenzie was

> Kim's self-restraint. I remember that he was wearing bright red braces. He came to while we were staggering up under his weight. Normally you'd expect someone so fuddled to forget himself and babble something out of turn. Not Philby. He just smiled and didn't utter.[42]

One discerning young American who worked in Angleton's

department was Christopher Felix. He found the Englishman from SIS a pleasant, courteous, unpretentious person, who smiled a good deal:

> His smile, suggestive of complicity in a private joke, conveyed an unspoken understanding of the underlying ironies of our work. Philby and I were engaged in jointly conducting an operation abroad, reports on which reached us separately from the American and British agents in the field. In those days American communications left much to be desired. The British worldwide communications network, on the other hand, was one of two invaluable assets which the British War Cabinet had retained at all costs during the war-time liquidation of British overseas holdings – the other was the British reinsurance business. On three successive occasions, Kim came into my office with urgent reports which I had not received through our channels. The third time, when I again had to confess ignorance, Philby, with an air of anxious helpfulness which had just the right degree of opacity, asked: 'Well, look, in these circumstances, wouldn't you like us to handle your communications for you?' The offer of the poisoned apple was adroit. (I of course had no idea that it was doubly poisoned.) In declining it, I laughed. The charm part was that so did he.[43]

Christopher Felix was not the only intelligence agent, American or British, to notice another odd fact: whether by design or accident, Philby displayed a curious ignorance of Russian current affairs. The shifts and turns in Soviet policy, which preoccupied and often excited others, appeared to leave him indifferent. As Felix later noted:

> It could be that he avoided all detailed discussion of these matters because, on one level, he did not wish to risk a slip over his illegitimate contacts and political beliefs; or that, on another level, which is less likely, he wished to avoid implications of even legitimate contacts. In retrospect and on balance, I don't think his ignorance was feigned.[44]

The unpretentiousness which visitors observed in Philby's domestic life, the sparse furnishings, the casual atmosphere of untidiness, the 'full martini pitcher' and whisky bottles perpetually to hand, had been extended by long practice to his professional attitudes. He could have invented no better camouflage in Washington than his posture as an urbane, classless

Englishman who wore no airs and graces. He carefully avoided showing off, except to tease Angleton, and only when the moment for teasing was judged right. He certainly deceived Aileen, trying to compensate by treating her tenderly and affectionately in the knowledge that she would probably find out one day that the man she loved was a stranger whose alien loyalties had always proved stronger than the natural bonds between husband and wife. By the second half of 1950, however, Philby's mastery of everyday deception had become a waning asset. The pressures on him grew perceptibly. He must have been grateful to his Russian friends for their reassurances that he would be spirited away to safety in any unforeseen emergency. His artistry lay in inducing the majority of his American and British colleagues 'to think for themselves what he willed them to think'. Up to a point the artifice succeeded. Only Angleton and perhaps half a dozen of his closest aides saw right through Philby but pretended to see nothing.

In fact, the first serious omen of impending disaster appeared one morning in October 1950. It came in the form of a personal letter to Philby from London. The writer was his awkward old friend Guy Burgess, who began characteristically: 'I have a shock for you. I have been posted to Washington. . . .' Could Philby put him up until he found a place of his own? At the British Embassy two formal, longer communications had meanwhile arrived from the Foreign Office, the first addressed to Derek Hoyar Millar (now Lord Inchyra), the Minister, and the second to Mackenzie in the security office. According to Mackenzie, the scribe was the head of Foreign Office security, a man who seldom minced his words:

> George Carey-Foster explained crisply why Burgess was getting this last chance to make good, and the character description that followed was withering. He left out nothing that mattered and listed some of Burgess' more glaring peculiarities, including his homosexual habits. I showed the letter to Philby. We agreed it was unusually explicit, then I remember asking Philby what Carey-Foster could possibly mean by hinting that we'd better take care as Burgess was capable of worse things: 'Surely he can't mean goats?' I said. Philby laughed, then said quite seriously that he'd be willing to look after this unwanted Second

Secretary and make sure he behaved himself. Burgess, he added, was an old friend. I must say everyone else was relieved.[45]

The Personnel Department in London had found it anything but easy to convince Burgess that he had little choice but to go abroad. The alternative was 'the sack'. They assured him that an overseas posting to a large embassy would be in his own best interests. This would definitely be his 'last chance'. If he fitted in, his precarious career prospects might just benefit. Burgess, however, did not want to go. He enjoyed the pattern of crazy living he had long grown used to. He kept telling his friends that he would resign rather than go. In the end, Hector McNeil exerted all his powers of persuasion to make him see reason and cooperate.

Goronwy Rees and David Footman attended the typically mixed and rowdy farewell party at the flat in Lower Bond Street the evening before Burgess departed for Washington; so did Hector McNeil, now in the Cabinet as Secretary of State for Scotland, as well as his successor at the Foreign Office, Kenneth Younger. Apart from Footman, Rees noted among the guests two other senior members of the security services, as well as Anthony Blunt and

a distinguished homosexual writer of impeccable social origins. There was a member of the German Embassy, also homosexual, who before the war had actively plotted against Hitler and now lives in the German Democratic Republic. There were two women who seemed to be even more out of place than anyone else. There was Jimmy, who so long ago had listened in to telephone calls and now lived in Guy's flat and acted as his general factotum. There were two very tough working-class young men who had very obviously been picked up off the streets. The drink flowed faster, one of the young men hit another over the head with a bottle, another left with the distinguished writer.[46]

What Rees called 'the Establishment figures' had tended to drift away early, before the 'wake' livened up. Footman happened to move off at the same moment as Hector McNeil. He stopped and listened to the Minister, who was earnestly offering Burgess a few parting words of advice as they stood in a group on the landing outside the open door of the flat. 'There are three basic don'ts,

Guy, to bear particularly in mind when you're dealing with Americans. The first is Communism, the second is homosexuality, and the third is the colour bar. Do please memorise them, won't you?' Burgess smiled his seraphic smile and at once quipped back: 'I've got it, Hector, so there, don't worry. What you're trying to say in your nice, long-winded way is – "Guy, for God's sake don't make a pass at Paul Robeson."'[47]

Aileen Philby abhorred the prospect of having Burgess as a guest under her roof. She foresaw correctly that, once settled in, the lodger would show no inclination to leave. From time to time her husband tried to remonstrate with her, pointing out that he had promised his embassy colleagues to keep Guy in order and therefore could not let him stray from sight. It was simpler all round to give up the basement and try to forget Guy's existence. Mackenzie, the security officer, gave Philby 'full marks' for sticking to his word: 'I was at their place several times when Burgess came staggering in, drunk and disorderly after a gay night out. On each occasion Philby got up at once and shepherded him firmly downstairs.[48]

Inside the British Embassy nobody had much time or patience to squander on a troublesome and unwelcome misfit whom everybody sought to sidetrack. Lord Greenhill, later to become head of the Diplomatic Service, was then a rising official. A war-time colonel in the British Army, Greenhill could vaguely recall this noisy, undisciplined individual whom he had sometimes seen "slouching about the Foreign Office" in McNeil's time as Minister of State. Burgess had evidently not improved:

> He was even more unattractive than I remembered. In his tobacco-stained fingers there was a perpetual cigarette, the ash from which he contrived unerringly to drop in the centre of one's papers. Beneath his blotchy face there was more often than not an old Etonian bow tie of which he was inordinately proud and to the uniqueness of which he constantly referred.[49]

Greenhill then worked in the British Embassy's Middle East

Department. After forceful objections by a succession of senior officials to having Burgess foisted on *them*, the Counsellor of the Far Eastern Department was approached. He, too, 'refused point blank' to accept Burgess, who was then sent to assist the reluctant Greenhill. Philby, incidentally, had already put in a good word for the newcomer. Seeking out Greenhill, he said that Burgess had been a contemporary at Cambridge and 'an intellectual prodigy'. It was sad that the brilliant promise of youth had not been fulfilled. Greenhill soon began to appreciate why. Burgess took no interest whatever in Middle East affairs, preferring to let others do all the routine work while he sat back and regaled the office with irrelevant banter and lightning cartoons. Greenhill freely acknowledged that

> his conversation was always entertaining and sometimes of arresting interest. He was at his most congenial on someone else's sofa, drinking someone else's whisky, telling tales to discredit the famous. The more luxurious the surroundings and the more distinguished the company, the happier he was. I have never heard a name-dropper in the same class.[50]

As the embassy's odd-man-out, Burgess cheerfully guided Anthony Eden, the shadow Foreign Secretary, round the sights of Washington early in November 1950. There were no subsequent complaints. On the contrary, Eden courteously wrote a warm note of thanks from Ottawa to his knowledgeable guide:

> I was so well looked after that I am still in robust health, after quite a stormy flight to New York and many engagements since. Truly I enjoyed every moment of my stay in Washington, and you will know how much you helped to make this possible. Renewed greetings and gratitude.[51]

When it suited him to be on his best behaviour, Burgess could turn on the charm like a tap. Gladwyn Jebb (now Lord Gladwyn) saw this likeable side of him on the fairly frequent visits paid to New York by the obviously underworked Second Secretary from Washington, Guy Burgess. Jebb was Britain's permanent representative at the United Nations and busy enough himself. The Korean war had been raging since the end of June. Under

General MacArthur, the United Nations forces were locked in combat with the Communist invaders from the Soviet-controlled North; unknown place names like Pusan, Inchon, Wonsan and Pyongyang had forced their way into the headlines of the American press as MacArthur's mobile strategy first caught the enemy in the rear, then gradually carried the struggle into enemy territory north of the 38th Parallel. Though Burgess's superiors steered him off Far Eastern problems, he made it his business to worm out every secret nuance of the 'Korean scandal'. Nor was he particularly diplomatic in his approach. Unlike Philby, Burgess could hardly contain the vehemence of his anti-American feelings. The contempt he expressed for President Truman's sharp response to the challenge of aggression in Korea was surpassed only by the intemperate language he used to describe the strutting MacArthur. The fear that American policy in Korea was dragging the world into a Third World War seemed to possess Burgess throughout the autumn and winter of 1950.

Two other dominant topics helped to heighten the notoriety of Burgess in polite company: the inability of Truman to exorcize the witch-hunting activities of Senator Joseph McCarthy; and the technical debate behind the scenes on atomic development, which ended with a presidential decision to accelerate production of the hydrogen bomb and experimental nuclear submarines. To a sharp-witted zealot like Burgess, in whom the fixations of the little Englander jostled with the certitudes of the unreconstructed Marxist dreamer, everything that could be wrong *was* wrong with the United States. Hard as Philby strove to calm him and keep him under wraps below stairs, the venomous tone of Guy Burgess's anti-Americanism began to mar domestic harmony. Even Aileen Philby, who had ruefully and accurately predicted that they would never see the back of this intruder once he set foot in the house, picked up the habit of thoughtlessly running down Americans and American ways. Yet Philby dared not let Burgess go, rash though it was to detain him.

Despite his sorry reputation at the office, the Second Secretary still had his clandestine uses. The compulsive inquisitiveness of Burgess, whose longing to be at the centre of things alone reconciled him to exile in Washington, no doubt added trimmings to the ampler sources of secret information already at Philby's disposal for Soviet consumption. The conspirators worked fairly well in harness; and their Russian friends doubtless agreed with Philby that the risks implicit in separating outweighed the risks of staying together. This mattered more than the received opinion of Colonel Valentine Vivian. Arriving for a visit in his role as Security Chief of SIS, Vivian suggested to Philby that Burgess appeared to be getting 'a bad name'. Philby admitted that his lodger was 'a great nuisance', adding lamely that Burgess had so far been unable to find a suitable apartment. Vivian, a shallow person whom it was easy to deceive, took Philby's word for it and dropped the subject.

On 4 December 1950, Clement Attlee flew into Washington at short notice for urgent consultations with President Truman. Britain's Prime Minister had several pertinent questions to ask about the conduct of the Korean conflict. He particularly disapproved of MacArthur's adventurous strategic notions about the surest way of winning it. Were the President and the General in accord? MacArthur's recipe for outright victory after the intervention on the enemy's side of overwhelming reinforcements of Chinese 'volunteers' was to knock out Soviet air and supply bases in Manchuria, then draw on Chiang Kai-shek's Nationalist troops in Taiwan as a further step towards regaining the initiative. The British Cabinet could not condone such a policy. It relieved Attlee to receive confirmation that the US Chiefs of Staff and the State Department were as firmly opposed to this perilous strategy as the President himself. Limited action to contain Soviet aggression was Truman's policy; nothing would deflect him from it. Yet the President still hesitated to remove the General. From December 1950 to April 1951, Truman kept as tight a grip as possible on MacArthur, turning a deaf ear to the strident campaign in the American press against the administration's attempts to curb a heroic anti-Communist crusader.

This was the cacophonous background accompaniment that jarred increasingly on the frayed nerves of the three British spies still 'in place', though only just. For not until the beginning of

November 1950 did Donald Maclean return to duty in the Foreign Office, London. His spasmodic psychiatric treatment had done him no lasting good, largely because he visited his chosen specialist rarely, and then only to deceive her and so steer clear of the official panel of 'head-shrinking' experts. Had he gone into a clinic as advised, instead of fitfully subjecting himself to shallow psychoanalysis, he might have blurted out too much for his own good. Melinda heard from him at infrequent intervals. She had spent the summer months of 1950 in Spain with her mother and the children, eventually receiving a despondent letter in which her husband castigated himself for being a bad father and worthless husband. The note concluded with the flat proposal that they ought to part forthwith. Melinda replied by flying to London. The talks she had, first with the psychiatrist, then with Maclean's Foreign Office superiors, induced her to stay. If she decided to leave him, they said, there would be every chance of the patient going 'completely to pieces'.[52]

Melinda, as before, allowed herself to be duped. She did not expect the reunion to bring unwonted happiness; things had gone too far to be retrieved by a fresh start. She suspected that Donald had not been cooperating with the psychiatrist. What she did not yet realize, but might have guessed, was how compulsively he had been drinking and consorting with male lovers behind everyone's back. Burgess, of course, had lost no time before his own marching orders came through in nosing him out; other and more considerate friends like Cyril Connolly now confessed to being aghast at the rapid deterioration in Maclean's composure:

> His hands would tremble. His face was usually a livid yellow and he looked as if had had spent the night sitting up in a tunnel. . . . In conversation a kind of shutter would fall as if he had returned to some basic and incommunicable anxiety.[53]

In a frank letter to her sister Harriet in Paris, Melinda acknowledged that she had taken the only possible decision, not so much on her own account as 'on account of the children'. She added that Donald 'has already benefited tremendously. . . . He is going back to the FO on November 1st – poor lamb.'[54]

The Foreign Office, ever indulgent to its own, made allowance. Now that Maclean's wife had returned to him, the prospects of a full recovery were at any rate marginally better. Besides, he had been absent on sick leave for nearly six months and would soon be put on half-pay if his convalescence were prolonged. His superiors considered that, on compassionate grounds among others, the American Department should be offered to Maclean. The workload would certainly not be light; indeed, so crucial were many of the daily policy decisions required of the incumbent that Maclean's stamina would be quickly tested. The post carried one incidental advantage: it involved relatively few social duties, and this appears to have been the clinching factor. Dispensed from routine attendance at official parties and receptions, Maclean could more easily avoid the temptation to drink in the line of business and suffer a relapse. His superiors, like Melinda, had little reason at first to question the wisdom of the appointment. Maclean's typically scrupulous application to his work could not be faulted; so his superiors breathed a sigh of relief. Shortly before the Christmas break of 1950, he announced that the family would be moving out of London into a large, rambling house called Beaconshaw, in the village of Tatsfield, on a slope of the North Downs not too far from Winston Churchill's country home near Westerham. Melinda was again pregnant; and Donald, in his renewed mood of solicitude, seldom missed the same early evening commuter's train from Charing Cross Station.

Yet Maclean, regardless of the common concern of wife and superiors for his health and career, had simultaneously and just as effortlessly resumed his former espionage activities. The sleeper had been reanimated. What or who roused him it is impossible now to say with certainty. If a Soviet 'neighbour' took the initiative, possibly using Guy Burgess as intermediary before the latter's move to the United States, there can be no question that Maclean required little prompting once he returned to the Foreign Office. Like his two fellow conspirators at the British Embassy in Washington, he genuinely feared that American policy in the Far East was endangering world peace. The highly confidential despatches on developments that crossed his desk daily seemed to stiffen his resolve to act at once and prevent a nuclear holocaust. He convinced himself that the Truman administration had lost control. The risk, as he saw it, of Britain's being dragged passively into a needless conflict against the Soviet Union had not been diminished by the negative outcome of Attlee's urgent flight to Washington early in December. The bellicose Douglas MacArthur was still calling the shots, as though he, not Truman, had the overall right to dictate strategy on behalf of the United Nations and their outnumbered troops in Korea. If it was the last deed Maclean did, he would prefer to be caught red-handed in the act of betraying secrets rather than sit back and condone a head-on collision. So he again provided for the Moscow Centre microfilmed copies of every vital document that passed through his hands. Plainly for Donald Maclean, as for Guy Burgess and Kim Philby, anti-American fanaticism came into its own as the motivating force which gave treachery an acceptable, quasi-virtuous face.

Until the dismissal of MacArthur by Truman on 11 April 1951, Soviet intelligence was probably better served by the still unsuspected Maclean in London than by the joint efforts of his fellow conspirators in Washington. For Philby and Burgess were already under loose surveillance. If there was a touch of grotesque irony in the accidental and quite unconnected reasons which first led the Foreign Office to push Burgess off to the United States, then find a suitable post at home for Maclean, the only Englishman in a position to savour it was Kim Philby; and Philby had by then become an exceedingly worried double agent. He knew that the Anglo-American security search for the war-time embassy source was approaching its climax. A short list of prime suspects had already been drawn up – and he had seen it. The names of several distinguished British diplomats were on it, including those of Michael Wright, Paul Gore-Booth and Roger Makins, apart from Donald Maclean's. Under tightly enforced restrictions, only Ernest Bevin, Britain's ailing Foreign Secretary, and at most half a dozen senior officials in MI5 and the Foreign Office, were being notified of progress. The elimination of individual suspects would soon start. How long the procedure would take before the inquisitors reached and cornered Maclean was anyone's guess; the FBI and American signal-intelligence sources had to be informed of every new move, and this coordination militated against speed. The Russians, for their part, were quite determined to squeeze the last drop of useful information out of Maclean. They were against any premature rescue operation. So Philby took it on himself to force the pace a little; in his uneasy state of mind he blundered by over-persuading his 'friends' that the improbable Guy Burgess would be perfectly adequate as a 'cut-out man', first to warn Maclean personally, then to supervise the last-minute arrangements for his flight to safety. Philby wrote:

> The decision to initiate him was taken after I had made two lone motor trips to points outside Washington. I was told that the balance of opinion was that Guy's special knowledge of the problem might be helpful. I therefore took Guy fully into our confidence, briefing him in the greatest detail, and the subject remained under constant discussion between us.[55]

What Philby did not know was that James Angleton, playing his usual unobtrusively deep game, had accumulated enough evidence, through 'Basil', whom the two British spies still trusted completely as 'one of ours', to hand over Burgess to the FBI for questioning. But that was scarcely Angleton's style; he preferred to wait until Philby, the bigger fish of the pair, hooked himself. He did not demur when Hoover's men concealed a listening device in the basement of the Nebraska Avenue house to eavesdrop on Burgess though it may well be doubted whether the sophisticated Angleton, a poet and a grower of prize orchids as well as a keen trout-fisherman, entirely approved of such crude methods. In fact, the FBI 'bugging' disclosed far less than the CIA counter-intelligence chief had already discovered through the indispensable 'Basil'.[56]

Mackenzie, the Foreign Office man in charge of regional security, had left Philby's home on the April evening when Burgess came lurching in very late after his customary nocturnal prowling. The lodger promptly insulted the wife of an FBI visitor by gratifying the lady's request for a pencilled drawing of her countenance. There was an unpleasant scene and the party broke up in disarray, only a few guests staying on. One of them, Dr Wilfrid Mann, finally decided to go home by taxi and return next morning to collect his car. 'Hearing voices upstairs he went up to find Kim and Guy in bed together, drinking champagne. They had already been down to the Embassy but not being able to work had come back.'[57]

Truman's deliberate care in removing the self-willed and outspoken MacArthur as UN Commander in Korea only when the moment seemed ripe was justified by events. An unbridled public controversy broke out in the United States when the President announced his decision on 11 April 1951. Few American Presidents had ever been forced to take such a difficult step in the thick of a desperate military struggle. One side effect of the General's sensational dismissal was, as Denis Greenhill has recalled, the flooding of the British Embassy with

> outraged letters attributing [his] fall to British influence. The Ambassador rightly said that those that were rational and temperately worded should be answered in similar vein. Burgess was deputed to do the job. He sat for some weeks in a haze of cigarette smoke in a small office, reading and re-reading the growing pile of letters. . . . He told me he wanted to write a personal letter to Donald Maclean, and in the end showed me a messy draft. . . . My recollection is that it was unexpectedly favourable to Truman's policy.[58]

It is conceivable that the impulsive Burgess might have inserted in this personal letter to Maclean a veiled hint of his own imminent return to London. For Philby, unwilling to let the grass grow under his feet, doubtless secured Soviet approval for his next dangerous and paradoxical move. This was a formal reminder to SIS headquarters that, more than ten years earlier, the Soviet defector, Walter Krivitsky, had provided evidence pointing to the probable presence in the Foreign Office of a young Englishman of ideals, good education and family background who had been recruited to spy for the Russians in the early thirties. Philby's reminder has been denounced by a former member of the Foreign Office, Robert Cecil, as a particularly scurvy and cowardly trick: 'Philby, to save his own skin, had pointed the finger at his "old comrade",' commented Cecil sourly.[59] In fact, Philby's elbow had been jogged by the action of General Walter Bedell Smith, the highly competent new Chief of the CIA, one of whose closest friends and confidants happened to be the taciturn, ever-patient Angleton. Bedell Smith had apparently just learned that Maclean was the man who had held an unauthorized pass to the headquarters of the US Atomic Energy Commission; and in deciding to inform the British, Bedell Smith was the one person in authority who could point an accusing finger at Maclean. Philby had no choice but to follow up Bedell Smith's protest as quickly and professionally as possible. He could hardly have lain low any longer without incurring the suspicion of Mackenzie and Patterson, his embassy security colleagues. For they knew as well as he did that the CIA had passed on this unexpected clue to the true identity of the mysterious embassy source. Angleton's secretive skill in paying out just enough line to induce the trout to bite was beginning to vindicate itself. The ex-Fifth Man 'Basil' had all but fulfilled his purpose as a compliant double agent under CIA control.

Philby also knew that British cryptoanalysts at Eastcote, the temporary centre near London now occupied by the former Bletchley specialists, had deciphered further fragments of evidence which would positively identify Maclean very soon. These telltale pieces proved that 'Homer', the Russian code-name for the helpful British diplomat, had not only been in the habit of calling twice weekly at the Soviet Consulate but that in September 1944 his wife had been expecting a baby. American intelligence was duly informed through Hoover of the FBI in accordance with agreed procedure; and by early April 1950 Maclean had become the prime suspect. Dick White and two MI5 assistants were detailed to supervise arrangements for keeping him under loose surveillance without rousing undue suspicions.

When Carey-Foster, the Head of Security at the Foreign Office, quietly broke the news to Strang, the Permanent Under-Secretary, that Donald Maclean was in all probability the guilty man, Strang's face turned pale. The two men were walking across St James's Park at lunchtime, and after a long pause the Permanent Under-Secretary said: 'I just can't believe it.' However, Strang promptly suspended disbelief. Maclean, he agreed, must be interrogated.[60]

Meanwhile, Philby had other official troubles on his mind. He had sat listening, for weeks past, to anguished post mortems, conducted by CIA and British colleagues, on the disastrous outcome of a secret Anglo-American military operation against Albania, perhaps the least stable and most vulnerable and accessible Soviet satellite in 1950–1. The brooding Angleton had contributed little to these exchanges. He was aware that somehow Moscow had been forearmed in good time. If he felt frustrated, he did not show it. There was no clear-cut evidence to test, still less prove, his belief that every detail of the joint operation had been given away, possibly by one of the planners, maybe in London, but much more probably in Washington. He was fairly sure that Philby had leaked it; but he said nothing. Given time, he would bait a trap for the perpetrator when the next joint operation was being prepared. For the moment he refrained from any rash or premature move, on the excellent counter-intelligence principle that inspired hunches never warrant over-hasty responses. Philby was rapidly becoming a special problem for the British. They still appeared to trust him far more than Angleton ever would. In the United States, spy fever and Red-baiting, stimulated by the smear campaign of Senator Joseph McCarthy, served as a corrective against moves that might misfire. Temperamentally, Angleton was not in the least addicted to rushing in and possibly compromising his own hidden sources. If the White House apparently had to bend over backwards, now and then, in its unwillingness to lend credibility to the most flagrant manifestations of McCarthyism, James Jesus Angleton had reasons of his own for letting Philby go on thinking that he was in the clear and above suspicion.

Besides, there had been too much Anglo-American wrangling over which political puppets should be installed in Tirana after the expected overthrow of the Albanian Communist régime. It was quite conceivable that careless talk among Albanian émigrés in the United States had contributed something to the fiasco which had cost many scores of lives among the would-be liberators who went ashore as an advance party. Philby had shared in the planning and remote control of the whole affair with three amusing men: Lord Jellicoe of the Foreign Office, Robert Joyce of the State Department, and Frank Lindsay of the CIA. 'Even in our serious moments,' Philby afterwards asserted, 'we Anglo-Saxons never forgot that our agents were just down from the trees.'[61] The glib moral he drew in retrospect that 'it is better to cut one's losses than to give hostages to fortune' was regretfully drawn in Washington and London, when the British dropped three groups of agents far behind the Iron Curtain later in 1951. The Americans were forestalled by the British on this second occasion. There had again been a good deal of squabbling over the rival merits of two Ukrainian leaders-in-exile, with London stubbornly backing its fancied man, Bandera, and Washington seeking vainly to impose its own particular favourite. However, one can only shudder now at Philby's macabre epitaph for the agents who parachuted down in the futile hope of linking up with Ukrainian underground resistance partisans of dubious validity: 'I do not know what happened to the parties concerned. But I can make an informed guess.'[62]

Christopher Felix of the CIA took equal exception to another tendentious remark of Philby's: 'Some eight years later, I read of the mysterious murder of Bandera in Munich, in the American zone of Germany. It may be that, despite the brave stand of the British, CIA had the last word.' To this Felix retorted drily: 'Is Philby hoping that we have all forgotten that in 1961 Bogdan Nikolaiavevich Stashinsky, one of Philby's Russian colleagues, defected to West Germany and confessed to having murdered Bandera on orders from his superiors?'[63]

There was something similarly unsubtle about Soviet acceptance of Philby's foolhardy proposal to entrust Burgess with the critical early stages of Donald Maclean's imminent rescue. Perhaps, almost at the end of his tether, the most influential spy of the harassed three simply panicked; perhaps, too, he was partly swept off his feet by the precipitate enthusiasm of the least responsible member of the trio. Certainly the manner in which Guy Burgess arranged his own departure from Washington in disgrace proved to be as spectacular and wilfully incongruous as anything the Marx Brothers could have devised. His passion for fast driving was by now a by-word among embassy colleagues who thought of it as one of his less harmful eccentricities. The huge twelve-cylinder Lincoln which he had bought second hand shortly after his arrival seemed to gratify that passion. 'He drove like Mr Toad,' Greenhill observed. 'In the end, it contributed to his undoing.'[64] That undoing was, of course, artfully pre-planned by the victim. On his way to deliver a lecture at an American military establishment in the South, Burgess stepped so hard on the throttle, also persuading a casual hitch-hiker whom he picked up to take his turn in the driving seat and travel even faster, that in a single day he received three tickets from the police for exceeding the speed limit. Pleading diplomatic immunity, Burgess insisted that his case should be forwarded to the Governor of Virginia. In due course, the irate Governor addressed an outspoken complaint through the State Department to Sir Oliver Franks, the British Ambassador. By another of those odd twists of coincidence which crop up again and again in this weird story, Franks had been awaiting some such opportunity to send for Burgess and pack him off home. This was it.

Greenhill noted:

> He came straight to my room after hearing his sentence from the Ambassador. He was apparently boiling with rage. He had been told that he 'lacked judgement'. Who did the Ambassador think he was to speak to him in those terms? . . . Then there was the question of the Lincoln. He would be lost without it. Would I help him on this, or at least keep an eye on the car when he had gone?[65]

Burgess left his Lincoln convertible behind in the British Embassy car park. It offered Philby an excuse for sending a wire nearly four weeks later to remind his self-centred friend of his forgotten part in the 'springing' of Maclean. Among his personal belongings Burgess carefully stowed away a lengthy, closely reasoned but untidily written critique of the American political situation. He had intended to submit this formally, through the Ambassador,

Franks, and the permanent Head of the Foreign Office, to Ernest Bevin's successor or at least to the junior Minister, Kenneth Younger; but Sir Oliver had refused to accept it. Perhaps the despatch might come in handy as ammunition in his own last-ditch defence, or so Burgess fondly believed. For he still nursed the hope of riding out the latest storm and, possibly with some discreet help from influential supporters, getting off with nothing worse than another reprimand. Before boarding the *Queen Mary*, he killed time gaily in New York. The detailed reconstruction of his career, compiled in due course by the FBI, indicated that he regaled one dinner party of friends there with recorded reminiscences, including a passable imitation of Winston Churchill's encouraging words to him at Chartwell after the Munich crisis. On the voyage to Southampton, a chance encounter with a young American, did much to rekindle his romantic ardour. As will be shown, this typically brief but strong attachment so distracted Burgess that he virtually lost all sense of urgency. But for some forceful eleventh-hour prompting, by Philby among others, he might well have failed his Soviet masters and abandoned Donald Maclean to his just deserts.

Goronwy Rees, who had exchanged a few letters with Burgess during the abortive American interlude, was not altogether surprised to receive a final note outlining the unfortunate scrape which had caused the delinquent's recall in disgrace. Stressing that he would be arriving at Southampton on Saturday 7 May, Burgess expressed the hope that Rees would not mind his coming to stay that first short weekend at his friend's home in Sonning, Berkshire. He duly arrived on the Sunday, with his luggage still unpacked, having spent the previous night in London. Rees thought Burgess looked 'much cleaner' and in far better shape physically and mentally than might have been expected:

> he gave us long, scurrilous and extremely amusing accounts of life in Washington and especially in the Embassy, and we were all delighted to find him in such good order and humour. But it was also evident that he was labouring under a tremendous sense of excitement, as if he were under intense internal pressures.

Crass American policy, British subservience to it, the menace of McCarthyism, the imminence of war, these obsessive themes seemed to stir the visitor to a frenzy. Eventually he produced the letter which Anthony Eden had written him and proudly showed it round; then he asked Rees to read his rejected despatch. Its manic lack of objectivity was as depressing as its shrill anti-American tone: 'I had the slightly queasy feeling,' said Rees, 'that I was talking to a lunatic.' Rees warned his guest that it would be a waste of time presenting the document in its existing form to Kenneth Younger or anyone else at the Foreign Office. Somewhat deflated, Burgess talked freely about his uncertain prospects. Of course, he said, he would prefer to resign rather than wait to be pushed. He did not greatly mind. He had enjoyed at least one lucky break in Washington. His old Etonian acquaintance, Michael Berry, had looked him up and hinted that a job might be found for him on the diplomatic desk of the *Daily Telegraph*. The thought gave him 'some twinges of conscience because, as he said, the paper's Conservative views were not exactly his own'.

One subject was sedulously avoided by Rees: his bizarre yet disquieting confrontation with Donald Maclean one winter's night at the Gargoyle Club not long after Burgess had left for Washington. A very drunken Maclean had been seated at the far end of this haunt of intellectuals when Rees arrived shortly before midnight, accompanied by his wife and two friends. 'I would not even have recognized him,' Rees declared, 'if I had not been told who he was. To my astonishment he lurched over to the table and then said in an extremely aggressive and menacing tone: "I know all about you. You used to be one of us, but you ratted."' For a moment Rees thought that the intruder was about to assault him. Suddenly, however, Maclean's legs seemed to buckle. He sank to his knees and shouted abuse at Rees across the table until, staggering to his feet, he lurched off. The horrid suspicion suddenly dawned on Rees that Maclean had given himself away in his inebriated state 'as a collaborator of Guy's in his espionage activities'. Only Burgess could have told Maclean of Rees's refusal to join the group of undercover agents to which 'Maurice', among others, still belonged; so Guy Burgess must have been speaking the truth, not inventing another fantastic Walter Mitty role, when he had revealed himself in the mid thirties as a Comintern representative. The consequences and implications were so appalling that Rees had tried hard ever since to erase Maclean's outburst from his memory.[66]

Maclean had meanwhile been emulating Burgess as an articulate anti-American fanatic out of office hours. One night a fellow diplomat of roughly the same seniority returned home after dining out with Maclean and said to his wife: 'Donald behaved so disgracefully and said such rum things at the club that I'll have to inform the FO in the morning.' Felicity Rumbold, who had always had a soft spot for Maclean, tried to talk her husband out of doing anything 'so beastly' as to jeopardize the career of an old friend. 'Don't forget that Donald has been unwell. And he was the best man at our wedding', she scolded. However, Anthony Rumbold argued that any diplomat as 'mad on Stalin' as Donald seemed to have become was simply asking to be denounced.[67] Certain phrases and fixed ideas kept bobbing up monotonously like corks in Maclean's mannered conversation. Because, when sober, he had a charming, mocking way of analysing problems, people who had known him for years were seldom shocked or startled when he would begin a sentence: 'Of course, viewed from my side of the barricades. . . .' Cyril Connolly confessed to being impressed at this time by the force of his criticisms. 'All colonial possessions are morally untenable,' Connolly once heard him intoning. 'Surely,' he said to Maclean, 'you aren't suggesting that Britain should get rid of Malaya and Hong Kong? These are vital dollar earners.' 'That's precisely why we should give them up,' said the intransigent Maclean.[68]

Rumbold's fitful sense of outrage was matched by the disbelief of another person, a writer and a close mutual friend of Connolly and Maclean who dropped in to discuss with Connolly one morning a heated argument he had been having with the head of the American Department towards the end of a long drinking session the previous evening. Maclean had turned on him finally and said defiantly: 'What would you do if I told you I was a Communist agent?'

'I don't kno .'

'Well,' Maclean persisted, 'wouldn't you report me?'

'I don't know. Who to?'

'Well, I am. Go on, report me.'

Connolly advised his friend to forget the incident which, in retrospect, certainly seemed not merely ridiculous but incredible.[69] It was as if Maclean, under the stimulus of whisky, his regular medicine against despair, found courage enough to throw all caution to the winds and flaunt his true credentials, invariably losing his temper when his companions refused even to look at them. For Maclean had learnt to live with the daunting knowledge that the security authorities were closing in to trap him. Had they not stopped the flow of classified documents to his desk? He did not mind dropping defiant hints in passing that he was 'working for Uncle Joe'. What he hotly resented was the kid-glove dissembling which his discreet Foreign Office superiors deemed suitable for someone already under suspicion. While denying him access to top-secret files, they lacked the spirit to offer any reason. In fact, Roger Makins (now Lord Sherfield), his immediate superior and one of the handful of senior officials 'in the know', would have dearly liked to confront Maclean and force the truth out of him. Makins suggested this one day to the Foreign Office's head of Security. 'Why can't we station an MI5 man at the door, then barge in and make him talk?' he said.

Carey-Foster pointed out that Sir William Strang had expressly forbidden any premature intervention. Formalities apart, every detail of this joint Anglo-American exercise had to be concerted with the FBI in Washington, down to the actual date of Maclean's interrogation. And for various puzzling reasons, the FBI appeared to be in no desperate hurry.[70]

Melinda could never reach her husband in his morose moods of frustration. Nor did he wish or seek to confide in her. Only at weekends would he occasionally shake himself out of the aura of self-pity which enveloped him like a thick, dank fog. His sister-in-law, Harriet, whose wedding in Paris to an American, Jay Sheers, he had attended with Melinda in January 1951, later heard him holding forth at length against the imbecilic policies of the

West, contrasting these unfavourably with the enlightened plans for world order of Soviet Communism. Harriet and Jay stayed at the Maclean's Tatsfield home for several days at the beginning of May, and Donald Maclean's self-mockery emphasized how weary he had become of travelling up to the Foreign Office each day in the regulation dark hat and suit, carrying his regulation briefcase and rolled umbrella. It made him feel like an over-dressed sheep. He longed with all his soul, he said, to 'cut adrift'.

Philby subsequently wrote the following remark about Maclean, and it is impossible to disagree with it:

> After his departure it was said blandly that he was 'only' Head of the American Department of the Foreign Office, and thus had little access to high-grade information. But it is nonsense to suppose that a resolute and experienced operative occupying a senior post in the Foreign Office can have access only to papers that are placed on his desk in the ordinary course of duty.[71]

Hemmed in as tightly as he was, Maclean undoubtedly made it his business to lay hands on all the documents available for his clandestine purposes. Because of his increasing tendency to go out on the spree and miss his last train, Maclean's secret work for Moscow piled up and occasionally had to be completed like homework at weekends. When guests came to Beaconshaw, he would drive into Westerham and rent the dark room above White's, the village chemist, by the hour. The proprietor at first thought this a little unusual, but complied. The customer explained that the films he wanted to develop were 'very sensitive' and that he would make it worth Ernest White's while. Only once did Maclean fail to clear up thoroughly afterwards. It was then that the chemist noticed the screwed-up portion of an over-exposed film through which the Foreign Office seal and heading were faintly visible. He wondered at the time whether he ought not to report the matter to the police, but thought better of it. White finally came forward with the information only after reading the sensational press story that two British diplomats had gone missing.

Melinda Maclean's reproaches failed to dissuade her husband

from indulging in bad old habits. She rightly feared that he might lose his liberty as well as his job. He ran too many risks. He did not tell her about his problems at the office, nor did she know that Guy Burgess had reappeared from Washington under a cloud. The two men met several times, at least twice in Maclean's room at the Foreign Office, between 10 May and 20 May 1951. By then Dick White and his two assistants were simply awaiting confirmation of the day on which to pounce. The few Foreign Office seniors who shared the secret longed for the ordeal of waiting to end. All the facts fitted. Those intercepts from the Soviet Consulate in New York demonstrated that the source, 'Homer', had visited his Russian contact there twice a week; and laborious Anglo-American checking had since confirmed that Maclean alone, a creature of habit, had travelled regularly up and down between New York and Washington both before and after his wife's confinements at her mother's home. More recently there was Philby's reminder of the Krivitsky file and that blunt protest from the CIA about Maclean's apparent dabbling in atomic secrets. If the natural reaction of Strang and his senior colleagues to this *prima facie* evidence of treachery within had been one of horrified scepticism, they were now glumly resigned to it.

Burgess, never an admirer of Maclean's, must have been shaken by the latter's air of cynical indifference on being told point blank that the game was up. The diplomat did not appear to be in the least concerned about what might happen to him. In view of the withholding of high-grade documents from him at work, and the unceasing vigilance of the Special Branch plain clothes officers who shadowed him as far as the ticket barrier at Charing Cross Station each evening, there was little point in talking vainly of trying to dodge the inevitable. Burgess earnestly begged to differ. He had business of his own to transact; but this would not fill all his time. He would himself be resigning from the Foreign Service as soon as he had completed alternative arrangements to get a steady, well-paid job in Fleet Street. In the meantime they must maintain discreet contact with one another. Until fuller details of the escape plan reached them, it would be just as well to behave quite naturally, as if neither of them had a care in the world.

Coming from Burgess, of all people, such advice had an unwelcome counterfeit ring.

The plain clothes sleuths from the Special Branch were led a merry dance to restaurants, nightclubs and the homes of respectable citizens until the second-last week of May 1951. It was Maclean, not Burgess, whom they had orders to trail. On at least four or five occasions, the pair set out to lunch or dine together with plain clothes policemen in discreet attendance. The charming insouciance of the diplomat would melt away like snow in the Sahara after his second drink. One evening, after feinting menacingly with clenched fists, he felled an argumentative friend who had the temerity to stand up for Whittaker Chambers in a rambling discussion about the Alger Hiss case. 'Which do you suppose is my hero, Hess or Hiss?' Maclean shouted angrily as onlookers helped the bleeding victim to his feet.[72]

At an earlier date, Lord Pakenham (now the Earl of Longford), at that time First Lord of the Admiralty in Attlee's reshuffled and weakened Cabinet, took mild exception to Maclean's hectoring tone both before and during dinner in the flat of a former Oxford pupil of his, the young diplomat Nicholas (now Sir Nicholas) Henderson.

> Maclean asked me as a prominent Roman Catholic for a short list of names of suitable chaplains, preferably intellectuals and good mixers, for the British community in Washington. He rounded on me rather insultingly when I hesitated and failed to produce one. Henderson, who was then working under him, seemed very embarrassed. He apologized. Next morning my host came and apologized again. Maclean, he told me, had gone out to the Gargoyle after dinner and had to be carried home to a spare bed.[73]

Ministers of the Crown were fair game to a diplomat who had long given up troubling about such bourgeois trifles as good manners.

'How else, at this moment of history, can anyone behave except badly?' was the excuse Guy Burgess offered to critical friends for his own more outrageous misdemeanours. On the other hand, Burgess could not bear the thought of living without the esteem of that dwindling group of understanding friends who still liked and cared for him. If Sir Oliver Franks's icy disapproval had merely enraged him, the actions of ex-friends like Sir Roy Harrod in reporting him to Franks at an earlier date had hurt him deeply. He was all the more grateful, therefore, to others like Lord Hartwell, Fred Warner, Cyril Connolly, Goronwy Rees and Anthony Blunt for their tolerance. Hartwell had asked to be shown a sample of his written work, partly to banish fears that Burgess might have forgotten how to string words together on paper. So Burgess entertained him at the Reform Club and let him have that lengthy despatch, marked 'Top Secret' and originally intended for the eyes of the Foreign Secretary until spurned by the unfeeling Franks. Hartwell read the document afterwards. Its sloppy construction convinced him that Guy would not be quite suitable for the diplomatic desk of the *Daily Telegraph*. Hartwell wondered how he could best break the bad news without hurting Guy's pride too much. So he arranged a small dinner party for 29 May, a Tuesday, at his town house in Westminster. He would inform him of his decision that evening. Apart from Burgess, the only other person invited was Blunt.[74]

Indeed, Burgess became so preoccupied with his private concerns that he gravely neglected his duty as an agent to smooth the way for Donald Maclean's escape. Had he been less allergic to the haughty, fatalistic manner of Maclean, less concerned with pleasure-seeking, and less anxious to redeem himself in the eyes of understanding friends, the normally sharp-witted Burgess would not have botched the job. He would have concentrated harder on finding out, for instance, that the Foreign Secretary, Herbert Morrison, had quashed the delaying tactics of his senior officials and had upheld the security authorities' request to begin their interrogation of Donald Maclean on Monday 28 May. Morrison's decision was a closely guarded secret. The suspect himself had no wind of it, nor had the distracted Guy Burgess. It was probably on Wednesday 23 May, or at the latest on Thursday 24 May, that Philby's agonized eleventh-hour wire reached Burgess. Alarmed by the misgivings of his Soviet control and by the sudden expectancy of his security colleagues, Philby had used the abandoned Lincoln convertible in the embassy car park as a pretext for reproaching his absent-minded friend direct and 'in pressing terms, telling him that if he did not act at once it would be too late – because I would send his car to the scrap heap. There was nothing more I could do.'[75]

To be perfectly fair to Burgess, he had not been utterly idle. Since his Russian friends would not put the escape plan into effect until he gave the word, and since the Foreign Office was firmly closed to him as a channel of inside information, he had to rely on the good will of friendly associates in, or with access to, the British security services. This was a desperate gamble, yet it did not fail. He was wily enough not to approach these associates personally. Instead, he induced the devoted 'Maurice', whose standing with most of his war-time colleagues remained high and above reproach, to discover whatever he could about the exact timing of the expected proceedings against the cornered Maclean. Having taken these elementary precautions, Burgess switched blithely to his own personal affairs as if nothing else mattered. One of his last journeys out of London took him back to Eton for tea with the headmaster, his former history teacher, Sir Robert Birley;

> He came to see me the very day before he went off to Moscow. He rang me up to say he had something important that he wished to discuss with me. I thought he looked well. He certainly sounded cheerful. He came to the point quickly. The Salisbury family, he said, had requested him to complete the biography of one of his great heroes, the Third Marquess of Salisbury, a work which Lady Gwendolen Cecil, his daughter, had left unfinished. Remembering Guy's innate abilities as a boy at school, I was suitably impressed. I asked why he wanted my advice. 'Ah,' he replied. 'Well, you see, whereas Salisbury was a convinced and practising Christian, I happen to be a total agnostic, and I'm afraid that might affect my judgement of him.' I thought his scruples were a bit far-fetched, so I told him my only advice was that he should talk about his difficulty to the present Lord Salisbury. That was more or less all Guy had to say. After exchanging a few pleasantries, he said goodbye and left.[76]

The next day, Friday 25 May, happened to be Maclean's thirty-eighth birthday. A number of his friends, including Cyril

Connolly, met him in a Soho street at lunch time. He appeared 'rather creased and yellow'; but his manner struck the observant Connolly as well as the hosts, old friends who were taking Maclean out for oysters and champagne by way of 'a birthday treat', as quite composed, genial, sober and thoughtful. The guest mentioned that, because of Melinda's advanced pregnancy, he hoped to go on compassionate leave the following week. He appeared to be quite unworried. With characteristic thoroughness, Maclean worked as diligently as ever for most of that day at the Foreign Office, another pointer to the fact that he had not yet heard from the heedlessly unconcerned Burgess that this would be his last day there or anywhere else in Britain. Robert Cecil, then in charge of the Latin American Section under Maclean's broad supervision, discovered afterwards

in Maclean's sloping script, a concise and accurate record of a visit paid to him on May 25th by the Argentine Minister-Counsellor, who raised an intricate point connected with current trade negotiations.

Cecil also unearthed in his late Chief's private filing cabinet

a numbered copy of the Cabinet Paper containing Prime Minister Attlee's account of his hasty visit to President Truman in December 1950, the aim of which was to ensure that General MacArthur should not be permitted to use the atom bomb in the Korean war.[77]

Burgess managed to reach Maclean by telephone late that afternoon before the diplomat left the Foreign Office to catch an early train home, dogged as usual by a detective. The message from Burgess was brief and non-committal, for obvious reasons; and while reflecting that his 'rescuer' must have better things to do than propose himself for dinner at Tatsfield on a Friday evening, Maclean realized with a start on the train journey that he had almost certainly been given the cue for the long-delayed escape operation. Burgess had come to his senses late that morning. He had fully intended to spend the weekend in Paris with the American friend he had recently acquired on the *Queen Mary* and had even toyed with the idea of going on from there to Italy for a spell in the sun. Then the telephone rang. The call cut short all such lotus-eating schemes. 'Maurice's' information was startling:

Maclean's interrogation would begin on Monday 28 May, so there was no more time to lose. Burgess left his flat, walked to the Green Park Hotel to explain to his American friend that the Paris jaunt might have to be postponed, made the necessary arrangements to hire a self-drive car, visited the Reform Club to ring up various friends, then went shopping, collected the hired car, and returned home to pack and ring up Maclean. He had the details of the escape plan. At that point Burgess had no serious intention of accompanying the cornered diplomat further than the quayside at Southampton to see him safely aboard the midnight cross-Channel steamer to Saint-Malo in France.

Driving through the southern outskirts of London in the rush hour, Burgess reached Maclean's home at Tatsfield less than half an hour after his host. Maclean introduced him to Melinda, who later claimed that she had never set eyes on him before, as 'Roger Stiles, a colleague from the Foreign Office'. While she was out of the room, Burgess quietly informed Maclean that they must leave together immediately after dinner. There was some banter and irrelevant 'shop' talked at table; but Maclean rose and excused himself as soon as the birthday meal was finished. 'Mr Stiles and I have to keep a pressing engagement, but I don't expect to be back very late. I'll take an overnight bag just in case.'[78]

Somewhere in the maze of narrow cross-country lanes leading to the main Southampton road, Guy Burgess, with two boat tickets in his pocket, originally intended for his friend and himself must have jumped to the understandable conclusion that Maclean could no longer be entirely trusted to continue his journey through France unaccompanied. Without sparing a thought for anything beyond the urgent task in hand, oblivious of Philby's parting message when they had said goodbye in Washington just over a month earlier: 'Don't you go, too, Guy!', he decided on the spur of the moment to escort the diplomat as far as French soil at any rate. Then their Russian friends could take over, and Burgess would resume his day-dreaming about the sweet life ahead and the exciting challenges of Fleet Street journalism. He was looking forward to meeting Michael and Pamela Hartwell over dinner the following Tuesday and had already asked Anthony Blunt to pick him up first inside the Reform Club at six o'clock that evening.

Unfortunately for his plans, the Russians had different and more realistic ideas about this unlooked-for emergency. Because Burgess, in a typically casual spasm of knight-errantry, had insisted on going a step too far, they regretfully decided that the over-zealous bungler had better accompany Donald Maclean all the way to Moscow too. There could be no going back, once he had abandoned his hired car, unlocked, on the quayside and dashed up the gangplank, escorting the runaway diplomat with minutes to spare before the ropes were cast off and the ship moved slowly away from the shore.

Only after the weekend, a breathing space immemorially sacred to the leisurely ways of British officialdom, would the alarm bells start belatedly ringing. If the Russians had been imprudent or callous enough to heed the protests of Burgess and let him find his own way back to British soil, he would have had far too much difficult explaining to do. So, quite by mischance, two agents instead of one had to be spirited away from the West by their Soviet friends, leaving Philby to face the music, alone and unprepared for what lay ahead. Angleton, too, would have cause to feel cheated and partly foiled by the folly of Burgess. Now that Philby's cover had been effectively 'blown', the British would have to take over themselves and deal with him in their own lackadaisical and half-incredulous way: the former Fifth Man could be stood down at last to enjoy the benefits of American citizenship with his wife and children. A useful, specialized job awaited 'Basil' in Washington. He had earned his reward; his role as Angleton's double agent had more than vindicated itself. Now, with the uncovering of Philby, 'Basil' had become expendable as a double agent.

11. EXIT THE THIRD MAN

At first, of course, nobody in Whitehall knew what to think. The consternation among senior ministerial advisers was widespread. It affected the Foreign Office in particular; but the Security Directorate itself, the new name for the old, refurbished MI5, did not escape the creeping contagion. Why should Burgess have vanished with Maclean? What had *he* to hide? Where could they both have gone? Such questions were anything but rhetorical. An embarrassed, suitably indignant British Cabinet demanded positive answers; but the bewildered Sir Percy Sillitoe, that 'honest copper' whose appointment as Security Chief in 1946 had been vigorously backed by the then Lord President of the Council, Herbert Morrison, was as yet in no position to oblige. Until some clearer indications emerged of the runaways' motives, their individual degree of culpability, their whereabouts and their itinerary, Parliament and public had better be kept in the dark: on that point at least there was unanimity. Premature statements would merely compound the confusion and excite the sensational press. And if, horror of horrors, Fleet Street managed to sniff out even part of this incredible story, there would be red faces and worse at Westminster and in Whitehall.

As for the political consequences, nationally and internationally, these did not bear thinking about. Sillitoe could not account for the comparative ease with which the missing diplomats had disappeared into thin air. Yet if neither he nor his aides had a coherent explanation, the FBI in Washington would quickly come up with the most obvious and disparaging one. The consequences of that peculiar distemper which had warped the minds of uncounted middle-class undergraduates in Britain during the

1930s were about to be calculated and paid for. The bill could not be settled until that mortifying legacy had been accepted, however reluctantly, by the British people and the ruling Establishment as a whole. Today, more than a quarter of a century later, the lesson has been more or less digested – and it has proved no end of a lesson. . . .

There had been a minor 'false alarm' on Saturday 27 May, when Maclean failed to appear for work. A detective had reported the fact to MI5; George Carey-Foster was alerted; and he immediately approached Roger Makins at home. An apologetic Makins explained that Maclean had, in fact, asked for that morning off. As there had seemed no good reason to refuse, the request had been granted. Makins was sorry to have caused unnecessary commotion at a weekend: he had meant to notify security at the time, but the matter had slipped his mind. Everyone concerned breathed a deep sigh of relief and settled down to enjoy an otherwise uneventful weekend.[1]

Melinda Maclean waited until the early afternoon of Monday 28 May 1951 before raising the alarm. She sounded tearful and distressed when she rang the Foreign Office. Had her husband, by chance, turned up for work? She had not seen him since the previous Friday night when he had rushed off with a colleague on 'urgent business'. She had no idea where they had both gone. George Carey-Foster, as head of Foreign Office security, listened in amazement. His department was undermanned and unloved. It had been grafted painfully on to the parent body after the unmasking of 'Cicero', a smooth double agent in German pay who had also served as valet to the British Ambassador in war-time Turkey. Carey-Foster did his best to calm Melinda down. At that moment her husband should have been facing his security inquisitors, in accordance with agreed Anglo-American arrangements: Herbert Morrison had signed the necessary order on Friday 25 May, the very day on which the suspect had apparently taken to his heels with Burgess. Carey-Foster advised Mrs Maclean not to worry, not to talk to outsiders, and not to stray too far from the telephone. He promised to ring her back.[2]

Guy Liddell, Sillitoe's number two, did not seem unduly put

out by the ominous news. He hid his feelings well. Of Maclean's guilt he had little serious doubt. During the past weeks first-hand reports of the diplomat's dissipated behaviour and extremist political remarks had strengthened Liddell's belief in a *prima facie* case of treachery. Maclean had been constantly shadowed in the company of Guy Burgess, especially towards the end; but Burgess, whom Liddell knew of old and rather liked, had not been considered worth shadowing. Nothing definitely incriminating was recorded against him. Sillitoe, a pedant for strict procedure, had insisted that not a finger should be laid on Maclean until the imminent Foreign Office enquiry brought in the expected judgement.

On his way through London to an official conference in Paris, Sir Robert Mackenzie, the regional security officer stationed in the Washington Embassy, had looked in briefly to see Liddell and others just two days before Maclean's unscheduled disappearance with Burgess. To Dick White, Liddell's assistant in charge of the case, Mackenzie had expressed the unwelcome opinion that the procedural guidelines were far too inflexible and cumbersome: 'From all I hear, Maclean is on the point of cracking up. If he's in anything like the poor shape of Burgess, you ought to pull him in at once and get the truth out of him without all this nonsensical kid-glove treatment.' White had replied shortly that they had their orders and must stick to them. So Mackenzie left for Paris, arriving there possibly twenty-four hours after the absconding diplomats. It was on Monday 28 May, not long after Melinda Maclean's telephone call to Carey-Foster, that Mackenzie hastily abandoned other business to take an urgent personal call from Carey-Foster in London. Two birds had flown the coop, not one, he was told. Special Branch officers of Scotland Yard had found on the quayside at Southampton the white car which Burgess had apparently hired on the Friday. Certain articles of clothing belonging to the missing men had been picked up from their cabin in the overnight cross-Channel steamer. Police were on the lookout at airfields and ports in Britain, but everything pointed to the likelihood that Burgess and Maclean might still be on French soil. Would Mackenzie approach the Sûreté Nationale and alert them at once?

Mackenzie lost no time. The instant incredulity of M. Vidal, a police chief whom Mackenzie had dealt with often in the past, came crackling infectiously down the line. '*Mon Dieu*,' said M. Vidal. 'It's grotesque. Two men from the Quai d'Orsay I'd have understood. But two *British* diplomats – *par bleu*. . . .'[3]

It soon became clear that, with two clear days in hand, Burgess and Maclean had broken clean away. Mackenzie, working in liaison with Vidal, was gradually able to reconstruct, stage by stage, the route taken by the defecting pair. A taxi-driver had driven them from Saint-Malo, a ticket inspector at Rennes had seen them through the barrier to an express bound for the French capital. But there the trail had gone cold. One piece of evidence came eventually 'from a clerk at the big post office near the Bourse'; a nondescript woman, certainly not French and possibly from the Soviet or a satellite embassy, had handed in two messages, one addressed to Melinda, the other to Lady Maclean.

'Had to leave unexpectedly,' the first message read. 'Terribly sorry. Am quite well now. Don't worry darling. I love you. Please don't stop loving me.'

The second message was couched in similar affectionate terms. Both had been sent at 10 p.m. on 6 June. By then, as Robert Mackenzie subsequently ascertained, the diplomats had reached Prague, via Zurich, en route to the Soviet Union. By then, too, an alert British correspondent in Paris had fastened on a conversational slip by a talkative contact at the Sûreté, eliciting the bare facts that two unidentified members of the Foreign Office were being sought for questioning by French and British police. On the morning of Thursday 7 June, the *Daily Express*, closely followed by the *Daily Herald*, carried similar versions of the mysterious search under bold banner-headlines.

Confusion and tight-lipped perplexity had meanwhile been mounting behind every executive office door in Whitehall. Since Melinda Maclean's original telephone call to Carey-Foster less than two weeks earlier, a touch of demoralization had also begun to set in. There was not a little recrimination. Senior officials in the departments directly involved, the Foreign Office and the Security Directorate, had been rudely shaken out of their normal complacency. Perhaps the worst effect of the resulting panic was suspicion, slowly settling like a plague spot on insiders known or believed to have been on friendly terms with the two missing diplomats, whether professionally or personally. And perhaps the earliest victim of this unhealthy, almost uncontrollable undertow of mistrust was Philip Jordan, the Prime Minister's press officer at 10 Downing Street. As one of Maclean's few reasonably intimate friends in Washington, Jordan suddenly came under a cloud that was partly of his own making, once the flight of the two diplomats had been confirmed by a discomfited Security Directorate. The strain of hushing up the bad news, of almost willing it to go away, proved insupportable. On 6 June, Kitty, the wife of Malcolm Muggeridge, was dining with Philip and Ruth Jordan at their home near Regent's Park. Malcolm happened to be out of London that day. Kitty Muggeridge said:

> During the meal Philip had to leave the table to take a telephone call. When he came back, his face was ashen. He muttered something inaudible to Ruth, then again excused himself, adding that there were urgent things he must attend to. I felt that some sudden calamity must have happened. Next day I knew what it was – the escape of Maclean and Burgess. Philip looked so tragically ill that it seemed the bottom had dropped right out of his world. I decided to go home there and then. The following morning Ruth, who lived near us, told me that Philip had suddenly cried out in the night. When she reached his bedside, he was dead.[4]

There was no question of suicide or foul play. The death certificate indicated that this was just another straightforward case of heart failure, possibly brought on by overwork and stress. However, it presently became plain to Malcolm Muggeridge that a deeper and less tangible worry must have been preying on Philip Jordan's mind. With a mutual friend and distinguished fellow journalist, Alan Moorehead, Muggeridge decided to approach the Prime Minister, inviting him in a personal letter to a memorial service for the late press officer and delicately hinting that Attlee might care to consider offering a discretionary pension to Philip's widow, who had not been left too well provided for. To both suggestions the Prime Minister responded with a peremptory

'No'. From now on, it seemed, the new factor of 'guilt by association' was being taken into account by an Establishment deeply worried and at bay.[5]

Guy Liddell, who would in time suffer the consequences of his own amiable regard for Guy Burgess, had received a wildly intuitive warning of the latter's possible defection late on Sunday 27 May. A colleague in MI6, David Footman, had rung Liddell at home to inform him of a peculiar call he had just taken from a mutual acquaintance of theirs and Guy Burgess's – the writer Goronwy Rees. It appeared that Rees had been at All Souls', Oxford, during part of that weekend. On returning to Sonning, Rees heard from his wife that Burgess had telephoned her from the Reform Club on the very day of his disappearance. He had talked for several minutes in a rambling, incoherent manner, which led her to suppose that Guy must be drunk; yet one or two of his repetitious thoughts forced her to revise that judgement. Burgess had stated, for instance, that

> he was about to do something which would surprise and shock many people but he was sure it was the right thing to do. . . . Guy had gone on to say that he would not see me [Goronwy] for some time and that was really for the best because we no longer saw eye to eye politically. But I would understand what he was going to do, and indeed was the the only one of his friends who would. . . .[6]

Brooding over these remarks with his wife, Rees suddenly jumped to an irrational conclusion which he passed on immediately to the disbelieving David Footman: 'I'm certain Guy's heading for Moscow,' he said. 'I'd be grateful if you'd tell Guy Liddell and ask him to get in touch with me.'[7]

Liddell arranged to interview Rees at the Security Directorate's headquarters. The appointment, deferred because of more pressing problems, did not take place until Wednesday 7 June, by which date the startling news of the missing diplomats had become public property. Rees had given much thought to the question of making a voluntary statement. On the night he originally decided to rouse Footman and Liddell, he decided to obey another impulse and talk to Anthony Blunt, undoubtedly the oldest and closest of

Guy Burgess's friends. Rees remembered the exchanges with Blunt in detail.

He was greatly distressed and said he would like to see me. On Monday May 28th he came to my house in the country, and on an almost ideally beautiful English summer day we sat by the river and I gave him my reasons for thinking that Guy had gone to the Soviet Union: his violent anti-Americanism, his certainty that America would involve us all in a Third World War, most of all the fact that he had been and perhaps still was a Soviet agent. He pointed out, very convincingly as it seemed to me, that these were really not very good reasons for denouncing Guy to MI5. His anti-Americanism was an attitude which was shared by many liberal-minded people and if this alone were sufficient reason to drive him to the Soviet Union, Moscow at that moment would be besieged by defectors seeking asylum. On the other hand, my belief that he might be a Soviet agent rested simply on one single remark made by him years ago and apparently never repeated to anyone else; in any case Guy's public professions of anti-Americanism were hardly what one would expect from a professional Soviet agent. Most of all he pointed out that Guy was after all one of my, as of his, oldest friends and to make the kind of allegations I apparently proposed to make about him was not, to say the least of it, the act of a friend. He was the Cambridge liberal conscience at its very best, reasonable, sensible, and firm in the faith that personal relations are the highest of all human values.

The protracted discussion between Rees and Blunt never became discourteous or heated, though Rees would not accept his visitor's firm defence of E. M. Forster's precept that betraying one's friend was worse than betraying one's country:

I said Forster's antithesis was a false one. One's country was not some abstract conception which it might be relatively easy to sacrifice for the sake of an individual; it was itself made up of a dense network of individual and social relationships in which loyalty to one particular person formed only a single strand. In that case, he said, I was being rather irrational because after all Guy had told me he was a spy a very long time ago and I had not thought it necessary to tell anyone. I said that perhaps I was a very irrational person; but until then I had not really been convinced that Guy had been telling the truth. Now I was....

Blunt spent hours doing his best to dissuade Rees from disclosing what he knew to the security authorities:

He even gently hinted, out of his own experience, that they might even wonder what on earth I was up to coming to them with so curious a story. I could not help wondering if this would have been his own reaction when he was a member of MI5 himself and for a moment I had a sense of how profoundly English he was; but I repeated that I now felt that the only thing I could do was to tell the security authorities what I thought I knew as full and precisely as I could and leave to them what use, if any, they might wish to make of it. . . . He did not disguise his disapproval of what I was going to do.[8]

Goronwy Rees duly kept his appointment at MI5. The experience purged his mind of all the lingering doubts, speculations, hesitations and recurring suspicions which had haunted his relationship with Burgess over the past nineteen years. Guy Liddell and Dick White listened to every word in a strained silence. Then Liddell stated that Guy Burgess had indeed left Britain. Nor did he travel alone. Someone else had disappeared with him.

'Who is it?' Rees said.

'Donald Maclean. They went together.'

Outside in the street the news vendors were selling their wares to queues of passers-by. The press headlines were already shrieking out what Liddell, an anxious man beneath the calm, apologetic exterior, had just confided as an afterthought before Rees rose to leave the room. For over a week Hartwell, too, had been wondering what had become of Burgess. The press lord had intended to tell Guy over dinner on Tuesday 29 May that there would be no immediate opening for him on the staff of the *Daily Telegraph*. When Blunt, the other guest, had arrived, alone and rather downcast, having waited in vain for Burgess to join him at the Reform Club as arranged, Hartwell said lightly that their friend was not noted for punctuality. They lingered, and there was an empty place at table when they sat down thoughtfully to dine. Blunt evidently did not enjoy the meal. He appeared sickly, pale and increasingly distraught. Suddenly, he got up and said apologetically: 'I feel I must go now and look for him.'[9]

Only the day before, Blunt had dismissed with disdainful logic the theorizing of Goronwy Rees about the likely destination of Burgess. Hartwell learnt later that the eminent art critic and connoisseur, prostrated by his unavailing efforts to solve the mystery of Guy's disappearance, had taken to his bed, sick with anxiety. As he had indicated to Rees, Blunt saw nothing to be gained by voluntarily approaching the authorities. So powerful indeed was the aversion of intellectuals generally to what they saw as 'playing the informer', that Sillitoe's Directorate obtained disappointingly little evidence from witnesses who individually could have shed light in various places. The popular press was having an unprecedented run of field days, openly attacking Whitehall and its mandarins for trying to cover up a scandal which plainly discomfited and indicted them. Rattled ministerial spokesmen in Parliament failed to allay spreading suspicions that there was an official conspiracy of silence and that this must be broken because the truth, however sordid, was the one thing that mattered. In their own determination to resist the intrusion of sensation-hungry 'gentlemen of the press', some intellectuals entered into a separate conspiracy of silence which effectively thwarted the security authorities.

Among the handful of volunteers who, like Rees, felt obliged to tell the security authorities their innermost thoughts about the two absconders were two other writers, Humphrey Slater and Rosamond Lehmann. Slater astounded his friend, John Lehmann, by admitting that 'he'd been almost certain for a long time that Donald had been a secret member of the Communist Party and had wondered whether he ought to turn him in'. Then Rosamond added to her brother's astonishment by saying that

> she had been trying to recall everything Guy had said and done in the years before 1945, when they had seen much of one another. She had been uneasy for a long time; now she was completely convinced that Guy, originally out of pure idealism, *had* become a Communist agent, but also that even if he had wanted to he had been unable later to get out of the one-way lobster pot, and that his flight – she felt sure – was due to the fact that the security net was closing around him. She further told me that she had already got in touch with the security authorities,

and though she had been mystified by the lack of urgency with which an eminent military figure had appeared to treat the whole affair, she had managed to obtain an appointment and was going to tell them all she knew – and all her deductions.[10]

Lehmann was imprudent enough to mention in passing the doubts of his sister about Burgess's loyalty, as well as Slater's independent doubts about Maclean's, in a brief note he wrote to the poet Stephen Spender, who was then on holiday at Lake Garda in Italy. The purpose of Lehmann's letter had been to obtain the Italian address of their mutual friend, W. H. Auden. However, through over-excitement and child-like trust, Spender handed over the letter from Lehmann to a badgering reporter from the *Daily Express* and thereby caused a rift in their relationship. As Lehmann has stressed, the 'hullabaloo' made by this newspaper, as

> self-appointed substitute for the security services [it] considered incapable, did not advance their desperate chase for the truth about Burgess and Maclean in the slightest. It only caused a great deal of pain to several totally innocent people who were trying to keep their heads and do their duty.[11]

This incident was typical of the confusion, misunderstanding and divisions which the escape of Burgess and Maclean helped to engender among the middle-class intellectuals who had known and befriended them. In the circumstances, a tacit agreement to sit tight and say nothing cannot altogether be wondered at, though, far from helping the security authorities, such a policy of elected silence obviously hampered them.

Sillitoe and his colleagues became more and more flummoxed. They drew the line at seeking evidence from knowing but unforthcoming witnesses. They plodded on, hoping for a break in the sullen clouds of misapprehension. A prompt search of Burgess's flat had disclosed 'surprisingly little of value in the way of leads'.[12] The police removed books and papers; that desperate wire from Philby about the forgotten car was there, but the expected haul of incriminating letters from friends had not been found. Despite signs of the tenant's frantic haste, Burgess or someone else had been far-sighted enough to take them away.

Nor would Melinda Maclean go further than the simple, bemused statement she had first blurted out on the telephone to Carey-Foster of the Foreign Office. The latter had implored Strang to dispense with kid-glove treatment in her case, only to be reminded firmly: 'We must not be harried into bullying tactics. After all, she's pregnant.'[13] As for routine interrogations of professional colleagues, these had so far yielded nothing new or revealing.

If there was cynical mirth in Moscow at the manifest discomfiture of British officialdom, there was little inclination on the part of the American intelligence community to see the joke and join in the mocking laughter. The escape of Burgess and Maclean merely seemed to seal the doubts long held by Hoover and the FBI about MI5's competence in handling security. The bungled affair also quickened Bedell Smith's resolve to wash his hands forthwith of Philby, the friend and confederate of Burgess, and here Angleton was wholly with him.

The SIS linkman with the CIA had been staggered by the news of Burgess's unplanned disappearance. It at once exposed him to even chances of being caught himself. Philby had striven to put a calm face on his inner turmoil; he had consulted his control; then he had driven out into the wooded countryside beyond the city to bury his compromising camera and other equipment. The composure with which he faced his inevitable expulsion did credit to his years of disciplined preparation for a crisis like this. 'It was most unlikely,' he wrote, 'that MI5 would put a foreign security service on to me without the agreement of MI6, and I thought that the latter would hesitate before compounding an implied slur on one of their senior officers.'[14]

In fact, Sillitoe, Liddell, Dick White and others had quite enough on their plate already. Philby's alleged complicity still begged far too many questions. Philby could wait. Besides, the Security Directorate's representative in Washington, Geoffrey Patterson, appeared only too happy to accept at face value his SIS colleague's stunned response to the news. The quizzical attitude of Sir Robert Mackenzie, who returned from Paris about a week afterwards, proved somewhat less to Philby's liking. Mackenzie greeted him with a long, searching look. 'I wanted Kim to realize,' said the regional security officer, 'that I knew that he knew or at least could guess that I had rumbled him. I wished to God I'd had some solid proof. If only Liddell or White had turned a blind eye to regulations, we might, between us all, have dug out sufficient by then.'[15] Mackenzie did not voice these suspicions, yet Philby was quick to spot 'the shrewd glint' in Mackenzie's eyes.[16] Bedell Smith, whether Philby yet realized the fact or not, had already asked London to recall the SIS linkman on the grounds that he was no longer acceptable to the CIA. The terse wire from Stewart Menzies, summoning Philby home, duly arrived. He bade farewell to Allen Dulles, Jim Angleton and others; he booked his ticket and flew back to London alone to face the music. These American colleagues of his were not sorry to see the back of him, though only Hoover had been brutal enough to say so to the embarrassed Sillitoe when the two met in the FBI building to compare notes on the scandalous affair of the missing diplomats. If the British Security Chief failed at first to grasp what Philby could possibly have to do with the matter, Hoover obligingly enlightened him. Bedell Smith and he were, for once, unanimous that there could be no useful cooperation between Washington and London while this particular SIS officer remained. The curt command to return had followed automatically as night follows day.

While Aileen stayed on in Washington with her four children (and the expected fifth) to clear up, pay outstanding bills, dispose of the house and pack the family belongings, her husband reported to SIS headquarters in Broadway. Air Commodore Jack Easton, the Assistant Chief of the service, who now occupied the desk where Dansey had once sat, greeted Philby formally and at once suggested that they should both go across to the Security Directorate in Curzon Street where Dick White was expecting them. Philby commented:

> I could not claim White as a close friend, but our personal and official relations had always been excellent, and he had undoubtedly been pleased when I superseded Cowgill. He was bad at dissembling but did

his best to put our talk on a friendly footing. He wanted my help, he said, in clearing up this appalling Burgess–Maclean affair.[17]

Bad at dissembling Dick White might be. Eager to preserve the decencies without letting Philby wriggle out of anything, the interrogator asked his questions quietly and almost casually. White had been uncertain of Philby's honesty and loyalty since the Volkov fiasco. Stewart Menzies had ruled against any enquiry then because, in his down-to-earth fashion, 'C' refused to damn an officer when a stroke of bad luck was sufficient excuse for a botched mission. White, relatively inexperienced though he was in field operations, would have liked to scrutinize minutely and in turn each element in that alleged chapter of accidents, simply because his instinct told him that Philby was an accomplished liar. Now, in the humiliating aftermath of the Burgess–Maclean defection, he intended to probe hard but with deceptive gentleness, in the hope of catching him out. White had already received reports from Patterson and Mackenzie in Washington, giving Philby's ingenious explanation for the flight of the diplomats. It exonerated Philby, of course, by placing the entire initiative and responsibility on Burgess, a person whose manifest unsuitability for the role of an undercover Soviet agent had taken in everybody from start to finish. Hoover and the FBI, apparently, had at first gratefully swallowed this plausible version, for it let them off the hook. It also showed up the professional inadequacy of their counterparts in Britain.[18]

However, Dick White was more interested to hear from Philby how long he had known Burgess, where and when their paths had crossed, and why the claims of past friendship should have blinded so seasoned a professional as Philby. The defendant, as he already thought of himself, talked discursively about the man and his flawed personality,

taking the line that it was almost inconceivable that anyone like Burgess, who courted the limelight instead of avoiding it, and was generally notorious for indiscretion, could have been a secret agent, let alone a Soviet agent from whom strictest security standards would be required. I did not expect this line to be in any way convincing as to the facts of the case; but I hoped it would give the impression that I was implicitly defending myself against the unspoken charge that I, a trained counter-espionage officer, had been completely fooled by Burgess. Of Maclean, I disclaimed all knowledge. . . . As I had only met him twice, for about half an hour in all and both times on a conspiratorial basis, since 1937, I felt that I could safely indulge in this slight distortion of the truth.[19]

White accepted Philby's offer at the end of the first interrogation 'to put a summary of what I had said on paper'. The accused feared that the room had been bugged and wished to correct, in writing, 'any bias that the microphone might have betrayed'. White grudgingly admired Philby's quick mental reflexes: compared with Fuchs and Nunn May, both of whom had been artless in their desire to make a clean breast of treasonable acts committed in protest against what they regarded as the unequal treatment of the Soviet Union by its allies, Philby was too hardened, altogether too slippery and crafty, to confess anything freely. He was not the stuff of which genuine martyrs are made. Yet even Philby might still trip himself up. And, on his own admission, Philby nearly did so during his second session with Dick White a few days later when, in describing his work as a war correspondent on Franco's side of the fighting line in Spain, he gave away 'a piece of gratuitious information, a slip which I bitterly regretted at the time'. Though he consoled himself that White or another inquisitor would have rooted it out in the end, it upset him to discover, as soon as the correction was out of his mouth, that MI5 had mistakenly supposed him to have been sent out in the first place by *The Times* as their own special correspondent.

White had pounced at once: how, he asked, had Philby financed himself? A freelance journalist of no independent means could hardly have lived on air. The simple question struck home. For Philby's upkeep had been paid for by 'the Soviet service' until he established his reputation and *The Times* signed him up. Moreover, Krivitsky had independently stated that a Soviet agent, whom he could not identify but who was an Englishman and a journalist, had been employed behind the battle-front in Spain. White's swift follow-up indicated that he also had read the Krivitsky file and was merely putting two and two together. So Philby fell back on the classic explanation favoured by many penniless graduates on the threshold of a career; he had sold all his goods – 'mostly books and gramophone records' – in an ambitious and ultimately successful attempt to break into the 'world of high-grade journalism'.

The preliminary investigation only deepened White's suspicions that Philby had instigated the defection of Burgess and Maclean. He lacked positive proof; but Stewart Menzies, under constant harassment by Attlee and Morrison, seemed more amenable now to the suggestion that Philby should submit to a judicial enquiry *in camera*. For 'C' had also received a personal letter from Bedell Smith. It denounced the irresponsible conduct of Philby for harbouring Burgess under his roof, to the grave detriment of both the American and British secret services. Sending for the culprit, 'C' told Philby, in effect, that his future hung in the balance. The Americans were very angry. Yet the Director of the CIA had confined himself carefully to generalities, even though he had received enough conclusive evidence from Angleton, via 'Basil', to sink Philby virtually without trace. Political and professional considerations prevented Bedell Smith in 1951, just as temperamental caution had deterred Angleton three years earlier, from divulging this damning evidence to Stewart Menzies. The British had forfeited their immediate right to American help. Having mishandled the Burgess–Maclean business, they should be left severely alone to redeem themselves by trapping Philby, the deadliest member of the trio, unaided. They would have to manage out of their own resources, without the direct or indirect testimony of 'Basil'. Otherwise the Russians would almost certainly get wind of it and 'spring' Philby, as they had 'sprung' the other two.

It may seem almost incomprehensible in retrospect that the once harmonious Anglo-American 'special relationship' in the field of intelligence should have deteriorated so greatly since the halcyon days of war. As has already been shown, however, the untimely abolition of OSS, followed by the painful breach birth of the infant CIA, had not conduced to a speedy restoration of the old spirit of confidence between Washington and London.

And the perverse SIS decision, as Bedell Smith saw it, to pick Philby, of all people, for the purpose of mending Anglo-American fences, now looked like unwitting sabotage. Small wonder, then, that Dick White was deprived of the one ace up the sleeve he sorely needed to trump a skilful, devious opponent who knew early all the cards in White's hand.

Stewart Menzies had little option but to sit tight. Conscious of the distinct coolness that had developed in working relations between London and Washington, mainly as a result of the Burgess–Maclean fiasco, 'C' prudently decided to ask no favours of Bedell Smith. Instead, he concentrated his mind on the twin problems of placating an uneasy, tetchy Attlee and of dealing sensibly and justly with Philby. He could see no merit in despatching another senior officer to Washington, bearing a limp olive branch. The gesture might have struck the hard-headed Director of the CIA as an overt confession of failure, and 'C' remained inordinately proud of SIS and its officers. He could not even bring himself to condemn in advance, as Bedell Smith had done, the seeming rashness of Kim Philby. Yet if Dick White, for instance, had been sent by 'C' to Washington simply to reassure the American intelligence community that Philby's possible involvement was being thoroughly investigated, it is just conceivable that White, for whom Angleton retained much admiration and respect, would have returned with irrefutable testimony to nail the suspect.[20]

The decision to ask Philby for his resignation from the secret service was a reasonably painless formality. Stewart Menzies summoned him again, thanked him for his past work, then offered fairly generous severance terms: a lump sum of £4000, half of it to be paid immediately and the rest doled out in half-yearly payments of £500. A disconsolate Aileen rejoined her husband in late July 1951, and the family moved into a small house near Rickmansworth in Hertfordshire. The word went round the charmed, tight circle of ex-MI6 officers that Kim Philby, of all improbable people, was in deep trouble. The sympathy expressed on his behalf was unfeigned. 'There must be some ghastly mistake,' summed up the common view, a tribute in itself to the esteem in which he was widely held. At a time when the press, the public and the Establishment were at one only in their search for ready scapegoats, it seemed utterly bizarre to such clannish supporters that the secret service should be busily hounding one of its smartest, most proficient and most likeable operators. Just because Beaverbrook and his like wanted publicly to flay the hides off the faceless mandarins in the Foreign Office, whose alleged ineptitude in letting Burgess and Maclean slip through their fingers was surpassed merely by their tight-lipped primness in striving to conceal their laxity, surely that did not excuse the harrying of Philby by the partisan ruffians of MI5. The ancient enmities between the services took on a renewed lease of life during the late summer of 1951 as rival factions, both inside and outside SIS, debated the rights and wrongs of the forthcoming 'secret trial' of Philby.

By then the political fortunes of the Attlee Government, weakened by Bevin's recent death, by Bevan's controversial resignation, and by the embittered feuding in the Party which ensued, were ebbing away fast. Another General Election was held on 25 October 1951, and the ageing Winston Churchill returned cheerfully to office with a slender majority. Among the politically vocal champions of the cornered Philby was the new Tory MP Dick Brooman-White, who had helped to smooth his original entry into SIS. However, the Tory Prime Minister had little time for all this secretive wrangling. According to Sir John Colville, Churchill's personal secretary, the restored tenant of 10 Downing Street lost no sleep over the rumbling Burgess–Maclean scandal:

> I don't think he was much interested in the case of Burgess and Maclean. In fact I had to press him to ask the Cabinet Office to provide a Note on the incident. I think he merely wrote them off as being decadent young men, corrupted by drink and homosexuality, and the whole story lowered still further his not very high opinion of the Foreign Office (I regret to say!). He certainly did not look upon it as an indication of widespread Communist infiltration – and I doubt if he had ever heard of Philby.[21]

Backbench MPs, of whom Brooman-White proved to be the steadiest and most persistent, compensated for Churchill's lofty indifference by interceding vigorously with Stewart Menzies. Malcolm Muggeridge remarked:

> This other Dick White, the politician, kept me well posted about the affair. He was a sensitive and charming person mistakenly devoted to Kim whose doings he would recount with a definite note of awe in his voice. Incidentally, the three authors of *The Philby Conspiracy* are hopelessly wrong about Brooman-White whom they present as a tough, money-grubbing, right-wing politician. Nothing could be further from the truth; he was diffident to a fault, comfortably off himself and almost childishly disinterested where money was concerned. . . . He saw Philby as a kind of Elizabethan in a world full of little prudent men, and he quite failed to realize that Philby's swashbuckling qualities were born, like his appreciation of them, of crude twentieth-century longings and frustrations.[22]

Barely a fortnight after Churchill's close electoral victory, Stewart Menzies rang up Philby at home. He wished to see him the next morning at ten o'clock, without fail. The interview was brisk and short: a judicial enquiry had been opened into the Burgess–Maclean affair, he said, and Philby would be required to give evidence and answer questions. A leading barrister, H. J. P. Milmo, a King's Counsellor who had worked for MI5 during the war, would conduct proceedings. The mention of Milmo's name caused Philby's heart to sink momentarily into his boots:

> A crisis was at hand. I knew him and of him. He was a skilled interrogator; he was the man whom MI5 usually brought in for the kill. . . . I was still confident that I could survive an examination, however robust, on the basis of the evidence known to me. But I could not be sure that new evidence had not come to hand to shoot at me.[23]

He need not have worried. Milmo, for all his bluster and intimidating sharpness, had no fresh facts at his disposal. His brief seemed to be a longer and more elaborate version of the Dick White approach. Not once did Philby stumble as the hectoring Milmo drove him back and forth across the same familiar landscapes of the past – from Cambridge, Austria, Spain, war-time St

Albans and Ryder Street, to Turkey, Washington and various points of interest between. There were two awkward moments for the accused. Why, Milmo demanded, had there been a significant increase in KGB signals traffic from London, firstly in 1945 after Philby took over the Volkov case personally, and secondly in late 1949 after Philby had been told officially about progress by American and British cryptoanalysts in tracing the source of the leaks from the British Embassy in Washington? Perhaps believing that the sudden stammering of the accused suggested guilt rather than nervousness, Milmo paused and repeated the question. He seemed infuriated by the disarming reply: 'I don't know.' The well-rehearsed, cooperative approach of Philby, his eagerness to oblige, his show of disappointment at not being able to help Milmo, exasperated the barrister more and more. At last, after three hours of cross-examination, Milmo stopped and solemnly left the room.

White had failed to break through Philby's guard. Now the formidable Milmo had failed in turn. The accused had good reason to feel elated as well as deeply relieved. He did not mind when the MI5 legal officer asked William Skardon, the interrogator who had coaxed the truth out of Fuchs by kindness, to accompany the accused to his home in an official car and there collect his passport. Skardon called at the Philbys' house half a dozen times more during the next few weeks of listless waiting, but the interrogator found it hard to lead on a man who stammered and usually chose to give monosyllabic answers to awkward questions, though Philby admitted:

> He was much more dangerous than the ineffective White or the blustering Milmo. . . . He was doubtless convinced that I was concealing from him almost everything that mattered, and I would have given a lot to have glimpsed his summing up.

Skardon eventually ceased his visits; but not until early 1952 was Philby recalled to Broadway for a final tussle with 'C's' deputy, the bluff but simple Major-General Sir John Sinclair, with the less than inspired Jack Easton in attendance. Both men made it plain that he was still under suspicion but that the case against him could not yet be proved. 'It was distasteful to lie in my teeth to the honest Sinclair', mused Philby retrospectively. 'I hope he now realizes that in lying to him I was standing as firmly on principle as he ever did.'[24]

Stewart Menzies at last decided to call a halt. For the next two years, Philby was left almost entirely to his own devices. His passport was sent back at once when he wrote to Skardon requesting its return; but gainful employment could not easily be found. He tried his hand, for want of anything better, at a desk job in the City office of an export–import agency owned by another ex-SIS friend. Between times he struggled to re-establish himself in journalism as a freelance. It was then that Dick Brooman-White, determined to place the fallen idol back on its pedestal, reappeared in the familiar guise of ministering angel. Having satisfied himself that Philby was 'in the clear', he enlisted the practical assistance of Malcolm Muggeridge, who recalled:

> Before going ahead I asked Brooman-White for an assurance that there was nothing against Philby other than imprudence, and received it, I am sure, in the utmost good faith. The notion, I was told, that Philby had tipped off Maclean that his exposure as a Soviet spy was imminent, thereby facilitating his escape with Burgess, was nonsensical. On that understanding I tried to get him taken on by the *Daily Telegraph*, whose deputy editor I then was, the idea being to send him to India. When that failed, I wrote to David Astor, proprietor and editor of the *Observer*, explaining how Philby came to be needing employment, and suggesting that he would be well worth talking to. While this was afoot I saw Philby once or twice. He struck me as decidedly subdued, which was scarcely surprising in the circumstances, and I was touched to find that he had already started reading up about India on the assumption that the *Daily Telegraph* job might come off. . . .[25]

As a result of other unpublicized inquisitions into the conduct of individual Foreign Office and intelligence service representatives, ten officials either retired prematurely or were invited to resign. More than twice as many were cautioned, staying on under a temporary cloud, and a senior Treasury official was unmasked and forced to go. The disagreeable task of cleansing the Whitehall stables had been discharged quietly and promptly enough by leading members of its tightly knit Establishment. A powerful working party of three high-ranking civil servants set to work, under the chairmanship of Sir Norman Brook, the Secretary of the Cabinet, to review methods of recruitment, selection, entry and promotion inside the Whitehall 'Club'. Sitting for months as judge and jury in its own cause, the powerful trio decided in the end to scrap the existing rule book and to introduce several overdue reforms calculated to outrage the sensibilities of many senior colleagues reared in the Club tradition of unquestioning trust and mutual respect. By far the most important innovation was a new system of 'positive vetting' applicable to every civil servant, old and new. Largely to set a good example to disgruntled subordinates in the Foreign Office, Strang, the Permanent Under-Secretary, volunteered to be vetted before anyone else, a gesture which did not altogether mollify a number of uneasy senior diplomats behind him in the queue. Indeed, at least four future ambassadors had a lot of explaining to do because of their admitted close associations with Burgess or Maclean. One of the four needlessly implicated himself by expressing the rash hope in a letter to a strategically placed colleague that 'we may all soon be reunited with our erstwhile friend, Donald'. The Whitehall reformers separately decreed that an internal security apparatus, broadly similar to Carey-Foster's small, reasonably efficient unit, should be gradually enlarged and extended to other ministries; and Carey-Foster himself was urged to remain at his post for two more troubled years.[26]

Not that this energetic and straightforward practitioner in an unpopular field managed to avoid harassment himself when, quite unexpectedly, an over-zealous member of Dick White's investigative team denounced him one day as a suspect. According to the MI5 informer, George Carey-Foster was the likeliest source of the suspected last-minute tip-off which had given Burgess and Maclean their head start. Had Carey-Foster not been seen repeatedly in grave discussion with Maclean whenever they walked across St James's Park together to and from their club at lunchtime? Obviously the Foreign Office Security Chief, possessing inside knowledge of the case, must have been less than judicious. Whether inadvertently or not, he might just have let slip to his friend the merest hint of the impending investigation, and therefore thoroughly deserved to be investigated himself. The accusation fell flat; the accuser duly silenced. It was symbolic of the tangled cross-purposes that flourished in Whitehall during those unhappy months.

The lofty and somewhat contemptuous attitude of Norman Brook towards the muck-raking press did little to repair the damage already inflicted on morale throughout the Civil Service. As secretary both of the Joint Intelligence Committee and of the Cabinet Security Committee, on the first of which Carey-Foster occasionally deputized for him, Norman Brook was content to ignore the wild charges of Fleet Street hacks, leaving it to ministers to reassure Parliament and the populace in their own good time. A public servant of all-round ability and the utmost rectitude, he did not care in the least about public relations. His doctrine, rigidly upheld and enforced, was that every matter handled by Whitehall bureaucrats would remain an official secret until their political masters decided otherwise.

Naturally, the Norman Brook doctrine of secrecy appealed to Sillitoe and the Security Directorate. It proved less than palatable to those members of SIS, past and present, who were determined to protect the 'innocent' Philby from his MI5 persecutors. Certainly, the provisional failure of Sillitoe's specialists to trap the cunning Kim added to their collective frustration and even seemed to whet their predatory appetite for easier game.[27] Perhaps the most notable casualty of all was Guy Liddell, that long-serving senior executive who had seen too much of Burgess without ever wholly seeing through him. Contrary to inaccurate rumours, Liddell did not depart in official disgrace. He was retired on the rather tenuous pretext that he had 'outlived his usefulness, since the Americans would no longer wish to work with him'.[28] Liddell moved on from Curzon Street to the Atomic Energy Centre at Harwell as its chief security officer, proof that he left without a stain on his professional reputation.

If there was more than a touch of injustice in Philby's successful parrying of repeated attempts by ex-colleagues to extract from him the slightest admission of treasonable guilt, he had other unsuspecting ex-colleagues to thank for sustaining him, first by muddying the waters and then by asserting and loudly insisting on his innocence. So far Philby's luck and nerve had held; but he was by no means out of the wood yet. The bare will to survive and emerge unscathed kept him going. He did not rage or plot against his enemies, as the irrepressible Guy Burgess might have done. Nor was it in his nature to surrender meekly, as the fatalistic Maclean would probably have done. His pride had been badly dented, but that was something he could put up with. Stripped of everything that had given life its savour, he clung like a prisoner in solitary confinement to the gossamer hope that the authorities would tire of the waiting game before he did. Dick White's parting words had been: 'You may think you've had the last laugh, but bear this in mind – we'll haul you back when we're ready, not before. Then the last laugh could be on you.'[29]

The sense of living from day to day, strictly on borrowed time, was depressing. Seldom did the born opportunist in Philby feel confident of being able to outwit White, Skardon and Milmo a second time. In his self-imposed isolation and greatly reduced circumstances, he slowly grew away from Aileen as the months dragged by. On rare visits to friends, his wife could not always be trusted to choke back her bitterness at 'Kim's folly'. Somehow, she had acquired the fixation that he had brought misery on himself and disgrace to the family by spying for Russia, and Aileen did not mind who knew it. Philby tried to pass off these outbursts with a pitying shrug.

Only now and then did major happenings outside his closed world touch him personally, though he continued to read the newspapers with the confirmed addict's eye for items offering crumbs of comfort. Otherwise the globe spun past like a distant planet. His old, mordant taste for the absurd enabled him to gloat a little over the humbling of the mighty in Whitehall, especially when Fleet Street's jackals turned up stale and often misleading morsels of evidence on the cold trail of the missing diplomats. Maclean's 'conscience money', sent home in two drafts of £1000 each, via two Swiss banks, came as a bitter-sweet reminder that the Russians took good care of their own. So did the messages from Burgess to his mother. His own contact with these 'friends' had ceased, perhaps the hardest of all the privations he had to endure.

Monarchs, Presidents, so-called statesmen and churchmen, like the ambassadors and the anonymous 'Great and Good' of Whitehall, seemed to come and go like mayflies, resigning, retiring or dying, then fading into well-deserved oblivion after the summary honour of fulsome obituaries in *The Times*. Philby had been too preoccupied with his own defence against the thrusts of White, Skardon and Milmo to notice the passing of Lord Inverchapel, the former Archibald Clark Kerr, towards the end of 1951. After King George VI died on 6 February 1952, people in their tens of thousands had filed mournfully past the catafalque in Westminster Hall. Fleet Street's leader-writers had gushed on sententiously about the ending of an epoch, then gushed on again about the dawning of a new Elizabethan age with the accession to the throne of the late King's young daughter. The King had died of cancer, like his father. Grief and shame at the humiliating consequences of the Burgess–Maclean scandal had not shortened his life by a day. Of that Philby could be quite sure, just as he would never have credited Inverchapel, for one, with dying of mere surprise.

No doubt the shock-waves were still rippling through the Foreign Office and perhaps disturbing the slumbers of Her Britannic Majesty's loyal and trusty servants in their spacious residencies abroad. The word 'surprise' was, however, less than exact to describe the mood of tight-lipped embarrassment which still oppressed not a few august envoys who had humoured and protected Maclean in his diplomatic prime. Sir John Balfour, less self-conscious than most of the breed, had moved from Buenos Aires to Madrid as British Ambassador when the astounding news first reached him. Not given to overstating things, Balfour was suddenly reminded of a classic phrase used in a difficult court case of long ago. A patient English judge, seeking to assess the varying degrees of responsibility for a collision offshore between a warship of the Royal Navy and a commercial vessel, had intervened to ask one of the ship's engineers: 'Tell me, were you really *surprised* when the crash happened?'

'Surprised, your honour,' replied the witness, 'I was so flabbergasted you could have buggered me through my oil-skins.'[30]

There were divided counsels on the surest ways of achieving Britain's modest, post-imperial goals in the second Elizabethan Age. The sun had set on the British Empire. Not even Churchill tried to resist the irresistible demands from colonial territories in Africa, Asia and elsewhere for the progressive ceding of independence; and the British public, inured to change, acquiesced without fuss or false regrets. The Mau Mau emergency in Kenya, like the Chinese Communist incursions against law and order in the Malayan jungle, imposed extra burdens on the heavily pruned defence forces of the Crown. Like gnats biting a mangy old lion, Malta and Cyprus asserted themselves too. Churchill's return to office made little difference to Attlee's original handiwork. Early jubilation over the rotund promise 'to make a bonfire of controls' did not last. The veteran Prime Minister was no longer imbued with the fiery, indomitable spirit of his greatest period, yet people did not seem to notice or truly to care. The loquacious Bracken found their indifference irritating, as he had written to Beaverbrook shortly before Churchill's return:

English history is marked by a continuous strain of what might be called rumbunctiousness. For nearly a thousand years the English have been prepared to pull down the arrogant and the strong from their thrones, and until this century they have always striven to limit the authority of their political masters. . . . Perhaps the change in the national character is due to loss of faith in what the Victorians described as 'Britain's Mission', plus a sense of bewilderment about the immensity and variety of ugly problems that are constantly thrust upon them. . . . When Henry Adams was here during the American Civil War he wrote a discerning though rather gloomy analysis of Britain's problems for the benefit of his prophetic brother, Brooks Adams. At the height of the mid-Victorian prosperity he declared that the English economy was based on the most fragile foundations and that the remedy for this evil lay in economic unity between Britain and her wideflung possessions beyond the seas. Is it too much to hope that hardship and suffering may in the end persuade the countries that are left in the Empire to understand that their best hope lies in creating a Commonwealth or Empire with the same measure of free trade within its borders that is enjoyed by the United States and the Union of Soviet Republics? . . .[31]

Such dreams belonged to stabler, ampler days, gone beyond recall. Churchill, generally acknowledged as 'the greatest living Englishman', lacked the means and the stamina to put the clock back. Only in private did he indulge in witticisms with a distinctive Victorian tang, as when he commented to his Colonial Secretary, Oliver Lyttleton, who had witnessed a riot in an African dependency: 'Ten thousand Africans, armed with staves, inflamed with drink and inspired by the highest Liberal principles – it must have been a formidable gathering.'[32] Churchill sought, first and last, the friendship of the United States, a superpower with an almost pathological mistrust of old-fashioned colonial ambitions and ideals. Truman had bowed out in 1952, making way for Dwight D. Eisenhower, the eminent soldier nominated by the Republicans as their leader. Nobody disliked 'Ike' at the start. The British regarded this war-time Supreme Commander in Europe, and recent military Chief of the North Atlantic alliance, with an affectionate respect, which endured no better than their regard for Churchill. Two men called Dulles were stamping the seal of their considerable power and authority on the foreign policy of the United States, John Foster at the State Department and Allen at the institutionalized CIA. Eisenhower tried to stand above the battle, deferring to them both until he forfeited much of his popularity. Then cynics, after Philby's taste, started to call the White House 'the tomb of the well-known warrior'.

Two events in 1953 impinged strongly on the mind of Philby. The first was the announcement on 5 March of the death of Josef Stalin; the second was the gratifying news in early September that Melinda Maclean had left her temporary home in Switzerland as mysteriously as her husband had done from the Foreign Office over two years before. The renewed discomfiture of the Establishment at her unforeseen departure, doubtless to rejoin her husband in Moscow, warmed the cockles of Philby's cold heart. Whether

Stalin's demise would mean some relaxing of tension in the Cold War, even some easing of restrictions inside the Soviet Union itself, he was in no position to say. Cold-shouldered by some of his former colleagues in the service, Philby could bear that slight with more equanimity than the abrupt decision of his Russian control to drop him until further notice. Only in an emergency was he authorized to signal his distress and arrange to escape; but he felt no urge to make a premature run for it.

Less than a month after the Queen's coronation, the ailing Winston Churchill had suffered another stroke. This physical setback on 23 June 1953, did not incapacitate him. Nor did it tempt him to retire from the fray. 'A week ago I was thinking of running the world,' Churchill said during his early convalescence at Chartwell, 'and now – while I sit still, I feel quite well.'[33]

His impatient heir-apparent, the Foreign Secretary Anthony Eden, had not been enjoying the vulgar if intermittent clamour in the press about the unsolved Burgess–Maclean scandal. The new system of 'positive vetting' was working reasonably well, he assured the House of Commons. About the missing diplomats, Eden had nothing fresh to say. He had his work cut out in any case, trying to restrain John Foster Dulles's enthusiasm for anti-Communist brinkmanship. Dulles thought of Eden as 'a weak sister' more to be scorned than trusted. This suited Churchill. Aware of the temperamental incompabitility between the pair, he gladly hung on as Prime Minister. He had no wish as yet to be parted from the red despatch boxes, those precious playthings of his second childhood, so long as he could influence American policy in Europe and the Far East. The encirclement of an outnumbered French garrison at Dien Bien Phu by Vietminh rebels was a challenge which, in Dulles's view, the free world could ignore only at its peril.

'Where do you the British stand on this?' asked Senator Lyndon Johnson when Admiral Radford, chairman of the Joint Chiefs of Staff, had outlined to a secret meeting of congressional leaders a plan for using carrier-borne aircraft to break the siege of Dien Bien Phu, deploying ground forces also if necessary. Congress drew the line at single-handed American intervention, while

Eden shrank from committing the reluctant British to an insane adventure.[34]

As Churchill's intuitive *alter ego*, Brendan Bracken already knew who was pulling the strings behind the hapless British Foreign Secretary:

> He [Winston] alone has the capacity to hold on to the excitable Uncle Sam's coat-tails. The volubility of Dulles and the pugnacity of the US Chiefs of Staff may destroy the possibility of an armistice in Indo-China. The Sino-Russian axis is far more formidable than the alliance forged by Hitler.

As for Churchill's plans to retire,

> our friend intends to give up before June. . . . Though his health is not worse, and he gets through a lot of work, the desire for office has diminished rapidly.[35]

Still Churchill hung on until advancing senility, stigmatized as a disservice to the nation by Malcolm Muggeridge in the pages of the irreverent weekly magazine of which he was now editor, eventually persuaded the Prime Minister to delay no longer.[36] Owing to an industrial dispute which had shut down the national newspapers, the belated retirement of Churchill in April 1955 received less extensive coverage than it merited. Had the printing presses been rolling as usual, there was another far more tantalizing development in distant Canberra whose significance no alert editor would have overlooked, if the news had leaked out as it so often did. The original defection of Vladimir Petrov, listed as a Third Secretary at the Soviet Embassy in Canberra, had caused an ephemeral sensation on 2 April 1954. If Philby had wondered at the time what it portended, the Security Directorate's new chief, Dick White, had learnt enough meanwhile from the Australian intelligence community to hope that this fresh and unexpected source of evidence might enable him to pull in Philby shortly for decisive questioning. Already, he knew, Petrov had confirmed that Burgess and Maclean had been recruited as Russian agents while still undergraduates at Cambridge, and that their escape from Britain in 1951 had been engineered by a 'third man' in Washington. Convinced that the British Government ought to publish some of the facts without delay, partly to allay public misgivings and partly to unsettle Philby, who would conclude that the net was again closing round him, White sought authorization to approach the Foreign Secretary and Prime Minister-designate, Anthony Eden, whose approval he needed and fully expected to get as a matter of course.

Alas, White's pleas fell on resolutely deaf ears. Eden would not consider any move which, as he put it, might create needless disturbance while he stood in the wings, waiting impatiently for Churchill to leave the stage. The next government, Eden stressed, would have more urgent business on its hands than re-enacting the wretched melodrama of the missing diplomats. If White wished to come back in two or three months, that would be time enough; the present moment was quite inopportune. The disconsolate White thus had to abandon a move which would probably have been premature in Sillitoe's day but certainly not in the spring of 1955. For the Security Chief foresaw the distinct likelihood that the press would 'nobble' Vladimir Petrov in the interval between his secret debriefing and the publication of the Australian Royal Commission's report on this Soviet defector's disclosures. In that event, Eden would have cause to regret an expedient snap decision – and the Russians as well as the Americans would marvel again at the unerring instinct of the British for standing clumsily in their own light.

Needless to say, Eden was far too preoccupied that summer to reconsider the 'untimely' proposal of White. The Prime Minister called an election in June 1955 to confirm his inherited mandate. Elated by the result, he still did nothing; then Parliament rose for the long recess, unprepared for the gathering storm which a heedless Prime Minister had wished upon himself.[37]

One can only speculate now, as Philby doubtless did at the time, on what finally prompted the Russians to get in touch with him again. He had recently moved the family home from his rented villa at Rickmansworth to a large, rambling and inconvenient Edwardian house, standing in two and a half acres of unkempt garden at Crowborough, on the eastern edge of Ashdown Forest between Kent and Sussex. Out of the blue, in the early summer of 1955, there had reached him 'through the most ingenious of routes, a message from my Soviet friends (urging) me to be of good cheer and presaging an early resumpion of relations'.[38]

Anything but well versed in the nuances of Soviet politics, Philby had no better insight than the average intelligent British layman into the power struggle which had been going on in Moscow since Stalin's death more than two years earlier. The defection of Petrov, nevertheless, had been undoubtedly influenced by it. For Petrov was an adherent of Beria, that dreaded Chief of the KGB and a favourite of Stalin's, who had since been liquidated by Malenkov. Faced with the choice between going home as ordered, and seeking asylum in Australia, Petrov had not hesitated. It appears probable that Philby, too, came under the balefully hostile scrutiny of the new régime in the Kremlin. Thanks to a German, Philby was eventually declared 'clean'.

In July 1954, on the tenth anniversary of the abortive bomb plot on the life of Hitler, Dr Otto John, the *Abwehr* agent whose war-time reports Philby had refused to accept (somewhat to Hugh Trevor-Roper's disgust), unexpectedly crossed from West Berlin to the East. According to his own account, Otto John went involuntarily, having first been drugged by a Russian agent. According to other accounts, Otto John was merely another defector fleeing to the Soviet side with the usual bundle of Western secrets. However, his prolonged endeavours subsequently to clear his name did produce one intriguing strand of evidence which underlined the suspicious interest of the KGB in the past activities of Philby. Indeed, Otto John went so far as to state that he was kidnapped in 1954 and subjected to lengthy interrogation by the KGB 'solely to determine' whether Philby was 'a double agent betraying the Russians to the British'.[39] Such suspicions invariably tend to fall on double agents, especially on double agents whose cover has been 'blown'. And though Philby, for propagandist purposes, has repeatedly spurned the title of double agent as applied to his own exemplary career in the KGB, one can sympathize with the protestations without artlessly swallowing the propaganda. How rich in its irony is the thought that Philby may have at least partly owed his rehabilitation in the Kremlin to the negative testimony extracted from Otto John by the post-Stalin KGB!

It is doubtful whether Philby learnt anything of these Byzantine manoeuvrings from his Soviet friends in England when they finally took him up again. What was past could best be forgotten. It was the immediate future that mattered, and Philby's future still looked unpromising. Much would depend on the Eden Government's handling of the so-far undisclosed secrets which Petrov had betrayed to the Australian security authorities. If Dick White got his way, and the Petrov evidence justified it, Philby knew that he could expect no quarter from his inquisitors next time. They would bait the trap and watch him fall into it. Then he would probably be tried *in camera* like Fuchs, and condemned to spend the rest of his life behind bars. What he could not comprehend was the deafening official silence. Was it an ominous or a hopeful sign? Philby could not be sure, though it seemed almost incredible that a defecting KGB agent of Petrov's calibre could have given away insufficient information for the determined Dick White to seize and act on. Perhaps it was the policy of White to let him sweat until the last minute, then move in coldly for the kill. Philby simply did not know.

There was a cruder and less credible explanation: White's hands had been tied behind his back in effect by a new Prime Minister primarily concerned with short-term political expediency. On Sunday, 18 September 1955, when Petrov's evidence was first published in the *People* newspaper, then eagerly followed up by the rest of Fleet Street, Philby could hardly believe the sudden turn in his luck. Someone in Whitehall had compounded, at one fell swoop, the blunderings of the past four years. Unless White already possessed some further damning evidence which had been withheld from the *People*, there was little now to worry about. In fact, the premature publication of Petrov's account fulfilled the darkest forebodings of Dick White. It did not console him in the slightest to reflect that Eden had been made to look very foolish indeed. For White knew that there would be another deafening and time-consuming outcry against this latest example of smug ineptitude in Whitehall. With Parliament still in recess, the British press would keep up the pressure, forcing the Government back helplessly on its heels. If Eden misjudged matters yet again and let his critics walk all over him, then the chances of catching Philby would dwindle and probably disappear. Somehow the situation had to be contained; otherwise only the Russians stood to gain from it.

The three most damaging facts which Petrov had announced to the British public and the world at large were these: that Burgess and Maclean had been recruited as agents before graduating from Cambridge; that their escape from Britain had been authorized and arranged by the Russians; and that the flight of Melinda Maclean from Switzerland in September 1953 had been similarly organized. The former Third Secretary at the Soviet Embassy in Canberra was not directly concerned himself in any of these exploits, though that did not detract from his accuracy. As White realized only too well, Petrov's informant, Filip Kislytsin, had previously served in London where he appeared to have acted as the mastermind behind Burgess from 1945 to 1948. Kislytsin also claimed to have participated in the 1951 escape plan. It was left to a Foreign Office spokesman to acknowledge lamely and belatedly that Petrov's disclosures in the press were substantially correct, adding a promise that the full version of the Burgess–Maclean case would be released in a White Paper on Friday 23 September.

The FBI, through its 'legal attaché' in London, was kept abreast of every hasty step taken by Whitehall. A message to J. Edgar Hoover enclosed an advance copy of the official document; there might be later revisions, Hoover was warned, since the Cabinet had still to approve its contents. 'This paper was prepared by the British Security Service (MI5)....' So Eden, five months too late, had saddled Dick White with the impossible task of answering justifiable public criticisms of the Government, while expunging anything that might be considered too sensitive from the strict security point of view. This miserable exercise utterly failed, as it was bound to. The FBI man in London cabled to Hoover:

Today press describes White Paper published late yesterday as a pathetic and unconvincing document, which reveals bungling, omits facts and tells little new. Press critical of long delay by security authorities in establishing subjects' identities and also for not making adequate arrangements at all ports to prevent their departure from England. Press dissatisfied with explanation re disappearance and now asks who in Foreign Office warned subjects, as they disappeared immediately after the security service was authorized by the Foreign Secretary to question [Maclean]. Bureau will be further informed.

Hoover's appetite was whetted further by his assiduous representative's next summary of British press reactions:

All Sunday papers continue attacking conformity and inefficiency and carelessness of security service. Criticism of White Paper omissions also continues. Sunday Pictorial headlines that both subjects were notorious sex perverts and asks why this was not mentioned in White Paper as it is one of the keys to the scandal. Press strongly pressing for disclosure of identity of Third Man who tipped off subjects, asking if he has been punished or fired, and if unknown to authorities, what action is being taken, suggesting that these are questions that will be asked when Parliament reassembles October 25. . . .[40]

The Foreign Office, rather than the Security Directorate, was singled out for most of the blame. Dick White could afford to smile grimly at Fleet Street's mistake. It did not help much, of course. White could do nothing now but wait, just as Philby must be waiting, for the floodtide of abuse to ebb. Normally balanced people, especially politicians, were starting to ask very awkward and searching questions. The possibility that someone might openly name Philby as the Third Man could no longer be ruled out. The Foreign Secretary, Harold Macmillan, to whom White confided his fears and frustration, could offer little more than conventional sympathy.

The rumours and insinuations were just as rife on the American side of the Atlantic. The FBI, and to a lesser extent the CIA, did little to discourage them. Instead of refusing to see a leading executive of the International News Service, who asked to discuss the matter with him on 29 September, J. Edgar Hoover spent more than an hour explaining the legal and other niceties that would flow from positively identifying Philby in print as the Third Man. The FBI had no conclusive evidence of its own to support the allegation, but Hoover naturally did not admit this. He informed three of his principal aides:

I advised X that he was on the trail of some very hot information but cautioned him that in the White Paper which has just been released by the British Government there was no mention of Philby's name, apparently because of lack of direct proof and the fact that Philby was in contact with lawyers and threatening heavy libel suits if any paper prints his name in connection with this matter.... I also mentioned that I believed Philby's name was known to one or two newspapers in London but they have been reluctant to use it because of lack of direct proof. I gave the brief background on Philby, to the effect that he had been living with Burgess while employed with British Intelligence in Washington, was a heavy drinker, and because of his association with Burgess was suspected of having tipped off Burgess to the investigation being conducted; that if Philby had not actually done so, he was at least in the position of having access to this and other highly confidential information....[41]

Hoover's confidential advice, which Angleton of the CIA could certainly have embellished in conclusive detail, seemed to set the seal of approval on unofficial American whisperings about Philby. Inevitably, the only press reports positively identifying Philby as the Third Man appeared in the United States, the *New York Daily News* being the first to take the risk. Meanwhile, the FBI representative in London notified Hoover that the British press was playing it more cautiously:

Philby has been besieged with telephone calls and visits from the press ever since name appeared in newspapers but continues to decline comment; this for reason that he has been prohibited from doing so under Official Secrets Act. He now appears relieved that name has been mentioned in press as he feels the burden is on the Government to reveal his position and at the same time enlighten him as to the strength of their case against him.[42]

In the midst of all the hullabaloo, death stalked in almost

unnoticed to claim another victim of 'guilt by association'. The former Minister of State at the Foreign Office, Hector McNeil, had spoken out only once since the publication of Petrov's findings. Within days of taking part in a BBC discussion programme, during which he inveighed against the prevailing tendency to mindless 'hysteria', this former friend of Guy Burgess sailed to the United States, collapsed on board ship, was rushed to hospital but did not recover. As in the case of Philip Jordan, the late press officer to Attlee at 10 Downing Street, McNeil's death, on 11 October 1955, was medically attributed to natural causes; but colleagues who knew him well believed that his end was hastened by strain mixed with remorse for his imprudent tutelage of Burgess.

Harold Macmillan's plea that ministers, not civil servants, should be held accountable for past blunders in security did not appease Parliament, press or public.

By now Philby had taken the cue and dispersed his family. He spent much of his time walking in Ashdown Forest to avoid the attentions of newshawks, or discreetly conferring in London with Brooman-White and other supporters who had the sympathetic ear of Sir John Sinclair, Stewart Menzies's successor as head of the secret service. Philby could not yet be sure that Dick White's hand had been forced. Nevertheless, if anyone dared to say openly that he, Kim Philby, was the Third Man and a traitor, his own hand would be forced. Perhaps the mere threat of slapping a libel suit on that person or organization might prove a sufficient deterrent. So, assuming the posture of a man aggrieved and much put upon, Philby waited for White to move.

One of the most persistent backbench MPs to harry successive Foreign Secretaries over the unedifying implications of the Burgess–Maclean affair was Lieutenant-Colonel Marcus Lipton, a Socialist lawyer of maverick temperament, who had sat for the London constituency of Brixton since 1945. Lipton, so his critics complained, could be read like a book but seldom closed so easily. On the first day of the parliamentary session, 25 October 1955, this Labour MP seemed for once to be voicing the misgivings of many colleagues, irrespective of Party, about the secretiveness and ineptitude of Whitehall and the government when he rose and asked a leading question: 'Has the Prime Minister made up his mind to cover up at all costs the dubious third man activities of Mr Harold Philby who was First Secretary at the Washington Embassy a little time ago, and is he determined to stifle all discussion on the very great matters which were evaded in the wretched White Paper, which is an insult to the intelligence of the country?'

Turning this thrust at Anthony Eden aside, the Foreign Secretary, Harold Macmillan, replied that the House of Commons would shortly have the opportunity to debate the issue. He would then deal fully with the honourable and gallant gentleman's points. However, Philby was by now too agitated to wait on tenterhooks until 7 November, the date fixed for this privileged parliamentary occasion. Nor, for somewhat different reasons, did Dick White intend to sit back passively if he could help it. Philby's SIS backers again warned him emphatically to say nothing out of turn which might prejudice his case. Reluctantly, he accepted their sound advice. Equally, to show a submissive spirit, he surrendered his passport and agreed to answer, with an air of injured innocence, an informal cross-examination by ex-colleagues of SIS, an ordeal less exacting than a similar encounter with Dick White's hounds would have been. Philby, according to his own account, was returning home from an assignation with his Soviet friends after dusk when he caught sight of his own name in the headlines of an evening newspaper, accidentally discovering what Lipton had been saying about him at Westminster that very afternoon. He indignantly rang 'my SIS friends' from his mother's flat, telling them that he had no alternative but to speak out. 'They agreed that I would have to say something sometime, but again urged me to postpone action until after the debate in the Commons.'[43] So Philby barricaded himself in for twelve more uncertain days.

Dick White was displeased on learning of Philby's renewed efforts to stir up ancient antagonisms by playing off SIS against the Security Directorate. Not for the first time in recent months, he privately implored 'C' to leave sentiment out of it and have the Philby case re-examined strictly on its merits. Had it not been for the Prime Minister's untimely decision to defer publication of Petrov's evidence, Philby might already have been lured into confessing his guilt. Events had since run out of control, but was that any reason for refusing to make a combined stand together? Sinclair resented White's self-righteous tone. He would not budge from his view that the Security Chief had yet to establish the presumed guilt of Philby; presumption and proof were rather different things. During these twelve days of suspense, while the hunted man lived on his nerves and the hunter gradually gave up hope of cornering his quarry, Harold Macmillan himself was in something of a quandary. In the Commons debate he would have to answer Lipton's unfortunately phrased question, and neither the House nor the press would be satisfied with an inconclusive or evasive reply. As matters stood, he would have to say that no proof had been found to implicate Philby in the escape of Burgess and Maclean, unless White could meanwhile suggest some acceptable alternative.

At a later stage in Macmillan's exchanges with the Security Chief, one positive suggestion was raised and almost immediately rejected by both. After a few moments' consideration, White had to acknowledge that an offer of a 'general amnesty', embracing everyone directly or indirectly involved in Communist subversion since the early thirties, might now prove counter-productive. The bonds between the remaining conspirators were still drawn tight. That wall of silence which the security authorities had so far been unable to penetrate would probably stand firm against so sudden and suspect a trumpet blast of forgiveness from Whitehall. So the idea of an amnesty was dismissed, and Dick White reconciled himself to the prospect of another humiliating setback.[44]

The mood of the Commons was solemn and expectant on Monday 7 November 1955. MPs thronged the benches as Foreign Office spokesmen fielded questions about Sudanese self-government and the current Icelandic fisheries dispute, fobbing off a number of oblique queries about Burgess and Maclean with reminders that all would presently be revealed. Harold Macmillan rose from the government front bench at 3.34 p.m.: 'It can rarely have happened in our long parliamentary history,' he began, 'that the political head of a Department should have had to unfold to the House of Commons so painful a story as that which it is our duty to consider today. To understand – though not, of course, to excuse – this story, it is necessary to cast our minds back to the 1930s and to recall the kind of background against which the two principal characters grew up. . . .'

Macmillan held back nothing. Without seeking to moralize on the sinister pull of circumstances which had led so many members of that generation to espouse extremist views, so that some 'could put the interests of another country before their own and commit the horrible crime of treachery', the Foreign Secretary defended the handling of the Burgess–Maclean affair by both Labour and Conservative governments. He did not accept the criticism that the recent White Paper had said 'too little and too late'. Nor did he accept that the Foreign Office should be supervised by the Security Directorate. He was not much attracted by suggestions 'that there should be a kind of NKVD or OGPU system in our public offices'. As to complaints that precautionary action against the spies was not taken soon enough, he felt strongly that these were 'based on a misapprehension of the rights of a citizen in a free society in time of peace. . . . Action against employees, whether of the State or anybody else, arising from suspicion and not from proof, may begin with good motives, and it may avert serious inconveniences or even disasters, but judging from what has happened in some other countries, such a practice soon degenerates into the satisfaction of personal vendettas or a general system of tyranny, all in the name of public safety. . . .'

Between May 1951 and April 1954, the 'first thought of those responsible had to be not how much they could tell the public but what they could do to minimise the harm that had been done. The Security [Directorate] still had extensive enquiries to make, not merely to reconstruct the story but to improve the Service. But when Petrov defected on April 3rd 1954, a whole new vista on the case was opened up.' Here Macmillan's explanation of his own leader, Eden's, unwillingness to pre-empt, as Dick White had strongly advocated, publication of the Petrov report by the Australian Royal Commission, appeared to strike a disingenuous note which must have made White inwardly wince. Recalling press statements as early as 28 April 1954 that Petrov had information on the Burgess–Maclean escape, he justified the refusal of the Foreign Office to be drawn at that time: 'Petrov let it be known that if, as soon as he said anything to the Australian security and intelligence organization, it was to be given publicly in this country, he would then refuse to say any more at all. This is a most important point. Since it was essential that Petrov should give his evidence before the Royal Commission, it was decided not to make any further announcements bearing on his testimony. The report of the Royal Commission is dated August 22nd 1955. It was laid before the Australian Parliament and first became public on September 14th 1955. It then became possible to answer questions which had hitherto remained unanswered, and that was done by the Foreign Office spokesman in reply to questions arising out of an article in the *People* on Sunday September 18th and the White Paper published nine days after the publication of the Royal Commission's Report.'

Macmillan was doing his best with a very thin case. To hint at Eden's error of judgement in disregarding White's advice to publish earlier, and to hell with Petrov and the cheque-book journalists lying in wait to tempt him, would have been unthinkable. White was possibly too experienced in the polite evasions and connivances of Whitehall to be shocked. Besides, he liked and admired the Foreign Secretary too much to begrudge him that deceitful little flourish. However, once Macmillan reached the crucial point of his statement, White's heart sank. He could not escape the bleak conclusion that the speaker had overstepped the limits of generosity, thereby letting Philby slip too easily off the hook.

'The possibility of a "tip off" had to be seriously considered,' said Macmillan, 'and searching and protracted investigations into this possibility have been undertaken and are proceeding even at the present time. In this connection the name of one man has been mentioned in the House of Commons, but not outside. I feel that all Honourable Members would expect me to mention him by name and to explain the position. He is Mr H. A. R. Philby, who was a temporary First Secretary at the British Embassy in Washington from October 1949 to April 1951 and had been privy to much of the investigation into the leakage. Mr Philby had been a friend of Burgess from the time when they were fellow undergraduates at Trinity College, Cambridge. Burgess had been accommodated with Philby and his family at the latter's home in Washington from August 1950 to April 1951; and, of course, it will be realized that at no time before he fled was Burgess under suspicion. It is now known that Mr Philby had Communist associates during and after his university days. In view of the circumstances, he was asked in July 1951 to resign from the Foreign Service. Since that date his case has been the subject of close investigation. *No evidence has been found to show that he was responsible for warning Burgess or Maclean. While in Government service he carried out his duties ably and conscientiously. I have no reason to conclude that Mr. Philby has at any time betrayed the interests of this country, or to identify him with the so-called "Third Man", if indeed there was one* [my italics]. . . . A number of Foreign Service officers who had associated, as office colleagues or outside, with Maclean and Burgess were examined by the Foreign Office security service. If, of course, any evidence not already available can be produced by anybody either inside or outside this House, I trust that it will be made available to the authorities.'

All politicians err; and their errors often deserve to be remembered and held against them. Harold Macmillan, magnanimously determined not to tilt the delicate balance between national security and an individual's rights under the law, went too far in the wrong direction. The facts never warranted this degree of generosity towards Philby, though no MP who took part in that long and absorbing debate disputed the ancient principle that a man must be presumed innocent until proved guilty. Herbert Morrison contented himself with a superfluous demand for a thorough enquiry into the Foreign Office. Other MPs, including the scathing Richard Crossman, condemned the élitist autonomy of that department and echoed Morrison's call. The impenitent Marcus Lipton would not, however, immediately withdraw his earlier charge in which he had named Philby as the Third Man.

Nor would he be gagged by indignant colleagues chanting: 'Say it outside.' Parliamentary privilege safeguarded Lipton from libel, but some sixth sense also told him that Harold Macmillan had badly overplayed his hand. 'I am absolutely convinced that I'm serving the public interest,' Lipton said, 'by forcing the Government, and in particular the Foreign Secretary, to provide much more information than has been provided hitherto.'

It fell to Dick Brooman-White to deplore the callow irresponsibility of a fellow Member for 'directing public suspicion on an individual against whom nothing at all has been proved. We must leave it to his own conscience to straighten out what that may cost in personal suffering to the wife, children and friends of the person involved. . . . In a very minor way, this is our Alger Hiss affair, and the remarks of the honourable and gallant Member have shown how near to the wind it is possible even for the House of Commons to sail.'

But the last dozen words uttered by Marcus Lipton, almost in a defeatist aside, rang on in Brooman-White's ears, while a nervous and subdued Anthony Eden wound up with an appeal for public confidence in the much-maligned Foreign Office and the promise of a Privy Councillor's enquiry into its administration. Lipton had said: 'Even Mr Philby has not asked for it to be repeated outside.'[45] That challenge could no longer be ignored. Brooman-White urged Philby that very evening to force Lipton to eat his words by inviting him to repeat them outside the sacrosanct arena of the Commons. The same idea had already occurred to Philby: 'I've arranged to meet the press, here in my mother's flat, tomorrow morning,' he said.[46]

The press conference proved a resounding personal triumph for Philby. 'C' had readily sanctioned it, much to the dismay of Dick White and his colleagues in security; and Philby prepared his lines with meticulous care. The journalists who crowded into his mother's flat were first handed a typed statement, aptly described since as 'a model of hypocrisy'.[47] The Official Secrets Act, fortified by Philby's natural desire to help the authorities, had sealed his lips and would necessarily continue to do so, regardless of his personal inclinations. His air of candour and geniality disarmed many of his questioners. Yes, he admitted, his association with Burgess in Washington had been imprudent and had led to his resignation. No, he stressed, 'I have never been a Communist,' despite holding leftish views: 'the last time I spoke to a Communist was, I think, in 1934.' He was safe enough trotting out such bare-faced lies since Dick White's boys alone could deny it – and Dick White's boys would never do so in public and in any case had already been hopelessly outmanoeuvred by events. As for old friends and acquaintances who knew parts of the truth about his past, they would be most unlikely to split hairs after Harold Macmillan's unexpectedly fulsome tribute to the so-called 'Third Man' in the House of Commons. So much in command was Philby that not once did he break into his accustomed stammer. Only when asked to comment on Lipton's charge against him, did he temper urbanity with a flash of anger.

'Ah, Lipton,' he said. 'That brings us to the heart of the matter.' The gallant colonel had two options: he should either tell the security authorities exactly what he knew; or, if he dared, repeat his accusation on an unprivileged occasion outside Parliament and take the legal consequences. Philby's statement made headlines. He could not complain of receiving a bad press, but the hoped-for withdrawal by Marcus Lipton did not come at once. The MP for Brixton met Roger Hollis, Dick White's enigmatic deputy, and had to acknowledge that his charge against Philby was based on hearsay evidence only. So very reluctantly, towards the end of that momentous week, Lipton rose in his place at Westminster and made honourable amends.

'I think Colonel Lipton has done the right thing,' was Philby's terse public comment. 'As far as I am concerned, the incident is closed.'[48]

Philby had slipped quite easily again through Dick White's fingers, but his sense of elation was well controlled. How he longed to put an ocean between himself and the place of his unnaturally protracted trial by public ordeal; and when he received an unlooked-for chance to work in Ireland as a literary collaborator with a well-wisher, he snatched it gratefully. The offer came from a former colleague at the British Embassy in Ankara, W. E. D. Allen, who had served there as press counsellor in Philby's day. Allen wanted help with the compiling of a history about his family's business firm in Cappagh, County Waterford. Philby's stay in this pleasantly relaxing Irish backwater lasted several months. The experience helped him gradually to recover his old zest and poise. It was a blessing to be out of Britain in February 1956, for instance, and again in April of that year. The official presentation to the world of Maclean and Burgess at a hastily arranged press conference in Moscow on 11 February gave Philby quite a turn, though he had little reason for astonishment, except perhaps momentarily to wonder at the timing. And if he did idly question why the Soviet Union had kept their guests in cold storage for so long, Philby soon found a ready answer in Anthony Eden's friendly invitation to the Russian leaders, Bulganin and Khrushchev, to visit Britain. Unfortunately, Anglo-Soviet harmony was somewhat strained in the event by the attempt of a British naval frogman, Commander 'Buster' Crabb, to examine, unasked and at close range, the hull of the Soviet cruiser peacefully anchored off Portsmouth on which the two leaders had sailed from Russia. The frogman was never seen alive again. Naturally, the Kremlin's new overlords protested fiercely to their bewildered hosts. Someone else had blundered again. In fact, what has been described to me since as 'an appalling failure in communications between SIS and the Admiralty' caused acute embarrassment to Eden and his Cabinet. It undoubtedly led to the early retirement of Sir John Sinclair as 'C' and to his replacement by the younger and more sophisticated Dick White, the first MI5 officer of non-military background to preside over the secret service.[49]

One of Sinclair's last kindnesses before his departure had opened up new and exciting vistas to Philby. The chance of permanent employment as a foreign correspondent was one he relished, and 'C' was prodded once more by the dogged Brooman-White into prodding other senior men in the Foreign Office to 'do the right thing'. Towards the end of his temporary Irish assignment, Philby learnt of these hopeful overtures. A discreet, informal approach had been made to David Astor, the editor of the *Observer*, whom Muggeridge had already sounded on Philby's behalf some four years earlier. Astor, a man of instinctive sensitivity, agreed that nothing could be less fair than that 'so able a man should find difficulty earning a living as a journalist, now that he had full clearance from the Foreign Secretary'. Through a joint arrangement with the editor of the *Economist*, Donald Tyerman, Astor agreed to share 'Mr Philby's services in the Middle East.'[50] The offer was too good to turn down. It was then that Sinclair, for reasons which somewhat baffled an old and once-valued colleague, invited Philby to drop in for a chat. It seemed amazing that 'C' should be so keen to right an imagined wrong that he, too, wanted to re-engage a reject for secret work on a freelance basis under his respectable journalistic cover. Yet so it proved, a weird turnabout which gave Philby food for careful thought.

His Soviet friends reassured him. They were not displeased, though Sinclair and SIS insisted that their newly re-employed operator should confine himself strictly to non-Communist targets. The two London editors, of course, were told nothing about their Middle East representative's clandestine commitment. Nor did Dick White discover the details until he took over from Sinclair towards the end of 1956. Anything but amused at his predecessor's soft-heartedness, White refrained from vetoing a transaction which, because of its very irregularity, could perhaps still serve to enmesh an undesirable adventurer whom the new 'C' still impenitently suspected of treachery.

Before the memory of Philby's Houdini-like escape from the tentacles of his Establishment persecutors had faded, two of his former colleagues, Graham Greene and Malcolm Muggeridge, chanced to be passing the time of day together in the vicinity of Crowborough. Knowing that only the spirit of Kim lived on in the place, they were guided by whimsical curiosity up the suburban road to the large, empty house surrounded by a jungle of unkempt garden. Aileen Philby, now separated from her husband and said to be mentally disturbed, had long ago given up the unequal struggle to make a home for the wanderer. Within a year of her husband's abortive trial-by-press-and-Lipton, she would return briefly, to die alone of neglect and an apparent overdose of drugs and alcohol in that cheerless, uncomfortable barracks.[51]

On the day Greene and Muggeridge walked up and peered through the letterbox at the piles of unopened circulars, empty milk bottles, spiders' webs and unpaid bills, the place already exuded an air of melancholy and total abandonment. Kim's caravan had moved on. Under the impetus of whatever devil possessed him, this man, of whom they were still fond if slightly unsure, was apparently settling down to another lease of life beneath his father's roof in an Arab village among the foothills above Beirut. How appropriate, Muggeridge reflected, that Harry St John Philby, too, should be on the run at his advanced age. Exiled from Saudi Arabia by one of the late King's less tolerant sons, who could no longer bear the waspish tongue and rank mismanagement of an arrogant English adviser and trader who had overstayed his welcome, Philby *père* had temporarily withdrawn to the white stone village house to which Philby *fils*, the journalist, had come for temporary refuge.

The two impish pilgrims to Crowborough felt sorry for Kim while reserving judgement on his innocence. Macmillan's testimonial had been altogether too glowing, leaving out Kim's inherent deviousness. They hoped Macmillan was right; but with their separate and highly sceptical views of human conduct in general, and of the extreme gullibility of the British political animal in particular, they could not help wondering. Scourges of the Establishment before the word itself crept into currency in the mid fifties, these improbable ex-secret servicemen derided the antics of the new breed of pygmies posing as Churchillian giants who had lately been entrusted with the nation's affairs. As Muggeridge expressed it: 'There's nothing on earth less edifying or more ludicrous than the spectacle of the ruling class on the run.'[52]

Eden's Suez 'adventure' in the dying months of 1956 epitomized Muggeridge's harsh verdict. The pathos of the affair lay only partly in the illusions of a Prime Minister seemingly afflicted by *folie de grandeur*. After the Egyptian leader's unilateral takeover of the Suez

Canal, Nasser became, in Eden's feverish eyes, an Arab reincarnation of Hitler. At all costs the shame of a Middle East Munich must be averted, even if it meant Britain's fighting alone. The prospect made his Chiefs of Staff tremble, since they lacked the conventional means in a nuclear age for long-range combined operations at short notice. Legally the British had no standing, having withdrawn from the Suez Canal Zone under the Anglo-Egyptian agreement signed by Eden in October 1954. The French, humiliated in Indo-China and heavily embroiled again in Algeria, were more eager for action than the British, while the Israelis, for narrow tactical reasons of their own, quietly colluded with the French: they simply wanted to clear the Egyptians out of Sinai.

Ironically, the British Cabinet at no point fully consulted or confided in the diplomatic and secret services.[53] John Foster Dulles and his brother Allen of the CIA were better informed from their own worldwide sources. Thus, like a stealthy megalomaniac, Eden led his ministers into what Sir Oliver Franks termed 'a collective aberration'; ignoring Eisenhower in the throes of his re-election campaign and bypassing the United Nations organization into the bargain. Eden's vain hope was that the normally amiable and amenable 'Ike' would understand. The Chancellor of the Exchequer adopted the same absurdly simplistic view. Macmillan, who had since moved from the Foreign Office to the Treasury, felt certain that 'once Great Britain took action Ike would "lie doggo" and let them get on with it'. As the Dulles's biographer noted, 'It was the costliest miscalculation the British ever made.'[54]

While the Anglo-French invasion force was sailing from Malta and Cyprus towards Port Said, closely observed by U2 reconnaissance aircraft and the United States Sixth Fleet, Frank Wisner of the CIA's Munich station felt deeply aggrieved. Eden's military adventure

> was in danger of sabotaging the best chance the CIA had had since the war to overturn Soviet hegemony in eastern Europe. . . . Now it was Hungary's turn. There the revolution was in full flood. . . . Anti-Soviet

rebels had taken over the Hungarian capital. . . . [Wisner] asked for an airlift to provide them with immediate supplies of arms and trained reinforcements. . . .[55]

Allen Dulles would not hear of it, certainly not at the climax of a presidential election campaign, though it must be doubted whether the United States would ever have intervened to prevent the crushing by Soviet tanks of the Budapest uprising. Eisenhower's annoyance with Eden for keeping him in the dark about Suez was hardly genuine. His own Secretary of State knew everything about the planned operation from the American Joint Chiefs of Staff, who had been duly informed at every stage by their hapless British counterparts. The scuttle from Suez after the United Nations' prompt call for a cease-fire was influenced less by threats of Soviet retaliation than by the slowness of the US Treasury in meeting Harold Macmillan's panic-stricken request for a billion dollar loan to prop up the tottering pound.

Philby took in the whole fiasco and its aftermath of bitter recrimination with understandable detachment. Suez had not been a traditional gentleman's war. A passive spectator now, he would go no further than to dissemble his thoughts for the benefit of subscribers to the *Observer* and the *Economist*. His eccentric father had no inkling whatever of the son's secret life. Kim was in his forty-sixth year, prematurely middle-aged, a tired adventurer who needed a respite to take stock of the future. When St John patched up his disagreement with the Saudi royal household, returning before the end of 1956 to the desert kingdom, the son did not leave his father's conveniently cheap and remote abode. His routine of work enabled him to divide the weeks and months unevenly between Beirut, with its bars and bustle and shop-talk, the Arab world beyond Lebanon whenever developments justified the journeys and expenditure, and the isolated village base in the hills. His paymasters recognized the professional touch in his well-informed despatches. These would go through to London punctually and without fail. So for the next three and a half years, interrupted only by rare flights back to Britain for such contingencies as the funeral of his wife Aileen, Philby led a half-hidden existence. Mentally he had slipped into neutral. He afterwards wrote:

> It has been generally assumed that I was working under journalistic cover for SIS. Indeed, it would have been odd if they had made no use of me at all. They habitually use journalists, and there I was, with a sound knowledge of their requirements and more anxious than anyone to be in their good books. I would like to assure my Arab friends who may read this book [that] I do not think I did their cause any disservice by telling the British Government what they really thought; in any case, the British paid scant notice. . . .[56]

To be fair to Dick White and SIS, there were more pressing matters to handle than keeping the solitary freelance Philby in play. Frayed links with the CIA had to be renewed and strengthened, damaged networks in eastern Europe repaired and reactivated. Under the benevolent eye of Britain's fourth post-war leader, Harold Macmillan, a politician whose patrician affectations concealed a compassionate heart and a cool, calculating brain, the nation began to adjust itself to a lower and humbler place among the Great Powers. In the aftermath of Suez, this process of slow adjustment to reality was not achieved without pain or regret. As citizens of a small, offshore island which, within living memory, had been the hub of a mighty worldwide Empire, the British people were in no bigger hurry than the outcast Kim Philby to decide where their future lay. Between nominal leadership of a disintegrating Commonwealth and a partnership in the new-fangled and currently unattractive European Economic Community of the Six, there seemed little advantageous to choose. They were suffering from deep psychological wounds, some of them recently self-inflicted. History had not merely caught up with them but appeared to be passing them by. Increasingly they were being forced to accept the status of poor second cousins in their so-called 'special relationship' with the United States, to become introspective onlookers rather than instinctive policy-makers. Since British influence had ceased to count for much in the unsettled Middle East, the Russians were moving in and vying with the Americans as the new friends and protectors of Arab nationalism. It was a useful arena for any double agent of Philby's experience and adventurous calibre.

> If it would have been odd of SIS not to take advantage of my presence in the Middle East, it would have been odder still if the Soviet intelligence service had ignored me. The fact is that the Soviet Union is interested in a very wide range of Middle East phenomena. Enjoying a wide margin of priority at the top of the list are the intentions of the United States and British governments in the area. For an assessment of such intentions, I was not too badly placed....[57]

Here Philby was putting the best face on the marginal value of any background information he collected in the ordinary journalistic rounds. No doubt he dressed up the material well, but its quality was always second hand and usually thin. Like Burgess in his pre-war role as a freelance purveyor of political intelligence to the British and Russians alike, Philby managed to line his pockets at the expense of London as well as Moscow. Whether the KGB thought they were getting their money's worth may be questioned. Certainly SIS often felt that, for so seasoned an operator, Philby was not trying too hard. Both sides now suspected him but paid on the nail, if not too cheerfully. There was no other method of keeping him in play and under scrutiny.

Then, all of a sudden, in early 1959, there came a sea-change in the style and pace of his hitherto easy and secluded existence. He had first encountered Eleanor, the wife of Sam Pope Brewer of the *New York Times*, at the bar of the St George's Hotel in Beirut, barely a month after his arrival. They at once took to one another; and presently Philby's apparently profound and deepening emotional dependence on this simple, affectionate but unhappily married American, some two years younger than himself, captivated her completely. Eleanor Brewer's retrospective account of their relationship, first as lovers and later as a wedded couple, underlines both the insidious charm with which he overwhelmed her and the skill with which he shut her out from the secret world he had for so long inhabited.

When Sam Pope Brewer, who remembered this English interloper from Spanish Civil War days, realized what was happening and finally barred Philby from his home, the couple started to live together openly and Eleanor sought a divorce from her husband. The couple endured with the impatient ardour of younger lovers the separations enforced by his intermittent journeying to Iraq, Saudi Arabia, the Yemen and other parts of his wide 'beat', then by her absence for a whole year in the United States. Their reunions were all the sweeter for the partings. Eleanor's Mexican divorce was granted on 4 July 1958, a portentous Independence Day indeed in the sad life of the third Mrs Philby. Because of legal delays and complications, she had six more months to wait before their civil marriage in London, on 24 January 1959. The two witnesses at Holborn Register Office were Tim Milne of SIS, an admiring friend of Kim's since their school days together at Westminster, and Jack Ivens, another devoted colleague of the war days who had been the first to extend a practical, helping hand during the bleak years of disgrace by offering Kim temporary work in his orange-importing business. The ever-loyal Dick Brooman-White, too, saw something of the newly-weds before their return to the Middle East; so did Nicholas Elliott, though somewhat more briefly, on one of his routine visits to headquarters from his SIS station in Vienna. Close mutual friends and advocates of Philby, both Brooman-White and Elliott remarked that he could now laugh off the memory of his ordeal by bureaucratic suspicion and procrastination as if it had been someone else's misfortune. At least all was well that ended well: in eight and a half years of sluggish and ineffectual endeavour, the Security Directorate had failed to substantiate its suspicions of Philby's alleged complicity in the espionage activities of Burgess and Maclean.

It is worth recalling here that Sir Claude Elliott, the Provost of Eton at this time, had once been responsible as headmaster of the college for rejecting a job application from the young Guy Burgess.[58] Sir Claude was the father of Nicholas Elliott; and the son took pride in possessing a similar dispassionate concern for truth and fairness. In the case of Philby, he had striven from the start to preserve 'an open mind', uncluttered by false sentimentality. Kim, in Elliott's judgement, had been unduly and unjustly harried. The suspect deserved a break. Ever since Dick White, the former Security Chief, had stepped into the shoes of Sinclair, there had been less bickering and bad blood between the rival branches of the service. Perhaps that was a sign of progress; only time would tell.

Pleasant and approachable as Dick White continued to be, the new 'C' was a deep and exceptionally patient person, who kept his own counsel. Unlike his near-namesake, Brooman-White, he was more than ever convinced of Philby's guilt. He believed that eventually positive proof of that guilt would come to light. With this in mind, and weighing Elliott's open-minded bias in Kim's favour against Elliott's integrity and quick-wittedness, Dick White presently took a bold decision. In the early summer of 1959, when the station director's post in Beirut fell vacant, he sent for Elliott and asked him whether he would like it. Perhaps because of, rather than in spite of, the intimate knowledge and experience he had acquired in recent years of Soviet and European affairs, Elliott wanted a change and accepted the offer gladly.

It naturally crossed his mind that his paths and Philby's would shortly converge again; but the newly appointed station director hardly expected to run into his friend as quickly as he did:

> On the very day I disembarked with my wife after the voyage through the Mediterranean to Beirut Harbour, we went to a restaurant I remembered from a holiday visit long before and found the Philbys lunching at a table nearby. It was a most agreeable reunion.[59]

And that chance meeting marked the opening of a fresh and seemingly carefree chapter in the personal and official relationships between them. For the next two and half sunlit years, nothing outwardly marred the sense of harmony and reciprocal trust. As Eleanor Philby noted, Nicholas Elliott at once said to her husband: 'Fill me in, old boy,' and leaned on Kim as his unofficial adviser on the bewildering complexities of Arab politics. 'They used to meet once or twice a week, vanishing into another room, and leaving me to gossip with his wife.'[60] Eleanor was idyllically happy. As for Kim, he seemed to relish the confidence reposed in him by a man he had always liked, emerging gradually from his previous seclusion without any apparent inhibitions. During this protracted honeymoon period his concern to help Elliott, sometimes at the expense of journalistic commitments which had begun to bore him, mesmerized and deceived nearly everyone, his Soviet friends and himself included. If Eleanor had no inkling whatever of the 'monstrous and prolonged confidence trick' that was about to be played on her, Kim's Russian mentors must sometimes have anxiously asked themselves which side this double agent, whom they jealously thought of as 'ours', imagined he was playing for, and when the strange confusion of his loyalties would cease.

Precisely how, when and where Dick White unearthed tell-tale evidence of Philby's continuing meetings with KGB agents in the area remains a well-guarded secret. Elliott had no suspicions, indeed, no grounds for any as yet. It is not improbable that the CIA, which sedulously kept its distance but had by no means lost interest in Philby's activities, provided White with a few early and useful pointers. Certainly, after Philby's escape and in the course of Eleanor's first visit to London during the late spring of 1963, Dick White astounded her when he said to her simply: 'We have definitely known for the last seven years that Kim has been working for the Russians.'[61] And as if to prove that he was not bluffing or merely being wise after the event, the head of SIS had shown her a plainly recognizable photograph of the same Soviet intelligence officer who had visited her flat not many days before in a vain attempt to persuade Eleanor not to fly to London but to rejoin her husband on Russian soil. Regardless of Philby's insistence, in self-justifying retrospect, that he never strayed from his true allegiance, spurning as undeserved and unfitting the very title of 'double agent', there can be no doubt that he played unwittingly into Dick White's hands by his over-generous response to Nicholas Elliott's reliance on Kim's grasp of local issues. He served both sets of masters, British and Russian, with as much or as little loyalty as the restless Burgess had done in his inglorious heyday. The restricted and 'marked' confidences he passed on methodically to his Soviet friends could hardly have failed to make Moscow wonder; but the dangers of his ambivalent position were obscured both by the approbation of Elliott and by the comforting warmth of an adoring wife whom he loved after his fashion.

Another startling development, unknown to Philby, had meanwhile happened at home. It passed off quietly inside SIS headquarters.

Harold Nicolson had written in his diary on 7 June 1951:

> If I thought that Guy was a brave man, I should imagine that he had gone to join the Communists. As I know him to be a coward, I suppose that he was suspected of passing things on to the Bolshies, and realizing his guilt, did a bunk. . . . I fear all this will mean a witch-hunt.[62]

There had been no witch-hunt, except by sections of the press against the palsied response of the Foreign Office and the helplessness of the security authorities. Few individuals had volunteered information since then. Yet thirteen years after the reappearance of Burgess and Maclean in Moscow, 'Maurice', the Fourth Man, belatedly called on the security authorities to confess all he knew about the past links between himself and his fellow conspirators. His motives for coming forward were mixed. Fear that Burgess might 'get in first' and reveal the worst to the world at large may well have clinched his decision to speak. No bargains were struck in advance: 'Maurice' was scarcely in any position to bargain. Nevertheless, like 'Basil' in Washington before him, he received in the utmost secrecy the equivalent of a 'Royal Pardon' for turning Queen's evidence and contritely unfolding his own secondary but guilty role in the nefarious exploits of Burgess, Maclean and, to a lesser extent, of Philby. Dick White had no authority to promise 'Maurice' unconditional favours; but those above him could and did exercise their discretion. Because 'Maurice' had owned up, quite of his own accord, submitting vital evidence which threw new light on the subversive practitioners of the past thirty-five years, leniency doubtless seemed the sensible and proper course. It was not a decision which either the popular press or the vigilantes at Westminster would have understood or endorsed. Whether legal opinion would have unanimously approved this extra-legal line of prudent clemency may equally be questioned. Nevertheless, what was the alternative?

A sensational arrest, then another somewhat tardy treason trial held *in camera*? It was too ghoulish for any British government to contemplate.

Britain had done enough agonizing over the distemper of the thirties. The Foreign Office as well as secret intelligence were all the better for the internal reforms and the 'positive vetting' procedure introduced after the Burgess and Maclean nightmare. A further complication which possibly clinched the case for a gratuitous pardon was the public eminence of the Fourth Man. Not that anyone suggested that equality before the law, any more than the prerogative of mercy, could be airily trifled with; it was simply that 'Maurice' had won such renown in his own field that he had been signally honoured. To drag him into court might fortuitously embroil many eminent people, perhaps even the Royal Family itself, in scandal and controversy. 'Maurice's' voluntary confession could not have been more awkward. It was as if an over-scrupulous Archbishop of Canterbury had felt impelled to admit that invincible doubts about the Thirty-nine Articles were the result of reckless dabbling in witchcraft and black magic as a young curate. In the case of 'Maurice', no equivalent of a consistorial tribunal could have been appealed to; common sense and a sprinkling of compassion had to be exercised instead. So 'Maurice' remained a free man, though not exactly a happy one.[63]

In the far more traumatic dénouement of the Philby case, the same delicate moral considerations still weighed with SIS and the Prime Minister. Macmillan wanted as far as possible to avoid another needless public sensation, with the inevitable retractions and all the eating of words that would obviously involve. Dick White, for his part, was just as determined to bring the accused home to face his just deserts as soon as the last bit of irrefutable evidence against him could be obtained. The confession of 'Maurice' had helped only a little. It enabled the security authorities to piece together some corners of the unfinished jigsaw. They now knew more about the invisible threads binding together the main conspirators from Cambridge days onwards, but they lacked conclusive proof of Philby's leading role later. Then, like a lightning flash, there came that stroke of good luck which the persistent White had long been awaiting. In the last days of 1961 another Soviet spy defected.

Anatoli M. Golitsin was no ordinary defector. A bigger and more important catch than Vladimir Petrov, he gave himself up to the CIA after disappearing from Helsinki and at once identified himself to American counter-intelligence experts as 'a major in the First Chief Directorate of the KGB working primarily against targets in the NATO alliance'.[64] James Angleton of the CIA was naturally interested in what Golitsin had to say about Philby; but his main concern lay in eliciting every particle of information to support the defector's allegation that the KGB had 'already planted an agent within the highest echelons of United States intelligence'.[65] The debriefing went on for weeks. Finally, Angleton handed the Russian over to SIS for further interrogation. By the early summer of 1962, Dick White's unremitting suspicions about Philby were duly confirmed, one by one, in the light of earlier defectors' testimony. The case against the accused was brought up to date. It thoroughly vindicated the new 'C's' unsupported hunch, even partly excusing those wild and, at the time, unhelpful charges of Marcus Lipton, MP. Only the manner of confronting the culprit now remained to be settled.

As the Prime Minister insisted, the British had no jurisdiction in Lebanon, so there could be no question of trying to assassinate, arrest or even abduct Philby there. Whether the CIA, still less the KGB, would have scrupled about such legal niceties is irrelevant and academic; SIS had no powers and precious few means to act otherwise than it did. Assassination, above all, was unthinkable. Yet White badly wanted to bring back Philby for the final round of cross-examination. He hoped, perhaps somewhat foolhardily, that Philby would agree to return of his own free will, once he realized that the game was up.

None of these disturbing developments reached the ears of the untroubled Middle East correspondent as he went about his routine work that summer. Characteristically, his Soviet friends, in particular the Counsellor at the local embassy whom he met most frequently, kept him in the dark about Golitsin and the probable consequences of his disclosures. They treated their agent much as he would have expected, indeed exactly as he himself had treated Maclean in his hours of self-doubting and uncertainty. For the same salutary reasons, Philby had 'no need to know'. He bore himself with his customary self-possession. Observant friends and acquaintances among the resident journalists and diplomats thought of him as a man without a care in the world, good at his job, happy with his new wife, an amusingly urbane host who deserved respect for the courageous way he had lived down the past and rehabilitated himself. Eleanor Philby adored him – that was clear to everyone. The couple sometimes travelled together when an assignment took Kim off to another part of the Arab world, not excluding Saudi Arabia where Kim's eccentric father had resumed his influential advisory post at the King's right hand. Her father-in-law had written at once on learning of the marriage: 'Welcome into the Philby family. And all my best wishes to you both for a long and happy life together.'

From early January 1959 the couple had occupied

> a fifth-floor apartment in the rue Kantari, whose main feature was a large, semi-circular terrace commanding a great sweep of mountain and sea. . . . This flat gradually filled with the loot of our Middle East trips, oriental rugs, pictures, archaeological treasures, and my own sculptures. . . . On Saturday mornings, when Kim would be on the alert for any last-minute news-break for the *Observer*, we would pick up our mail at the Normandy Hotel before going across at noon to the St George's to see what the other journalists were up to. But the Normandy was our home base – it was like an extension of our own flat.[66]

Eleanor now accepted that there was a hidden side of her husband's life from which he debarred her. His secretiveness about the extra work she presumed he was doing for British intelligence did not trouble her at first; it struck her as a conventional pose rather than a natural ingrained habit. Only slowly was she forced to revise that kindly judgement. Their early years together were, she admitted, the most blissful she had ever known. It was after the sudden death of Kim's father, on the way home from a conference of Orientalists in Moscow, that Eleanor began to notice that her husband appeared to be undergoing exceptionally heavy strain. As his sole remedy for this was excessive drinking, she began to worry as well. Two days of extreme conviviality had preceded, and no doubt precipitated, Harry St John Philby's fatal heart attack as he lay in bed at the Normandy Hotel, Beirut, on 30 September 1960. On the other hand, the old eccentric had enjoyed a good innings. He breathed his last with the mild complaint on his lips that he was feeling 'bored'. While Eleanor recognized Kim's unbounded affection for this exceptional father, whose independence the son strove to emulate in his own fashion, she could not understand the extremity of his reaction: 'Kim,' she declared, 'was shattered and drank himself senseless. It was several days before he could settle down to answer letters of condolence.' There was worse to come. This sentimental lover, so kind to animals, as attentive to her only daughter as to his own children, so enthusiastic a cook and a conversationalist, showed increasing signs of instability. Yet his wife could never reach him when he fell to brooding introspection. Only the bottle – 'snakebite' was his word for it – could ease the mysterious pain by drowning it.

It was hardly astonishing that the climactic year of unhappiness was the year 1962, notably its final quarter. By then Eleanor had grown used to manifestations

> of strange, unexplained tensions in his life. As the year wore on, these became worse and were reflected in bouts of deep depression and drinking. Now I know that he sensed the net closing around him and that his active career as a Soviet agent was drawing to a close.[67]

The recall to London in April 1961 of George Blake, a secret agent Philby knew of but had barely met, and whose espionage exploits for Soviet Russia were unknown to him, served as an early warning of the occupational risks run by all double agents. The savage sentence of forty-two years' imprisonment passed on Blake must have forcibly convinced Philby that he could expect no mercy from British justice if he were unlucky enough to be unmasked, trapped and brought to court. There could never be any bargaining with a man as unrelenting as Dick White; and if Philby knew the man, White would wait until he had the necessary evidence to put him away for life. So during the fifteen months that passed before the Russians decided to confide the grim news of Golitsin's defection and of the damning testimony he had undoubtedly given to the Americans and the British, Philby's nerve progressively gave way. Though he did not much care for the prospect of ending his days like Burgess and Maclean as a Soviet pensioner in an alien land, the new 'C' left him precious little choice.

One of his sons, Harry, was staying with Kim and his wife during the second half of 1962. Eleanor's daughter, Annie, was good company for the boy. Solicitous for the feelings of the young, Philby put himself out to amuse them and behaved perfectly almost until the end. Their last happy outing together was a sight-seeing trip to Jordan early in September. Eleanor had a slight premonition that something untoward had cropped up when Kim came in one evening and casually announced that he would have to return alone to Beirut at once, leaving her to bring back the children leisurely. She packed up and went home next morning only to find Kim hopelessly drunk and incoherent with grief on the terrace of the flat. The ostensible cause of his terrifying despondency was the death of their pet vixen, which had either fallen, or been pushed, from the balcony to the ground below; but Eleanor knew that something more dire had driven him to drink. She did not press him to tell her what it was. That, she knew, would have been utterly useless. Whatever the real cause of his dread, he took his own remedy for killing the pain more and more frequently afterwards.

Dick White pondered hard before deciding how best to confront Philby with the truth, far away and on neutral territory. The ideal person for the task, he concluded, would not be Nicholas Elliott's successor in Beirut, with whom Philby had seemingly little or nothing in common. Who else could be sent? White was still casting about carefully for the most acceptable substitute when Elliott knocked on his door one day and, without beating about the bush, volunteered to go out himself and bring the miscreant to heel. He admitted that Philby had taken him in, not only during the recent Middle East assignment but ever since 1951. Elliott swore not to exceed his brief, coldly angry though he now was. He would first make Philby confess that he had spied for the Soviet Union by producing the evidence. His second and more exacting objective would be to draw him out on precise targets and methods used so as to assess the damage Philby had done. The third would be to persuade him, without making false promises, that the only sane course left was to return with Elliott and take his medicine.

White had no doubts about extracting a general confession. Golitsin's evidence was clear-cut. The big uncertainty concerned Philby's present state of mind. By all accounts he appeared to be on top of his work and living a reasonably quiet life, apart from his freelance spying activities for the British and the Russians. Provided that Elliott played him along skilfully, Philby might cave in completely. Nothing on the file, none of the information White had acquired in twelve painstaking years of examining and re-examining the man's tastes and habits, suggested that Kim Philby was an ideologue who would willingly cut his losses, bolt, and cheerfully settle in Moscow.

By early January 1963, when Elliott had prepared himself for a battle of wits he was determined to win, his adversary and erstwhile friend had lost his stomach for a dramatic personal confrontation. The ex-station director arrived, unannounced, on 10 January. Elliott rang up Philby, not from the British Embassy, but from a private flat he had rented. 'You owe me a drink,' said the unsuspecting Kim at their first encounter. 'I haven't had one since my birthday on New Year's Day.' His head was still swathed in a bandage, and he explained how, after celebrating not wisely but too well at an American party, he had fallen down and cracked his skull against a radiator in the bathroom at home. The wound had had to be stitched in hospital. The preliminary pleasantries over, Elliott went to the attack brutally and without a shred of compunction. 'You took me in for years,' he said. 'Now I'll get the truth out of you even if I have to drag it out.' Philby was thunderstruck. He listened without a word to Elliott's unanswerable indictment, delivered in a suddenly calm, business-like manner, on the basis of the latest Soviet defector's detailed testimony. He seemed to be crushed by the weight of it, the sheer bulk of it, the fatal accuracy of it. The accuser kept reminding the accused of his unforgivable personal duplicity: 'I once looked up to you, Kim. My God, how I despise you now. I hope you've enough decency left to understand why.'

Having softened him up, Elliott started to interrogate Philby, forcing him step by step to describe how, when, and where he had been recruited, his espionage training and activities before the war, his work as a double agent for the KGB and SIS during the war and since. The cornered Philby did not try to deny his complicity with Burgess and others in the escape of Maclean; and he recounted his own fears after Burgess's unintended departure with Maclean that nothing could save him then from falling into the trap, except the over-caution and scrupulosity of his interrogators. The confused circumstances leading to his premature trial-by-newspaper in 1955, at the time of the Petrov disclosures, had let him off the hook again, admittedly with the support of people like Elliott who still trusted him implicitly. Nor did he contest in further sessions the charge of having worked since in double-harness for both sides, though with far less scope and effect than previously.

If Philby still hedged about his contacts and methods and targets, that was natural enough. The details could wait, important as they were for evaluating damage done. Elliott had at any rate succeeded in extracting the general confession he had come for. There and then he asked Philby to write it down and sign it. He could not offer a blank cheque; but he could say that this voluntary written statement might stand Kim in good stead, especially if he would now agree to take the next sensible step of returning to London and clearing matters up once and for all. Philby hedged again. He would like more time, he said, to think it over. Perhaps they could resume their discussion at a later date? Elliott consulted with his superiors and had to leave it at that, returning alone to London after dining out with Eleanor and her husband and trying to appear as if nothing had intervened to destroy an old and treasured friendship.[68]

The Russians realized Philby's predicament. They may also have become as apprehensive about his continuing loyalty to them as about his declared inability to ward off the charges levelled by his interrogator. Perhaps the Russians, like Eleanor, were taken aback by the badly shaken nerves and extreme vulnerability of this formerly unflappable English agent of theirs. At any rate they would not hear of his waiting any longer, still less of his going back to London as Elliott had recommended. Once in London, they surmised, Philby would probably crack and break down. The time had come to set in motion the long-rehearsed emergency plan for spiriting him out of the country. Philby's relief was deep. Whether Nicholas Elliott would be more or less disappointed than Dick White to have seen the last of him, there could now be no way of telling. For the next few days, while the helpless Eleanor endeavoured to console him, he lay low. The recently appointed station director, Elliott's successor, was imprudent enough to invite him over for an interview at the British Embassy. Philby declined, pleading that he was unwell, but went on filing his copy as usual to the two editors in London. He was on the point of making a run for it; all he needed was the signal. The Russians kept him on tenterhooks. Not until the evening of Wednesday 23 January 1963, did he receive final clearance. He disappeared at once, cutting an invitation to dine with Eleanor and a number of other guests at the home of Glen Balfour-Paul, the First Secretary at the British Embassy.

'Daddy's going to be late,' his thirteen-year-old son, Harry, called to his stepmother when the telephone rang. 'He says he'll meet you at the Balfour-Pauls at eight.'[69]

When Philby failed to turn up, Eleanor's feelings were terribly confused. It had been a day of howling winds and torrential rain. She feared at first that he might have suffered a fatal accident. The embassy intelligence staff hung on, then informed Dick White in London that their quarry was missing, and White could not pretend to be completely surprised. Within the humane limits prescribed by traditional democratic procedures, SIS had gone as far as practicable to hold him. He had already confessed. Now he had compounded that act by fleeing to his so-called friends. It would have been more satisfactory had he given himself up, of course, but probably his nerve had failed him. One thing was certain: Kim Philby's grilling by the KGB would be as thorough and unrelenting as the grilling he would have undergone at the hands of SIS. He would have at least as much explaining to do as Burgess before his Soviet protectors finally accepted him at face value.

EPILOGUE

The CIA, which had been shadowing Philby for months, were convinced that his disappearance from Beirut had been hurriedly arranged by the Russians for his own safety; and Dick White's SIS colleagues were ruefully inclined to agree. Nicholas Elliott was recalled urgently from a tour of Central Africa and ordered back to Beirut, wondering whether Dick White had ever forewarned the American counter-intelligence specialist, Jim Angleton, of that recent and decisive confrontation with the downcast Kim.[1] The British Government, no doubt anxious to buy time, pretended that nothing at all had happened until the *Observer* forced Macmillan's hand. Their Middle East correspondent was missing. The newspaper could not explain how or why. The editor would have to replace him; so readers had the right to be informed. Naturally, after the initial announcement in the *Observer*, questions were asked in the House of Commons. It fell to the then Lord Privy Seal, Mr Edward Heath, to answer them somewhat dismissively. 'Since Mr Philby resigned from the Foreign Service in 1951,' he assured MPs, 'he has had no access to any official information.' Rumour and gossip could not be so easily stilled. Yet the press moved more circumspectly than of old. Had not Philby been handsomely cleared by the present Prime Minister? Clare Hollingworth of the *Guardian*, who had attended the dinner party at which the missing guest failed to arrive, at once filed a speculative story (on which her editor firmly sat), implying that Philby had enhanced his claims to the title of the Third Man by vanishing so abruptly, presumably aboard a Soviet freighter which had left Beirut homeward-bound late that same stormy night.[2]

Clare Hollingworth contained her frustration as best she could. It was appeased towards the end of June 1963, when the US magazine *Newsweek* declared positively and fearlessly that Philby was indeed the Third Man, that he had worked as a spy for the Soviet Union since early manhood, and that he was now almost certainly in Moscow. Heath returned to face questioners at Westminster and made a brave show of eating his words. Yes, he admitted, the Government could at last confirm the identity of the Third Man. However, with considerable political adroitness, Harold Macmillan averted the expected political tempest. Taking the Opposition leaders, Harold Wilson and George Brown, fully into his confidence, the Prime Minister briefed them on the background facts and managed to persuade them both that a touch of soft-pedalling would be in the public interest. Unfortunately, the story simply would not lie down or go away. The Soviet Union naturally saw to that, and the public throughout the free world did not complain unduly. The last illusions of Philby's dwindling bodyguard of admiring supporters in Britain were dispelled on 30 July 1963, the day on which Moscow sounded a triumphant fanfare for their latest hero. The Supreme Soviet had not merely granted Philby's request for political asylum, reported Tass, but had conferred on him the privileges of Russian citizenship as well.

Dick Brooman-White, MP, perhaps the most ardent believer in Philby's innocence, was severely shaken. His health had never been robust. He went into a decline and died on 25 January 1964, a year and two days after his own betrayal at Kim's hands. Eleanor Philby, though broken by the discovery that she had loved and married a fantasy, would not give him up without a fight. 'She really proved herself a woman as "gutsy" as Aileen, her predecessor,' said Nicholas Elliott.[3] Twice, in answer to her husband's pleas, she rejoined him in the Soviet capital. Twice she displayed a spirited independence of mind by returning alone to the West, the second time for good when it had become embarrassingly and sickeningly plain that the fickle Kim was bestowing amorous favours simultaneously on Melinda, the discontented wife of the morose, cuckolded Donald Maclean. Eleanor had noticed from the start how hard Philby worked to adjust himself to the grey, regimented monotony of existence in an alien environment. An abstraction which he had served from afar since youth with blind devotion had suddenly materialized as his home, his shrine, his final place of refuge. The handful of KGB agents selected for his initiation were not inconsiderate to Eleanor, though such was their relief at her refusal to stay with Kim in those dreary surroundings as just another concubine that they saw her off for the last time at the airport with a large bunch of tulips.[4]

The third Mrs Philby had also noticed in passing how pathetically hungry Kim always seemed to be for the 'approbation' of his hosts: throw him a few crumbs of praise, and his spirits would rise and respond like the tail of one of Pavlov's dogs. In remarking on this trait, Eleanor touched on one of the keys to his strangely warped character. Philby's Soviet protectors have exploited it shrewdly since for their own political and propaganda purposes.

Only once did he try to arrange another meeting with Nicholas Elliott, the colleague who had forced him to admit openly the extent of his double-dealing as an undercover spy. The letter was couched in friendly, persuasive terms. Philby wanted to clear up any lingering misunderstandings, so he suggested that Elliott should contrive to visit him at some convenient neutral point like Helsinki, but on no account to inform his superiors in advance. Elliott was tempted; then he showed the letter to Dick White, who promptly forbade him either to answer or act on it.[5]

The process of Philby's beatification as a spy-hero has gone on almost without interruption from 1963 until the present. Nor will it cease with his death. Given the modern cult of spy fiction, the Soviet propagandists were on fairly safe ground from the outset. Yet they had other intentions beside the routine one of denigrating the American and British secret services. In a sense, they have been driven by reasons of state to inflate the Philby legend out of all proportion to the slender merits, mixed motives and debatable exploits of the man himself. In fact, as Hugh Trevor-Roper alone among articulate Western critics has aptly stressed, the Soviet Union finds it necessary as well as expedient to create a new mythology of all their spies, including Burgess, Maclean and Philby, no matter how they came in from the cold to the promised land:

Recent events in Russia have revealed a situation which contrasts strikingly with the situation in the 1930s. Then the young intellectuals of the West, like Burgess, Maclean and Philby, dissatisfied with the social and moral 'contradictions' of their own society, looked east and saw an idealized Russian Communism as the hope of the future. Today the situation is exactly reversed. Today the young Russian intellectuals, impatient of the hypocrisy and tyranny of the Communist Party, look to the West, which they also perhaps idealize. The trial of Sinyavsky and Daniel, and its consequences, clearly show the disillusion of a generation....

A decade and more has passed since 1968, when Hugh Trevor-Roper was writing. There have been many more trials of dissidents, and not a few defections to the West, in the meantime. Building up the legends of Philby and other pseudo-heroes may have helped slightly to offset the more fundamental problem posed by dissident intellectuals inside the Soviet Union. The credibility gap between true heroes and false has been bridged partly because of the West's insatiable appetite for glamorous fiction about spies. Nevertheless, it is the average, servile Soviet citizen whom the propagandists are most anxious to brainwash and mislead. For, in Trevor-Roper's words, the dissidents have exposed a fossilized and repressive régime's 'waning power of attraction'. Hence the importance of spurious idols like Philby to bolster up morale:

Against the idealists at home, who goggle at the flickering multi-coloured lights of the West, it [the régime] points to the uncorrupted idealists of the West who, having looked more deeply into their own society, find that they prefer the pure, steady, incandescent eastern light....[6]

The trouble, of course, is that the Philbys, Macleans, Burgesses, Blakes, and other fugitive agents, alive or dead, are as outmoded and fossilized as the régime itself. And if the Soviet authorities cannot afford to recognize that fact, Soviet dissidents are not so willing to be deceived.

Philby himself has contributed to the perpetuation of his own legend by describing his adventures in *My Silent War*, an autobiography which understandably became a bestseller. For the attempts of successive British governments since 1951 to cover their confusion and embarrassment behind a cloak of silence merely goaded good investigative journalists to dig out as much of the truth about the careers of Britain's three known spies as could be dug within the limits of the Official Secrets Act. Philby's skilful but doctored personal account was perhaps meant to be the last, authoritative word on the subject. The praise heaped on his book by some critics was altogether too lavish and undiscriminating. It helped to place him, temporarily at least, among the immortals of the spy cult, much as his Soviet masters wished. To quote one of his former friends and colleagues, Malcolm Muggeridge:

> In the climate of ideological conflict, the spy is king. From Bulldog Drummond to James Bond, from Kipling's Kim to Kim Philby is the course our world has run. Philby, in other words, may be regarded as a real-life James Bond. His boozy amours, his tough postures, his intelligence expertise, are directly related to the same characteristics in Fleming's hero. . . .[7]

To that extent, Soviet propaganda has been successful, largely in the West. To scale the mythical hero down to ordinary life size, to see him as he really is and was, rather than in the glamorized terms his masters wish us to go on seeing him, should be the prime task of any contemporary historian worth his salt.

Another of Philby's war-time colleagues, the novelist Graham Greene, went clean overboard in a slightly mischievous effort to catch the paradoxical radiance of a traitor's tarnished halo. He asserted in the preface to the British edition of Philby's memoirs:

> Like many Catholics who, in the reign of Elizabeth, worked for the

victory of Spain, Philby has a chilling certainty in the correctness of his judgement, the logical fanaticism of a man who, having once found a faith, is not going to lose it because of the injustices or cruelties inflicted by erring human instruments. How many a kindly Catholic must have endured the long bad days of the Inquisition with this hope of the future as a riding anchor. Mistakes of policy would have no effect on his faith, nor the evil done by some of his leaders. If there was a Torquemada now, he would have known in his heart that one day there would be a John XXIII. . . .[8]

This was surely to exaggerate the quality of Philby's faith and the spiritual integrity of the man himself. Undoubtedly, his conversion to Communism was irreversible; but the trail of deliberate deceptions, the havoc of broken lives, the violent deaths, and the litter of falsehoods marking his nonchalant progress through adult life, suggest that Philby's faith was principally a corrupting and destructive force from early manhood onwards. It remains so still. Trevor-Roper properly rejects Graham Greene's far-fetched religious analogy as 'an engaging historical fantasy. . . . An argument which depends on telepathic foreknowledge of events 400 years later illustrated the ingenuity of the author. It does not illustrate much else.'[9]

It is reasonable to infer from the impressive catalogue of Philby's misdeeds that this pseudo-hero was drawn to Communism not so much by the crude simplicity of its dogma as by his own gargantuan appetite for power. The Soviet Union as such remained an abstraction; yet Stalin was far more real and attractive than the Gods of Christians and Muslims, for instance, since Stalin stood out as the embodiment of naked and absolute despotism. To serve that dictator and his successors, in the natural expectation of being rewarded here instead of hereafter, became Philby's *raison d'être*. As a result, not only his character but his mental and emotional growth were stunted. His spirit was hollow. Only a superman or a saint could have entered his secret world and emerged with faculties whole and unimpaired. Philby was neither. In that world where the partitions between reality and fantasy eventually overlap, causing such mental and moral confusion that even the subject's identity may easily become blurred, he behaved at times more like a devil in a gentleman's disguise.

Philby seems to have suffered less than most from the occupational hazards of the 'great game'. A sophisticated and charming veneer enabled him to take in nearly everyone who crossed his path. He was a very cool and calculating customer indeed. A born nihilist, who flourished in a nihilistic period, he was probably lucky to spin out so much time in the West. Had he been forced to escape, say, in 1951, the eve of Stalin's final purges, Philby's end might have been sudden and sticky. Since both Burgess and Maclean remained in some danger of liquidation while the dictator lived, the additional flight of the third and most important member of the central spy ring operating inside the British Establishment would not have amused the vengeful Stalin. Philby, according to his wife, was allowed to see his old friend Guy Burgess only once, and then very briefly, while Burgess lay on his deathbed. Under what Eleanor called the 'rigid discipline' to which her husband was subjected during his elaborate and lengthy debriefing, permission to attend Guy's funeral, at which Donald Maclean delivered the oration, was denied him. Characteristically, Philby did not complain, 'but I suspect,' said Eleanor, 'there were few things in life he would have liked more than a long, intimate, allusive dialogue with Burgess – just like old times. It might even have kept Burgess alive a little longer.'[10]

Unlike the compliant Philby and the conformist Maclean, Burgess never pretended to enjoy the drab anonymity of life in his Russian exile. Moreover, he loved the system and hated the people. According to the late Tom Driberg, who wrote his apologia and incidentally introduced him to the 'large underground urinal' in the centre of Moscow, which was 'open all night and frequented by hundreds of questing Slav homosexuals', the nonconformist Burgess nonetheless did command some respect from his official superiors. His political flair had not come amiss early in 1956, after the Suez fiasco and Eden's enforced retirement, when Burgess had advised, contrary to the prevailing wisdom, that Macmillan, not R. A. Butler, would be Britain's next Prime Minister.

'How on earth did you get it right?' Driberg asked him.

'Oh,' he replied, 'from a study of the life of the great Lord Salisbury. . . .'[11]

His work for the foreign department of the State Publishing House had not stretched his talents sufficiently, proud as he was of having persuaded his bureaucratic masters that the novels of E. M. Forster and Graham Greene deserved to be translated into Russian. Driberg remarked on his fondness for the English classics, which he would read over and over again, and for picking out, 'with two fingers', on a decrepit upright piano, hymn tunes remembered from schooldays at Eton long ago. Nostalgia for things past, regret at being cut off in an ice-bound backwater from the mainstream of bohemian gaiety, made Burgess more of a misfit in Moscow than he had ever been in London or Washington. The sensational articles, based on original material supplied by Goronwy Rees, which had appeared in the *People* before the end of 1956, did not unduly distress him: 'He probably needed the money,' Burgess said. 'He always did.'[12] Only the allegation that he had once made love to Maclean as a means of strengthening the latter's Communist views now seemed to offend his aesthetic sense: 'The idea of going to bed with Donald!' he spluttered. 'It would be like going to bed with a great white woman' – the lady in mind being Dame Nellie Melba.

Burgess had a retentive but highly selective memory, as became such a skilled embroiderer of mundane truth. His homesickness for England led Jim Andreyevitch Eliot, the Russian pseudonym he chose for himself, to enquire whether the British Government would ever give him a safe-conduct to return for a visit.

The very suggestion displeased the British authorities, though England had his cremated bones in the end. They lie in the cemetery at West Meon in Hampshire close to his father's grave. Burgess's enquiry also alarmed a number of former accomplices, including the badly scared 'Maurice'. The salutary effect on the Fourth Man of Guy Burgess's threat to 'spill the beans' has been referred to earlier. Maclean's dour pride forbade him indulging in any such extravagant and empty gestures. Like the solemn Scots determinist he had always been, he resigned himself mutely to his fate, on rare occasions displaying the better side of himself to chance callers like Lady Felicity Rumbold, but more frequently drowning his private sorrows in alcohol, as Philby still does.[13]

King George V's premonitions on his deathbed were not so wildly off the mark. Within the lifetime of his second son and his granddaughter, the old British Empire ceased to exist. The looser association of a multiracial Commonwealth, consisting mainly of independent republics owing no direct allegiance to the Crown, steadily replaced it. The British people themselves, after experiencing more than one sharp rebuff and after spending a further decade in doubtful hesitation, voted to become a member state of the European Economic Community. The US elder statesman Dean Acheson had pointed out in late November 1962, barely two months before Philby's escape from Beirut, the uneviable political and psychological dilemmas facing the old country: 'Britain,' he said, 'has lost an Empire and not yet found a role.' It was a discerning judgement. To a lesser degree than the three symbolic figures, who had plotted and spied with others in the fond hope of turning Britain into a Soviet satellite, thoughtful British citizens had long recognized that imperial pretensions could have no place in a small, heavily populated, freedom-loving island kingdom off the mainland of Europe. Had there been a Welfare State in the 1930s, the political distemper which afflicted so many young intellectuals then might not have become a severe epidemic. Had the government of the day been better led, had ministers been alert to the nature of Marxism, to the aims and tactics of the Comintern, the conspirators might have been detected and decontaminated before the disease got out of hand. Because Communists preached class warfare, the authorities watched out only for card-carrying Party members; they were ill-advised enough to believe that the chief threat to security came from the working classes and their extremist champions.

The security authorities and the police woke up too late. Brilliant old-guard Soviet revolutionaries like Maxim Litvinov, who knew from experience the tight web of loyalties, friendships, family and club relationships binding together the sprawling but complex fabric of Britain's ruling class, were responsible for the master plan. They somehow overcame the hard-line opposition of orthodox Bolsheviks who maintained that no good would ever come of relying on the effete offspring of bourgeois decadents: to penetrate an Establishment from within through such agents was to invite failure; nevertheless, the ruse was attempted. Who can now deny that it did not justify itself? The failure of the British authorities sprang from complacency, poor leadership, inertia and ignorance. They still believed in the past. Unworthy inheritors of old imperialist ideals that were no longer valid, they underrated the quasi-religious attraction of Communism for young men and women of their own kind who no longer believed in anything else. The professional slackness of the security authorities was more than matched by their excessive secretiveness, itself a reflection of the immemorial refusal of British officialdom to unveil the arcane processes of decision-making in Whitehall. Why ever should the uninitiated multitude be told the mysteries of the inner circle? The divine right to withhold classified information of every kind from the public, and to let the Prime Minister be the sole judge of what should be declassified, became the unquestionable working rule when the Official Secrets Act was passed in 1911. That rule has gone virtually unchallenged in Britain for the past sixty years and more. Had there been more openness in government, there would have been better public understanding of the country's problems in every sphere, not excluding the difficulties which the small, neglected yet overrated secret and security services created for themselves.

Though it has never been officially confirmed that the Communist pasts of Philby, Burgess, Maclean, the Fourth and Fifth Men, Nunn May, Fuchs, Pontecorvo and not a few others were quite unknown to MI5 when the Second World War broke out in 1939, this scandalous fact happens to be largely true. In fairness, the security services have since been drastically reformed; and in their laudable endeavours to retrace both the recruitment of covert Communists and the infiltration of the recruits into positions of influence, they have compiled an imposing array of information which may be instructive to future historians, if the files are ever declassified and released. Whether these records will prove as complete as the American dossiers on the British subjects known to have spied for Russia may well be doubted. The FBI and the CIA did not start researching thoroughly into the careers, of Philby, Burgess, Maclean and others until the early summer of 1951. The results of their research, or at any rate those voluminous sections open to public scrutiny under the US Freedom of Information Act, provide an object lesson in meticulousness.

The first casualty of the expulsion which shook the foundations of Whitehall after the flight of Burgess and Maclean in 1951 was the traditional public school convention of mutual trust obtaining between colleagues who shared the same privileged social backgrounds. Nobody could be considered safe any more. King George V would probably have been less perturbed, in view of his dark premonitions in old age, than Clement Attlee and his fellow ministers in the first post-war Labour Cabinet. That a Communist conspiracy could have so atrophied the normal impulses of patriotism that men in positions of responsibility would betray their country's secrets to the Soviet Union out of conviction seemed quite incredible. Alas, an official conspiracy of silence set in. Shock, embarrassment, grievance, bewilderment, these and other negative responses to inconceivably bad news were fortified by the age-old instinct of the British ruling class to sit tight and say nothing when in doubt or difficulty. The stiff upper lip technique irritated the general public and was derided by the press. Fleet Street finally nosed out, bit by bit, an unsavoury tale of omissions which the authorities would have been happier to bury and forget.

As for the reluctance of friends, acquaintances and left-wing associates of the British spies to disclose what they knew to the security authorities, this, too, was understandable if unedifying. Conspiracies of silence on high unfortunately tend to beget conspiracies of silence below. Just as Hugh Trevor-Roper quite reasonably assumed, without asking, that MI5 must have been already aware of Philby's Communist past when MI6 recruited the newcomer in 1941, so Goronwy Rees assumed with equal reasonableness in 1951 that, in offering to recount everything he could remember about the activities of Burgess, he was simply mouthing facts with which the security authorities had long been familiar. Examples of such misunderstandings could be multiplied. The self-effacing, often mediocre, members of MI5 in Stewart Menzies's day had little conception of the magnitude or meaning of the Communist ferment among the middle-class intellectuals of the thirties. The men and women who could have enlightened them were later reluctant to do so, partly out of a sense of stubborn if mistaken loyalty to their own kind, partly from a collective sense of guilt. Despising Fleet Street's unbridled passion for sensation, they held back so that confusion became worse confounded.

The men and women of that generation are now an ageing and dwindling race. Like Philby and Maclean, the two exiled survivors in Moscow, they are unlikely to live much longer. No doubt they look back on the events of those far-off days with mixed feelings. To the new generations that have grown up and taken their places since, the conspiracy of the thirties is utterly remote and unreal. The young have developed subcultures of their own. Post-imperial Britain may not yet have found her precise role in a nuclear age, standing upright but dwarfed in the shadows of the two superpowers; yet the social climate of this small, poorer, stabler, less class-ridden Britain is perhaps slightly healthier and saner than it was between the two world wars which drained the country of so much blood, treasure and self-confidence.

History, it is said, never repeats itself exactly; but then historians are seldom right, never infallible. Some cynics contend that patriotism no longer counts as an acceptable virtue among the young, that Western society is uncertain what it believes or what it values, that God is dead, that the era of nihilism is here to stay, as the hijacking of aircraft and the amoral outrages perpetrated by international terrorists and lesser fry in their millions indicate all too frequently and gruesomely. It may be even true, as outstanding, though gloomy and retired American intelligence specialists like James Angleton still fear, that the United States has become the prime target for Soviet penetration, just as Britain in her decline as a Great Power undoubtedly was nearly half a century ago. If so, we can only trust that the Americans have learnt from the melancholy experience of the British, who almost certainly have little worth spying for any more.

In spite of that, and regardless of Philby's misplaced sneers at the continuing incompetence of the British Secret Service, the instrument refashioned by Dick White and his successors since the mid 1950s is said to be envied by rivals for its compact efficiency, notably on the counter-intelligence side. There may be merit in the Angleton thesis, which represents the Soviet Union as a formidable and unrelenting antagonist bent on weakening the United States from within as the first step towards world conquest; but the Angleton thesis should not be seen in isolation. It should be set against the Trevor-Roper thesis of a harassed Kremlin, using irrelevant 'fossils of the past' like Philby, Maclean and other Western spies 'to advertise its waning power of attraction'.[14] An optimist, I personally prefer Trevor-Roper's thesis to Angleton's; it has more 'bottom' and better perspective, even in this era of Soviet military growth and undiplomatic intervention in backward but strategically important parts of Asia and Africa. Viewed in proper historical context, the complex chain of events which led first, to Britain's decline as a leading imperial power, then to the emergence in the 1930s of a handful of middle-class Englishmen whom the Russians recruited as long-term agents, has an untidy inevitability about it. Other agents may be still at large. If so, it is more than probable that the security authorities have already accounted for them, one by one, at their own mysterious discretion. The deplorable conditions of that period, giving rise to the distemper which turned future pillars of the Establishment into spies, then into transitory pseudo-heroes of the Soviet Union, have long since passed away. Like debris on the ebb tide of change, they have been swept out to sea, never to return.

NOTES

CHAPTER 1: RULING-CLASS RADICALS (pages 27–41)

1 Neal Wood, *Communism and British Intellectuals* (Gollancz 1959), pp. 22 ff. This slim but meticulously researched book, which deserves to be better known, is less tendentious than James Klugman's *History of the Communist Party of Great Britain*, vol. 1, *Formation and Early Years 1919–1924* (Lawrence & Wishart 1960).

2 Hyndman, an agreeable if somewhat naïve collector of political geniuses, had abandoned Mazzini for Marx, by then an old man. In his *Record of an Adventurous Life*, Hyndman recounted this snippet of conversation with his friend: 'I remarked [to Marx] that as I grew older I became more tolerant. "Do you?" he said. "Do you?"' See also Isaiah Berlin, *Karl Marx* (Oxford University Press 1978).

3 David Marquand, *Ramsay MacDonald* (Jonathan Cape 1977), p. 89.

4 Marquand, p. 96.

5 Raymond Postgate, *The Life of George Lansbury* (Longman 1951), p. 138.

6 Francis Meynell, *My Lives* (Bodley Head 1971), p. 107.

7 Meynell, p. 119.

8 Meynell, p. 128.

9 Harold Nicolson, *King George V: His Life and Reign* (Constable 1952), p. 341.

10 *Daily Herald*, 22 July 1919.

CHAPTER 2: THE YOUNG MISFITS

1 See A. J. P. Taylor, *English History 1914–1945* (Oxford University Press 1965), p. 120.

2 Evelyn Waugh, *A Little Learning* (Chapman & Hall 1964; as quoted here, Sidgwick & Jackson 1973), p. 114.

3 Hugh Thomas, *John Strachey* (Eyre Methuen 1973), pp. 5–17 *passim*.

4 Information to the author from Joan Robinson, a disciple and fellow economist of Maurice Dobb at Cambridge.

5 Malcolm Muggeridge, *Chronicles of Wasted Time*, vol.1, *The Greenstick* (Collins 1978), p. 78.
6 Muggeridge, p. 205.
7 *Dictionary of National Biography, Supplement 1931–40*, Sir Donald Maclean (Smith, Elder), p. 583.
8 Personal information from Christopher Gillie to author.
9 Information to the author from Logie Bruce Lockhart, headmaster of Gresham's.
10 Information to the author from James Klugman.
11 John Pudney, *Home and Away* (Michael Joseph 1960), p. 48.
12 Pudney, p. 49.
13 Information to the author from Logie Bruce Lockhart.
14 Information to the author from Logie Bruce Lockhart.
15 Information to the author from Professor Leonard Forster.
16 Information to the author from the Rt Hon. J. Enoch Powell, MP.
17 Information to the author from Robert Childers.
18 Information to the author from Professor Leonard Forster.
19 Christopher Gillie's notes to the author.
20 Information from Christopher Gillie to the author.
21 Patrick Seale and Maureen McConville, *Philby: The Long Road to Moscow* (Hamish Hamilton 1973), p. 39.
22 Graham Greene, 'The Apostles Intervene', *Collected Essays* (Bodley Head 1969; Penguin 1971), p. 230. See also Peter Allen, *The Cambridge Apostles* (Cambridge University Press 1979).
23 Information from James Klugman to the author.
24 Information from Christopher Gillie to the author.
25 Information from J. O. Roach to the author.
26 Christopher Gillie's notes to the author.
27 Information from Sir Herbert Butterfield to the author. Confirmed by Charles Fletcher Cooke, MP.
28 Sir Herbert Butterfield's notes to the author.
29 Roy Harrod, *John Maynard Keynes* (Macmillan 1951), pp. 450–1.
30 Information from Goronwy Rees to the author. See also Rees, *A Chapter of Accidents* (Chatto & Windus 1977), pp. 110 ff.
31 Information to the author from Joan Robinson and others.
32 From a letter of Charles Madge to the author.
33 Information from Sir Robert Birley to the author.
34 From the personal file of Commander M. K. de Moncy Burgess, available at the Public Record Office from 1 January 1978.
35 From the personal records of the Royal Naval College, Dartmouth.

36 Confidential information to the author from a close friend of Burgess who prefers to remain unnamed.
37 From the records of Eton College in notes to the author by Patrick Strong.
38 Information to the author from Sir Robert Birley.
39 Information to the author from Michael Berry (now Lord Hartwell).
40 Sir Robert Birley's notes to the author.

CHAPTER 3: THE TALENT SPOTTERS

1 Neal Wood, *Communism and British Intellectuals* (Gollancz 1959), p. 172.
2 Information to the author from Joseph Grigg.
3 From the Westminster School magazine the *Elizabethan*, spring 1926.
4 Information to the author from Laurence Tanner.
5 From a letter to the author by Evan James.
6 *Varsity Weekly, An Undergraduate's Diary*, 27 February 1932.
7 From a letter to the author by the Hon. Mrs Miriam Lane (*née* Rothschild).
8 Kim Philby, *My Silent War* (McGibbon & Kee 1968; Panther 1969), p. 15. Among a few of the surviving letters he wrote to his parents is an affectionate but non-committal note about his future career prospects, dated April 1934 and addressed to his mother. By then he had partly 'proved himself' as a Soviet probationary agent in Vienna. This and other unrevealing glimpses of Harry St John Philby's son can be seen in the letters deposited at St Anthony's College, Oxford.
9 Confidential notes to the author incorporating original material provided by Guy Liddell of MI5 to the late E. H. Cookridge.
10 W. G. Krivitsky, *I was Stalin's Agent* (Hamish Hamilton 1939), p. 70.
11 A. J. P. Taylor, *English History 1914–1945* (Oxford University Press 1965), p. 255, footnote.
12 *Parliamentary Debates: Official Report*, 24 May 1927, cols. 1842–54, and 26 May 1927, cols. 2195–2310.
13 Information to the author from James Klugman.
14 Wood, pp. 182–3
15 Confidential information to the author as attested in E. H. Cookridge's notes from Guy Liddell of MI5.
16 Confidential information to the author from a source that must remain anonymous. See also Alexander Orlov's *Handbook of Intel-*

ligence and Guerrilla Warfare (University of Michigan Press 1963), pp. 108 ff.

17 From a letter to the author by John Lehmann.

18 Information to the author from Joseph Grigg.

19 Information to the author from Cambridge colleagues of Sir Dennis Robertson.

20 Information to the author from Sir Richard Clarke and others. See also Patrick Seale and Maureen McConville, *Philby: The Long Road to Moscow* (Hamish Hamilton 1973), p. 53.

21 From a letter to the author by Charles Madge.

22 Information to the author from Christopher Gillie.

23 Information to the author from several eye-witnesses and participants, including Gillie and Patricia Parry (now Lady Llewelyn-Davies).

24 Christopher Gillie's notes to the author.

25 *Granta*, 8 November 1933, p. 90.

26 Geoffrey Hoare, *The Missing Macleans* (Cassell 1955), pp. 135–6. Clare Hollingworth, journalist and widow of Hoare, confirmed that her late husband found the inscription and marked passage in that particular volume on Maclean's bookshelves at Beaconshaw, his last home in Britain.

27 Information to the author from Elizabeth Rea (now Lady Clapham).

28 Christopher Gillie's notes to the author.

29 Information to the author from Mrs Jo Grimond, Lady Clapham, Lady Felicity Rumbold, among others.

30 From a letter to the author by the Hon. Mrs Miriam Lane (*née* Rothschild).

31 Information to the author from Nicholas Elliott, whose father, the late Sir Claude Elliott, was Headmaster of Eton from 1933 to 1949 and then Provost of the College.

32 Information from Goronwy Rees to the author. See also Rees, *A Chapter of Accidents* (Chatto & Windus 1977), p. 117.

33 From a letter to the author by the Hon. Mrs Miriam Lee (*née* Rothschild).

34 Hugh Thomas, *John Strachey* (Eyre Methuen 1973), p. 34.

CHAPTER 4: THE DEVIL'S DISCIPLES

1 Tom Jones, *A Diary with Letters* (Oxford University Press 1954), pp. 194 ff.

2 Lord Vansittart, *The Mist Procession* (Hutchinson 1958), p. 483.

See also, for an amusing account of the true inventor of the 'Cliveden Set', Claud Cockburn, *I, Claud* (Penguin 1967), pp. 179–80.

3 Frances Donaldson, *Edward VIII* (Weidenfeld & Nicolson 1974), p. 196.

4 Personal communication to the author by the late E. H. Cookridge, then Eric Gedye's freelance assistant in Vienna. For a fuller account of Cookridge's contact with Philby, see E. H. Cookridge, *The Third Man* (Putnam, 1968), pp. 29–34.

5 Personal communication to the author by Naomi (Lady) Mitchison.

6 Extract from Naomi Mitchison's diary.

7 Patrick Seale and Maureen McConville, *Philby: The Long Road to Moscow* (Hamish Hamilton 1973), p. 67.

8 Vansittart, pp. 490–1.

9 Information from Mrs Jo Grimond to the author.

10 Cyril Connolly, *The Missing Diplomats* (Queen Anne Press 1952), p. 19. In a forward to this book, Peter Quennell declares that 'neither Burgess nor Maclean was a close associate' of Connolly. Nevertheless, the two men thought of this patron as a friendly sympathizer.

11 Robert Bruce Lockhart, ed. Kenneth Young, *The Diaries of Sir Robert Bruce Lockhart* (Macmillan 1973), pp. 285 ff.

12 Vansittart, p. 455.

13 Lockart, pp. 283–4.

14 Vansittart, pp. 460–1.

15 Malcolm Muggeridge, *The Thirties* (Hamish Hamilton 1940; Collins 1967), p. 14.

16 Stephen Spender, *World Within World* (Faber & Faber 1951 and 1977), p. 190.

17 Donaldson, p. 191.

18 Personal communication to the author by Sir Roger Chance.

19 Kim Philby, *My Silent War* (McGibbon & Kee 1968; Panther 1969), pp. 14 and 17.

20 Information from Malcolm Muggeridge to the author.

21 Lockhart, p. 348.

22 Donaldson, p. 211.

23 Vansittart, p. 544.

24 Arthur Koestler, *The Invisible Writing* (Hutchinson 1969), p. 382.

25 A. J. P. Taylor, *English History 1914-1945* (Oxford University Press 1965), p. 396. See also Robert Graves and Alan Hodge, *The Long Weekend: A Social History of Great Britain 1918-1939* (Faber & Faber 1940).

26 Elisabeth K. Poretsky, *Our Own People, a Memoir of 'Ignace Reiss' and His Friends* (Oxford University Press 1969), pp. 128 and 151.
27 Poretsky, p. 213.
28 Philby, pp. 16–21.

CHAPTER 5: THE TIME SERVERS

1 Information to the author from Frank Gillard.
2 Cyril Connolly, *The Missing Diplomats* (Queen Anne Press 1952), p. 20.
3 A. J. P. Taylor, *English History 1914-1945* (Oxford University Press 1965), p. 233.
4 Information to the author from Goronwy Rees. See also Rees, *A Chapter of Accidents* (Chatto & Windus 1977), pp. 134 ff.
5 Information to the author from Goronwy Rees.
6 Information to the author from Lady Felicity Rumbold.
7 Connolly, pp. 20–1.
8 Sir Basil Liddell Hart, *Memoirs*, vol. 2 (Cassell 1965), p. 149.
9 W. G. Krivitsky, *I Was Stalin's Agent* (Hamish Hamilton 1939), p. 117.
10 T. E. B. Howarth, *Cambridge between Two Wars* (Collins 1978), p. 222.
11 Peter Kemp, *Mine Were of Trouble* (Cassell 1954), p. 106.
12 Kim Philby, *My Silent War* (McGibbon & Kee 1968; Panther 1969), p. 23.
13 Philip Toynbee (ed.), *The Distant Drum* (Sidgwick & Jackson 1976), pp. 72–3.
14 Wilfrid Hindle (ed.), *Foreign Correspondent* (Harrap 1930), p. 254, footnote.
15 *The Times*'s 'Parliamentary Report', 23 February 1938.
16 Krivitsky, pp. 96–7.
17 Arthur Koestler, *The Invisible Writing* (Hutchinson 1969), p. 445.
18 Koestler, pp. 448–9.
19 Lord Vansittart, *The Mist Procession* (Huchinson 1958), pp. 442–3.
20 Tom Driberg, *Guy Burgess: A Portrait with Background* (Weidenfeld & Nicolson 1956), p. 41.
21 Andrew Boyle, *Montagu Norman* (Cassell 1967), p. 306.
22 Harold Nicolson, ed. Nigel Nicolson, *Diaries and Letters*, vol. 1, *1930-1939* (Collins 1966; Fontana 1969), pp. 354–5.
23 Nicolson, p. 374.
24 Asa Briggs, *The History of Broadcasting in the United Kingdom*, vol. 2, *The Golden Age of Wireless* (Oxford University Press 1965), p. 145.

25 Correspondence and discussions between the author and Ian Trethowan and others. Though the BBC's official archivist did try to answer a number of questions relating to the contents of Guy Burgess's personal file, the replies scarcely answered the purpose. It is a matter of record that Asa Briggs, the BBC's official historian, was also denied access to personal files for volumes 2, 3 and 4 of his monumental work.
26 Confidential information to the author.
27 See Patrick Seale and Maureen McConville, *Philby: The Long Road to Moscow* (Hamish Hamilton 1973), p. 101, and Bruce Page, David Leitch and Phillip Knightley, *Philby: The Spy Who Betrayed a Generation* (Sphere 1977), p. 35.
28 Communication to the author by Malcolm Muggeridge.
29 Information to the author from Goronwy Rees. See also Rees, pp. 149–51.

CHAPTER 6: THE CONFIDENCE TRICKSTERS

1 Keith Feiling, *The Life of Neville Chamberlain* (Macmillan 1946), p. 403.
2 J. M. Keynes, interviewed by Kingsley Martin, 'Democracy and Efficiency', *New Statesman and Nation*, 28 January 1939.
3 T. E. B. Howarth, *Cambridge between Two Wars* (Collins 1978), p. 206.
4 Information to the author from Goronwy Rees.
5 E. M. Forster, *Two Cheers for Democracy* (Penguin 1965), p. 76.
6 Elisabeth K. Poretsky, *Our Own People, a Memoir of 'Ignace Reiss' and His Friends* (Oxford University Press 1969), p. 82.
7 Hugh Thomas, *John Strachey* (Eyre Methuen 1973), p. 202.
8 Christopher Sykes, *Evelyn Waugh* (Collins 1975; Penguin 1977) p. 285.
9 Geoffrey Hoare, *The Missing Macleans* (Cassell 1955), p. 59.
10 Hoare, pp. 48–9.
11 Winston Churchill, *The Second World War*, vol. 2, *Their Finest Hour* (Cassell 1949), pp. 39 and 60.
12 Kim Philby, *My Silent War* (McGibbon & Kee 1968; Panther 1969), p. 25.
13 Asa Briggs, *The History of Broadcasting in the United Kingdom*, vol. 3, *The War of Words* (Oxford University Press 1970), pp. 185–7.
14 Bickham Sweet-Escott, *Baker Street Irregular* (Methuen 1965), p. 36.
15 Philby, p. 31.

16 Hugh Dalton, *The Fateful Years: Memoirs 1931-1945* (Frederick Muller 1957), p. 378.
17 Dalton, pp. 379 ff.
18 Philby, p. 30. Compare Winston Churchill, *The Second World War*, vol. 4, *The Hinge of Fate* (Cassell 1950), p. 497.
19 Philby, p. 34. F. H. Hinsley, E. E. Thomas, C. F. G. Ransom and R. C. Knight, *British Intelligence in the Second World War*, volume 1 (HMSO 1979), p. 278.
20 Churchill, *Their Finest Hour*, p. 121.
21 Harold Nicolson, ed. Nigel Nicolson, *Diaries and Letters*, vol. 2, *1939-1945* (Collins 1966; Fontana 1969), p. 95. See also Goronwy Rees, *A Chapter of Accidents* (Chatto & Windus 1977), p. 153, regarding Burgess's letter about his proposed Moscow *démarche*.
22 Nicolson, p. 122. Also personal information to the author from Sir Isaiah Berlin.
23 W. L. Langer and S. E. Gleason, *The Challenge to Isolation* (Harper 1955), p. 644.
24 FBI/CIA files, incorporating testimony of Isaac Don Levine and Walter Krivitsky. Apart from the Lothian report to the Foreign Office, earlier evidence had been submitted on Krivitsky's behalf by Wilfrid le Gallienne, a British diplomat. In this evidence the unnamed 'idealist of good family' had already proved his value by providing photocopies of proceedings of the Committee of Imperial Defence, seen by Krivitsky on his final visit to Moscow before defecting to the West. The photocopying was done in a Pimlico flat.
25 Arthur Koestler, *The Invisible Writing* (Hutchinson 1969), p. 483. But see also Poretsky, p. 270.

CHAPTER 7: THE DOUBLE PATRIOTS

1 Winston Churchill, *The Second World War*, vol. 3, *The Grand Alliance* (Cassell 1950), pp. 286 and 297.
2 Churchill, p. 299, Colville's note.
3 Information to the author from Foreign Office colleagues of Maclean. See also Robert Cecil's article in *Encounter*, April 1978, p. 10.
4 Information to the author from BBC sources and Goronwy Rees.
5 Asa Briggs, *The History of Broadcasting in the United Kingdom*, vol. 3, *The War of Words* (Oxford University Press 1970), pp. 300–92.

6 Andrew Boyle, *'Poor, Dear Brendan': The Quest for Brendan Bracken* (Hutchinson 1974), pp. 275 ff.
7 A. J. P. Taylor, *Beaverbrook* (Hamish Hamilton 1972), p. 515.
8 Information to the author from Harman Grisewood.
9 Harold Nicolson, ed. Nigel Nicolson, *Diaries and Letters*, vol. 2, *1939–1945* (Collins 1966; Fontana 1969), pp. 239–40.
10 Hugh Thomas, *John Strachey* (Eyre Methuen 1973), p. 219.
11 Nicolson, pp. 311–12.
12 Information to the author from Sir William Haley. See also Asa Briggs, *The History of Broadcasting in the United Kingdom*, vol. 4, (Oxford University Press 1979), p. 620, for evidence of Sir Harold Nicolson's extravagant estimation of Burgess's potential uses as a BBC specialist.
13 A. J. P. Taylor, *English History 1914–1945* (Oxford University Press 1965), p. 542.
14 The FBI/CIA files confirm the surmise of several colleagues and acquaintances that Maclean was first blackmailed before setting foot in the United States. Undoubtedly the information came from 'Basil' the Fifth Man, who later gained Maclean's complete confidence.
15 Douglas Hyde, *I Believed* (Heinemann 1950), pp. 144–5.
16 Malcolm Muggeridge, *Chronicles of Wasted Time*, vol. 2, *The Infernal Grove* (Collins 1973), pp. 106–7. Supplemented by personal information to the author.
17 Evidence of Vladimir Petrov to the Australian Royal Commission, 1955, afterwards repeated *ad nauseam* in the British and world press.
18 Elisabeth K. Poretsky, *Our Own People, a Memoir of 'Ignace Reiss' and His Friends* (Oxford University Press 1969), p. 74.
19 Robert Bruce Lockhart, ed. Kenneth Young, *The Diaries of Sir Robert Bruce Lockhart* (Macmillan 1973), p. 97.
20 Information to the author from Mrs Morell-Smith and others.
21 Kim Philby, *My Silent War* (McGibbon & Kee 1968; Panther 1969), p. 55.
22 Confidential information to the author from several former members of SIS.
23 Hugh Trevor-Roper, *The Philby Affair* (William Kimber 1968), pp. 27–9 *passim*.
24 Muggeridge, p. 126.
25 Ronald Lewin, *Ultra Goes to War* (Hutchinson 1978), p. 45.
26 Trevor-Roper, pp. 72–3.
27 Philby, p. 71.

28 Philby, p. 70.
29 Philby, pp. 74–5.
30 Patrick Seale and Maureen McConville, *Philby: The Long Road to Moscow* (Hamish Hamilton 1973), p. 114.
31 Information to the author from personal friends of Aileen Philby (*née* Furse).

CHAPTER 8: THE ENEMIES WITHIN

1 Arthur Bryant, *The Turn of the Tide* (Collins 1957), pp. 323–4.
2 Winston Churchill, *The Second World War*, vol. 3, *The Grand Alliance* (Cassell 1950), p. 22.
3 Hugh Trevor-Roper, *The Philby Affair* (William Kimber 1968), p. 38. According to Felix Cowgill, Trevor-Roper's principal fault, which Menzies himself could not overlook, was 'by-passing normal channels and giving secret intelligence direct to Churchill's friend and adviser, Lord Cherwell, to "C"'s subsequent embarrassment and genuine annoyance'.
4 Anthony Cave Brown, *Bodyguard of Lies* (W. H. Allen 1976), pp. 311 and 313.
5 Trevor-Roper, p. 78.
6 Brown, p. 315. See also Robert E. Sherwood, *Roosevelt and Hopkins. An Intimate History* (Harper, New York, 1950).
7 Winston Churchill, *The Second World War*, vol. 5, *Closing the Ring* (Cassell 1951), p. 543, minute to Sir Alexander Cadogan.
8 Churchill, *Closing the Ring*, p. 542, joint-minute to Minister of State and Sir Alexander Cadogan.
9 Douglas Hyde, *I Believed* (Heinemann 1950), p. 203.
10 Cyril Connolly, *The Missing Diplomats* (Queen Anne Press 1952), p. 25.
11 Churchill, *Closing the Ring*, p. 312.
12 Margaret Gowing, *Britain and Atomic Energy, 1939-1945* (Macmillan 1964), p. 37.
13 Martin J. Sherwin, *A World Destroyed: The Atomic Bomb and the Grand Alliance* (Knopf, New York, 1975; Random House, New York, 1977), p. 34.
14 Personal communication to the author from Sir Rudolf Peierls.
15 Confession of Dr Klaus Fuchs, as released to the public after his trial.
16 Connolly, p. 26.
17 Confirmed by the FBI/CIA files on Burgess, Maclean and Philby.
18 Kim Philby, *My Silent War* (McGibbon & Kee 1968; Panther

1969), p. 93. Cowgill, in retrospect, accepts, while still abhorring, the substance of this combined operational intrigue to oust him.

19 According to Trevor-Roper and others, quoting Philby's version of the interview with Stewart Menzies, 'C' is reported to have said of Cowgill: 'And to think, Kim, that only yesterday I was recommending him for the CBE!' See Trevor-Roper, p. 40.

20 Information to the author from Colonel Felix Cowgill.

21 Information to the author from Mrs Felix Cowgill.

22 Information to the author from James R. Murphy and others.

23 Personal communication to the author from Malcolm Muggeridge.

24 Personal communication to the author from Malcolm Muggeridge, confirmed by other colleagues in SIS.

25 Extract from Graham Greene's interview with Louise Dennys, *Sunday Telegraph*, 12 March 1978. Greene, however, retained an ambivalent sense of admiration and compassion for Philby as a man of 'divided loyalties'. In words used elsewhere by this novelist and ex-colleague of the spy: 'He betrayed his country – yes, perhaps he did. But who among us has not committed treason to something or someone more important than a country . . .?' In a letter to the author Greene also stated that he had never seen Philby the worse for drink.

26 Personal communication to the author from Malcolm Muggeridge.

27 Malcolm Muggeridge, *Chronicles of Wasted Time*, vol. 2, *The Infernal Grove* (Collins 1973), pp. 250–1.

28 Personal communication to the author from Malcolm Muggeridge.

29 Harold Nicolson, ed. Nigel Nicolson, *Diaries and Letters*, vol. 2, *1939–1945* (Collins, 1966; Fontana, 1969), p. 439.

30 Winston Churchill, *The Second World War*, vol. 6, *Triumph and Tragedy* (Cassell 1953), pp. 498–9.

31 A. J. P. Taylor, *English History 1914–1945* (Oxford University Press 1965), p. 596.

32 Philby, p. 120.

CHAPTER 9: ENTER THE FIFTH MAN

1 Foreign Relation of the United States (FRUS), *The Conference of Berlin*, p. 225. See also Stimson's diaries, 22 July 1945.

2 Martin J. Sherwin, *A World Destroyed: The Atomic Bomb and the Grand Alliance* (Knopf, New York, 1975; Random House, New York, 1977), p. 224. See also Harry S. Truman, *Memoirs*, vol. 1, *Year of Decisions* (Doubleday 1955), p. 416.

3 *The Memoirs of Marshal Zhukov* (ANP, New York, 1971), pp. 674–5.
4 Harold Nicolson, ed. Nigel Nicolson, *Diaries and Letters*, vol. 3, *1945–1962* (Collins 1966; Fontana 1969), p. 29.
5 Andrew Boyle, *'Poor Dear Brendan'* (Hutchinson 1974), p. 308.
6 A. J. P. Taylor, *English History 1914–1945* (Oxford University Press 1965), p. 599.
7 Hugh Dalton, *The Fateful Years: Memoirs 1931–1945* (Frederick Muller 1957), p. 483.
8 The same barbed gibe, however, was also levelled by Bevin at Herbert Morrison and Emanuel Shinwell, among others. See Michael Foot, *Aneurin Bevan*, vol. 2, *1945–1960* (Davis-Poynter) 1972), p. 31, footnote.
9 Roy Harrod, *John Maynard Keynes* (Macmillan 1951), p. 717.
10 Nicolson, p. 42.
11 Douglas Hyde, *I Believed* (Heinemann 1950), p. 312.
12 One of many current witticisms, almost certainly not apocryphal, uttered by Churchill at the expense of the self-effacing Attlee.
13 Information to the author from Sir Frederick Warner.
14 Information to the author from David Footman.
15 Information to the author from Goronwy Rees. See also Rees, *A Chapter of Accidents* (Chatto & Windus 1977), p. 169.
16 Nicolson, pp. 38–9.
17 Information to the author from Sir Frederick Warner.
18 Information to the author from Goronwy Rees. See also Rees, p. 170.
19 Information to the author from Sir Frederick Warner.
20 Information to the author from Sir Frederick Warner.
21 Information to the author from George Carey-Foster.
22 Information to the author from Malcolm Muggeridge.
23 Patrick Seale and Maureen McConville, *Philby: The Long Road to Moscow* (Hamish Hamilton 1973), pp. 181–2.
24 George Orwell, *The Lion and the Unicorn* (Secker & Warburg, 1941), pp. 70–1.
25 Information from several of Maclean's colleagues in war-time and post-war Washington.
26 Information to the author from Sir Isaiah Berlin.
27 Geoffrey Hoare, *The Missing Macleans* (Cassell 1955), pp. 53–4. Confirmed by Clare Hollingworth and others.
28 Confidential information to the author from CIA sources in Washington.

29 Personal communication to the author from Lord Sherfield (the former Roger Makins).
30 Information to the author from George Carey-Foster.
31 Harry S. Truman, *Memoirs*, vol. 2, *Years of Trial and Hope* (Doubleday 1955), pp. 10–11.
32 Lewis L. Strauss, *Men and Decisions* (Macmillan 1962), p. 256.
33 The declassified CIA/FBI files indicate clearly the awareness of the US intelligence community that Maclean had been blackmailed.
34 Information to the author from James R. Murphy in Washington.
35 Information to the author from Sir John Balfour.
36 Information to the author from Lady Balfour.
37 Information to the author from Walter Bell.
38 Information to the author from Malcolm Muggeridge.
39 Information to the author from Sir Robert Mackenzie.
40 Hoare, p. 54.
41 Information to the author from James R. Murphy in Washington.
42 Confidential information from a former CIA official who prefers to remain anonymous.
43 N. A. Rose, introduction to Blanche Dugdale, ed. N. A. Rose, *Baffy: The Diaries of Blanche Dugdale 1936–1947* (Vallentine Mitchell, 1973), p. 20.
44 Confidential information to the author from the same CIA source as note 42.
45 Confidential information to the author from separate CIA sources. For the sole fleeting reference in print to Angleton's coup in unmasking Britain's spies for Russia, see William R. Corson, *The Armies of Ignorance* (Dial Press/James Wade, New York, 1977), pp. 327–8.

CHAPTER 10: THE RUNAWAY AGENTS

1 Andrew Boyle, *'Poor Dear Brendan'* (Hutchinson 1974), p. 316.
2 Harry S. Truman, *Memoirs*. vol. 2, *Years of Trial and Hope* (Doubleday 1955), pp. 153–4.
3 Truman, pp. 115–16.
4 Truman, p. 116.
5 Harold Nicolson, ed. Nigel Nicolson, *Diaries and Letters*, vol. 3, *1945–1962* (Collins 1966; Fontana 1969), pp. 107–8.
6 Truman, p. 122.
7 Nicolson, pp. 140–1.
8 Information to the author from Sir Frederick Warner, David

Footman and Goronwy Rees, confirmed by George Carey-Foster.

9 Goronwy Rees, *A Chapter of Accidents* (Chatto & Windus 1977), p. 164.

10 Rees, p. 162.

11 Herbert Morrison, *Autobiography* (Odhams, 1960), pp. 276–7.

12 Information to the author from Sir Frederick Warner.

13 Information to the author from Christopher Mayhew.

14 Information to the author from SIS colleagues of Philby.

15 Information to the author from Foreign Office contemporaries of Burgess.

16 Cyril Connolly, *The Missing Diplomats* (Queen Anne Press 1952), p. 27.

17 Geoffrey Hoare, *The Missing Macleans* (Cassell 1955), p. 55.

18 Information to the author from Malcolm and Kitty Muggeridge.

19 Hoare pp. 56–7. Confirmed by Clare Hollingworth.

20 Bruce Page, David Leitch and Phillip Knightley, *Philby: The Spy who Betrayed a Generation* (Sphere 1977), pp. 235–6. Confirmed by George Carey-Foster.

21 Information to the author from Clare Hollingworth and Walter and Tanya Bell. Confirmed by Foreign Office and CIA evidence.

22 Information to the author from George Carey-Foster and other officials.

23 See Robert Cecil's article in *Encounter*, April 1978, p. 11.

24 Rees, pp. 184–5.

25 Information to the author from Lord Hartwell.

26 Information to the author from Goronwy Rees.

27 Rees, p. 179.

28 Information to the author from Goronwy Rees. See also Rees, p. 175.

29 Information to the author from George Carey-Foster.

30 Extract from a letter to the author by the Hon. Mrs Miriam Lane (*née* Rothschild).

31 Nicolson, p. 171.

32 Information to the author from Malcolm Muggeridge.

33 Information to the author from the Rt Hon. Jo Grimond, MP.

34 Extract from letter to the author by one of the senior diplomats involved.

35 Kim Philby, *My Silent War* (McGibbon & Kee 1968; Panther 1969), p. 133.

36 Confidential information to the author.

37 Stowers Johnson, *Agents Extraordinary* (Hale 1975), p. 189.
38 Confidential information to the author.
39 Philby, p. 134.
40 Philby, p. 139.
41 Philby, pp. 147–8.
42 Information to the author from Sir Robert Mackenzie. Confirmed in Washington.
43 Christopher Felix, *New York Times*, 9 May 1967.
44 Felix.
45 Information to the author from Sir Robert Mackenzie. This squares with Philby's recollection. See Philby, p. 152.
46 Rees, pp. 188–9.
47 Information to the author from David Footman.
48 Information to the author from Sir Robert Mackenzie.
49 Lord Greenhill, *The Times*, 7 September 1977.
50 Greenhill.
51 Extract from letter to Guy Burgess by Anthony Eden, an exhibit seen and noted by several of Burgess's friends.
52 Information to the author from some of Maclean's Foreign Office superiors at that time. See also Geoffrey Hoare, *The Missing Macleans* (Cassell 1955), p. 70.
53 Connolly, p. 29.
54 Hoare, p. 71.
55 Philby, p. 152.
56 Confidential information to the author from CIA sources.
57 Patrick Seale and Maureen McConville, *Philby: The Long Road to Moscow* (Hamish Hamilton 1973), p. 210. Confirmed by the same CIA sources.
58 Greenhill. For a sober, informative but inconclusive account of MacArthur's reasons for believing that the enemy's 'uncanny knowledge' of UN troop deployment had been due to intelligence leaks, see William Manchester, *American Caesar: Douglas MacArthur 1880–1964* (Hutchinson 1979), pp. 596–8.
59 Robert Cecil, *Encounter*, April 1978, p. 14.
60 Information to the author from George Carey-Foster.
61 Philby, p. 143.
62 Philby, p. 146.
63 Felix.
64 Greenhill.
65 Greenhill.

66 Information to the author from Goronwy Rees. See also Rees, p. 191.
67 Information to the author from Lady Rumbold, but officials contend that no formal complaint was ever laid against Maclean.
68 Connolly, p. 30.
69 Connolly, p. 31.
70 Information to the author from George Carey-Foster and Lord Sherfield.
71 Philby, p. 154.
72 Information to the author from a witness who prefers to remain anonymous. See also Connolly, p. 33.
73 Information to the author from the Earl of Longford.
74 Information to the author from Lord Hartwell.
75 Philby, p. 152. Philby's cable was later found in Burgess's flat and used in evidence against him – unsuccessfully.
76 Information to the author from Sir Robert Birley.
77 Cecil, p. 16.
78 Confidential information to the author from Foreign Office sources, based on Melinda Maclean's testimony.

CHAPTER 11: EXIT THE THIRD MAN

1 Information to the author from George Carey-Foster and Lord Sherfield.
2 Information to the author from George Carey-Foster and Lord Sherfield, supplemented by Geoffrey Hoare, *The Missing Macleans* (Cassell 1955), p. 10.
3 Information to the author from Sir Robert Mackenzie.
4 Information to the author from Kitty Muggeridge.
5 Information to the author from Malcolm Muggeridge.
6 Goronwy Rees, *A Chapter of Accidents* (Chatto & Windus 1977), p. 205.
7 Information to the author from Goronwy Rees. Confirmed by David Footman.
8 Rees, p. 209.
9 Information to the author from Lord Hartwell.
10 John Lehmann's autobiography, vol. 3, *The Ample Proposition*, (Eyre & Spottiswoode 1966), p. 128.
11 Lehmann, p. 131.
12 Confidential information to the author from security sources which must remain anonymous.
13 Information to the author from George Carey-Foster and others.

14 Kim Philby, *My Silent War* (McGibbon & Kee 1968; Panther 1969), p. 158.
15 Information to the author from Sir Robert Mackenzie.
16 Philby, p. 162.
17 Philby, p. 165. As White was attached to Allied HQ in Germany at the time of Cowgill's supplanting, Philby is guilty of inventing this.
18 The FBI in 1968 repudiated the Philby document as non-existent. An internal memorandum declared: 'A search of our files relating to the Maclean–Burgess matter has failed to disclose any information that Philby advanced such a theory or that he had ever discussed the Maclean–Burgess case with the Director.' It is more probable that Philby's self-exonerating paper was *discussed* with Hoover by Sillitoe.
19 Philby, p. 165.
20 Confidential information to the author by CIA sources in Washington. Needless to say, SIS sources reject this as 'retrospective wisdom'.
21 Extract from personal communication to the author from Sir John Colville.
22 Malcolm Muggeridge, extract from article in *Esquire*, April 1967.
23 Philby, p. 167.
24 Philby, p. 170.
25 Muggeridge.
26 Information to the author from George Carey-Foster and others.
27 Confidential information to the author.
28 Information to the author from David Footman. Confirmed by CIA sources.
29 Confidential information to the author.
30 Sir John Balfour in conversation with the author.
31 Andrew Boyle, *'Poor Dear Brendan'* (Hutchinson 1974), pp. 327–8.
32 The Earl of Swinton (collab. James Margach), *Sixty Years of Power* (Hutchinson 1966), p. 141.
33 Lord Moran, *The Struggle for Survival* (Constable 1966), p. 412, also p. 786.
34 Leonard Mosley, *Dulles: A Biography of Eleanor, Allen and John Foster Dulles and Their Family Network* (Dial Press/James Wade, New York, 1978), p. 356.
35 Boyle, p. 333.
36 Moran, pp. 523 and 527.
37 Confidential information to the author.

38 Philby, p. 171.
39 Otto John, trans. R. H. Barry, *Twice through the Lines* (Macmillan 1972), pp. 314–15.
40 FBI papers, file on the Philby case, September–October 1955.
41 FBI papers, internal memorandum from Hoover, 29 September 1955.
42 FBI papers.
43 Philby, p. 174.
44 Confidential information to the author. In the graphic words of one senior security official to the author: 'There was no way of piercing the liberal cloud of unknowing.'
45 *Parliamentary Debates, Official Report*, 7 November 1955, cols. 1483–1611.
46 Information to the author by former members of SIS who must remain anonymous.
47 Patrick Seale and Maureen McConville, *Philby: The Long Road to Moscow* (Hamish Hamilton 1973), p. 230.
48 Philby, p. 176.
49 Confidential information to the author.
50 Extracted from joint press statements by David Astor and Donald Tyerman.
51 According to her doctor, a distinguished Harley Street specialist, Aileen Philby may not have committed suicide. Such an end was, in his opinion, 'wholly out of character'. Whether the KGB played any part in her death, as he suspected, remains a matter for conjecture.
52 Malcolm Muggeridge to the author. See also Graham Greene's Introduction to Philby, p. 9.
53 Confidential information to the author.
54 Mosley, p. 407.
55 Mosley, p. 419. James Angleton, for once, was misled by his Israeli associates into thinking that there would be no Suez adventure: see Mosley, p. 414.
56 Philby, p. 178.
57 Philby, p. 178.
58 See page 116 of this book.
59 Information to the author from Nicholas Elliott.
60 Eleanor Philby, *Kim Philby: The Spy I Loved* (Pan 1968), p. 3.
61 Eleanor Philby, p. 56.
62 Harold Nicolson, ed. Nigel Nicolson, *Diaries and Letters*, vol. 3, *1945–1962* (Collins 1966; Fontana 1969), p. 191.

63 Confidential information to the author, duly confirmed by various ex-members of SIS in the course of the author's researches.
64 Edward J. Epstein, *Legend: The Secret World of Lee Harvey Oswald* (McGraw-Hill, New York, 1978; Hutchinson, 1978), p. 27.
65 Epstein, pp. 27–9.
66 Eleanor Philby, p. 51.
67 Eleanor Philby, pp. 47 and 54.
68 Information to the author from Nicholas Elliott.
69 Eleanor Philby, p. 2.

EPILOGUE

1 Information to the author from Nicholas Elliott.
2 Philby's escape route has never been disclosed, but Clare Hollingworth's presumption that he left Beirut aboard a Soviet freighter was widely shared. Bruce Page, David Leitch, and Phillip Knightley, *Philby: The Spy Who Betrayed a Generation* (Sphere 1977), p. 318, opt for a land route across Syria and Turkey into Soviet Armenia.
3 Nicholas Elliott in conversation with the author.
4 Eleanor Philby, *Kim Philby: The Spy I Loved* (Pan 1968), p. 154.
5 Information to the author from Nicholas Elliott.
6 Hugh Trevor-Roper, *The Philby Affair* (William Kimber 1968), pp. 96 and 98.
7 Malcolm Muggeridge, *Esquire*, September, 1967.
8 Graham Greene, Introduction to Kim Philby, *My Silent War* (McGibbon & Kee 1968; Panther 1969), p. 7.
9 Trevor-Roper, p. 100.
10 Eleanor Philby, p. 74.
11 Tom Driberg, *Ruling Passions* (Jonathan Cape 1977), pp. 231 and 235.
12 Driberg, p. 233. The ostracizing of Goronwy Rees thereafter by many members of Britain's academic and literary establishment was one of the least edifying instances of the prevailing mood of reticence and hypocrisy.
13 Nevertheless, in token of his unabated Marxist faith, Maclean produced a somewhat ponderous book on the aberrations of his native country's foreign policy. This literary swansong, *British Foreign Policy since Suez, 1956–68*, was published by Hodder & Stoughton in 1970.
14 Trevor-Roper, pp. 98 and 100.

INDEX

Q